ARMS MAKING
in the
CONNECTICUT
VALLEY

A Regional Study of the
Economic Development of the
Small Arms Industry
1798-1870

by FELICIA JOHNSON DEYRUP

GEORGE SHUMWAY, Publisher

York • *Pennsylvania*

Library of Congress Catalog Card Number 76-79610

Printed in the United States of America

1970

SBN 87387-023-9   500 copies

GEORGE SHUMWAY, *Publisher*

R. D. 7   York   Pennsylvania   17402

FOREWORD

Felicia Johnson Deyrup's economic study of arms making in the Connecticut Valley was first published in 1948 as Volume XXXIII of the Smith College Studies In History. In this form it was of course available to interested scholars willing to seek it out in libraries where it might be available, but to the large group of people who developed an interest in America's antique arms during the 1950's and 1960's it has for the most part remained unknown and unappreciated. This is unfortunate, for the study contains an abundance of information concerning the manufacture of U.S. martial arms during the flintlock and percussion eras that is not available elsewhere.

Twenty-one years have passed since the first publication of this work but it remains as sound today as when it first appeared. The bulk of the study is based upon primary sources, chiefly the well-kept records of the Springfield Armory. Being an economist and not an arms collector or arms student, the author has the healthy advantage of being able to view the data with a different eye than the arms student might use. This can be both an advantage and a disadvantage, but in this particular case it seems to be an advantage.

The importance of this study, and the great scarcity of copies of the original edition of 1948, call for republication. This present small edition is reprinted in facsimile from a copy of the first edition.

This study originally was titled ARMS MAKERS OF THE CONNECTICUT VALLEY. A small modification of this title seemed desirable to eliminate a possible implication that this is a biographical study, therefore, with the author's permission, it has been re-titled ARMS MAKING IN THE CONNECTICUT VALLEY.

George Shumway

ABOUT THE AUTHOR

Felicia Johnson Deyrup, A.B. Barnard College, 1938, M.A. Columbia University, 1939, Ph.D. Columbia University, 1946, was appointed Fellow of the Council of Industrial Studies of Smith College, 1940-1941. She was research assistant, 1942-1943, to Professor Alpheus T. Mason of Princeton University in the preparation of his biography of Louis D. Brandeis, and is at present instructor in economics at Brooklyn College.

CONTENTS

ACKNOWLEDGMENTS v
INTRODUCTORY NOTE vii
PART 1. INTRODUCTION 1
    I. The Place of Small Arms Manufacture in American History   3
    II. The Technical Development of Small Arms, 1770-1870 .. 17
    III. The Roots of the Industry 33
PART 2. DEVELOPMENT UNDER GOVERNMENT PATRONAGE, 1798-1830 39
    IV. Early Nineteenth Century Arms Makers 41
    V. The Contract System 55
    VI. Raw Materials 68
    VII. Interchangeability and Machine Tools 87
    VIII. Labor 100
PART 3. INDUSTRIAL INDEPENDENCE, 1831-1860 115
    IX. The New Manufacturers 117
    X. Raw Materials 133
    XI. Interchangeability and Machine Tools 144
    XII. Labor 160
PART 4. EXPANSION AND ADJUSTMENT, 1861-1870 175
    XIII. The Civil War 177
    XIV. Post-War Adjustment and Development 202
Conclusion 215
APPENDIX A. GENERAL STATISTICS AND MISCELLANEOUS DATA 217
    Table 1. Statistics of Small Arms Manufacture Derived from the United States Censuses of Manufactures, 1850-1940 217
    Table 2. Statistics of the Small Arms Industry Selected from the United States Censuses of Manufactures, 1850-1940 217
    Table 3. Concentration of Small Arms Manufacture in New England: Percentage Figures Based on the United States Censuses of Manufactures, 1850-1940 218
    Table 4. Data on Connecticut Valley Small Arms Manufacturers Selected from the United States Censuses of Manufactures of 1810 and 1822, from the Reports of the Federal Census Enumerators, and from Other Sources 220
    A List of New England Small Arms Manufacturers and Gunsmiths, 1770-1870 221
    Representative Federal Small Arms Contract, 1822 227
APPENDIX B. STATISTICS OF COST, PRICES AND PRODUCTION OF SMALL ARMS 229
    Table 1. Costs and Prices of the Springfield Musket and Breech-Loading Rifle, 1798-1870 229
    Table 2. Annual Production at the Springfield Armory, 1795-1870 233

CONTENTS

APPENDIX C. STATISTICS OF RAW MATERIALS 234
  Table 1. Prices of the Main Raw Materials of Small Arms
    Manufacture, 1800-1870 234
APPENDIX D. STATISTICS OF LABOR 240
  Table 1. The Growth of Occupational Specialization Among
    Production Workers at the Springfield Armory, 1806-1870 .. 240
  Table 2. Piece and Time Work of Production Workers, Assist-
    ant Master Armorers, Foremen, Assistant Foremen and In-
    spectors at the Springfield Armory, 1806-1870 240
  Table 3. Mean and Modal Monthly Money Wages of Springfield
    Armory Production Workers, 1802-1870; Real Wage Index of
    Springfield Armory Production Workers, 1802-1861; Moul-
    ton's Index of Average Real Wages in the United States,
    with Shifted Base, 1802-1870 241
  Table 4. Employment of Production Workers at the Springfield
    Armory, 1802-1870 245
  Table 5. Productivity of Barrel Welders at the Springfield
    Armory, 1806-1870 247
  Table 6. Piece-Rates for Barrel Welding at the Springfield
    Armory, 1806-1870 248
  Table 7. Average Monthly Wages of Small Arms Workers and
    Machinists in the Connecticut River Valley, 1822-1870 249
BIBLIOGRAPHY 250
REFERENCES 255
INDEX 284
CHARTS
  1. Comparison of Small Arms Industry and All United States
    Industry, 1850-1940 6
  2. Average Annual Wage of Small Arms Workers and of All
    United States Industrial Workers, 1850-1940 8
  3. Small Arms Manufacture, 1850-1940 10
  4. Concentration of Small Arms Manufacture in New England,
    1850-1940 12
  5. Distribution of Gunsmiths and Arms Manufacturers in New
    England, 1770-1870 15
  6. The Development of Small Arms 18
  7. The Development of Ammunition 20
  1, Appendix C. Prices of Raw Materials of Small Arms Manu-
    facture, Cole's and Mitchell's Commodity Price Indices and
    the Premium on Gold, 1800-1870 238
  1, Appendix D. Monthly Money Wages of Springfield Armory
    Workers, Real Wage and Cost of Living Indices, 1802-1870 .. 244
  2, Appendix D. Productivity and Piece Rates of Springfield
    Armory Barrel Welders, 1806-1870 246

ACKNOWLEDGMENTS

For aid and encouragement given me in preparing this study I wish to express my gratitude to Dr. Constance McLaughlin Green, Director of Research of the Council of Industrial Studies, Smith College; to Professors Carter Goodrich, Louis M. Hacker and Leo Wolman of Columbia University; to Professors Esther Lowenthal, Harold U. Faulkner and William Orton of Smith College. I am indebted to Brigadier-General G. H. Stewart, Ordnance Department, A. U. S., for giving me access to the Springfield Armory records. Major Alonzo Gaidos, Ordnance Department, A. U. S., has generously prepared the illustrations of small arms and ammunition especially for this study, and has read and criticized the chapter on the technical development of small arms. Major James E. Hicks, Ordnance Department, A. U. S., gave me most valuable assistance in the early part of my research and has permitted me to quote passages from his books, *Nathan Starr* and *Notes on United States Ordnance*. Mr. Maurice W. Cruze of the Department of Industrial Relations of the Springfield Armory has been very helpful in making the Armory records available. Mr. Edwin Pugsley, Vice-President of the Winchester Repeating Arms Co., has given me important information on the early history of the small arms industry. Through the courtesy of Colt's Patent Fire Arms Manufacturing Co. and especially of Mr. Harold G. Hart, Curator of the company's Arthur L. Ulrich Museum, I have had an opportunity to examine the museum's manuscript materials. I am under obligation to Mr. Henry Bacon, Secretary of the Middlesex County Historical Society, Middletown, Conn., for the privilege of studying the Starr and Aston papers in the Society's possession. Mrs. Margaret Brainerd Rolfe, a former fellow of the Council of Industrial Studies, has allowed me to use some notes on the Springfield Armory records. For the preparation of the charts I am indebted to my sister, Dr. Ingrith Deyrup. To Mr. O. C. Lightner, publisher of *Hobbies*, I am grateful for permission to reprint part of a letter by Samuel Colt.

INTRODUCTORY NOTE

This study is based in large part upon the records of the federal Armory at Springfield, Mass. The writer has also made use of the records of the Ames Manufacturing Co. of Chicopee, Mass., in the possession of the late Mrs. Edward Hale of Chicopee; the records of Colt's Patent Fire Arms Manufacturing Co., housed in the company's Arthur L. Ulrich Museum, in Hartford, Conn.; the papers of Henry Aston, of Nathan Starr Sr. and Jr., and of E. W. N. Starr, in the possession of the Middlesex County Historical Society, Middletown, Conn. Records of Valley arms manufacturers which are known to exist, but were unavailable to research workers at the time the material for this study was collected, are some papers of Samuel Colt, in the possession of the Connecticut Historical Society, Hartford, some letters of Eli Whitney Sr., and some early records of the Winchester Repeating Arms Co. of New Haven. Officers of the Winchester Repeating Arms Co. have stated that the business records of the Whitney Armory were destroyed, and officers of the J. Stevens Arms Co. of Chicopee Falls, Mass., believe that the early records of this company also were destroyed. The Smith & Wesson Co. of Springfield may have some early business records, but the writer has been unable to obtain any information on this. The writer knows of no other records of early Connecticut Valley small arms manufacturers.

This study has been extended to the Valley arms industry as a whole, rather than limited to the manufacturers whose records have been examined, since it seems apparent that these manufacturers are truly representative of the Valley industry, and the discovery of any additional sources of information would probably support the conclusions reached in this study.

PART 1
INTRODUCTION

CHAPTER I

THE PLACE OF SMALL ARMS MANUFACTURE
IN AMERICAN INDUSTRY

Small arms manufacture has played in the history of American industry a rôle of incalculable importance in the development of modern production methods. In this field the principle of making the parts of a weapon, tool or machine fully interchangeable with those of others of the same model, for factory production and for inexpensive repair, was first recognized and realized. The small arms industry also developed a variety of metal-working machine tools, adapted to specific tasks, at a time when elsewhere machine tools did not exist, or were crude or of only generalized function. Finally, because of the emphasis upon interchangeability of parts, precision measurement was greatly advanced in small arms manufacture. Interchangeability, machine tool production and precision measurement, three of the salient features of modern American industry, were well established in arms plants when much of this country's production was still on the handicraft level, or only slightly above it.

The development of the Connecticut Valley arms industry holds much of interest for the student of general American economic history. Small and self-contained though it has been, the industry has attained signal importance through its position at the key point of machine tool manufacture. In many respects its history has been typical of that of American manufacture generally. Small arms making only waited for sufficient capital to be available to spring from the level of a handicraft to that of an industry. As was elsewhere the case, it acquired important international markets within a very few decades after coming into existence. The history of small arms manufacture involves also specific problems characteristic of American industry as a whole, such as those connected with the development of cost accounting, with the use of machines and steam-power, with changes in product design, and with the technical lag which has so often occurred between inventions and their industrial application.

In some respects the history of arms making is unique. The unusual sensitivity of the industry to changes in political and foreign affairs is obvious. Arms manufacture was launched with government aid, and through its formative years could not have survived had government support been withdrawn. This gave it an integrated quality not usually present in early nineteenth century industry. One result of government domination was that private manufacturers were required to conform to public standards of production and cost. Another was the development of a strong spirit of cooperation among the early arms makers.

3

Unlike other industries, arms making did not benefit conspicuously from reduced cost as a result of mass production. And although real wages of many Connecticut Valley armorers seem to have paralleled closely those of American industrial workers as a whole, the industry is unusual in regard to the type of labor it has employed. Many arms workers, to be sure, as industrialization advanced became nothing more than semi-skilled machine tenders. But a large number retained much of the skill of the all around gunsmith, and as a group arms workers have remained among the most highly skilled and highly paid of American workers. The fact that industrial strife has been at a minimum in the industry is no doubt largely owing to this situation.

From the standpoint of economic theory, the history of small arms manufacture has some bearing on the economics of overhead cost. The production of interchangeable weapons has necessitated heavy investment in machine tools, as well as the employment of highly skilled workers. Yet the nature of the market for small arms is such that, except in wartime or in response to sporadic demand for military arms, the industry has never been able consistently to produce arms in sufficient quantities to reduce overhead cost to a reasonable proportion of unit cost. The combination of an unresponsive demand and burdensome overhead cost has frequently proved fatal to small arms concerns. Diversification of production, through manufacture of additional articles requiring the same type of labor and equipment as those used in arms making, has been the only even partially satisfactory means of coping with the problem of overhead cost.

This study attempts to record the economic development of small arms manufacture from its first appearance as an offshoot of gunsmithing in 1798 to its emergence by 1870 as an essentially modern industry. For purposes of orientation a brief discussion is given of the technical development of small arms from 1770 to 1870, followed by a chapter dealing with the period from 1770 to 1797, when the foundations of arms manufacture were being laid. The history of the industry from 1798 to 1870 has been divided into three periods. The first, from 1798 to 1830, covers the time in which arms manufacture was developing under government patronage. The second, from 1831 to 1860, deals with the years in which it achieved its independence. The third period, from 1861 to 1870, includes the extreme expansion of the Civil War and the years of readjustment immediately following. In each of these periods the significant aspects of the industry have been treated under topical headings corresponding with one another to facilitate comparison of the periods.

In geographic scope this study is limited to the Connecticut River Valley of New England, since this region is both the area in which the bulk of American small arms manufacture has normally been located, and, more significantly, the center from which most of the achievements of the industry have sprung. The characteristics of arms making as well as the nature of the data available have thrown the emphasis in this study upon the productive rather than upon the financial aspect of the economic development of small arms manufacture.

Particular attention is given to the United States Springfield Armory. As one of the two federal factories for the manufacture of complete small arms during the early nineteenth century, this armory served as an early yardstick for measuring the performance of private industry. The importance of the Armory was not, however, limited to the establishment and maintenance of standards of quality and cost to which the industry as a whole, through the contract system, was compelled to conform. Of still greater value in the growth of small arms manufacture was the Armory's function as a laboratory in which was developed a body of knowledge of improved weapon designs and better manufacturing methods easily accessible to the other arms makers. The Armory lost its preeminent position only when the industry attained its independence from government influence.

The records of the Springfield Armory, upon which this study is in large part based, afford unusually appropriate material for economic study. These records have been kept with a preciseness and detail uncommon in early American enterprise, and unique as far as New England arms manufacture is concerned. This in part derives from the position of the Armory as a government establishment subject at any time to a public accounting. In part it is a by-product of the yardstick function, which demanded a careful analysis and recording of all matters affecting standards of performance. The vast amount of correspondence carried on over the years between the Armory and other arms makers, all of which has been preserved in the Springfield Armory records, gives access to information on the Valley industry as a whole which would have been otherwise unattainable in view of the fragmentary nature of the surviving records of private manufacturers.

Important as small arms manufacture has been as the field in which some of the essential features of modern production arose, and indispensable as it is in guaranteeing the military position of the United States, quantitatively the industry has been an insignificant and diminishing item in the total of American manufacture. During peace small arms making has amounted to no more than three-tenths of one per cent or less of all American industry, when the census figures of the factory production of

6

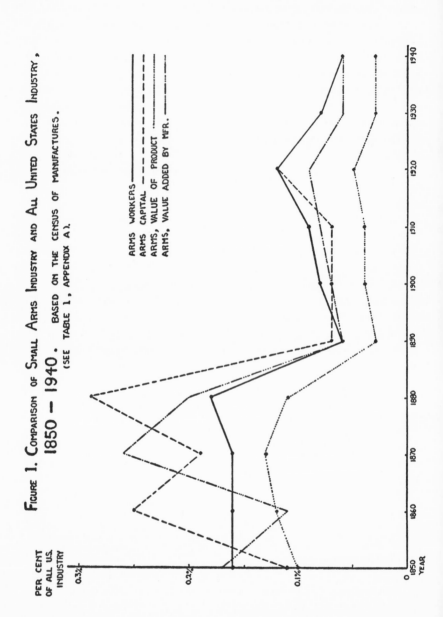

FIGURE 1. COMPARISON OF SMALL ARMS INDUSTRY AND ALL UNITED STATES INDUSTRY, 1850 – 1940. BASED ON THE CENSUS OF MANUFACTURES. (SEE TABLE 1, APPENDIX A).

PER CENT OF ALL U.S. INDUSTRY

0.3%

0.2%

0.1%

0

ARMS WORKERS
ARMS CAPITAL
ARMS, VALUE OF PRODUCT
ARMS, VALUE ADDED BY MFR.

1850 1860 1870 1880 1890 1900 1910 1920 1930 1940

YEAR

small arms are separated from those for ammunition manufacture, gun-smithing, and the making of heavy ordnance.* Data derived from the United States Censuses of Manufactures clarify the statistical position of small arms in American industry.** Figure 1 shows the proportion represented by the small arms industry relatively to United States industry as a whole in the items of capital, value of product, value added by manufacture, and number of workers employed. The year 1850 was taken as a point of departure for this chart since the Census of Manufactures for that year was the first sufficiently complete to be usable. As this chart shows percentage figures, it is unaffected by inflationary trends.

The most significant aspect of the four curves is their consistency with one another. Their course might lead to the conclusion that arms manufacture declined during the period under study to a third or less from its high point. This assumption, however, is unwarranted, for arms manufacture has grown rapidly, but has lost its relative position in total American industry by reason of the enormous development of other industries.

This chart shows that in arms manufacture none of the four items of measurement under consideration ever reached three-tenths of one per cent of the corresponding measurements of American industry as a whole, and that from 1890 onward rarely did any one exceed one-tenth of one per cent. It cannot be assumed, however, that this was constantly so in periods between the census years. The Civil War, the Spanish-American War, and the first World War fell between census years, so that their influence in the data is not clearly indicated. Had a census been taken in 1865, the figures on small arms would doubtless have far surpassed the peaks of the industry in 1870 and 1880.

In all four items of measurement the high point of the small arms industry occurred in 1870 or 1880. This is evidently in part the result of the expansion stimulated by the Civil War and by the development of foreign markets. The drop in the curves in the following years must be

* The term small arms industry may be defined for the purposes of this study as the factory production of weapons carried on the person. It must not be confused with the trade or handicraft of gunsmithing, from which it is historically derived and to which therefore some attention must be given. Throughout this study, as well as in the census statistics presented in Appendix A, an effort is made to keep the distinction clear between the arms industry and its related craft of gunsmithing. At no point have ammunition or heavy ordnance, which includes machine guns and cannon of all varieties, been included with small arms.

** The use of census figures necessarily subjects the statistical results which are here presented to all the limitations of the census. For example, handicrafts were included in the census figures for 1850. Businesses falling below certain size limits have always been excluded from the census. Statements for capital are excluded from the censuses of 1930 and 1940. In this study the official census year, falling on the first year of each decade, has been used for the sake of clarity and uniformity. As the study ends with 1870 it seemed unnecessary to include in Appendix A data from the more frequent censuses of the twentieth century.

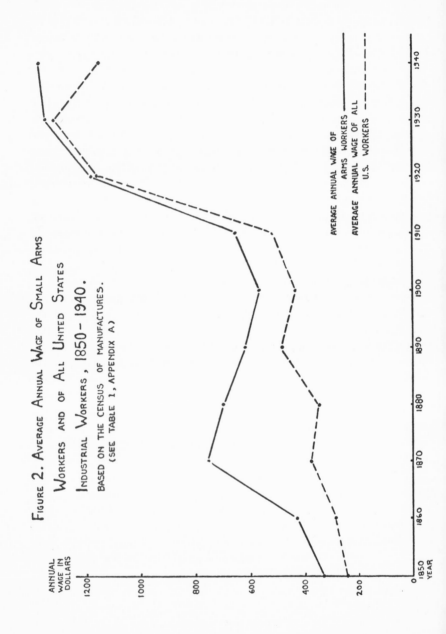

Figure 2. Average Annual Wage of Small Arms Workers and of All United States Industrial Workers, 1850–1940.

Based on the census of manufactures.
(See Table 1, Appendix A)

mainly attributed to the rapid growth of other manufactures after 1890, which compressed arms manufacture to a still smaller percentage of American industry as a whole. It is notable that on the eve of the second World War the small arms industry was, relatively to other industries, at a low point equalled only by its position in 1890 and 1920.

Of the four curves, those representing the number of workers and the value of the product show the least fluctuation. The value added by manufacture, covering the difference between the value of the product and the cost of materials, fluctuates almost as much as capital. Capital is consistently well above the value of the product, indicating that for a given amount of value of product heavier investment is required in small arms than in most industries.

An outstanding characteristic of small arms manufacture is its high annual wages. Figure 2 shows annual wages of arms workers and of all American industrial workers for 1860-1940.* As these figures are expressed in dollars, the effect of long-term inflation is conspicuous. The points at which the difference in wages is greatest are 1870 and 1880, the years in which the small arms industry was at its peak in proportion to all American industry. Wages of arms workers began to lose ground compared with average wages in 1910, barely keeping ahead of them until the depression of the 1930's again widened the gap between the two sets of wages. Arms workers, since they were in an industry at the key point of small metal products manufacture, were in an exceptionally favored position and did not receive the cut in money wages which the average worker suffered in the 1930's.

Arms workers' wages from 1850 to 1940 made a less remarkable rise than other aspects of small arms manufacture. Figure 3 shows the increase in dollars, of capital, value of product, and value added by manufacture in this period. Here the effect of secular inflationary tendencies, intensified by wars, is conspicuous. As a result of Civil War expansion and general price rises, value added by manufacture was more than quadrupled, and value of product doubled in the decade 1860-1870. Capital was not quite doubled. Like the percentage figure for capital shown in Figure 1, capital in dollars rose steadily to 1880. The three items dropped in 1890, only to begin a spectacular rise in the decade from 1910 to 1920 to fourfold the original figures. After 1920 no information relating to capital is available. Naturally in the twenty years of peace that followed, a rapid drop took place.

In American small arms manufacture early in the nineteenth century

---

* It must be borne in mind that part of the difference in the two wage curves is attributable to the fact that the bulk of American small arms manufacture has been carried on in New England, a region of high average industrial wages.

10

Figure 3. Small Arms Manufacture, 1850 - 1940.

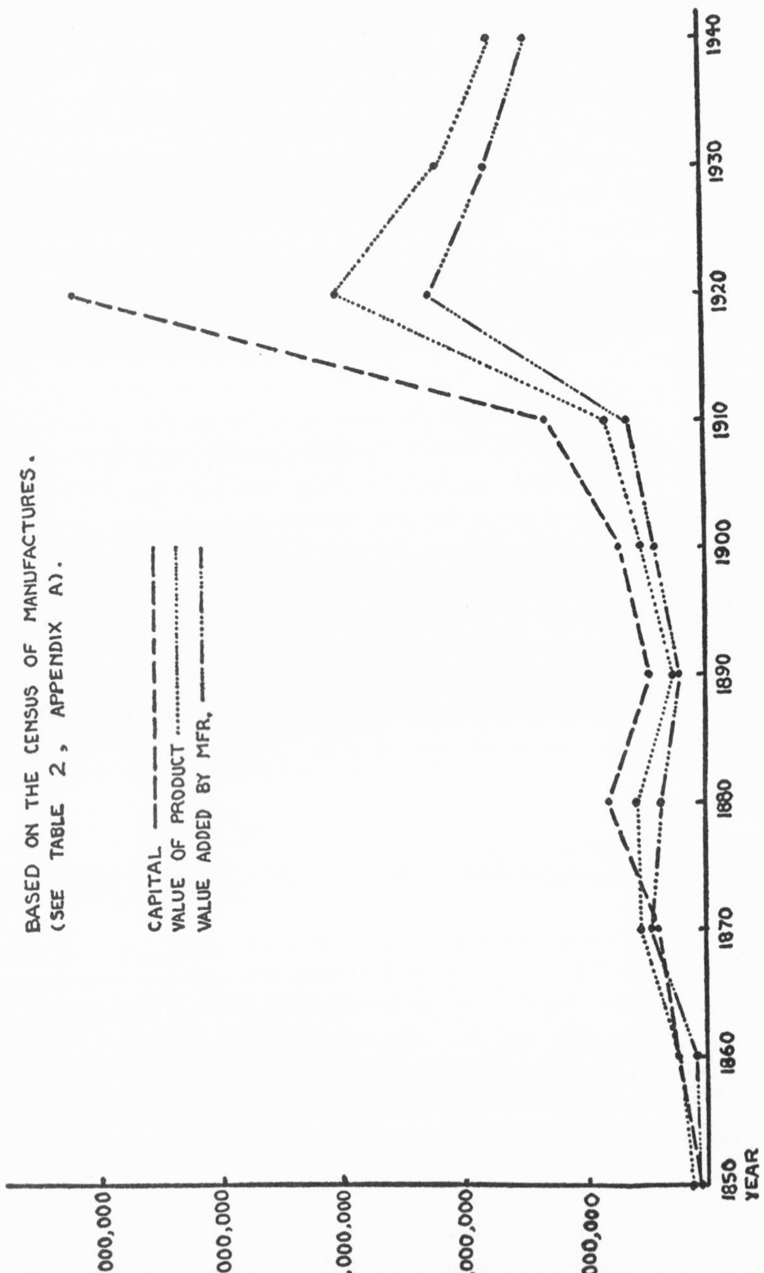

Based on the census of manufactures.
(See table 2 , appendix A).

CAPITAL ----------
VALUE OF PRODUCT ....
VALUE ADDED BY MFR, -----------

DOLLARS

50,000,000

40,000,000

30,000,000

20,000,000

10,000,000

1850 1860 1870 1880 1890 1900 1910 1920 1930 1940
YEAR

practical interchangeability, or uniformity of parts, was first deliberately aimed at and achieved. This had been attempted in the French small arms industry in 1717 and again in 1785, but it had been impossible to overcome deep-seated prejudice, the lack of suitable machinery, and faulty factory organization.[1] In England interchangeability had been closely approached shortly after 1800, when at Portsmouth ships' blocks or pulleys were made interchangeable through the use of machinery. But the true significance of this achievement was not realized at the time, for uniformity in blocks was of comparatively slight importance. In this instance interchangeability was the result of good manufacturing methods rather than a deliberate objective.[2]

Interchangeability was introduced in the United States arms industry after the War of 1812.[3] Eli Whitney, important as a New England arms maker as well as inventor of the cotton gin, was prominent in the development of the system. His workers filed the parts of the gun lock to hardened jigs or forms in which the parts were held, and thus made them identical.[4] At other plants, such as Simeon North's armory at Middletown, Conn. and the federal Springfield and Harper's Ferry Armories, the interchangeable system was also developing. It was the cumulative work of the large gun makers, rather than the contribution of one man. Once introduced, interchangeability proceeded along the lines of increasing refinement through the use of machine tools and of gages of closer tolerance. By the middle of the nineteenth century the "American System," as it was now called, had become famous throughout Europe. England sent a commission to the United States to study the system. The resulting orders for small arms with parts that could be interchanged and for gun machinery with which to make such weapons opened up world markets to American gun makers and tool builders.[5]

Elsewhere in American manufacture interchangeability developed at much later periods, nor was it always a main objective of the industry. In the manufacture of clocks uniformity was introduced for the benefit of wholesale production and because of the need of uniform gearing.[6] This was probably the second industry to achieve uniformity, but the contribution of clock manufacture to interchangeability in metal products was of limited value.[7] Watch makers did not attempt interchangeability until 1848.[8] After 1846 it was established in sewing machine manufacture, where it became of first importance.[9]

In contrast to development in these industries, interchangeability was long delayed in the manufacture of other metal products, for example, locomotives. The comparatively small market for locomotives and the enormous investment for machinery required for introduction of interchangeability explain the lag. Not until about 1860 was the system established at the Baldwin locomotive works.[10]

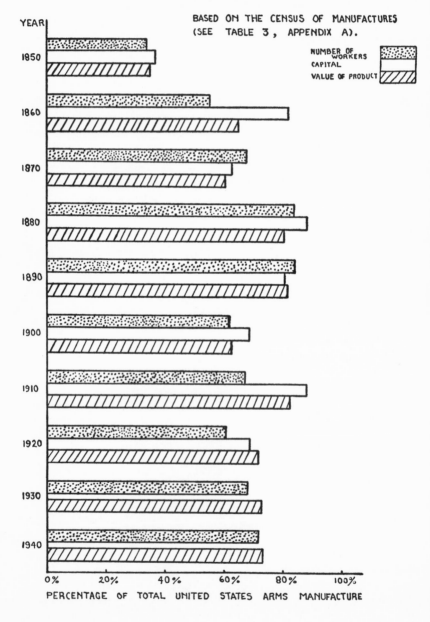

FIGURE 4. CONCENTRATION OF SMALL ARMS MANUFACTURE
IN NEW ENGLAND, 1850 – 1940.

BASED ON THE CENSUS OF MANUFACTURES
(SEE TABLE 3, APPENDIX A).

NUMBER OF WORKERS
CAPITAL
VALUE OF PRODUCT

PERCENTAGE OF TOTAL UNITED STATES ARMS MANUFACTURE

The early development in machine tools was in large part the result of pioneering work in the small arms industry. Although the cotton industry developed the American general machine tool,[11] the invention of certain highly specialized machines and the application of important mechanical principles are directly attributable to small arms manufacture. For example, Christopher Spencer, inventor of the Spencer rifle, introduced the cam control by which the operation of lathes was made automatic. F. W. Howe and Henry D. Stone, builders of machine tools for arms manufacture, introduced the turret lathe into American industry. The underlying principles involved in the cam control and the turret lathe are among the most vital in modern mechanized production.[12] Furthermore, many of the most influential machine tool firms of the country grew out of small arms manufacture.

The third contribution of small arms to American industry, the establishment of precision measurement, was integrally associated with interchangeability. To achieve the close fit required in small arms parts, manufacturers early developed and constantly improved a system of gages. These gages evolved from the cruder ones used by the early federal inspectors of arms to gages of extremely close tolerance, and included such types as receiver gages, limit gages, and for especially delicate work, vernier calipers and micrometers.[13] The linkage of interchangeability, machine tool production and precision measurement with standardization of product and therefore with the system of mass production characteristic of modern American industry is so obvious as to need no emphasis.

An outstanding aspect of the industry is its concentration in the northeastern section of the United States, particularly in New England. Unlike its kindred industry, ammunition manufacture, it is dependent upon the presence of a large number of highly skilled workers. Its kindred handicraft, gunsmithing, because of its character as a service, is more dependent upon population concentration than is arms manufacture. For this reason gunsmithing is far more widely distributed throughout the country than is ammunition manufacture, which in turn is more widely distributed than small arms manufacture.

The extent to which the industry was concentrated in New England from 1850 to 1940, as calculated from the statistics of the Censuses of Manufactures, is shown in percentage figures in Figure 4. Capital, number of workers, and value of product are here again taken as representative measurements. It will be noted that with a few exceptions two-thirds or more of these items have represented the New England branch of the industry. An exception are the figures for 1850, a year in which less than 38 per cent of capital, workers, and value of product was attributed to New England. This is because the Census of 1850 included gunsmithing in small arms manufacture, while later censuses distinguished clearly between the industry and the handicraft. Thus the 60% of the industry lying outside New England in 1850 must represent gunsmithing rather than small arms manufacture. This conclusion is borne out by the figures for 1860, which show a great increase in the percentage of the industry, and in particular a heavy concentration of capital, in New England. 1860 marked the end of a ten-year period of remarkable machine tool development and plant expansion, during which, for the first time, American arms and arms making machinery were being exported in great quantities to Europe.

The figures for 1870 reflect the influence of the Civil War on the arms industry, and show a diminution of the concentration in New England. This indicates not so much a decline in the number of New England plants after the war but rather a wider distribution, incident to expansion of the industry during the war. This inference is confirmed by the figures for 1880 and 1890, both years representing the close of peaceful decades, in which arms making subsided in other states and left the industry once more highly concentrated in New England. The figures for 1900 again represent expansion of the industry in other states in response to the demands of the Spanish-American War. 1910 shows a swing back to peace time conditions, with the New England concentration once more heavy. 1920, following the first World War, shows a wider distribution, which persisted through 1930 and 1940, and which may indicate that the proportion of the industry in New England has been substantially and permanently reduced.

Within New England there has been marked concentration of the industry in the Connecticut River Valley. Figure 5 shows the distribution of important arms makers and arms companies in New England during the period 1798-1870. This chart is based on published lists of arms manufacturers, and includes only those individuals, firms and corporations that appear to have carried on businesses of factory proportions. Many of these concerns were short lived, so that at no time more than a fraction of all the manufacturers here presented were active. The chart shows that most of the important arms makers were located in the vicinity of the Connecticut River.

The Connecticut River Valley may be considered, for the purposes of this study, to extend about thirty miles on either side of the river, and to include New Haven and Norwich, but not Worcester. These lines of demarcation have been fixed upon because of the close economic relations which developed among the arms makers directly located on the river and those no farther away than New Haven and Norwich. The arms industry at Worcester, on the other hand, was completely independent of that along the Connecticut.

FIGURE 5. DISTRIBUTION OF GUNSMITHS AND ARMS MANUFACTURERS IN NEW ENGLAND, 1770 - 1870.

(SEE APPENDIX A).

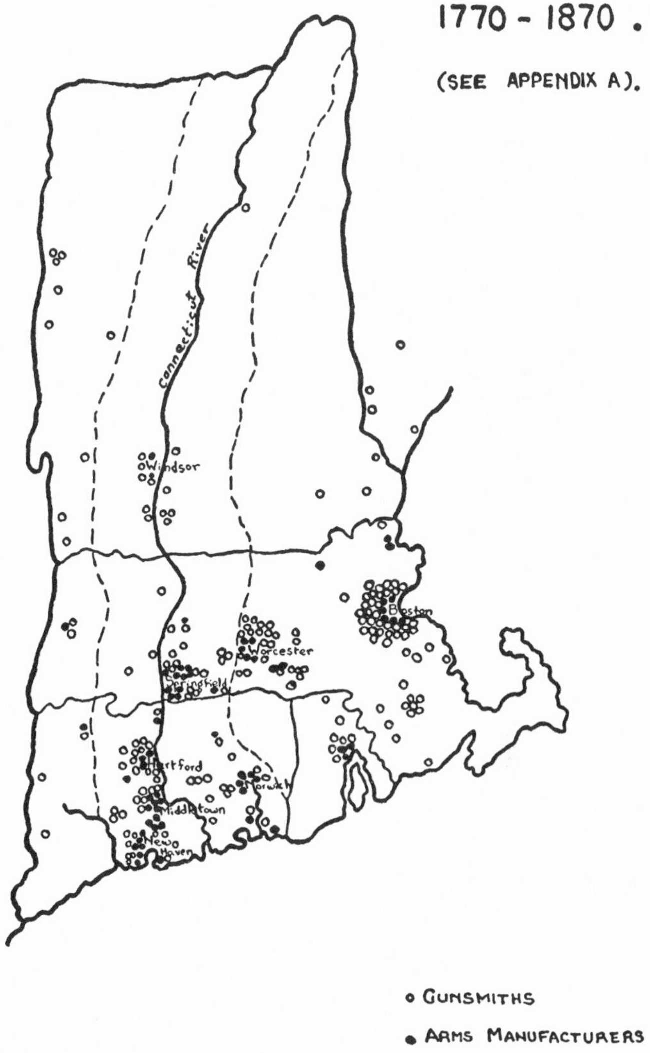

o GUNSMITHS

● ARMS MANUFACTURERS

For the sake of comparison, and also because small arms factory production developed from gunsmithing, the location of New England gunsmiths for the period 1770-1870 is included in Figure 5. The data are from the same sources. It is evident that the large centers of gunsmithing, as well as of small arms manufacture, have been New Haven, Norwich, Middletown, Hartford, Springfield, Worcester, Providence and Boston. Gunsmithing was also important in eastern Massachusetts, southern Maine, southern Vermont and New Hampshire, and along the entire western border of New England. Many of the large arms makers and arms factories found a footing in various centers where gunsmiths had been before them. It is notable, however, that Boston and its vicinity, while far surpassing any other single center in number of gunsmiths, had few large arms concerns. This emphasizes the point made earlier that gunsmithing is more vitally affected by population conditions than by the factors which govern the location of the small arms industry.

CHAPTER II

THE TECHNICAL DEVELOPMENT OF SMALL ARMS, 1770-1870

In the century between 1770 and 1870 American firearms achieved a perfection in design which their previous history would hardly have led one to believe possible.* The astounding rapidity of this technical development epitomized the enormous advance of American industry and invention occurring within this period. On the one hand, as in other industries, gradual improvements in manufacturing techniques made it possible to produce goods of high quality in much greater quantities than under a handicraft system. On the other hand, invention and refinement in design progressed by leaps and bounds, from flint to percussion lock, from muzzle- to breech-loading system, from single-shot to magazine or repeating gun, from powder and ball to center-fire metallic cartridge—so that by the end of this period much of the accumulated knowledge which has gone into the development of firearms of the twentieth century was in the possession of gun designers and inventors.

These hundred years may be divided into specific periods during which one or another type of improvement in firearm construction was introduced. It must be borne in mind, however, that in the course of continuous experimentation many improvements were developed which only later were to play their part in revolutionizing the industry. In fact most of the outstanding innovations in design were recognized as valuable for years before the industry generally accepted them. Their adoption was delayed because of weaknesses in experimental arms not inherent in the inventions applied to them, and because of the crudeness of models, difficulty in securing sufficient financial support for refinements of inventions, and conservatism among the manufacturers and the buying public.

Keeping in mind, then, the time lag between the introduction and the adoption of improvements, one may differentiate between the era of the flintlock, which preceded the Revolution by many years, and that of the percussion lock, which began about 1842. Revolvers became generally accepted in the 1840's. With the development of metallic ammunition, breech-loading arms became of practical use just before the Civil War.

---

* The discussion in this chapter is concerned with firearms alone, for early in the nineteenth century edge weapons sank into comparative insignificance. The use of swords by army and navy officers and by cavalry, and of pikes by seamen, became greatly restricted as firearms increased in variety and accuracy. The bayonet was the only edge weapon that did not become obsolete as hand-to-hand fighting was limited by the development of guns with increased range. The potentialities of edge weapons had been fully explored earlier, and changes in their design hold little of interest compared with the changes which took place in firearms during the nineteenth century.

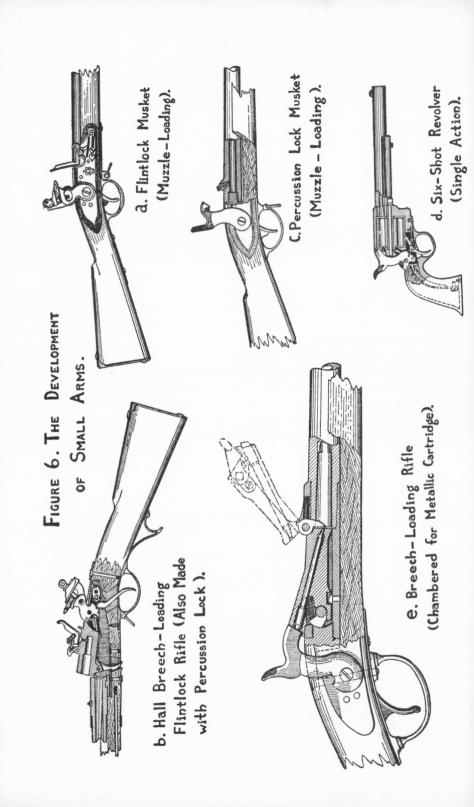

Figure 6. The Development of Small Arms.

a. Flintlock Musket (Muzzle-Loading).

c. Percussion Lock Musket (Muzzle-Loading).

d. Six-Shot Revolver (Single Action).

b. Hall Breech-Loading Flintlock Rifle (Also Made with Percussion Lock).

e. Breech-Loading Rifle (Chambered for Metallic Cartridge).

Like breech-loaders, repeating and magazine rifles* depended for their success upon the metallic cartridge, and it was not until shortly before the Civil War that they began to appear. The most important period in their development did not occur until after 1870, when the potentialities of single-shot arms had been thoroughly exploited.

1. The Flintlock Period.

The flintlock, a firearm of Spanish origin dating from about 1630, was the type of small arm characteristic of colonial America[1] (Figure 6a). The essential mechanism of the flintlock consisted of a cock under spring tension, holding between its jaws a flint, which, when the cock was released, struck a piece of steel—the frizzen—placed above the priming or flash-pan. The sparks which were generated ignited the powder in the pan and a flash of fire travelled through a small hole into the barrel, reaching the charge of propellent powder behind the ball. For military arms the ammunition consisted either of paper cartridges containing powder and a round ball, or, in the case of United States rifle regiments and dragoons, loose powder and balls[2] (Figure 7a).

There were two dominant types of flintlock weapons—the smooth-bore musket of New England and the rifle of the central and southern colonies. The clear-cut geographical distribution of these arms is notable. From Lancaster in eastern Pennsylvania the manufacture of the rifle spread south and west, including the whole of Pennsylvania, Kentucky, Ohio, and, to a less extent, Virginia, Maryland, Georgia and Louisiana.[3] New England, on the other hand, specialized in the manufacture and use of the smooth-bore musket to the almost complete exclusion of the rifle. One authority holds that New Englanders did not "take" to the rifle, so that prior to the Revolution no rifle shop existed east of the Hudson River. It was only by inducing migration of Pennsylvania gunsmiths that Sir William Johnson started some rifle manufacture shortly before the Revolution around Kingston, Schenectady, Johnstown and Canajoharie in New York.[4] Another expert in the history of small arms succeeded in discovering only three rifle makers in New England prior to the Revolution, although he believes that the rifle was to some extent used there.[5] A third claims that, with the exception of some of the Green Mountain Boys and a few veterans of earlier wars who had served in the middle colonies, New Englanders as late as the Revolution were unacquainted with the rifle.[6]

So clear-cut was this geographical specialization that in 1792 and 1793 the new federal government contracted for "rifle guns" with gunsmiths located in the southern, or Pennsylvania, region.[7] It is true that muskets

* No attempt is made in this discussion to differentiate between repeating and magazine rifles.

as well as rifles were repaired in the Philadelphia area in the period between the Revolution and 1800, but there is no indication that any were made in this region at that time.[8] The military muskets made on contract and by the federal government, on the other hand, came almost exclusively from New England.[9]

The difference between these two localities of manufacture may be

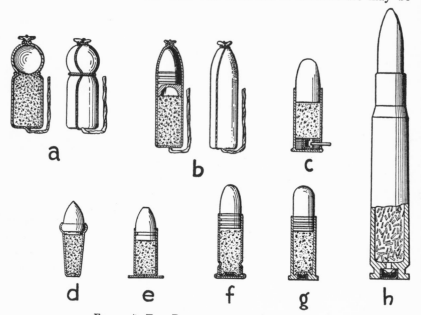

FIGURE 7. THE DEVELOPMENT OF AMMUNITION
a. Ball and Powder Encased in Paper or Linen. 1794.
b. Conical Ball and Powder Encased in Paper or Linen. 1812-1865.
c. French Pin-Fire. 1820-1870.
d. Burnside Metallic Cartridge Fired by Separate Percussion Cap. 1861-1865.
e. Maynard Metallic Cartridge Fired by Separate Percussion Cap. 1861-1865.
f. Folded Head Primed Cartridge. 1866-1870.
g. Berdan Primer. 1870.
h. Modern Cartridge with Boxer Type Primer.

partly accounted for historically. Rifling, invented in the fifteenth century, had fallen out of general use on the continent, and only in central Europe were rifles made in large numbers.[10] In the first decade of the eighteenth century German and Palatine Swiss immigration brought many rifle makers to eastern Pennsylvania, and the industry flourished in that colony to such an extent that by the middle of the eighteenth century the famous Kentucky rifle had been developed in Pennsylvania. This was a graceful weapon, long, slender, with a small bore, using a ball wrapped in a piece of greased buckskin or linen, known as a "greased patch," for rapid fire.[11]

It was a custom-made gun, no two specimens being alike or capable of having their parts interchanged. The value of the Kentucky rifle lay in its accuracy in shooting game and in Indian warfare, and in its economical use of ammunition.[12] In general, the barrel had a .45 inch bore, which was reduced, as the big game was killed off and the Indian menace subsided. The length of these early rifles ranged from about four and a half feet to more than six feet.[13]

New England, receiving the majority of its early gunsmiths from England, naturally adopted the musket, which was in general use in that country. For military purposes it surpassed the rifle. Except where a greased patch was used, the early rifle could not be re-loaded indefinitely without cleaning, because of leading or fouling the bore.[14] A round ball, such as was commonly used in both rifle and musket, did not "take" the rifling as well as the elongated ball, which came into general use only many years later, and therefore the rifle was not of much greater value than the musket. It was supposed that great force was needed to ram the ball into the rifle, and the resulting slowness in loading limited its usefulness, so that only a few picked troops were equipped with it after American independence.[15] Rifling was cut at considerable expense of time and effort, and required a skilled armorer's attention. It is also probable that the rifling did not stand up under continuous and at times careless use in the field.[16]

During the Revolution the colonial governments were perforce catholic in their tastes in small arms and used any sort of firearms available, including muskets, rifles, pistols and even blunderbusses and fowling pieces.[17] But with independence the problem arose of choosing a standard set of weapons for military purposes. The French government had furnished this country in the course of the war with large quantities of muskets, most of them Charlevilles, the standard French military musket, of the model of 1763. It was this model which was adopted by the United States government at the end of the eighteenth century for manufacture at its armory at Springfield and on contract with private arms makers.[18] From the model of 1799 to the model of 1818 the government musket had a .69 inch bore.[19] The Charleville musket continued as the official American military smooth-bore weapon until 1842, though it was modified in length, weight, caliber, and in details of construction.[20] The United States government also adopted models of other arms. Most important after the musket was the rifle, in two forms, one loading at the muzzle and the other close to the breech. Other weapons adopted were a carbine, rifled but lighter than the regular rifle; a musketoon, lighter than the musket and like it smooth-bored; a pistol and edge weapons.[21]

While the single-shot, muzzle-loading flintlock arm, either rifled or smooth-bore, dominated this period in the history of firearms, there were several significant variations from this standard. Most renowned, although by no means the most remarkable from the point of view of the later development of small arms, was the Hall breech-loading rifle, first made at Harper's Ferry in 1819[22] (Figure 6b). This weapon was not a forerunner of the modern breech-loading arm, but rather a muzzle-loader which, by the device of a barrel sectioned in parts—the rear part, or receiver, being movable—loaded closer to the breech than did the gun typical of the time. The receiver tipped upwards for loading, but the charge was put in from the front of the receiver, not, as in the modern breech-loader, from the rear.[23] John H. Hall, the inventor, worked at the government armory at Harper's Ferry on this rifle and on a carbine based on the same principle. For these two arms and for the use of the machinery for their manufacture the government paid Hall and his heirs about $37,000.[24] The rifle was made in considerable quantities, not only at Harper's Ferry but also by government contractors.[25] But it showed little tendency to displace the older muzzle-loading arms. Probably the fact that it was not truly a breech-loading gun gave it little superiority over regular muzzle-loaders.*

Another interesting development of this time was a flintlock revolver. Between 1800 and 1817 Elisha Collier, a Boston gunsmith, developed such a weapon, which met with considerable success in operation. This revolver might have become widely used had not its price been prohibitive. Collier moved to England and no one in the United States for many years thereafter developed a successful revolver.[26]

Most noteworthy of all innovations was the invention of "detonating" or percussion caps by Joshua Shaw, who received a patent for this in 1822. A letter written in that year describes the gun which he made to use these caps.** It seems almost incredible that so workable a scheme of ignition,

* Variations of the Hall breech-loading rifle were the North improvement and an experimental carbine patented by Nathan Starr in 1839. In each of these a lever operated the breech system. The Starr arm was similar to the Hall weapon, except that the breech or receiver was opened by an eccentric or cam operated by a lever. This device also cocked the gun. A variation of this, also made by Starr and patented in 1839, included a tie rod attached to the cam, which directed the action of the receiver and no doubt greatly increased its steadiness. Like the Hall weapon, the front of the breech piece was elevated for loading, rather than the rear, as in later breech-loaders.[27]

** Among the papers of the Springfield Armory is the following letter, written by a man named Hobbs and entitled:

Remarks Relative to Mr. Shaw's Detonating Gun, July 11th, 1822
Directed to the Editor of the Hampden Patriot.

Mr. Joshua Shaw of Philadelphia has made an improvement in Fire Arms which promises to be of considerable public utility. It is termed "the Detonating which was later to become the accepted method of firing all small arms, should have taken a score of years to win its way in the industry.

2. The Percussion Period.

Shaw's percussion cap was the basis of the second stage of development in small arms in the United States.* Yet the percussion cap's full value was recognized only tardily, for not until 1845 did the government pay Shaw $20,000 for this invention, and 1842 is the year commonly accepted as marking the beginning of the percussion period.[28] The time lag between the invention and the general adoption of percussioning was owing to distrust and conservatism, faulty manufacture of percussion caps, and the fear of shortages of caps in wilderness campaigns.[29]

There had been considerable early experimentation with the percussion principle before 1842. The percussion lock is said to have been invented early in the nineteenth century,**[30] but one authority believes that it was not until 1837 that the first percussion lock musket appeared in the United States.[31] Percussioning in rifles was apparently adopted at a somewhat

---

Gun." It differs from the common gun by having attached to the barrel a kind of pan called the Antechamber which is screwed into and communicates with the chamber in the barrel, to this is attached what is called the priming tube which is a piece of case-hardened iron or steel about half an inch in length and about $\frac{1}{4}$ of an inch in diameter next to the pan and a little smaller at the other end where it receives the cock with a small hole through it lengthwise into the antechamber, on this tube is placed the priming cap which is a small piece of copper made in a form so as to exactly fit the tube, and has on the upper part of the inside a small quantity of the oximuriate of potash and some other ingredients, which on the percussion of the cock explodes and communicates to the charge in the barrel with the rapidity of lightning. A gun fired on this plan is much less likely to miss fire than one that fires with a flint. It is said that the priming cap with the composition will not be so expensive as the flints and the powder required for priming a common gun. One great advantage of this invention is that it is perfectly water proof, which has long been a desideratum in the manufacture of fire arms. The lock is less expensive than the common lock as there is no need of a hammer or hammer spring nor the screws which attach them to the plate of the lock, and it is thought the pan will balance the expense of the other additions, the writer of this is not in the habit of falling in with every new invention which is offered to the public by the numerous patentees of the present day for it is believed nine-tenths of the patent rights prove to be of very little use either to the public or the proprietors but he was forcibly struck with the operation of Mr. Shaw's gun and is inclined to the opinion that it may be a valuable improvement, but it is expected a gun of this description will be sent to this vicinity and an opportunity afforded of testing its use by actual experiment. Further remarks therefore are deferred until that shall confirm his opinion or diminish the prospect of its advantages.

* Shaw applied for a patent for his percussion cap as early as 1814, but owing to a technicality failed to receive one at that time.[34]

** In 1807 a Scotch clergyman, Alexander Forsyth, patented a method of igniting powder by a percussion powder rather than by a percussion cap. Forsyth's material, which contained fulminate of mercury, was poured into a tube connected with the chamber of the barrel and was exploded by the falling of the hammer.[35]

earlier date; at least Nicanor Kendall's percussion Kentucky squirrel rifle, notable for a patent under-hammer lock, was used in Texas as early as 1835.[32]

The federal government was slow in adopting percussioning. The first percussion arms accepted for the United States service was the Model 1833 carbine, a Hall breech-loader manufactured by Simeon North and adapted to percussioning at the time it was made.[33] But once having undertaken the manufacture of percussion arms, the government accepted them with few reservations. By the beginning of 1845 over 5,000 percussion arms had been made at Springfield, and the figure for the fiscal year ending June 30, 1846 was more than 14,000.[36]

The manufacture of percussion arms was even longer delayed in private than in public armories. It was not until 1848 that flintlock musket production ceased in private arms works.[37] The distribution of these new arms was also exceedingly slow. As late as 1847 Captain S. H. Walker, who, with his company of Texas Rangers was to bring fame to the Colt revolver, was furnished with flintlock pistols only.[38] The weapon characteristic of the Mexican War was the flintlock.[39] In 1848, the Chief of Ordnance informed the Secretary of War:

As yet but few of our troops, other than cavalry and riflemen, have percussion arms. Flint-locks are still in the hands of most of the infantry.[40]

The means by which the lock was adapted to percussioning varied (Figure 6c). Shaw's gun made use of a nipple, over which the percussion cap was placed. A hollow metal tube or shank screwed into the barrel. Through the interior of this tube, called the flash hole, the sparks from the exploded percussion cap reached the charge in the barrel. The piece of the lock formerly called the cock now became the hammer, which exploded the cap by striking it. Flint, flash pan and frizzen were discarded.[41]

This was the standard method used in percussioning. It necessitated placing a new percussion cap on the nipple every time the gun was fired. Just how such a system might be made most efficient was a matter for further experimentation. Thus an Ordnance board recommended in 1846 that government flintlock muskets be altered to percussion by a method used at Harper's Ferry in which the seat of the nipple or cone was a little tipped and the nipple inserted into the barrel in a plane parallel to the plane of the sight.[42] When converted government muskets were rifled, however, this method was found to be unsatisfactory, and instead the end of the barrel was cut off and a new breech piece, including the nipple bolster, was added. This was the manner in which percussioning was applied to most of the United States arms in the Civil War.[43]

Many efforts were made to feed the caps on to the nipple automatically rather than by hand, from magazines placed in the lock, stock or barrel. Of these methods the one most widely known was the Maynard priming system, invented by a Washington dental surgeon and patented in 1845. The Maynard primer consisted of a coiled tape made of two strips of paper glued together and containing fifty percussion caps spaced at equal distances. The tape was placed in a magazine on the lock plate, and was automatically fed, one cap at a time, into the position in which it was struck by the hammer and the cap exploded.[44] This system was adopted by the government in 1845 for its converted flintlock muskets,[45] and the model of 1855 was designed from the outset to make use of it.[46] For several years the Springfield Armory made or converted guns to use the Maynard primer. But experience in the field showed that it was not entirely satisfactory, and when the Civil War broke out the Ordnance Department returned to the manufacture of arms with the earlier single percussion cap and nipple.[47]

It was during the percussion period that rifling became widely, if not universally, adopted,* while at the same time important developments in ammunition occurred. Improvement in each of these lines was greatly advanced by that in the other.

Until the early 1840's United States military arms had used a spherical bullet, but as rifling began to invade the field of smooth-bore weapons experiments in bullets shaped to take the rifling were made (Figure 7b). In France Captain Claude Minié successfully introduced in 1849 a conical bullet with a hollow base, which trapped the gases from the explosion of the powder and expanded the bullet to take the rifling. This caused the bullet to rotate in its flight and greatly increased the range and precision of the rifle. An additional characteristic of the Minié bullet was its small diameter when unexpanded before firing, compared to the bore of the rifle in which it was used. When the bullet—still wrapped in the paper in which it and the powder charge were furnished—was rammed into the barrel, the fit was not so close as to require great effort in loading, yet the paper carried the fouling from the gun down into the chamber, just as was the case when the greased patch of the Kentucky rifle was used. Thus a rifle using a paper-wrapped Minié bullet could be fired repeatedly without cleaning.

As a result of these developments, rifled arms rapidly supplanted

* Reference is frequently made in the records to the Springfield rifle—or rifled-musket. This was merely the standard percussion musket in which the bore had been rifled. The rifle-musket was similar in all essential points to the military percussion rifle. The term rifle-musket has been used in this study, particularly in connection with the Civil War, for the purpose of keeping clear the distinction between the percussion rifle and the breech-loading rifle.

smooth-bore muskets, and no more of the latter were made by the United States government after 1856.[48]

3. Revolving and Repeating Arms.

Like the percussion lock, revolving and repeating arms had been experimented with for many years before they became generally accepted in the late 1840's and early 1850's. The development of the revolver was particularly important in this period, for multishot shoulder arms did not really take hold in the industry for some years after the Civil War.

The Jennings repeating rifle was an early multi-shot arm. It had a sliding, self-priming lock, and, as improved by Reuben Ellis, was manufactured as a military gun for the State of New York about 1828.[49] It must, however, have been cumbersome or unreliable, as it offered little competition to single-shot arms. Simeon North made a repeating rifle in 1825 capable of firing ten shots without reloading,[50] but it, too, failed of general adoption. The failure of the Collier flintlock revolver has been mentioned. Not until the experimentation with the Colt revolver began in the 1830's did multi-shot arms promise to achieve an important position in small arms design (Figure 6d).

The manufacture of the Colt revolver began in Paterson, N.J., in 1836, but came to an end a few years later because of the difficulties of manufacturing so complicated a weapon.[51] In 1847, however, Captain Samuel Walker contracted with Colt for 1,000 of his "six-shooters," and their excellent record in the Mexican War, as well as improvements in their construction, made it possible to form a new company which made of their manufacture an astonishing financial success.[52] This revolver worked on the principle of a revolving cylinder, bored with six chambers containing the charges. It was a percussion arm, loaded from the front of the chambers. Even at the time of the Paterson factory, Colt had succeeded in making a few repeating rifles working on the same principle.[53]

Experimentation in revolving arms branched out in many directions, meeting with varying degrees of success. For example, in the 1850's Leonard's "pepperbox" pistol was being made. This weapon contained a cluster of barrels which were fired by a revolving hammer, but as it had no center of fire, it was very inaccurate.[54] A certain Colonel Porter invented another type of revolver having a wheel containing chambers bored inward in the rim. Above the wheel were magazines of powder and bullets, which emptied a charge into each chamber as it passed under them. When a chamber was in line with the barrel the gun was discharged by a Maynard primer. But as it was difficult to discharge one chamber without discharging another, and as a spark might explode the whole magazine, the weapon proved a total failure.[55]

Another revolver, made under the Leavitt patent, was manufactured by the Massachusetts Arms Co. in 1849. This was apparently a practical weapon, but was adjudged an infringement of the Colt patent.[56] Remington made workable revolvers under the Beal patent in the 1850's.[57]

An outstanding contribution to revolver design was made by Rollin White. This was a revolver with chambers bored clear through the cylinder. Cartridges were loaded into this weapon from the rear. Unfortunately this gun never reached the stage of actual production, because of weaknesses in its ammunition. White used loose powder and bullets or ordinary paper cartridges, and closed the rear of the chambers with a wad pierced with a hole, so that fire would pass through it from a percussion cap exploded on a nipple in the frame. It was necessary to put a cap on the nipple every time the revolver was to be discharged, and fire from one chamber might pass to the others, causing premature explosions.[58]

Horace Smith and Daniel Wesson secured White's patent on the bored-through cylinder, and received a re-issue of it which did not expire until 1872. It was in connection with this development that metallic cartridges first came into use, marking another outstanding advance in small arms design. Smith and Wesson introduced the .22 inch short rim-fire metallic cartridge in 1856, but gave it up to devote their efforts to their revolver. B. Tyler Henry, who became associated with Smith and Wesson, developed the metallic rim-fire cartridge. But although Smith and Wesson did the arms industry a signal service in introducing the metallic cartridge, their patent delayed for several years its use in arms other than their revolvers. Thus even as late as 1871 the Colt revolver was being altered to take metallic cartridges, while the Smith & Wesson .22 caliber revolver had been built from the outset to use them.[59]

The repeating rifle was slower in development, and while, as with the revolver, important preliminary work on it took place before the Civil War, much remained for further refinement, and designers of the late nineteenth century were to concentrate their attention on this type of gun. Prior to 1850 repeaters remained in the experimental stage. The Jennings rifle was an early, and probably unsatisfactory repeater. Another early type was Cochran's repeating rifle, which made use of a cylinder with several chambers.[60] Strong's repeating rifle, supposed to be superior to Cochran's, also used a revolving, multi-chambered cylinder, and could be fired fourteen times without being reloaded.[61] Colt's revolving rifle, as noted earlier, resembled his revolver.

In 1851 a further improvement in ammunition at last made possible the practical development of repeating arms. In that year Richard S. Lawrence of the Windsor, Vt. firm of Robbins & Lawrence, introduced grooved bullets, lubricated with tallow. This did away with the leading of the barrel, which had caused successive shots from a repeater to decrease in accuracy, and had therefore greatly restricted the usefulness of the early repeaters. Immediately after Lawrence's demonstration of the lubricated bullet it came into general use.[62]

Besides the lubricated bullet and the metallic cartridge a third line of development reached its peak after the Civil War. This was the introduction of breech-loading arms. As a result of these advances inventors were amply prepared for a period of intense activity in perfecting repeating shoulder arms in the decades after the Civil War.

4. Metallic Cartridges and Breech-Loaders.

Improved ammunition design was an integral part of the development of breech-loading arms. No weapon with a movable breech could be completely satisfactory as long as paper cartridges were used, for not even with the closest fitting breech system could leakage of the gases caused by the discharge of the gun be prevented. This leakage not only reduced the power of the charge behind the bullet, but also caused strains within the breech system, which was not unlikely to explode.

Breech-loaders became practical only when the metallic cartridge, the case of which provided a seal to hold in the gases, was introduced. Arms experts recognized the limitations of the breech-loader which used non-metallic ammunition, as is shown in the report of an Ordnance officer, made after a visit to Europe in 1855 and 1856:

But notwithstanding the acknowledged advantages of this [the breech-loading] principle, it is remarkable that no method of making a practical application of it has yet been suggested which can command general, or even extensive, approbation; mechanical ingenuity seems to have been thus far incapable of removing all the difficulties of having an opening or joint exposed to the action of the charge of powder.[63]

A forerunner of the metallic cartridge* was used by the Volcanic pistol put out by Smith, Wesson and Oliver Winchester when they were associated in the early 1850's. This was a bullet with a hollow base containing fulminate for priming. There was no powder present, nor a metallic cartridge case, and these factors were largely responsible for the failure of the Volcanic pistol.[64] This type of ammunition was significant, though itself unsuccessful, as it showed that arms designers were close to discovering the values of the metallic cartridge.

* The French pin-fire cartridge, one of the earliest forms of ammunition in which the primer was contained in the cartridge, was discharged when the hammer of the gun struck a pin in the cartridge which transmitted the blow to the primer (Figure 7c). Although designed for breech-loading weapons, this cartridge apparently had little influence on the development of American small arms.

As was noted earlier, the work on the metallic cartridge began about 1850, and was carried forward rapidly, especially by B. Tyler Henry. The cartridge was made of copper or brass, which allowed for expansion at the time of its explosion to form a gas-tight seal in the chamber, and for contraction on cooling, making it possible to slip the empty cartridge case easily out of the gun. The first successful metallic cartridges made in America were rim-fire, and were formed of metal tubes folded over at the head—or rear—of the cartridge (Figure 7f). The fulminate or priming substance was placed in the rim of the cartridge so that if the firing pin struck the rim at any point the priming would explode the powder charge within the case.[65]

While metallic cartridges were eagerly accepted by the industry, their value did not pass unquestioned. As late as 1865, for example, when the rim-fire metallic cartridge had been in use for almost fifteen years, the *Scientific American* cast suspicion on it by declaring that it was unreliable in cold weather. This, however, was immediately disproved by Major T. T. S. Laidley, Commanding Officer of the Springfield Armory.[66] The federal government itself was extremely conservative in officially adopting the metallic cartridge, delaying until 1865, when it selected the Martin cartridge to be used in the new Springfield breech-loading rifle.[67]

The rim-fire cartridge, though a remarkable advance over the paper cartridge, was not entirely satisfactory. The fold in the head created a weak spot which was liable to burst. Then, too, the presence of the primer around the rim made the cartridge subject to accidental discharge.[68] Probably the experience gained by arms designers in the Civil War caused the displacement of the rim-fire by the center-fire cartridge, or at least only after the war could ammunition makers devote themselves to the experimental work necessary for the latter's development.

The new cartridge had the primer in the center of the head, which was no longer folded over but made in one piece (Figure 7g).[69] The danger of accidental discharge was thus greatly reduced. At a very slight cost rim-fire weapons could be altered to use center-fire cartridges, principally by changing the position of the firing pin so that it would strike the center, rather than the rim of the cartridge.[70] Much of the improvement of center-fire design was carried out by the government, and the government rifle Model 1866 used such a cartridge.[71] A large part of the work done by contractors for the government after the close of the Civil War consisted in altering new or used arms to take the center-fire metallic cartridge.[72]

The importance of the metallic cartridge to the development of breech-loading arms is clearly demonstrated by the fact that several successful breech-loaders appeared in the early 1850's at a time when the metallic cartridge had recently been invented. Maynard, the inventor of the tape primer, patented an improvement in breech-loading in 1851, and at the end of fourteen years' additional work his rifle was widely used throughout the world both as a military and a sporting weapon.[73] Although Christian Sharps invented a breech-loading rifle in 1848, not until 1851, when the metallic cartridge had appeared, was a company formed in Hartford to manufacture it.[74] By the middle 1850's breech-loaders had developed to the extent that the Ordnance Department bought several types in small quantities for experimental purposes. These included Sharps, Perry, Gibbs, Merrill, Burnside, Symmes and Howe arms.[75] The results of the Department's examination were apparently inconclusive. At about this time the Chief of Ordnance reported to the Secretary of War:

The practical test of breech-loading arms, undertaken to ascertain the relative merits of the various arms of this description, and their fitness or unfitness for military service has made but slow progress and has reached as yet no definite result.[76]

One type of breech-loader, however, the Morse gun, attracted the favorable attention of the government. The War Department decided that a few government muskets and rifles and some Colt army pistols should be converted to breech-loaders by the Morse system,[77] and in 1858, the Department made an agreement with the inventor under which he was to supervise these alterations. The Civil War intervened before the system could be developed sufficiently to be considered worthy of adoption by the government.[78]

While the government's failure to accept officially a breech-loading system left the majority of the federal troops equipped with nothing but muzzle-loaders, the war stimulated experimentation with and refinement of breech-loading arms, and the government proved an excellent customer for the makers of many types of these weapons. For example, in 1863 the Remington Company perfected a breech-loading rifle and received a government order for 10,000.[79] It is estimated that from January 1, 1861 to June 30, 1866 the government bought or made 406,856 breech-loading arms of nineteen different kinds. Most of them were issued to mounted troops.[80]

The war had produced so many new kinds of breech-loaders that immediately upon its close the War Department convened a military board to examine them for the purpose of adopting one for the army. Among the more outstanding arms tested were Allin, Ballard, Ball, Burnside, Cosmopolitan, Gallagher, Joslyn, Lindner, Maynard, Merrill, Palmer, Peabody, Remington, Richardson, Sharps & Hankins, and Starr breech-loaders.[81] Numerous guns which were barely past the experimental stage and not yet in actual production were also submitted to the board.[82]

The breech-loading system invented in 1866 by Erskine Allin, Master Armorer of the Springfield Armory, won the board's warmest approval, and according to this plan and later refinements of it the Springfield muzzle-loaders were altered to breech-loaders.[83] The conversion was made by milling open the breech section of the barrel and placing in this opening a hinged breech-block attached to the top of the barrel by two screws.[84] A firing pin in the breech-block replaced the percussion cap and cone or nipple. The hammer, instead of exploding the primer directly, as in the percussion muzzle-loading gun, struck the firing pin, which transmitted the blow of the hammer to the primer in the cartridge.[85]

The Springfield rifle-musket Model 1868, also of the Allin breech-loading type, differed from the 1866 model in that the receiver was a separate unit into which the barrel screwed[86] (Figure 6e). It was characteristic of these breech-loaders that they had the firing pin in the swinging breech-lock. This arrangement continued until the development of the Springfield magazine rifle in 1892, in which the firing pin was in the bolt.[87]

As the result of eight months' use in the hands of the United States Army, the Springfield rifle-musket, altered according to the Allin breech-loading system, was declared to be powerful, accurate and serviceable.[88] By 1869 the infantry, heavy artillery and engineers were equipped with these weapons.[89]

The Allin system did not completely monopolize the field in military arms in the United States, although it did so as far as the Springfield rifle was concerned. The Navy Department preferred the Remington plan for altering its weapons to breech-loaders,[90] and adopted the Remington rifle, slightly modified.[91] The Army also adopted both the Sharps and Spencer carbines.[92] The relative value of the Allin system was soon called in question by the report of another board of officers convened in 1869 to examine breech-loading arms. The board considered four variations of the breech-loading system: the lever and vertical breech-block; the horizontal breech bolt; the swinging breech-block; the Remington system, in which the breech lock pivoted below the level of the chamber and which had neither lever, bolt nor trough-like receiver.[93] The board placed the leading weapons submitted to it in order of merit, ranking the Remington first, the Springfield second, and the Sharps third. It held that these only were good enough to warrant adoption by the United States, after certain changes had been made. The board considered the Remington single-shot pistol to be the best breech-loading pistol, and put in second place the Smith & Wesson revolver, which it felt to be superior to any other revolver submitted.[94]

The final step in the development of the single-shot breech-loader in the years immediately following the Civil War was the reduction and standardization of caliber. There had always been variations among weapons, with .50 inch bore perhaps the most widely used in military shoulder arms, while revolver and pistol calibers were somewhat smaller. The Ordnance Department did not fail to realize that the efficiency of a gun was directly affected by its caliber, and in 1872 ordered a military board to conduct experiments at Springfield to determine the proper caliber for small arms.[95] Swiss, Austrian and Prussian, as well as American guns, were submitted for the board's consideration.[96] As a result of its investigations a new model breech-loading rifle and carbine were adopted for the military service. The rifle was in most respects similar to the Springfield weapon which had been in service since 1867, but the caliber was reduced from .50 to .45 inch.[97] The caliber of the Smith & Wesson army revolver was also set at .45 inch, and this apparently became the standard for all military small arms for the next twenty years, when the United States rifle, caliber .30, Model of 1892, was produced at the Springfield Armory.[98]

CHAPTER III

THE ROOTS OF THE INDUSTRY

Little is known of the details of arms making in the Connecticut River Valley in the late eighteenth century.* It is necessary to depend for a study of this period on four types of information: official records of contracts and correspondence between government—particularly federal—agencies and arms makers; the records of the federal Springfield Armory of the last few years of the eighteenth century; evidence gleaned from contemporary weapons; and genealogies of arms makers. Each of these sources of information is limited, and the last two are of little value to the economic historian. Collectors have been able to establish the location of arms makers and the periods of their activity because the name and residence of the maker and the date of manufacture were frequently stamped on weapons. Where the name only was stamped, the type of arms has served to establish its probable date of manufacture. The genealogies usually give no detailed information on arms making.

The Revolution failed to raise arms making above the level of a handicraft, so that until the emergence of the federal contract system in 1798 the craft remained in approximately the same economic and technological condition in which it had been since the settlement of America. As a craft, in which skill was transmitted to a few apprentices over a period of years, arms making had a strong tendency to descend from father to son, occasionally remaining in one family for several generations. A remarkable example of this occurred in the Pomeroy family, which carried on arms making mainly in Northampton and later in Pittsfield from 1630, when Eltweed Pomeroy emigrated from England, to the middle of the nineteenth century.[1] The Waters family of Millbury, Mass. also made arms for about two hundred years.[2]

Gunsmithing was dependent upon population concentration, as has been noted, and before 1800 much of the craft in New England was located in the vicinity of Boston, and to a less extent around Hartford and Springfield. There was also throughout New England a thin scattering of arms makers who often combined general blacksmith work and the making of agricultural implements with gunsmithing. The market for any one smith's

* Before 1800 the practice of keeping accounts and business records was probably limited for the most part to money-lending and merchandising. Those manufacturers who did keep books were frequently engaged in more than one business, and their account books might confuse the record of one with that of another. Then, too, at this time arms making was an occupation in which the productive unit was so small that the value of keeping accounts might have seemed negligible. Even if such records had been made, the probability of their surviving a century and a half of flood and fire and careless destruction is slight.

33

arms was limited to the village or town in which he worked and to the surrounding countryside. The wide reputation which the guns of General Seth Pomeroy acquired was exceptional. It is said that before the Revolution Indians from as far away as Canada came to barter furs for his weapons.[3]

General purpose arms only were made to any great extent in America before 1800. Few pistols were made here before the Revolution, and until 1812 swords were mostly imported.[4] Many rifles and muskets were also imported, mainly from England.[5] Though apparently few early colonial smiths made their own gun locks,[6] by 1770 the colonies were probably self-sufficing in the production of hunting weapons.

Arms shops were doubtless financed, like other enterprises conducted on a handicraft scale, through the small savings of the smith himself, or possibly with the aid of one or two partners. One authority holds that the prices paid for arms were excessive, and that gunsmiths rapidly became rich.[7] But highly skilled labor and expensive raw materials, mainly imported, were required in the production of any weapon, and where arms makers became rich other factors, such as land speculation, may be in some cases more properly assigned as the cause. An exceptional method of financing arms making was used in 1769 by a group of Boston merchants, who, foreseeing an extensive demand for small arms, created a fund for developing an arms "manufactory."[8]

The New England system of production differed from the English. In England during the American Revolution it was the exception to make a complete musket within one shop. The gun maker commonly distributed the parts of a weapon among several journeymen, each of whom made a given part in his own home. The parts were brought to the armorer's shop for assembling.[9] This type of production survived in Belgium as late as the middle of the nineteenth century.[10] In New England, on the other hand, throughout the eighteenth century the rare cases of occupational specialization remained within one shop. It is supposed that in large city arms shops one man forged barrels, another made locks, a third stocks, and so on. But they all worked within one shop, and usually there was not even this degree of specialization, and a gunsmith worked, by himself or with an apprentice or two, on all parts of a gun.[11] The unspecialized character of the work explains why the Springfield Armory records before 1800 show no evidence of piece-work, which later became established as the basis of wage payment in arms manufacture.

As in other handicrafts, the use of apprentices prevailed in arms making. The Springfield Armory, established in 1795,[12] used in addition to journeymen numerous apprentices, who were provided with board and lodging, clothes and spending money.[13] In 1794 $20 was allowed for the cost of clothing an apprentice for a year. The Armory's journeymen were paid an average of $15 a month, and, like the apprentices, were allowed per day one and a half army rations—each ration being rated at twelve cents.[14]

Most arms shops were equipped with grindstones, driven by water, for smoothing the surfaces of the parts of weapons. Hugh Orr, a Scotch gunsmith who came to Massachusetts in 1738, is supposed to have built the first trip-hammer in the region.[15] By the early 1790's there were seven in use in the naileries, scythe, hoe and ax shops of the town of Sutton, Mass.[16] It is improbable, however, that trip-hammers were used at this time in arms making.

No machine tools were used in Connecticut Valley arms making in the eighteenth century. The southern branch of the handicraft was farther advanced in this respect, for at the site of the town of Lancaster, Pa. as early as 1719 there was a boring mill for smoothing the interior of barrels after welding.[17] Lathes for cutting the threads of press screws were built in Rhode Island in the last decade of the century.[18] Only two definite references to machine tools appear in the Springfield records prior to 1800. In the last months of 1799 one man worked on an unspecified machine, and others made two lathes, one of them for turning barrels.[19] These were perhaps merely experimental, or at any rate were probably not in use before 1800. The Secretary of War, reporting on the operations of the Armory in 1799, mentioned "labor-saving machines operating to great advantage" there.[20] But as the only form of depreciation of plant was listed in the same report as "wear of grindstones," it seems probable that he failed to differentiate between machines and machinery.[21]

The raw materials of arms manufacture up to the close of the eighteenth century were chiefly of domestic origin. The principal ones were iron for barrels, lock parts and scabbards, hard wood for stocks, steel for springs, ramrods, sword and bayonet blades, and oil for tempering and lubricating and for finishing gun stocks. Coal, emery, grindstones, files and other tools were also essential. The iron used by the Springfield Armory was chiefly from the Salisbury hills,[22] though imported iron was more important to the more eastern arms makers. The Salisbury region included the western borders of Massachusetts and Connecticut and the eastern border of New York. At least seven furnaces were in operation there in 1770.[23] This iron, considered better than most of American manufacture,[24] was generally used by arms makers of the Connecticut Valley.

Gun stocks were also of domestic origin. While the Springfield Armory used black walnut stocks exclusively,[25] other arms makers used also cherry, red birch, red and curly maple, and dogwood.[26] By 1803 the Armory was ordering stocks from Philadelphia,[27] and even before the opening of the new century the supplies of suitable walnut trees within easy reach of the Connecticut River had perhaps been exhausted.

The finest quality of steel was imported. Of 22,000 pounds of steel bought by the Springfield Armory from November 1798 to June 1800, only slightly more than 500 pounds were certainly of domestic origin.[28] Charcoal was the common fuel of the trade. Great quantities of chestnut, and to a more limited extent oak, pine and maple wood were made into charcoal along the river. Bituminous coal, known at the time as sea, pit or stone coal, was brought in small amounts by water from Virginia and the neighboring states.

With the exception of whale oil, used for tempering and lubrication, most of the other materials for arms making were imported. Files, anvils and vises were brought from England. Emery was imported from England and zinc from France. Grindstones came from Nova Scotia in the early nineteenth century and no doubt in the late eighteenth century as well. Raw materials of minor importance were also imported, either because they were not available in America, or because of the poor quality of the domestic product.[29]

The outbreak of the Revolution stimulated small arms making in America, but not sufficiently to allow an industry to develop. In 1774 Great Britain prohibited the export of arms to the colonies, and in the same year Massachusetts appointed a well known arms maker, Richard Falley, master armorer of a public arms factory. Arms factories were established by Virginia and Pennsylvania in 1775 and 1776. In addition to these public enterprises many of the Committees of Safety of the colonies engaged gunsmiths and blacksmiths to make arms under contract.[30] The colonies further tried to encourage arms production by offering premiums for guns of domestic manufacture,[31] and the Continental Congress in 1776 asked the colonies to exempt from military service all persons engaged in making arms or military stores.[32]

But the trade did not expand rapidly enough to meet the needs of the armed forces. Not only did shortage of skilled labor make it necessary to assemble many weapons from English, French and American parts,[33] but also America had to lean heavily on importation of entire weapons. The most important source of small arms proved to be France, and it is estimated that during the Revolution about 80,000 French military muskets, of models from 1717 to 1763, were imported.[34] Without these foreign arms the American armies would have been seriously, if not disastrously crippled.

The war left arms making in much the same state in which it had found it. In the early 1780's the federal government, then established at Philadelphia, dealt only with small gunsmiths for the manufacture, repair and cleaning of government weapons.[35] The small scale upon which arms making was conducted is shown by a set of Treasury warrants for 1792 and part of 1793. Of seven suppliers of "rifle guns," who were probably paid on delivery, none received at a time more than $1,200, and one received as little as $72.[36] The exact price of these guns is not known, but military muskets cost at least $12, and rifles somewhat more, so that these guns must have been supplied in very small quantities.

The small output of the trade caused great concern to the new federal government. Congress passed an act in 1791 forbidding the export of arms and ammunition, and another act admitting duty-free arms of foreign manufacture.[37] While the Secretary of War favored domestic manufacture rather than importation of small arms,[38] in 1795 the government decided to buy locks, which were the most complicated parts of military muskets, in England. These locks were distributed among small gunsmiths in the Philadelphia region for assembling to stocks, barrels and mountings.[39]

The government found one way to help meet its arms shortage when in 1794 the Secretary of War gave Congress an estimate of the expense of establishing a national armory, manned by a superintendent, seventy workmen and thirty apprentices, and capable of producing 4,200 muskets a year.[40] By an act of Congress of the same year the armory was established at Springfield, Mass. and production began in 1795.[41] The site of the armory had originally been selected by George Washington, who had been impressed by Springfield's water power resources and its strategic location on the main waterway of New England, but so far inland that hostile sea-going vessels could not sail up the shallow river to attack it. An arsenal for making cannon carriages and ammunition, and for repairing muskets, had been built here during the Revolution, and afterwards had become a depot for the storage of federal military supplies. There were already several workshops, storehouses, and barracks available for the new armory. In addition, a number of gunsmiths and blacksmiths who lived in Springfield and who had perhaps been employed in a loose combination as a Massachusetts state armory between 1791 and 1794, served as a nucleus of skilled workmen.[42]

Though the establishment of the Springfield Armory was a notable step toward making the government independent of foreign arms, the shortage of military small arms continued critical. In the five years from 1795 through 1799 a total of only 7,750 muskets was produced at Springfield.[43] About 1794 the War Department bought 2,000 rifles and, in an effort to increase domestic production, contracted for 7,000 muskets.[44] But only in 1798, when danger of war with France became acute, did the government overhaul its policy toward private arms makers. In that year Congress appropriated $800,000 for the purchase of cannon, small arms and ammunition.[45] Twenty-seven private contractors received two-year contracts for 40,200 stands of small arms,* at the rate of $13.40 per stand.[46]

* The Springfield Armory records show that at this time a stand of arms consisted of musket, bayonet, ramrod, flint, and for every twenty muskets twenty screw drivers, two ball screws for extracting bullets from the musket, and two spring vises for compressing lock springs which had lost their resilience.

The size of the contracts ranged from 200 to 10,000 stands.[47] Ten of the twenty-seven contractors consisted of groups of two or more men who agreed to supply arms under joint contracts.[48]

The inauguration of the contract system in 1798 established small arms making on an industrial footing. The government's steady and growing demand for high quality weapons offered arms makers a dependable market. Financing problems were eased, mainly because the government made generous advances to establish the plants of its contractors. In fact, few of the contractors of 1798 could have engaged themselves to supply such large quantities of arms if federal financial aid had not been forthcoming. The War Department's tendency in the following decades to consider reputable armories as quasi-public institutions, and therefore to be strongly inclined to continue its dealings with them, increased the security of the contractors. The nineteenth century opened with the arms industry barely developed, but established on a firm foundation.

PART 2

DEVELOPMENT UNDER GOVERNMENT PATRONAGE, 1798-1830

CHAPTER IV

EARLY NINETEENTH CENTURY ARMS MAKERS

1. Government Policy.

The importance of public support to the small arms industry during its formative period in the beginning of the nineteenth century was clearly recognized at the time. Tench Coxe, who, as Purveyor of Public Supplies, negotiated arms contracts on behalf of the government, attributed to government policy the revival of what he termed the "industry" after a dormant period lasting from the Revolution to 1801.[1] While a distinction should be drawn between the handicraft of arms making and the industry—the latter emerging only after 1798—Coxe was justified in emphasizing the importance of governmental subsidies to the development of the industry.

The exclusion of foreign arms, though somewhat at cross purposes with the military needs of the country, was an obvious type of encouragement of the domestic industry. The gunsmiths of Lancaster County, Pa. protested violently, and apparently successfully, against a House resolution of 1803 exempting imported arms from duties.[2] As late as 1808 only a few locks and unmounted sword blades were imported for filling government contracts.[3] It was as well for the United States that it did not rely upon imports, for by 1809 foreign relations had deteriorated to such an extent that no European country was willing to supply this country with arms.[4]

Aside from the exclusion of foreign arms, the government took no further positive action for several years after making the contracts of 1798 and 1799. It is true that small contracts for rifles and pistols, specialties of the Pennsylvania gunsmiths, continued to be made,* but the small arms industry as a whole received no direct governmental aid until 1808, when Congress passed a law providing for an annual appropriation of $200,000 for arming and equipping the militia.[5] Five-year contracts were granted to eighteen firms and individuals—ten of which were in New England and three in the Connecticut Valley—for delivery of a total of 82,200 muskets.

---

* The southern branch of the small arms industry lagged behind the northern one in its development. Up to the War of 1812, and perhaps afterwards, the government made contracts in Lancaster County, Pa., the center of the southern industry, for as few as 25, 50, 100, or 200 guns. The master gun makers divided the manufacture of the guns among themselves, each smith making a small number of complete guns. Where even as few as 40 or 50 rifles were to be made this division nevertheless took place. The contractor did not act as a middleman, as he made a portion of the guns in his own shop. Contracts could be filled quickly, either by means of this division of manufacture or from stocks of the rifles commonly used by the government which had been built up by the contractor at his leisure. In some cases manufacture was hastened by the use of ready-made government owned locks, which had probably been originally imported from England. The name of the maker of the gun, not necessarily the contractor, was stamped on the finished weapon.[6]

The government made advances of from 50¢ to $2.00 per musket to enable the contractors to establish or expand their businesses.[6]*

The contracts of 1808, for reasons which will be later discussed, proved unsatisfactory to the government. There was division of opinion within the government as to what was the best mode of meeting the persisting shortage of arms. Purchase in the open market of arms which had not been made according to official specifications and which could not be thoroughly inspected was never attempted.[7] Government manufacture alone was proposed, with the establishment if necessary for increased production of a third federal armory somewhere in the west.[10] Another plan, suggested by Tench Coxe in 1807, would have limited lock manufacture to the federal armories, while the contractors made the other parts and assembled the guns.[11] A fourth plan, which was actually put into effect about 1817, though not to the exclusion of the system of contracting for complete arms, made use of contracts for supplying parts of weapons, which the public armories assembled. This was the method used at the time in England, where parts of arms were delivered to the Tower of London for assembling and stocking. It was supposed that this method would not only aid in the detection of imperfections, but would also increase total output.[12] Barrels, bayonets and ramrods were contracted for by the Ordnance Department at a price which was supposed to allow "a liberal Profit to the Undertakers, that they may have no Pretence to slight the Work."[13] It was the hope of the Ordnance Department,** which had been established in the War Department in 1812 to handle matters pertaining to arms and ammunition,[14] that in time locks and mountings would also be made on contract. Unlike the contracts for the complete gun, parts contracts involved no advances.[15]

Many of the regular contractors undertook parts manufacture,[16] while at the same time small gunsmiths who stood no chance of obtaining contracts for complete arms were in this way able to contribute to the production of military weapons.[17] But though it was continued for many years as a means of increasing the output of the national armories, the system of contracting for parts proved unworkable in the field of contract arms and was promptly abandoned. The Ordnance Department reverted to contracts for complete arms, a method which had never been wholly discarded. Yet the department continued to pin its hope for an adequate supply of small arms of good quality on government manufacture. Ac-

---

* Early contract arms went exclusively to the militia, although in the War of 1812, when the regular army was increased from over 5,700 to more than 35,000 men contract arms had to be supplied them. Otherwise the two federal armories, at Springfield and Harper's Ferry—the latter coming into production in 1801 and later specializing in rifles—supplied the army.[9]

** In the beginning this was called the Ordnance Office, but to avoid confusion the title Ordnance Department has been used consistently throughout this study.

cordingly for some years after 1820 only renewals of old contracts were made and the system was not extended.[18]

2. Origin and Location of Arms Makers and Industrial Organization.

Almost without exception the arms contractors of this period were experienced gunsmiths or blacksmiths, or otherwise closely acquainted with arms manufacture, who for the most part had carried on their business on a very limited scale prior to receiving their government contracts. The only conspicuous exceptions in New England were Eli Whitney òf New Haven, who had attended college and had acquired manufacturing experience in connection with his cotton gin, and Daniel Gilbert of Mansfield, Mass., a prominent lawyer, politician and manufacturer.[19]

The contractors generally were men of originally modest position. Nathan Starr, who, with his son, Nathan Jr., built up one of the most important American sword factories, had been a regimental armorer in the Revolution.[20] He received his first government contract in 1798,[21] and the following year he returned from Hartford to his native Middletown, bringing with him the essentials of his trade—bellows, vises, hammers, sledges, a few other blacksmith's tools and supplies, and a lock for his shop door.[22] With a partner he started a scythe factory at Middle Haddam, and almost simultaneously a sword factory in Middletown.[23]

Simeon North, Middletown contract pistol maker, was at first a farmer and later a maker of agricultural implements. Like Starr, he carried on scythe making concurrently with arms manufacture, discontinuing the former occupation only in 1811.[24] Robert and J. D. Johnson, government inspectors of contract arms, established themselves about 1818 in Middletown as rifle contractors.[25] Oliver Bidwell, a contractor who lived in Hartford and later in Middletown, had apparently been a gunsmith all his life.[26]

The smaller contractors of the Connecticut Valley were also probably gunsmiths or blacksmiths. These included Elisha and Enos Buell of Marlborough, Ard Welton of Waterbury, Amos Stillman of Farmington and Burlington, Abijah Peck of Hartford, and, in Massachusetts, Asher and Pliny Bartlett of Springfield and Richard Falley of Montgomery.[27] At Walpole, N.H. there were two groups of contractors, one consisting of Joseph Bernard, Amasa Allen and Samuel Grant, and the other of Gurdon Huntington, Josiah Bellows, Daniel Stone and John Livingston.[28]

The location of arms makers in the Valley was determined by physical conditions as well as by the organization of the industry. The river was needed for transportation of coal, stocks, grindstones and imported tools, and for the shipment of finished weapons. Some measure of the importance of the river is indicated by the difference in direct cost of arms made at the Springfield and Harper's Ferry Armories. Because of the inaccessibility of Harper's Ferry both raw material and labor costs were much greater than at Springfield, though the supplies of Virginia coal and Pennsylvania stocks were much closer to Harper's Ferry. It was estimated in 1818 that transportation accounted for the fact that a musket made at Harper's Ferry cost $14.33 while one made at Springfield cost only $12.40[29]

The Connecticut Valley was strategically located in relation to the Salisbury iron region. In addition, the river's tributaries provided excellent water power sites for the heavy machinery required for arms manufacture. Even small streams, if harnessed efficiently, were of great value. Thus one sixteen-inch water wheel at the Springfield Armory, with a head or fall of water of only three feet nine inches, generated eleven and one-half horse-power and operated ten small buff wheels for polishing gun mountings, one large buff wheel for polishing barrels, one smooth boring bank for smoothing the interior of barrels, two drill presses carrying five shafts, one machine for slitting and milling pins, one machine for boring barrels, one for boring bayonet sockets and one for turning and milling side pins.[30]

The organization of the industry had a direct bearing on the location of arms contractors. Few were prepared from the first to manufacture small arms in all their parts, and the presence in the vicinity of small concerns which might relieve them of the heavier work was of considerable importance. The barrel was the part which could be most advantageously made on sub-contract. It had been Eli Whitney's plan to import barrels, but an epidemic of yellow fever in Philadelphia in 1798 shut off this port of entry, and he was forced to depend on a domestic supply.[31] He advanced Isaac Hollister & Sons, one of three barrel making firms in Litchfield County, Conn.,[32] sufficient funds to establish it in the business of barrel making. He planned to have all his barrels furnished by this firm, although he later found it necessary to buy them from other sources as well.[33] Nathan Starr of Middletown, the Springfield Armory, and Lemuel Pomeroy of Pittsfield likewise contracted with Isaac Hollister & Sons for barrels.[34] The Springfield Manufacturing Co. of Ludlow, Mass. supplied the Armory with barrels and bayonets.[35] Hezekiah Scoville of Haddam, Conn. furnished Whitney and Starr with barrels.[36] Until he became fully established in rifle manufacture, Starr bought from a small firm the component parts of rifles—that is, the lock work and possibly the mountings.[37] Simeon North was perhaps unique among the larger Valley contractors in being unwilling to put out the parts of his pistols on sub-contract. He considered such action a form of speculation.[38]

Though the Ordnance Department accepted the parts contracting system, it prohibited the regular contractors from importing parts from Europe with which to fill their contracts. It held that this defeated its object of encouraging the American industry, and also was a violation of the terms of the contracts.[39] In time parts contracting died out, although throughout the first three decades of the nineteenth century some barrels were made on contract. The practice was abandoned as the Valley contractors became more capable in handling all phases of factory production, and as the emphasis upon uniformity of parts increased.

3. *Problems of Financing.*

Armories were highly specialized and could be used for little else than arms making,[40] and a prospect of long continued demand was required to warrant the heavy investment necessary for large scale production. Eli Whitney, who had a thorough understanding of the industry, estimated that an arms factory took two years to establish, and twenty years' operation to warrant making the investment.[41] The Ordnance Department recognized this situation, and usually gave manufacturers five-year contracts and the assurance of continued patronage of contractors who fulfilled their obligations satisfactorily. It was acknowledged that this assurance acted as a strong inducement to bring contractors into the field.[42]

The investment required for an armory was for the times very great. The Ordnance Department in 1829 calculated that it varied between $20,000 and $40,000.[43] The accuracy of the Department's estimate is borne out by the fragmentary Census of Manufactures of 1822, in which the plants of the important New England contractors can be easily identified. This census lists capital investment in that year as follows:

Name of Contractor	Plant Capital
Lemuel Pomeroy	$30,000
Eli Whitney	50,000
Simeon North	75,000
R. and J. Johnson	30,000
Nathan Starr	50,000[44]

The source of this capital was not in the first instance the entrepreneur. It is true that when making its contracts the government was anxious to deal with "men of property." Tench Coxe refused a contract to a certain experienced gunsmith on the ground that he lacked property, although if he had connected himself with other gunsmiths and capitalists he would have been satisfactory. On the other hand, a man of "character" and property only was undesirable because he lacked practical experience.[45] It seems probable, however, that this property qualification was made with a view to the possibility of suits for non-performance, rather than to insure the successful establishment of an armory.

The contractors were not capitalists. Eli Whitney most nearly filled this rôle, but his resources were of a shadowy nature only, for the money he received from his cotton gin was spent in fighting infringements of his patent.[46] Nor was capital brought into small arms firms through partners. Neither Whitney nor Pomeroy had partners. The partnerships between Nathan Starr and his son, between Simeon North and his brother-in-law Elisha Cheney, between Robert and J. D. Johnson, between Nathan and Henry Cobb of Norwich, between Asher and Pliny Bartlett of Springfield, were obviously formed for division of managerial functions and for continuity of the firms.[47] Nor is there any evidence that merchant capital from the commercial centers of New Haven, Middletown, Hartford and Springfield, which proved invaluable in establishing other industries, flowed into arms manufacture at this time.[48] The joint stock company, later the chief source of capital in arms making, was unknown in the industry in this period.

The sole source of capital in the early Valley arms industry was apparently the federal government. From 1798 on it became almost unvarying procedure to advance contractors considerable amounts, without requiring interest payments, deducting the advances later from the purchase price of the arms. Advances were made for the purpose of establishing or expanding armories. No doubt an advance was made to Simeon North on his first pistol contract in 1799, and the following year he received an advance of $6,000 on a contract for 1,500 pistols priced at $6 each.[49] On a contract for 20,000 pistols at $7 each, made in 1813, North received a $20,000 advance.[50] When in 1816 an alteration was made in the pistol, he received an extra dollar for each altered pistol and an additional advance of $25,000.[51] On a contract made in 1819 for 20,000 pistols valued at $8 each he was given a $20,000 advance.[52]

Eli Whitney likewise received very liberal advances. At different times in the early 1800's $5,000, $10,000 and $15,000 were advanced him,[53] and by 1817 the Ordnance Department had lost track of the total amount he had received.[54] The final balance due Whitney out of a total of $134,000 for his first musket contract was only $2,400.[55] Rarely contracts were made which did not stipulate that the government make advances.[56]

As the United States government was the only customer that contractors of this period were allowed,[57]* financing through advances seems fully justified. Evidence of the trustworthiness of the prospective contractor was demanded through bonding him for performance of the contract. The bond—which had no connection with the advances made on the contract—was a separate document from the contract, executed on one side by the

---

* Occasionally a problem arose when arms makers whose contracts had run out and who had not received new ones had to seek other customers. After the War of 1812, for example, Nathan Starr wrote to commercial firms in New York and Philadelphia in an effort to dispose of his swords through civilian channels, and even shipped a few to Cartagena, Colombia. He wrote to the governors of Maryland, Virginia, North and South Carolina, Georgia, and Ohio to solicit state patronage. But new government contracts saved him from being forced to leave the ranks of the federal contractors.[58]

appropriate government official or his deputy, and on the other by the contractor as principal and his sureties. These sureties were supposed to be of good character and either individually or as a group worth at least the sum of the bond.[59] When Whitney was first bonded, ten sureties signed the bond, each stipulating that a total of ten or twelve would sign, and securing themselves with a mortgage on Whitney's farm and factory.[60] On one occasion North was bonded for $40,000, his son Reuben, his brother-in-law Elisha Cheney, and Josiah Savage acting as sureties.[61] Samuel Russell of Middletown is said to have endorsed North's notes so that he could expand his plant, but considering that there is no other evidence to show that this means of financing was ever used, it seems probable that he acted rather as a surety on a bond for a new contract.[62]

As far as short-term funds were concerned, the Valley arms industry ran on a system of ninety-day credit supplied by the merchants who furnished materials and tools. Even the parts makers granted three, or very rarely four months' credit to the contractors.[63] It is true that by 1819 Nathan Starr was using the banking facilities of Middletown,[64] but it is not clear that he received short-term credit from it. Wage payments depended on the rapidity with which the government accepted and paid for parcels of arms, and were often irregular, though probably no more so in private plants than at the Springfield Armory, which was frequently several months behind in meeting its payroll.

The credit system as a whole revolved around the regularity and promptness with which the government accepted arms. Whitney considered that an armory could not function normally unless arms were turned in and paid for every ninety days.[65] Throughout this period the records of the Springfield Armory show that any delay on the part of the government in inspecting and accepting parcels of arms met violent protests from the contractors on the ground that their creditors were dunning them for payment.

4. Early Failures, Profits and Costs.

In spite of steady government patronage many arms manufacturers failed in this period. It was the opinion of the Ordnance Department that Eli Whitney was the only one of the contractors of 1798 who could be considered successful.[66] Many of those of 1803 also failed. Later contractors, the Department believed, were saved only through government support,[67] but even these had a spotty record. By 1810 deliveries of arms had fallen in arrears to such an extent that Tench Coxe found it necessary to "address all the [contractors'] sureties in severe & urgent manner,"[68] and to institute suits against delinquent contractors.[69] Nineteen contractors of 1809 and 1810, who had received a total of $94,792 in advances on

85,200 stands of arms, had delivered only 53,560 stands, or 63 per cent of the total, by the fall of 1812, when all the contracts but one had only a year longer to run.[70] Failures were so common that, although many men attempted contract arms manufacture, by the 1820's in the entire United States the government could depend upon a mere handful of contractors— Whitney, North, Starr and the Johnsons in the Connecticut Valley; Pomeroy and Waters just outside it; Marine T. Wickham and Henry Derringer of Philadelphia; Alexander McRae of Richmond and Adam Carruth of Greenville, S.C.[71]

Several factors contributed to the failure of the early contractors, some of which were clearly recognized at the time. Tench Coxe supposed that the difficulties encountered by the contractors of 1809 were caused by an acute shortage of skilled labor, brought about by an expansion of the national armories occurring at a time when many new contracts were being made.[72] To meet this problem contractors were forced into division of labor and the invention of machine tools, which, though of incalculable benefit to the industry, delayed them in filling their contracts. Eli Whitney took eight years instead of the two originally stipulated to complete his first contract.[73] The low price of contract arms, which from 1807 to 1810 was $10.75 per musket, was later recognized as contributing to failures. Callender Irvine, the Commissary General, believed that at no time in the history of the United States could a good musket have been bought in the open market at this price.[74]

High wages, heavy capital investment, lack of experience and poor judgment were assigned as additional causes of failure. The Chief of Ordnance reported to the Secretary of War in 1817:

High wages makes the business unprofitable to the Contractors, and ultimately in many instances has occasioned their ruin. A great capital is required for commencing the business, and the returns are slow. The Contractor should be a man of great capacity, ingenuity and experience. Many men are tempted by the encouragements of the Gov't. aiding them with the advances of money have totally failed and be reduced [sic] to abject poverty or seriously injured in their circumstances.[75]

Unfamiliarity with large scale arms manufacture, coupled with inadequate prices, was a fundamental cause of early failures, and it was recognized as such by the Chief of Ordnance when he wrote in 1829:

In 1809 and 1810, Tench Coxe, then Purveyor of Public Supplies, made a number of contracts for muskets. But as there were then but few persons in the country acquainted with the business, and as the prices of labor and materials soon after increased, but few of the contractors were able to fulfill their engagements. Most of them failed and were ruined, and but one or two of them were able to continue in the business up to the close of the war in 1815. Those who first engaged in the business at a later period, when higher prices were given, were more successful.[76]

A clearer understanding of the causes of the widespread failures among early contractors may be gained by examining contemporary concepts of costs and profits, and the relation these had to the prices of contract arms. In the industry generally little effort was made to estimate costs accurately. Not even at the national armories, where a strict accounting of public funds was required from the first, was much attention paid to costs until 1817, when perhaps the recently organized Ordnance Department put into effect more rigid methods of bookkeeping. There was no uniform method of determining costs, and certain items of cost, notably depreciation and insurance, were neglected or unrecognized. This made it possible on the one hand for the government to buy contract arms below full cost—since price was based on an inadequate understanding of cost—and on the other hand for contractors to receive apparently reasonable profits from such contracts. But this resulted in the destruction of the productive capacities of private armories, and no doubt accounted for the majority of early failures.

Although cost determination was sketchy and lacking in uniformity, a recognized function of the national armories was to establish standards of costs by which prices of contract arms might be regulated. Costs at the Springfield Armory served as the standard for the musket contractors, and those at Harper's Ferry as that for rifle contractors. The cost of a pair of pistols was usually reckoned as equivalent to that of a musket, and therefore its price was fixed at the amount paid for a musket. The prices of swords, sabers and pikes, which were not generally made at the national armories, were fixed by bargaining between the Ordnance Department and the contractors, but were also affected by labor and material costs at the national armories. The Ordnance Department's conception of the items of cost which properly affected the contract price is contained in a letter of 1820 from the Chief of Ordnance to the Superintendent of the Springfield Armory:

In renewing our Contracts with Mr. Wickham and Mr. Pomeroy for fabricating small arms it has been stipulated that in case any material Reduction should take Place at the National Armouries during the Continuance of the Contract, either in the Wages of Labour or the Price of Materials, a correspondent Reduction should be made in the Prices of the Arms to be made and delivered by them.[77]

Contractors were allowed access to the government's cost figures.[78] But there was no relief for contractors who worked less efficiently than the national armories, or who were in less favorable positions in regard to labor and material supplies. It is in fact remarkable that any musket contractors succeeded under the prices established at the Springfield Armory, for the latter from the end of the War of 1812 to the early 1830's was outstanding for its excellent management and high efficiency.

Though the government had no consistent doctrine as to what constituted cost, it carried out its estimates with a precision which seems overly nice in view of the frequent neglect of the less conspicuous items of cost. At the Springfield Armory calculations were often made down to the last mill and to the last fraction of a pound of material, covering even the smallest screw and pin in the musket.[79] Two tendencies developed in cost analysis. The method more widely used was to figure what was called "actual expense." This included only labor and raw material costs, with in some instances supervisory costs added.[80] As late as 1818 the Ordnance Department assigned the cost of making a musket two-thirds to labor and one-third to materials.[81] The other method, which was for the time remarkably advanced but rarely used, covered in addition interest, insurance and depreciation charges. In spite of the high degree of development which this second method of cost determination implied, it was in general the government's policy to allow contractors only the direct cost of a weapon, with a dollar or so thrown in to cover all other items of cost and profit.

The less obvious items of cost once recognized were not always included thereafter. The experience of the Ordnance Department in this matter is illuminating. In 1817, for example, the cost of a musket was divided among the items of labor, materials, wear and tear, waste, and profit.[82] In the same year the Superintendent of the Springfield Armory distinguished between "actual expense," or direct costs, and "cost," which included interest.[83] In 1822 the cost of a musket was considered as being made up of "cost," which was the direct cost, interest, insurance on perishable property, and a two per cent depreciation allowance.[84] In the same year a separate estimate was made to which were added items for loss or waste in manufacturing and wear and tear of tools and machinery.[85] In 1825 costs were held to include interest and insurance on capital invested.[86] Finally, in 1829 the Ordnance Department made an excellent estimate of cost. It included "cost," or labor and material expense, six per cent interest on capital invested in land, buildings, machinery, tools and stock on hand; insurance at one-half per cent on perishable property, and an allowance for wear and decay of plant. Supervisory cost was not specifically mentioned, but might have been included in the first item of cost.[87]

The two trends of thought in cost determination are reflected in contemporary figures compiled by the Ordnance Department. They were originally made up at the Springfield Armory, where much effort was concentrated on keeping costs small, so that usually only direct and possibly supervisory costs were covered. In Washington the Chief of Ordnance added about a dollar per musket to the Springfield figure, apparently in an attempt to make a rough allowance for other costs, before presenting his annual reports to the Secretary of War. These figures, collected from the Springfield Armory records and from the Ordnance Reports, appear in Table 1 of Appendix B. It is evident that many of these figures were derived *ex post facto*, simply by dividing the total cost by the total number of arms produced in a given number of years. Even though these cost figures do not include certain items of cost they are not always below the prices paid for contract arms which appear in the same table.

In view of the obvious shortcomings in the methods by which the Ordnance Department usually determined costs, and the consequent unreliability of its cost series, it seems necessary to work out a new cost series. From the Springfield Armory statistics gathered under the direction of Colonel G. Benton for presentation to the Ordnance Department in 1880[88]—the only available data from which costs in early small arms manufacture can be determined—the writer derived the cost figures which appear with those of the Ordnance Department in Table 1 of Appendix B. Benton listed expenditures of the Springfield Armory under eight headings: lands, permanent improvements, miscellaneous expenses, manufacture of arms, manufacture of appendages—which was carried on on behalf of the arsenals—repairs of arms, manufacture of arms chests, and altering flintlock arms to percussion. For this cost series the writer used three categories of expense only—lands, permanent improvements and manufacture of arms. The other categories were considered either as connected with the Armory's function as an arsenal for the repair and storage of arms, or of such minor importance that they would be of little value in the construction of a cost series.

In deriving this cost series the writer has considered capital to be equivalent to the amounts spent under the heading "Lands" and "Permanent Improvements." Six per cent interest was calculated for the original amount invested plus the annual increment under these two headings for each year. Depreciation of two per cent and insurance of one-half per cent were taken on permanent improvements, the combined two and one-half per cent being calculated anew for each year, as in the case of interest, so as to include the annual increment as well as the investment in permanent improvements of all the preceding years. These particular percentages have been chosen since they were used by the Ordnance Department in its most thorough cost analysis of this period, which was made in 1837.[89] It is recognized that these percentages are too small by modern standards of cost analysis, but inasmuch as buildings and machinery were at this time operated for much longer periods than they would be under modern conditions, a low figure for depreciation and insurance seems logical. Interest, depreciation and insurance have been calculated for each year, and have been added to the annual expense for the manufacture of arms. This sum, divided by the number of arms produced annually, is considered as a fair estimate of the average cost of the musket made at the Springfield Armory.

A cost series arrived at in this manner is not without defects. The Armory bought some land which had no direct connection with the manufacture of arms, yet, because it was included in Benton's report it was considered part of the capital invested in arms manufacture. Permanent improvements perhaps covered the cost of such miscellaneous items as the Superintendent's residence and other living quarters, the elaborate iron fence surrounding part of the grounds, walks, drives, and the like—unless these were lumped under "Miscellaneous Expenses," another heading in Benton's tabulation. Strict accounting would allow for interest on capital invested in tools and materials in process, but there are no data for calculating precisely the time interval involved in the process of manufacture in the industry at this time. Inspection costs at Springfield doubtless fell into the category "Manufacture of Arms." For contract arms, inspection, usually estimated as costing $1.00 per gun, was paid for by the government and did not enter into the contractor's costs, so that the writer's cost series is not fully comparable with costs of privately made arms. It must therefore be recognized that these figures in some ways overestimate and in other ways underestimate costs. But at least the errors in this series are consistent with one another, and the method by which the figures were arrived at is unchanging from year to year.

Some figures in this cost series are greatly out of line with the series as a whole. The high cost of arms before 1800 was owing to the fact that the Armory was not yet in full production.[90] The very large figures for 1813, 1815 and 1816 were clearly the result of wartime inflation followed by curtailment of operations after the peace.

These cost figures help to explain the numerous failures among early contractors. The average cost of government muskets in the thirty-three year period 1798-1830, as calculated from the writer's series, was $12.88. This was sometimes well above the prices paid for contract muskets. These prices, collected from the Ordnance Reports, are recorded in Table 1 of Appendix B. In 1798, when Springfield Armory costs were $16.28 per musket, the contract price was only $13.40. It is true that Springfield exhibited the high costs of a newly established factory, but the contractors were confronted with like problems. From 1807 to 1810 inclusive, the contract price was $10.75, and cost at the Armory, with the exception of that for the year 1807, which was only $8.48, was always over $13.00. In the following decade Armory costs were reasonably in line with the contract price, except for 1813, 1815 and 1816, which, as has been said, were atypical years. The contract price was raised to $13.00 or $14.00 in this period. The 1820's showed cost at Springfield substantially below the contract price.

Few data exist concerning profits in arms manufacture. Perhaps close familiarity with the business rather than deliberate secrecy caused arms makers to carry records of their profits in their heads rather than in their account books, or perhaps they saw no reason to record them. At any rate there is no direct information concerning the gains they made. There are, however, clear indications that arms making was believed a profitable occupation, although the margin between the cost of muskets made at Springfield and their contract price was at best narrow. The prices of parts of arms were believed both by their makers and the Ordnance Department to be very liberal,[91] and it is improbable that they were out of line with prices of complete arms.

Some contractors made considerable fortunes from arms manufacture. As early as 1808 Nathan Starr had acquired enough excess capital, presumably from his sword factory, to buy a share in a ship. This was a common form of investment among Middletown capitalists.[92] The ship was in the Caribbean and South American trade, and carried a cargo of flour, tar, pitch, codfish, hams, butter and cheese, from which the owners expected a net profit of about $7,000. The following year Starr planned to sell an $8,000 cargo of Kentucky tobacco, flour, beef and pork in Spain or in the Malay Archipelago. He expected a gross profit of $10,000 from this venture.[93] In 1810 he travelled to Ohio, probably seeking new opportunities for investment.[94] Western lands were another type of investment of the Connecticut Valley capitalists,[95] and Starr's son, Nathan Jr., owned a farm in the west in the early 1840's on which he bred high grade live stock.[96]

It would seem inconsistent that on the one hand the contractors' costs were barely or not at all covered by the contract price of arms, and on the other hand that contractors received profits which at the very least were liberal enough to encourage them to stay in the industry. A reasonable solution to this problem lies in the contemporary definitions of costs, which, as has been pointed out, usually included only direct and perhaps supervisory costs. Under such definitions arms makers were able to take as profit the money which should have gone to meet depreciation and insurance charges. This explains at once the apparently adequate profits received under an unwarrantedly low contract price, and the failures of seemingly prosperous arms makers.

A definition of profit made by the Springfield Armory in 1817 lends support to this view. From contract barrels priced at $3.25 the Armory deducted $2.67 for material and labor costs, about a twelve per cent item for "wear and tear, waste, etc.," and allowed the remainder, amounting roughly to 24¢, for profit.[97] "Wear and tear" in this context covered wear and tear of tools and possibly of machines, but not of the plant as a whole. Nor was any allowance made for insurance. Where the Springfield Armory officials failed to reckon all items of cost, private manufacturers could hardly have been expected to do better.

The case of Simeon North illustrates the absorption by profit of money that should have gone to meet costs. About 1813 North invested $100,000 in his Middletown pistol factory.[98] By 1822, according to the Census of

Manufacturers of that year, his investment had fallen to $75,000. In 1828 he was reduced to such financial straits that he was forced to assign his contract and its profits to his creditors.[99] Nevertheless he remained in good standing with the Ordnance Department and received a new contract, and, no doubt on the basis of new government advances for fresh investment, he was able to continue his business. With his death, however, it came to an abrupt end.

It could hardly have been through mismanagement that North fell into such difficulties, for he was widely known among arms makers and in the Ordnance Department for honesty and efficiency. The conclusion seems inevitable that through the withdrawal as profits of sums which should have gone to pay for renewal charges, he squeezed his factory dry of its productive capacity, and was forced after some years to start over with new investment. This perhaps explains also the regular granting of government advances on contracts, even to well established contractors, which continued throughout this period. With such continual wearing out of arms plants, new capital for replacement was necessary even where no radical alteration in gun design or heavy investment in machinery occurred.

Eli Whitney was exceptional in his understanding of costs. The codicil to his will directed that his two nephews, who ran his armory after his death during the minority of his son, should receive in addition to a daily wage of $1.25 each, twenty per cent of the net profits of the contract he held. He required that the profits be determined by deducting from the price of his arms all "costs"—that is, direct costs—and also interest and insurance on capital invested, as was done on occasion at the United States Armories. It was probably no accident that the Springfield Armory, which was liberally supported by government funds, and Whitney's factory were the only New England small arms plants started before 1830 which survived the Civil War.[100] Inadequate prices and failure to make allowance for plant renewal led to the dissolution of the others within the lifetime of their owners or shortly afterward.

CHAPTER V

THE CONTRACT SYSTEM

The federal contract system not only served to bring the small arms industry into existence, but also caused it to acquire certain distinctive characteristics. Constant pressure on the part of the government for arms of high and uniform quality materially aided technical progress. The system of proof and inspection, although by no means completely objective, focussed the attention of arms makers on the importance of precision measurement. Finally, the contract system fostered the development of close personal and business relations among the arms makers, so that the early industry acquired a spirit of cooperation and mutual helpfulness which was one of its most conspicuous features, and which disappeared in later years only when the industry became independent of government aid.

1. The Form of the Contract.

Contracts were not always negotiated by the same official of the government. At first they were arranged by the Commissary General of Military Supplies,[1] but by 1806 Tench Coxe, Purveyor of Public Supplies, was handling them.[2] Callender Irvine, Commissary General, assumed this function from 1812 to 1815.[3] Finally in 1816 the Ordnance Department became the government's representative in making military contracts.[4] Comparatively few small arms were made on contract for the Navy. The Navy was represented in 1816 by the Navy Agent in the negotiation of contracts.[5] By 1826 the President of the Board of Navy Commissioners was dealing with the contractors, and in later years contracts were turned over to the Chief of Navy Ordnance.[6]

The complexity of the contract varied according to whether it was new or merely a renewal of an earlier contract, also according to the type and number of weapons contracted for, as to whether allowance was made for changes in model, and as to whether advances were made. Every contract, however, unless it merely extended the terms of an earlier one, was specific as to the parties involved, the number and kind of arms to be manufactured, the rate and dates of delivery, the type of inspection to be used, and declaration as to freedom from Congressional interference.[7]

A contract of the more elaborate type, made in 1822 between the Ordnance Department and Marine T. Wickham of Philadelphia, appears in Appendix A. It is atypical in that its duration is for two and one-half years, rather than for five years, and that it allows the contractor no advances. Requirements covering the rate of delivery of arms allowed several months for the manufacturer to make any necessary adjustments of equipment before the first date of delivery. The arms were required to conform in quality and form to the pattern musket furnished by the Ordnance Department to the contractor. Proof and inspection were to be carried out at the expense of the United States by a person appointed by the Ordnance Department, and the methods used were to be no more severe than those established for the federal armories. The arms were to be proved and inspected in parcels each consisting of not less than 250 stands.

This contract fixed the price of each stand of arms at $12. If, however, later contracts for similar arms were given out at a higher or lower price, the price stipulated was to be adjusted so as to conform with the new price. The contract required that arms be properly boxed and transported to the Frankford Arsenal—the arsenal nearest the contractor—at the expense of the United States. Payment was to be made on delivery of parcels of not less than 250 stands. If the model should be changed during the life of the contract the arms covered by it would be likewise changed, and the contractor would be allowed reasonable compensation for any extra expense caused by the alteration. The United States retained the right to nullify the contract whenever the contractor failed to deliver the number of arms specified for a particular year. The contract required that no member of Congress share in any of its benefits.

2. The System of Inspection.

Pattern arms were used instead of blue prints to hold manufacturers to contract specifications, which always required that contract arms be equal in quality to those made at the national armories.[8] On receipt of a contract an arms maker asked the Ordnance Department for a pattern arm, which, as far as New England was concerned, was furnished by the Springfield Armory and usually was made there.[9] The use of pattern arms, which will be discussed in detail later in connection with interchangeability, was a workable method of achieving uniformity but by no means entirely satisfactory. In practice it was impossible to obtain pattern arms identical with one another in all their dimensions, so that the arms of each maker varied slightly from those of others. Through constant checking of contract arms with his pattern the contractor wore away the latter so that its dimensions, and consequently those of his arms, became increasingly unstandardized. With every change in the model of the gun new pattern arms had to be made and distributed among the manufacturers, and machinery and tools had to be altered. These changes were often so expensive and difficult to make that the national armories resisted the introduction of changes in models. This reluctance to accept change is shown in a letter from Roswell Lee, a very able Superintendent of the Springfield Armory, to his superior in the Ordnance Department. The letter reads in part:

A model is fixed upon, after which it is our duty to work until another is adopted. Whether the present one is the best that could be devised is not for me to say. It is difficult for a pattern musket to be made by any one, to *please everybody. Faults* will *really* exist, and *many imaginary ones will be pointed* out. After experiencing the inconveniences and noticing the immense expense of frequently changing the model of muskets in this establishment, I have come to the conclusion that it is better to adhere to an uniform pattern than to be frequently changing; although the model may not be the most perfect.[10]

In order to insure a reasonable similarity to the pattern in contract firearms, the government instituted a system of inspection, which consisted of preliminary proof of the barrels and a later inspection of all the parts of weapons. Before the parts of the musket, rifle or pistol were assembled, the barrels were tested or proved for flaws in the iron or defects of workmanship. Those condemned by the government proofmaster could not be used in filling the contract. The proofmaster was held accountable for all barrels bearing his stamp of approval, subject however to the proof and examination of the inspector.[11] By 1829 the proof charge was required to be three times as strong as the service charge, and it was thought that this would guarantee that the arm would not explode in the field.[12]

Musket barrels were proved by weighing them, checking their dimensions with internal gage plugs and external gages, and then by closing the breeches, clamping the barrels in a frame, and firing them with a first charge which consisted in 1823 of 1/18 of a pound of powder, a lead bullet weighing 1/15 of a pound, and two paper wads; this was followed by a second charge of 1/22 of a pound of powder, one bullet and two wads. The proof powder was of a strength established by the Ordnance Department. Those barrels which stood the proof were next stopped up and filled with water and allowed to stand for several hours. If they were water-tight, they were accepted and the letters U S P, and the initials of the proofmaster's name were stamped upon them.

Inspection was a more laborious process than proving. The musket was taken apart, and every piece carefully examined for visible defects. The straightness of the interior of the barrel was checked by "truing by line," which consisted of stretching a string through the barrel and applying it to at least four sides of the bore. The caliber was checked by two gage plugs, of which one would pass freely through the barrel, while the other would not. The exterior of the barrel was checked at the breech, middle and muzzle by gages.

The parts of the lock were carefully examined to make sure that they were of proper shape, well filed, strong, and had good threads where necessary. The entire lock was put in a lock gage—apparently a form containing recesses and elevations corresponding with the formation of the lock of the model arm. The action of the lock was tried to make certain that all parts moved freely, that they fitted together accurately and that the springs were neither too strong nor too weak. The inspector also made certain that the lock fitted into the stock correctly.

The inspector tested the form and dimensions of the mountings, which included the three bands and their springs for holding the stock and barrel together, and the guard, side, and heel plates, which took much of the wear of handling the gun from the stock. These parts were checked by gages and by comparison with the pattern weapon.

The stock was examined to make certain that it fitted the other parts. A gage was used to compare its dimensions with those of the pattern stock. No stock could be accepted which contained cracks, splits, or worm holes. The wood used had to be hard black walnut, and thorough seasoning was of the utmost importance. If, when the lock was first unscrewed from the stock its inner surface was rusted, it indicated that the stock was too green. The ease with which a thin sliver cut from the stock crumbled, and the smell of a fresh cut on the surface of the stock were helpful to the inspector in deciding whether or not the stock was well seasoned.

The dimensions of the ramrod were checked by trying it in the barrel for length, and by gaging it in three places for diameter. Its temper was tested by springing it in four directions. If the ramrod was hung by a thread and struck with a piece of metal, the sound indicated the presence or absence of flaws which could not be detected by the naked eye.

The flexibility of the bayonet blade was tested by driving its point under a staple, resting the blade on a block of wood and bearing down on its end. The neck of the bayonet was acceptable if it did not bend when the bayonet was fixed to the musket, its point on the floor, and the inspector bore down on the musket. The general dimensions of the bayonet were measured with a scabbard gage, into which the bayonet had to fit.

Rifles and pistols were proved and inspected in the same manner, except that they received lighter proof charges. Arms which had passed inspection were stamped with the inspector's initials, the contractor's name and location, and the date of manufacture.[13]

Edge weapons had to be put to a severe proof of their blades with additional attention paid to their handles and accessories. The following regulations governed the proofmaster:

The swords are to undergo the following proof, viz., they are to be sprung nine inches from the center each way, and to return to the original shape without setting or breaking. They are to be taken by the handle and three blows made with the edge of the sword and two with the back on a block of wood at equal distances from the point to the hilt. The force of the blow must be discretionary, but ought to be such as to insure the detection of any defects that might be in the blade. The sword should be well finished and every way equal to the pattern and agreeable to the contract.[14]

Condemnations of barrels during proof varied among manufacturers and from one year to another. The Springfield Armory inspection book for the New England contractors, which covers the period from 1818 to 1830 inclusive,[15] lists a total of 78,483 barrels proved during those years, of which 9,432 or 13 per cent were condemned. This percentage changed from year to year, being at its highest, 17.8, in 1827, and at its lowest, less than 1, in 1829 and 1830. That the rate of condemnations was not much affected by improvements in methods of manufacture at this time is shown by the fact that there was no tendency for it to decline during the twelve year period. As to the loss resulting from inspection, as distinct from proof, Roswell Lee believed that the barrels burst in proving were only about one-half the loss, since many were condemned because of faults discovered only on inspection.[16] If this estimate is applied to the New England contract arms made at this time the percentages of loss under proof would be doubled, with the result that of the 78,483 barrels proved from 1818 to 1830, 26 per cent would have been unacceptable for the government service. Lee estimated that the total loss in proof and inspection at the Springfield Armory was only 10 or 12 per cent.[17]

3. Problems of Inspection.

Detailed though the regulations governing proof and inspection were, it is obvious that they were not truly objective, and much room remained for the exercise of individual judgment on the part of the proofmaster and the inspector. They were cautioned by their superiors to fulfill their duties in "a fair, candid, and impartial manner, and not proceed to extremities, but give a proper degree of attention in examining the work."[18] But this was by no means a simple thing to do. Even conscientious arms makers were liable to fall below the government standards. Lee explained: "It is extremely difficult to keep contractors to the pattern. In the absence of the inspector errors will creep in; he is unwilling to reject it for a trifling fault. . . ."[19] Added to this was a strong tendency on the part of some contractors to fill contracts with defective arms, and an equally strong tendency on the part of certain inspectors to be prejudiced in favor of or against individual contractors. The result was that the system of inspection was a source of such bitter and continuous dispute that the office of Chief of Inspectors was one which men who were at once upright and peace-loving avoided.

Even within the government armories inspection was a most unpleasant duty. When barrel inspection became more rigid at Springfield in 1830, the foreman who was appointed to carry it out protested to the Superintendent:

Sir I presume you are well aware (as the welders have not been subjected to this rule) that let who will undertake a performance of this duty it will be attended with no very pleasant feelings towards the person so employed . . . I cannot believe it to be in *my* power to give satisfaction to both parties—and I think I have also reason to believe that there are some persons should I undertake [barrel inspection] who would do their best to destroy my reputation (if I have any) for even any business.[20]

Inspection was not always directed by one agency. As long as the Purveyor of Public Supplies attended to contracts he was in charge of inspection of contract arms, and both duties passed simultaneously to the Commissary General of Purchases.[21] When the Ordnance Department took over the negotiation of contracts inspection of New England contract arms fell to the lot of the Superintendent of the Springfield Armory, while inspection of contract arms in the southern states presumably was carried out by the Superintendent of the Harper's Ferry Armory.[22] In 1831 contract inspection was put under a separate officer, the Chief Inspector, who sent out his assistants whenever contractors called for them.[23]

Disputes over the inspection of contract arms were greatly aggravated when the officer in charge lacked a high degree of diplomacy and tact. The controversy which arose during the War of 1812 between Callender Irvine, in charge of inspection, and Eli Whitney is interesting not only on account of its intensity, but also because of its potentially if not actually deleterious effect on the country's armament program.

Shortly after the declaration of war on England Whitney received a contract for 15,000 muskets, as a result in part of a favorable impression the Secretary of War had received from a visit to his factory.[24] Gossip, quickly passed on to Whitney by the Master Armorer of the Springfield Armory, had it that Irvine was "very sorry" that Whitney had received the contract.[25] Mutual antagonism of the most vicious sort complicated the situation. Irvine's scorn of Whitney is only too apparent in many of his official letters and reports,[26] and for his part Whitney detested Irvine. Whitney was obviously portraying him when, several years later, he described the type of officer of inspection most objectionable to him, by whom he would feel himself "martyred" if he were "subjected for a number of years to the quibbling and caprice of a little narrow mind groping along thro' a cloud of ignorance, prejudice and jealousy."[27]

A dispute arose between the two in connection with the advance to be made to Whitney, who did not hesitate to go over Irvine's head. In describing the incident several years later, Whitney wrote:

Having given up all hope of anything like justice or fair dealing on the part of Irvine, I went on to Washington and laid this correspondence before the Secretary of War Gen.l Armstrong, who informed me the business, relating to my contract had, a few days before, been put into the hands of the comptroller of public accts.—A copy of this correspondence between me and Irvine was shown to the Secy of State and by him laid before the President, with both of whom I had several interviews on the subject.[28]

Whitney failed to meet his first delivery date, and many months passed before any of his muskets reached the stage of inspection. Towards the end of 1813 Irvine could no longer restrain his exasperation, and protested to the Secretary of War:

If Govt. relies on individual contractors for supplies of arms it will be greatly disappointed. Whitney's contract is vague on its terms, very advantageous to himself and the reverse to the Govt. It is founded on many thousand muskets furnished by him to the State of New York, all of which were defective. The best musket he could select, is exceedingly exceptionable. The breechings are so miserably fitted as not to be water tight. Such are unfit for service he has not complied with his engagements as to time inasmuch as five hundred stands should have been delivered in May last [sic]. I have accordingly told him that I consider his contract at an end. He is in high dudgeon and we are at loggerheads, this I don't regard a straw. He has imposed on the Govt. and people long enough. I have informed him that we do not want any more apologies for arms, having plenty such already.[29]

Two years after Whitney's contract had been signed, 500 stands were at last ready for inspection. Irvine chose to send two, rather than one inspector to New Haven, declaring that he "apprehended difficulty with this man."[30] He gave careful instructions to the inspectors, warning them to take their own proof powder with them.[31] Whitney was incensed with the inspectors' actions. In his account of the matter he wrote:

After two days' conversation on the subject, in which Wickham and Perkins [the inspectors] both declared that they considered that it rested entirely with them to decide what kind and quality muskets I should deliver on my contract, without any regard to the terms of the contract itself—that they had an entire right to say that I should make and would cost me or any other person 30, 40 and even 100 Dollars a piece to manufacture [sic]— That they had secret instructions in writing from Irvine by which they were to be regulated in accepting or rejecting the arms and which instructions could not be submitted to my inspection, etc., etc., with many other things, equally absurd—I told them, if I must be bound by writing, to which I was not a party, which I had never seen and which I must never be permitted to see, my situation was certainly extremely deplorable—that tho' I was excessively anxious to deliver the arms, (the Enemy being then in sight of N. Haven Harbor and reports every day in circulation that they were coming to destroy my manufactory) I could never consent, under any circumstances to submit to an inspection of that sort—A few days after this the British came to Washington and *blew up* Armstrong.* The business of the Armories and contracts for arms was placed under the care of the Ordnance Dept. . . .
I have good reason to believe that it was in consequence of this nefarious conduct of Wickham and Irvine that the business of the Armories and

* General John Armstrong was Secretary of War from 1813 to 1814. He resigned because of ill feeling resulting from the capture of Washington and from the failure of the Canadian expedition.[36]

contracts for arms was put over into the charge of the Ordnance Dept; and it is nothing strange that Irvine should have a grudge against me, as I certainly had no inconsiderable agency in defeating his abominable projects.[32]

In view of such disputes as that between Irvine and Whitney, it is not surprising that almost as soon as contract arms were put in charge of Roswell Lee, a man of great firmness but of pacific intent, he was anxious to shift the onus of inspection to someone else. As early as 1818 he was petitioning the Ordnance Department to appoint a permanent chief inspector.[33] The repeated demands of the contractors for inspectors from the Springfield Armory staff interfered with the Armory's work.[34] But more important, Lee could not close his eyes to the dishonesty of the contractors, nor did he wish to antagonize them. He explained his position with frankness:

. . . I was unwilling to take the whole responsibility of all the arms made on contract; and I was much more anxious on the point after visiting Waters' and Pomeroy's works in February last. I have no wish to injure them or to make them my personal enemies, but if I am made responsible for the quality of their muskets, my *duty* requires that I should insist upon their executing their work agreeable to the terms of their contract.[35]

With many of the contractors Lee had a warm personal friendship, which ran the risk of impairment whenever, as director of inspection, he was forced to censure the quality of their arms. On one occasion he felt compelled to warn Whitney, with whom he had an especially close friendship:

In confidence I hasten to give you the following information. When I reported to the Ordnance Officer, Col. Bomford enquired particularly about your arms and stated that every time he saw Col. Irvine he was speaking about your muskets, and gave it as his opinion that the arms you were making was [*sic*] inferior to any made on contract. . . .
. . . I feel it an indispensable duty to remove, far as I can this unjust, unfounded prejudice.[37]

Again, Lee generously gave Simeon North an opportunity to redeem his reputation, writing him:

It is with regret that I hear you have suffered your pistols to be of far inferior workmanship than when I was at your works. In fact our inspectors are very much opposed to examining your pistols at all, because they are sure to be censured if they receive them; if they do not, then hard thoughts would ensue . . . tread backward without delay to place where you was two years since, and retrieve if possible what you have lost in eighteen months past. My ideas relative to your work I have not stated to anyone but yourself, and should we be able to get the works in a situation that it *should* be, I shall be happy in continuing to recommend your work and works; otherwise it will become my duty however unpleasant to report the true state of your pistols. Believe me, Sir, I send you this not to injure, but to benefit you.[38]

The Ordnance Department was fully aware of the methods by which a contractor might cheat the government. Lee wrote to his superior in the Department:

I would however take the liberty to observe that the Contractor has it in his power to deceive the Inspector in various ways if he is so disposed. After a musket is faithfully examined and approved and stamped, he may take some of the parts and replace them with condemned work. To guard against such an unwarrantable proceeding, the arms must be inspected in a room with a lock and key and the door always secured when the Inspector is absent. But I should much rather withhold contracts when such a course is necessary.[39]

The seriousness of this problem is apparent when it is realized that the inspectors examined parcels of arms at the factories of the contractors and then went on for other inspections or returned to their posts. This meant that except when inspection was taking place, the muskets remained in the hands of their manufacturer, who packed and shipped them to the arsenals.

The contractors showed considerable ingenuity in palming off inferior arms on the government. Several years after their manufacture a set of muskets was found to be full of defects that had been skillfully hidden in a manner which the examining officer described as follows:

The defects are principally in the barrels: Some having been plugged, others have deep flaws extending for some length and penetrating nearly through the barrels, and others again having extensive and deep cavities, on the outside, the thinness of the metal not allowing them to be worked out. Those injuries are generally, if not always, on the under part of the barrel, and concealed by the stock, and thus escaped detection when the arms were cleaned before, as it was then done without starting [i.e. disassembling] any of the limbs. Our armourer gives it as his opinion, that many of the barrels were fabricated from old ones, and states that about the year 1821 Mr. Waters [the manufacturer] purchased a number of old muskets. To judge from the appearance of many of the arms, I cannot avoid thinking that his conclusions are right. Besides the defect in the barrels, there are many flawed and broken barrels, and ramrods.[40]

A serious case of substandard arms concerned muskets furnished by Lemuel Pomeroy of Pittsfield. In 1818 some of his muskets which had originally passed inspection were reexamined and found to be of poor quality. Pomeroy exonerated both himself and the inspector who had accepted them, saying that if such was the case it was due to a few split stocks which his stockers had glued together and which had appeared satisfactory to the inspector. He added that a few locks had been over-hardened by an inferior workman, but that he had replaced them at his own expense whenever they gave trouble.[41] The charge against Pomeroy involved theft as well as fraud. Lee wrote him:

Many reports are in circulation relative to the circumstances of your condemned work being crowded in, and sent off as good. The report states further that you have in one case at least, when arms were sent to your works to be cleaned and repaired, that you kept the bayonets belonging to them, and put on the muskets such as were not good.[42]

But as was his wont, Lee was willing to give the contractor a chance to justify himself. He informed Pomeroy:

I have not yet written to Government on the subject nor shall not until the point is proved to my satisfaction which I hope may not be the case. . . . And while duty compels an investigation, I trust you will not consider me as an enemy, for such I can assure you I am not; though if the facts should be established, I shall not of course have the same respect for you as I have heretofore entertained.[43]

Pomeroy answered the accusation with a denial of guilt, explaining that any reports circulating about poor muskets of his maufacture either concerned muskets bought eight or ten years earlier by the State of New York, or others made on his first contract with the United States, which "went into the hands of new recruits at this post and with all their jamming and breaking—for 16 or 18 months" were damaged, but which he had repaired free of charge.[44]

For some reason the case was dropped, but in 1824 new charges were made against Pomeroy. Over five hundred stands of his muskets were sent to the Watervliet Arsenal, but the officer who received them reported them to be "so roughly fabricated, and in my opinion so foreign from the spirit of the Contract that I could not without doing violence to my feelings receipt for them."[45] Listing the defects as including badly turned and flawed bayonet shanks, bayonets so soft they could be bent by hand, rough barrels, poor lock plates, poor case-hardening, disproportioned bands and triangular ramrods with only their edges rounded, the officer concluded that they were the "worst arms that have been made for many years."[46]

Pomeroy denied knowledge of the alleged faults, putting the blame on the laxity of the inspector, whom nevertheless he considered a "very honorable and careful inspector and a good judge of a musket." He admitted that the bayonets were "too light—two or three lockplates were crooked from the sear spring hole to its edge and several other things were out of order to his [the examining officer's] eye, which a good judge of a musket would conceive of no importance." He blamed the iron used for the barrels as being badly made, and finally asked that the arms be reinspected.[47]

Lee appointed another inspector who turned in a very drastic report.[48] Pomeroy protested violently,[49] and as the difference in the findings of the two inspectors brought the honesty of the first one into question, a former foreman of Eli Whitney, who was satisfactory to both Lee and Pomeroy, was selected to give the disputed arms a third inspection.[50] This inspector, though he declared that he had "ever considered the duty of an Inspector as an unpleasant one, especially where there is bad work offered and a disposition on the part of the maufacturer to crowd in everything good or bad,"[51] carried out the reinspection with diplomacy as well as integrity, and turned in a report much more lenient than the previous one, owing in part, at least, to the fact that Pomeroy had replaced many of the condemned parts of the arms.[52] This final report probably saved Pomeroy from being stricken from the list of government contractors.

In an effort to improve the quality of contract arms, a few years later the government reinspected sample arms made by the different contractors. Reports on the arms were sent to their makers, and the inspectors were warned to increase their vigilance.[53] The reports were badly received and one inspector who took the manufacturers' part, and who was incidentally the man who had made the final inspection of Pomeroy's defective arms, remarked:

I could wish that a board of *disinterested* Inspectors (if any such could be found) were appointed to examine one or more boxes of arms made at the National Armories, as well as those by private individuals and report the result. I doubt whether such a board could be found, for I am fully satisfied from what I have seen and heard, that a considerable degree of prejudice exists, towards contractors, in the minds of the good folks at Harper's Ferry and Springfield, tho' in the latter place much less than formerly.[54]

The general antagonism over inspection was not appreciably abated as time went on, and Lee finally persuaded his superiors in the Ordnance Department to place inspection under a separate army officer.[55] The plan met with serious objections revolving about the difficulty of finding a man who was sufficiently experienced and who was at the same time *persona grata* to all concerned. Whitney's former foreman who was quoted in the preceding paragraph emphasized in a letter to Lee the need on the part of the proposed chief of inspectors for great mechanical knowledge and experience, and added:

In the next place where can you find an inspector who is *now* competent, entirely free from bias and prejudice? Will you send a New England Inspector into Pennsylvania or a Pennsylvanian into New England?

If a sufficient number of impartial, competent inspectors could be suddenly created "that knew not Joseph" that is, were ignorant of all the remarks and jealousies that have prevailed and circulated in the different armories among inspectors and contractors; in this case perhaps justice might be done between Government, Contractors and Inspectors.[56]

The plan was nevertheless adopted and the new Chief Inspector of contract arms, after serving an apprenticeship of a few months observing methods of inspection as carried out at the contractors' plants, took office in 1831.[57] Thus inspection problems dropped out of the Springfield Armory records at this point. It would be unrealistic, however, to assume that they came to an end or even were materially reduced in number.

4. *The Effects of the Contract System.*

Inspection difficulties were not the only disadvantage of the contract system. It was recognized by the Ordnance Department that contract arms were generally inferior in quality to those made at the national armories, and, since the government had to pay for inspection, their cost—as cost was figured at the time—was greater than what the Department supposed the cost of government made arms to be.[58] Further, the granting of subsidies was a continual drain on the government. From the manufacturers' point of view also the contract system had serious disadvantages. Those who lacked the necessary qualifications for the successful manufacture of arms on a large scale, and who nevertheless were lured into the business by the hope of advances and good profits, might be ruined. Once arms makers accepted contracts they had to continue to receive them or suffer serious loss through idle plant facilities.[59] At the expiration of a contract they had to retain their workers, even if this occasioned a loss, so that they might be prepared for new contracts.[60] Finally, as the Ordnance Department was habitually dallying with the alternate scheme of complete government manufacture of small arms, contractors could never be certain that there was a future in the business.[61]

Despite these difficulties the contract system was of immense value both to the government and the contractor, for aside from bringing the industry into existence it promoted a spirit of cooperation and mutual aid unique among early American manufacturers, which had much to do with the rapid development of the industry in the first thirty years of the nineteenth century. This spirit of mutual helpfulness, which was most strongly expressed in the relations between the New England contractors and the Springfield Armory, extended to many aspects of arms manufacture. The Superintendent of the Armory openly aided contractors by advising them of strategic times for applying for contracts.[62] Trade secrets apparently did not as yet exist in the new industry, and the Armory and the contractors exchanged advice and information relative to interchangeability, gun design, manufacturing processes and machine tools.[63]

The exchange of raw materials was widespread. Supplies were occasionally bought and inspected by the Springfield Armory for a contractor or vice versa.[64] Unfinished stocks were the commonest raw material exchanged, and were either paid for in money or exchanged for other stocks which because of requirements as to size, shape, or extent of seasoning were usable by one party only.[65] Tools which were difficult for a contractor to acquire or limited in their uses were loaned by the Springfield Armory.[66]

Patterns for machines were frequently exchanged in the industry.[67] Specialized services, such as difficult forging or grinding, were also exchanged.[68] A very common service with which the Armory favored contractors was rolling the bar iron they obtained from the Salisbury region into the various sizes required for making the different parts of the gun.[69]

A valuable type of cooperation was the lending of skilled workers. In this case it was usually the Springfield Armory which accommodated the contractors. Contractors paid the transportation expenses and the regular Springfield Armory rate of wages to the workers they borrowed. Afterwards workers might return and continue in their positions at Springfield unless the Armory was willing that they should leave its service. Thus the contractors were able to acquire the services of highly skilled pattern makers and tool makers, useful for a short period only.[70] In this connection Lee informed the New England contractors in 1818:

Should you be in want of any workmen in your establishment such as first rate barrel welders—trip hammers men—forgers, filers, stockers or finishers, you can probably be supplied from this place, by giving me information, mentioning the number and description you may want.[71]

The most noteworthy type of cooperation between contractors and the Springfield Armory in regard to labor was their open understanding not to outbid one another in the labor market. This arrangement was first entered into in 1816 and continued throughout this early period. Probably the scarcity of highly skilled labor, as well as the desire to keep wages low and reduce labor turnover, led the manufacturers to take this action. It is surprising that Lee, so enlightened in other respects, introduced the system, but it must be remembered that he was at least as anxious as any private manufacturer could be to keep the expenses of the armory under his charge as low as possible. He wrote the Chief of Ordnance in 1816:

I have agreed with Mr. Whitney, Mr. Stubblefield,* North, Starr, and all the Masters of Manufactures to the South of this, not to employ each other's workmen, without a recommendation from the person who last employed them.

Permit me, Sir, to suggest the propriety of adopting this method at all the establishments under your charge.[72]

In contrast to this condition of cooperation within the New England industry was the isolated state of the other federal armory at Harper's Ferry. It was much inferior to the Springfield Armory as far as manufacturing techniques, costs and prestige in the industry were concerned. Its remoteness from other arms makers was recognized by the Ordnance Department as the cause of its general backwardness.[73] There is no doubt that the contract system, through the cooperative spirit it induced among plants within fairly easy access of one another, accelerated by many years the technical development of the industry in New England.

* James Stubblefield, Superintendent of the Harper's Ferry Armory.

CHAPTER VI

RAW MATERIALS

1. Transportation.

Before considering in detail the raw materials of small arms manufacture it may be helpful to examine briefly the problems of their transportation to the Connecticut Valley. In the early nineteenth century three types of transportation were employed—hauling overland by wagon or sled, carrying by inland waterways, and shipping by sea. Wagoning or sledding of raw materials was laborious as well as expensive. The transport of iron was difficult, and even finished arms had to be moved in ox carts instead of the regular country wagons.[1] In special instances compact and urgently needed articles could be carried by stage coach, although in the earliest part of the century this method was considered undependable.[2]

In regard to cost overland transportation made a poor showing beside water carriage. The Salisbury iron masters found that it cost five dollars more per ton to haul their iron the forty or fifty miles to Springfield than to send it to New York, although the latter course meant either a twenty-mile overland haul to the Hudson and a barge trip down the river, or a good hundred and thirty mile boat trip down the Housatonic and through the Sound.[3] Iron makers in southern central Pennsylvania, using the Susquehanna and whatever smaller streams and canals might be accessible to them, found it necessary to charge a differential of ten dollars for land-and-water freight as compared with straight water freight to Baltimore.[4] Some Pennsylvania forges were so located that straight water carriage was possible only once in the year, during the spring rise.[5] This dependence on overland hauling put Pennsylvania iron at a serious disadvantage compared with New England iron in regard to the Connecticut Valley arms industry.[6] Susquehanna bituminous coal, shipped by water for use in New England arms manufacture, was cut off from the nearby Philadelphia market because of the land carriage involved.[7]

For local raw materials the Valley arms makers were dependent upon land carriage. Charcoal, firewood, lumber, and miscellaneous items such as cast iron, powder and lead, were easily acquired in the countryside and hauled by land to arms factories. Salisbury iron was transported partly, at least, by land. Such was the preponderance of local raw materials that about 1829 the Springfield Armory received annually an estimated 2,464 tons hauled by wagon or sled from the region extending fifty-four miles to the east and sixty-five miles to the west of the Connecticut River, as compared with 1,229 tons of water-borne materials.[8]

The river was the main artery of traffic for the arms manufacturers of central New England. Up to Hartford, to which sea-going vessels could sail, the river could be considered an adjunct of the ocean. Canals built at South Hadley and Turner's Falls, Mass., at Bellows Falls, Vt., and at Enfield Falls, Conn.—the last finished in 1829—opened up the higher reaches of the river.[9] At Hartford freight was transhipped to river boats of twenty to twenty-five tons, equipped with sails. By 1828 a steamboat was handling traffic between that city and Middletown.[10] In 1825 gunstocks were carried by water the twenty-five miles from Hartford to Springfield for one cent apiece, and most raw materials for $2.50 a ton.[11]

River and canal transport, although having distinct advantages over land carriage, had severe seasonal limitations. The value of even the Connecticut was reduced through the presence of ice from December to March.[12] Sea transportation was least affected by weather and was as well the least expensive method of moving raw materials. Eli Whitney calculated that it would cost him three times as much to ship gun stocks down the Connecticut from Springfield to New Haven as to procure them from Philadelphia or Baltimore.[13] Freight charges on stocks in 1829 were 1½¢ from Baltimore to New York, 1½¢ from New York to Hartford, and 1¢ from Hartford to Springfield.[14]

In sea transportation the sailing vessel was predominant, although on urgent occasions steamboats might be used. As early as 1815 a steam packet sailed from New Haven to New York and possibly to Philadelphia,[15] and in the late 1820's the Hartford packet ran regularly between Hartford and New York.[16] New York and to a slightly less degree Boston were the chief importing centers with which the Valley arms makers dealt.

2. Terms of Purchase and Means of Payment.

The records of the Springfield Armory of this time afford the only fairly complete information on raw materials used in arms making, and are probably representative of Connecticut Valley arms manufacture as a whole. The fragmentary records of Nathan Starr substantiate the Springfield Armory records as to type, price and origin of raw materials. As the different arms makers exchanged information concerning raw materials, and even raw materials themselves, it may be assumed that these were fairly well standardized as to quality and price. The fact that the Springfield Armory accounted for a large portion of the Valley's arms production* gives additional value to its records on raw materials.

Most raw materials were bought by the Armory on contract with importers or dealers in Boston, New York, Philadelphia, New Haven and

* It was calculated in 1818 that the two federal armories, of which Springfield was consistently the larger producer, were capable together of making 25,000 stands of arms a year, while only 8,000 to 10,000 were made annually on contract throughout the United States.[20]

Hartford.[17] An extract from the 1822 report of Superintendent Lee to the Ordnance Department describes the methods by which raw materials were purchased, and indicates that the purchaser exercised considerable control over the price of locally produced materials:

The contracts have generally been made at the superintendent's office, without public notice, except for coal. For this article proposals have been publicly requested by notice in the papers. Relative to imported articles, I have made it a point to inquire of the most respectable hardware importers in New York and Boston, and request their prices for such articles as were wanted in the armory, and have made their lowest prices the standard for making the contract, taking into consideration the quality of the materials and the time of payment, and have generally procured them at the New York and Boston prices, delivered at the armory and warranted. I have generally made the purchase with the stipulation that, if the articles did not prove good, they were to be returned. This is particularly the case with iron, steel, files, coal, and gun-stocks, and all the heavy materials used in this establishment.

It has been an object to keep so large a supply of those articles on hand, that it might not be in the power of the sellers to impose on us an unreasonable price. By this management we have reduced the prices of most of the articles, viz. iron from $10 to $7 per cwt., charcoal from eight and nine cents to five and six cents per bushel, pit-coal from fifty to forty cents per bushel, etc.[18]

Especially in the case of imports it was considered good policy for arms makers to build up large stocks of raw materials against possible embargoes and wars.[19] Lee estimated that the Springfield Armory, through failure to have on hand sufficient supplies, had lost at least $50,000 during the War of 1812.[21]

With the exception of gun stocks raw materials were purchased under one-year contracts.[22] No advances were supposed to be made to raw materials contractors by the Springfield Armory,[23] and they were prohibited by law in 1823.[24] Payment was almost universally made within ninety days after delivery, or quarterly.[25] Payment for materials was complicated in the first few years of the century by an unreliable postal system, and throughout the period under discussion by unstable currency. Post notes of the Bank of the United States, used around 1800 by the Springfield Armory, to be carried safely through the mails were torn in two and sent separately. This was a widespread custom in the Valley. The Springfield Armory paymaster commented:

This appears to be a safe way for in case one half is stolen they become of no value to the villain who takes them, the other half being in possession of the lawful owner serves as a check—on substantiating his character, I should presume he would be able to procure new Bills of the Bank from which the former were issued for the half he retains—in case of no miscarriage the two parts being pasted together they have the same currency as before.[26]

The absence of a uniform currency complicated commercial transactions in the early nineteenth century. In 1806 Connecticut Valley banks handled notes of the Bank of the United States only at a discount, but the United States Treasurer's drafts on Boston banks did not require discounting, as they were "current" in the Valley.[27] Accordingly the Springfield Armory for many years paid some of its creditors through Boston banks.[28] United States Bank notes became more acceptable in 1810 when a number of eastern banks failed.[29] But again early in 1815 the public's confidence in the government's ability to pay had been so much shaken as a result of the war that the paymaster of the Springfield Armory hesitated to accept funds for the Armory in the form of treasury notes.[30] Yet in the same year treasury notes began to appreciate, so that by the fall of 1816 they were equal to specie and Boston bank notes, and they remained in good standing from this time on.[31]

Problems affecting the different state bank notes were at least as numerous. One Boston merchant, in 1805, could not be paid for supplies sent the Springfield Armory because he would not accept a draft on a Hartford bank.[32] A ton of steel could be had in 1814 for $300 in Boston bank bills or $360 in New York bank bills.[33] Springfield and Hartford bank notes were frequently at a discount not only in New York City,[34] but also in upstate New York. One Albany creditor of the Springfield Armory declared in 1827: "It is a fact we could not pay our debts with Springfield money at all."[35]

Merchants could depend on United States Bank notes and Boston and New York bank notes carrying the lowest discount rate or the highest premium,[36] but the interrelations among these three currencies were subject to constant change. In later years the Springfield Armory met this problem in part, at least, by paying those creditors who would not accept Springfield bank notes by drafts on a New York firm.[37]

3. The Course of Prices of Raw Materials.

Prices of the more important raw materials of small arms manufacture, as collected from the Springfield Armory records, appear in table and chart form in Appendix C. In order to relate these prices to the general price structure, the writer has superimposed upon the chart Arthur H. Cole's index of wholesale prices of commodities in New York City, with variable group weights, for the month of January from 1800 onward.[38] In view of the fact that the Springfield Armory bought its materials at New York or Boston prices the use of this index seems appropriate.

While no close comparison can be made between relative and actual prices, a glance at the chart shows the presence of parallel trends between the prices of all raw materials which were imported or produced outside New England and Cole's index. A period of high prices occurred before the War of 1812, followed by inflationary peaks from about 1812 to 1816, and a general levelling off towards a lower price structure in later years. Two exceptions are the prices of iron and charcoal, both of which rose very slowly with only minor fluctuations. This is accounted for by the local production of all charcoal and most iron. As will be shown later, the arms makers exercised considerable influence over the prices they paid for these products. Where Pennsylvania or imported iron was used, it had to conform with the price of Salisbury iron in order to compete with it.

4. Iron.

In the early nineteenth century iron was used extensively in firearms. All metal parts were made of it, with the exception of the ramrod, bayonet, springs and frequently the pan.[39] Thus iron was of all raw materials, with the possible exception of steel, the cause of greatest concern to the arms makers. Those who could afford it were constantly seeking, through trial and error or through deliberate experimentation, to discover sources and types of iron which would fully meet their requirements. But, as shown by the experience of the Springfield Armory, these efforts resulted in only partial success.

Wrought iron refined from pig iron, and therefore known as "refined" iron, was the only iron used in the manufacture of small arms. Bloomery iron, commonly wrought iron made directly from the ore,[40] could not be substituted on account of impurities remaining in it. Nor was all refined iron suitable, but only the purest portion of it, called the "head of the loup."[41] After being wrought the iron was hammered or rolled to the desired sizes and shapes either at a forge or rolling mill close to the furnaces, or, more rarely, at the arms factories themselves. Hammering was the older method, but rolling was preferred because it resulted in iron of greater uniformity of width and thickness.[42] Nevertheless there was difference of opinion on this point. Roswell Lee observed in 1825, long after rolling had become a well established practice:

I have always had my doubts whether iron manufactured by rolling would be equally pure, sound and tenacious, as when wrought by hammering, believing the hammer the most capable of discharging the vitrious oxyd, other impurities and the excess of carbon, and rendering the iron more firm in its texture than can be effected by rolling.[43]

Iron reached the arms maker in the form of rods of various sizes, according to the size of the gun parts to be forged from them, and in the form of barrel skelps, known at the time as "shapes" or "scalps." These skelps were flat slabs with "scarfed" or bevelled edges, for smooth junction in welding. A skelp was bent by sledge-hammer or trip-hammer around a mandrel or metal bar, and the edges welded together to form the gun barrel.

Three sources of iron were important to New England arms makers in the early nineteenth century. By far the most prominent one was the Salisbury mountain region of western Connecticut and eastern New York. The ore hills of central Pennsylvania furnished a considerable amount of iron. Some was imported from Russia, but while Boston gunsmiths and those along the coast perhaps depended on it, it was used only experimentally in central New England. Deposits of iron at Franconia, N.H., Danbury, Conn., and in eastern New York, especially around Lake Champlain, supplied only the local gunsmiths and did not enter into the Connecticut Valley industry.

The Salisbury iron industry was at the peak of its productive capacity at this time. About 1800 there were between forty and fifty forges in Litchfield County, Conn. alone,[44] of which thirty-nine were still extant in 1819.[45] The iron was heated with charcoal and refined under a cool or warm blast.[46] It was free from sulphur, and was described by Lee, a connoisseur of iron, as being remarkably pure, malleable, tenacious and strong —in short, the best gun barrel iron in his experience.[47]

Salisbury iron had been used at the Springfield Armory from its very beginning, as indicated by early records, and the Armory's correspondence shows that it was relied on by all the contractors of central New England. Up to and during the War of 1812 the Armory used no iron from any other region, except experimentally. But after the war, owing to an increase of one-third in manufacturing costs, the price of Salisbury iron rose from $7 or $7.50 per hundredweight in 1813 and the years before the war to $8 or $9 in 1814.[48] The immediate result was that arms makers began a persevering search for new sources of iron.

Although Pennsylvania iron had earlier been found to contain too much copper to be used in arms making,[49] in 1816 the Springfield Armory ordered 120 tons of it.[50] From then on iron from the south and central portion of the state, especially Huntingdon, Centre and Blair Counties, was established. as a formidable competitor of the Salisbury product. During the first third of the nineteenth century, however, there was no likelihood of its replacing Salisbury iron, since it was used principally in order to destroy the monopolistic position of the Salisbury iron masters. Lee had written in 1815 with this purpose in mind:

When I first took charge of the Armory, $10 pr Cwt. was fixed for Iron. With great difficulty [I lowered] the price to $8.50 per Cwt. which is too high; but from peculiar circumstances cannot be obtained for a less sum, except I can form a powerful competition by contracting for that article in the interior of Pennsylvania; Which in conjunction with Mr. Whitney (of Connecticut) I think may be accomplished, and be very advantageous to the public.[51]

A month later he mentioned another attempt to take the determination of the price of Salisbury iron out of its producers' control:

I had conferred with all the principal iron masters in this quarter and endeavored far as I could to create a competition between them, which has had a good effect; but as the pigs of which most of our good iron is made, are all cast at one furnace, it is difficult to obtain that article for its real value, without placing ourselves in a situation, in some measure independent of them. I think it expedient soon as practicable to procure (at least) a year's stock of every kind of article necessary for the manufacture of arms.[52]

Experiments were made in 1816 with foreign iron rolled to the correct size after importation.[53] For a time Russian iron promised to compete seriously with domestic iron. A sample of it was considered at the Armory as the best barrel iron used there in twelve years.[54] But after 1816 Russian iron is not mentioned specifically in the Armory records, nor is there any indication that imported iron was used there except in 1818.[55] Either a sharp decline in its quality or increased duties account for the discontinuance of the use of Russian iron. Duties were imposed on wrought iron by 1810, if not earlier, and were increased in 1821.[56] Of a total of 50,000 tons of bar iron used in the United States in 1810, only about 4,500 came from Russia. An equal amount was brought in from England, but was unsuitable for small arms making because it had been manufactured with mineral coal.[57]

Salisbury remained the chief source of iron for the large New England arms makers, with Pennsylvania in a secondary position. The price of Salisbury iron and the quality of Pennsylvania iron were sources of continual difficulty. In 1816 Lee forcibly lowered the price the Springfield Armory paid for Salisbury iron from $170 to $160 a ton.[58] The iron masters recouped the losses imposed by their powerful customers from their more helpless ones. Eli Whitney described the difficulty in which Isaac Hollister & Sons, a small firm from which he received barrels, was placed by Holly & Coffing, the most outstanding Salisbury iron concern. Whitney wrote Lee:

Holly & Coffing, I think, have imposed hard terms on them in the supply of iron for the barrels which they have made for me—They have required I. H. & Sons to pay them the same price for the iron at the forge where it was made as they rec'd. for iron of the same quality delivered at Springfield—H. & C. ought by no means to charge I. H. & Sons more than 6.25 per Cwt. for the best scalp iron, delivered at the forge. . . . If Holly & Coffing bind them down to such terms that they cannot live without slighting their work, no advantage will result to anyone from the undertaking.[59]

Yet relations between the arms makers and the Salisbury iron firms continued with comparative smoothness for a few more years, aided by the fact that the former actually preferred Salisbury iron to other iron because of its higher quality.[60] The Salisbury iron masters had been so much subdued that in 1819 Lee made the following declaration to them:

We hold it as our privilege and right to alter the quantity of any article contracted for, by giving sixty days notice (foreign exempted). But it must be admitted, that this point ought to be understood at the time the contract is made. And as it is probable nothing of this kind has passed between us, I shall not urge it the present year. But from the first of January 1820 you will please to understand, that I hold it as my right and privilege, as U. S. Agent, to alter the quantity and price by giving *ninety days* previous notice. On these terms, and no other shall I contract for the Government.[61]

Lee even felt himself in so strong a position that he gave notice of his intention to contract for iron in 1820 at $140 a ton, when the price asked was ten dollars more. "I should think," he informed the six Salisbury firms with which he dealt, "from the present reduced prices of the necessaries of life & almost every other article, as well as wages, that good refined iron ought not to be higher than $140 per ton delivered at the works."[62] The iron masters were caught between the mill stones of their desire for good profits and their unwillingness to lose so steady a customer as the Armory. Adding to their distress was the knowledge that the Armory's action would almost inevitably lead to reductions in the price which other large arms makers would pay. The Salisbury firms protested with vehemence and logic, but Lee insisted on the price reduction.*

* The following extract from a letter in the Springfield Armory records from Holly & Coffing to Lee, Dec. 20, 1820, is an excellent example of the iron masters' arguments against the price reduction:

We regret that you should have an idea of reducing the price of our iron of the best quality below $150 per ton delivered at the Armory, as we cannot possibly afford to make it, of the quality which we send you, at a less price. And we believe that a few plain facts, fairly stated, will lead you to think that we cannot. In the first place, the proprietors of the Ore hill, the principal of whom, are Gen.l Livingston and Esquire Forbes, have been regularly advancing the price of the ore, ever since we commenced the manufacture of iron. When we began, they charged us four shillings per ton duty—then one dollar, and for 3 or 4 years past, we have paid them one dollar and twenty-five cents per ton which is the present price, and no probability of its being reduced. The only deduction in the price of ore which has taken place since the late peace, is 25 cents per ton, which was taken off from the price of digging it, last spring. There is, therefore, no probability, that this part of our raw materials will receive any deduction from the present price. Secondly—our coal costs us but fifty cents per hundred bushels less, now, than it did during the war. And we cannot expect that this article will be materially reduced in price, as we are, every year, obliged to go farther from the works after it; and the men who manufacture it barely get a living now, by their labour; and the only reduction reasonably to be calculated on must arise on the labour of making, and drawing it to the works. The first, if made, must be supplied by a more rigid economy in the workmen—which you know is difficult to effect in that class of people, and cannot be done untill after many changes of laborers; and these changes are always attended with some loss to the owners of works. The reduction from the other source, in consequence of the increased distance, must necessarily be small.

The Armory's policy of exerting pressure on the iron firms continued, and it was wholeheartedly supported by the contractors. In 1821 Eli Whitney gave Lee his opinion of the situation, which was none too indulgent to the iron masters. He wrote:

Thirdly, the price we pay for making the iron is but two dollars per ton less, now, than it was during the war, and this cannot be much more, if any, reduced, because good refiners are so scarce, not only in our neighborhood, but throughout the country, so far as we can learn, that we cannot dismiss them when we please, and procure others in their place, but we must of necessity keep them, upon the best terms we can make for ourselves.

We are very sensible that the necessaries of life are much reduced in price, but we know also, that labor has not been, and cannot be, at present, reduced in the same proportion. It was slower in its advance, than the produce of the country, and will always be slower in its decline; and the ore, as before observed, is fixed, and cannot be reduced in price. For these reasons, it is obvious that the price of iron, relatively to that of the necessaries of life, cannot be regulated by the same rule that many other manufacturers, as for instance, cotton, and wool, where the raw materials rise and fall very much in union with the necessaries of life. But there is another reason why our iron should not be reduced in price, which we consider of great weight, and we hope you will consider it so likewise.—This is, that our iron is *better in quality* than you receive of others. It is, we believe, well known that the Winchester [Litchfield County, Conn.] gentlemen, and others, except ourselves, who have furnished iron for the armory, have not selected the best part of each loup to send to you, but have uniformly drawn the whole into scalp iron, and sent it on in that way. This has been practised for years, and we have received no higher price for our iron, which has been uniformly acknowledged to be better, than others have for theirs, which was inferior. In this way they have had none on hand, of an inferior quality, to dispose of as they could, while we have had about one third of all we made, except the small portion of lock iron which you have received, to sell at a considerable discount. We have no doubt but that it is for the interest of the United States, generally, and in this case particularly, to encourage the manufacturing of iron of the very best quality; the reasons for this, you are as well acquainted with as any man. If then, one man does manufacture an article of better quality than others, but can get no better price, what encouragement has he to proceed in perfecting his manufacture? And as difference in quality constitutes difference in value, why is not the best article sold cheapest in market? In short, how is justice dispensed, in this way, to the different manufacturers? While you paid us a price for our iron, that we could live by, it was of little consequence to us how much you paid others for iron of inferior quality; but now, when the price is about to be reduced below what we can afford to make it for, we hope to offer you such reasons as to induce you not to reduce the price of our best quality, as we cannot but believe it to be, still, the interest of the United States to have the iron selected, and pay the present price, in preference to having the whole loup drawn out, as has generally been done. If you will receive ours in the latter way, we will very cheerfully furnish it at the reduced price which you mention, leaving ourselves as well off, as to select the best of it at $150 ton. We still feel desirous of supplying you with all the iron we can, provided your prices will do, and of doing everything in our power to accommodate you, in every respect—as we have always been pleased with your mode of doing business, and the result has always been satisfactory on our part; and we hope it has been on yours. Indeed from the good character which you have always given us, and our iron, abroad, so far as we have heard, we have good reason to conclude that you have been satisfied.

You may not, perhaps, have reflected, that we pay fourteen dollars per ton for transporting the iron to the Armory—and that we always, almost, have discount and interest to pay on our accepted accounts. We know that in one or two instances you have added that into the account.[64]

It is my candid belief that 7 Dlls per Cwt. for the best Salisbury iron is a fair price and that it can be very well afforded for that price—that is, that it will give to the faithful manufacturer a fair profit at that price—a better profit than it did at any time, in a period of ten years, next preceding the late war. Holly & Coffing are certainly very honorable dealers. I have uniformly found their iron to be of the best quality and I have no doubt it will continue to be so, in all cases where they engage to supply the best quality—Though there is not the least shadow of reason to doubt their honesty, still there is a stronger appearance, that they will keep up the quality of their iron, to be derived from their *intelligence*, than from their personal *integrity*—They understand their *own interest*, too well, to suffer the quality of their iron to depreciate. . . .

You certainly have it in your power to fix the price of iron and I think it will be fair to fix it at 7 Dolls per Cwt which is full 40 percent higher than the price of good common refined iron, by the quantity—I have no doubt that Holly & Coffing will furnish it at that price and I think them entitled to a preference.[63]

But a new complication arose. Either the arms makers' demands for a lower price than the iron masters could accept, or a definite tendency towards exhaustion of the ore hills resulted, in the early 1820's, in a distinct deterioration in the quality of Salisbury iron. At earlier times complaints had sometimes been made by the arms manufacturers,[65] but in 1822 iron supplied by Holly & Coffing, the best of the Salisbury concerns, proved very unsatisfactory to Lemuel Pomeroy. He wrote Lee:

Will you have the goodness to inform me whether you are using Messrs Holly & Coffing's iron in your musket barrels and what the proof is and about what time you rec'd the iron you have worked. Within 3 or 4 months past my proof has been for 3 months very bad—I have had 200 barrels from Mr. Hollister [a barrel manufacturer] and his proof has been as bad as ours. . . . I presume the burst will average 20 per cent. . . . If you have much the same proof and have in use no stronger powder than the standard I shall conclude the difficulty to be in the iron—and shall try some other iron for barrels. . . . I could better pay them [Holly & Coffing] for such iron as they made in 1816 and 17 than to have the iron they now furnish for nothing.[66]

This situation brought another search for more satisfactory iron. In 1824 Lee left the Armory for several months to investigate Tennessee iron.[67] During his travels he examined several Tennessee iron works and ore banks and gained a favorable opinion of their potentialities,[68] but nothing came of this project, probably because of the undeveloped state of the region and the inadequacy of transportation. The Tennessee iron used at the Armory in 1825 was only in experimental quantity.[69]

Inquiry was made into other sources of supply. Iron was examined from forges at Taunton and South Bridgewater in Massachusetts, at Franconia, N.H., near Danbury, Conn., in New York at Crown Point and Westpoint.[70]

The iron industry of Huntingdon and Centre Counties in Pennsylvania was more thoroughly canvassed.[71] But iron from most of these sources proved unsatisfactory. Although Lee admitted that Pennsylvania iron could bear a high welding heat, was soft, malleable and tenacious, free from chemical impurities and in itself an excellent metal, it continued to be so poorly refined that he felt it not equal to Salisbury iron.[72] That the latter was still preferred by arms makers is indicated by the fact that at this time Lee introduced Salisbury iron to the Harper's Ferry Armory, where it was found to be superior to any ever used there.[73] As late as 1825 arms makers could have excellent Salisbury iron if they were willing to pay the price demanded. Lee wrote:

I find no difficulty in obtaining any quantity of iron of a good quality, but I had some reason to suspect the iron masters were calculating to raise the price, already very high. This led me to make some further examinations into the resources of the country for producing iron.[74]

But the best days of the Salisbury iron had come to an end. After continued complaints,[75] in 1829 Lee issued a sharp ultimatum to the principal concerns which had been supplying the Armory:

The unprecedented bad quality of this article that has been received at the Establishment for six months past, render it indispensably necessary that great precaution should be observed in receiving Iron [in] future, for the loss is too great to be suffered, even by the United States. The poor quality of the Iron is not furnished by any one person or firm, but appears to be common to all, that have delivered the article here for the last year; and except much better Iron can be furnished, recourse must be had to some other quarter for the purpose of obtaining an article of better quality.

With a view to ascertain the quality of the Iron, I propose to send a man to inspect it at the forge, and to have the Iron broken into suitable sizes for Gun Barrel Scalps, and have it examined in that state, and none to be received but such as shall be approved by the Inspector. The bars to be broken at the expense of the Iron Master. Please inform me by return mail if you will or will not agree to this proposition.[76]

The iron masters submitted meekly to his demands, and inspection began immediately.[77] The first inspection report is worth inserting as showing the basis of Lee's discontent and the extent to which the famous Salisbury iron had deteriorated:

Firm Inspected	Bars of Iron Broken and Inspected	Of Which the Following Number Were Rejected
Holly & Coffing	940	102
" " " (another forge)	1351	130

	Scalps Broken and Inspected	Of Which the Following Number Were Rejected
Canfield & Sterling	248	16
Solomon Rockwell	579	54
R. Cook	220	9[78]

With the close of the 1820's the New England iron industry entered into a period of steady decline. While for some time Connecticut Valley arms makers continued to buy Salisbury iron, in the following decades their patronage shifted more and more to imported iron.

5. Steel.

The military musket in 1817 contained only two pounds and two and one-half ounces of steel, costing 43¢.[79] This had increased by 1829 to three pounds, costing 55½¢.[80] Yet there was no part of the musket on which the life of its user so much depended as on the few parts made of steel—the main spring, the hammer spring, the sear spring, the bayonet and the ramrod.

Prior to the War of 1812 arms makers used two types of steel, "blistered" or blister steel, so called because of its appearance and made from wrought iron by the process of cementation, or fusing with heated charcoal; and German steel, made from bog ore.[81] Rarely small amounts of expensive cast steel were used. Blister and German steel, delivered to arms makers in "fagots" or bundles of rods of undesignated diameter, sold at approximately the same price per pound, although in the 1820's the price of German steel dropped below that of blister steel.

A few years after the War of 1812 steel began to be made for special uses in arms manufacture. Rod, bayonet and spring steels were imported from England and Germany in large amounts. Although the bulk of the steel used continued to be the undifferentiated German and blister, shear or laminated steel—made by repeated heating, rolling and tilting of fagots of blister steel—was used for sword and bayonet blades.[82] In regard to its form when delivered, steel was altered, being rolled to the exact measurements required for the different parts of the weapon. Thus an 1826 order sheet of the Springfield Armory specified bayonet steel rolled to $19/40$ of an inch square in cross section, main spring steel $23/40$ x $11/40$ of an inch, hammer spring steel $14/40$ x $12/40$ of an inch, and both sear spring steel and ramrod steel of $1/4$ inch square cross section.[83]

New England small arms manufacture was almost completely dependent on foreign steel in the first thirty years of the nineteenth century. Frequent attempts were made to introduce domestic steel, but it did not become really established in the industry. As early as 1799 the Springfield Armory received some steel from a Salisbury iron firm, but to judge from the record of this transaction it was for experimental purposes only.[84] From the first the two sources of foreign steel were Germany for German steel and England for blister steel made from Swedish iron.[85]

The War of 1812 gave domestic steel a temporary advantage over foreign steel. England cut off supplies and her control of the seas made undependable the importation of German steel, which was carried on via France.[86] It is true that inexpensive Swedish steel sometimes appeared in the American market, but it was probably of inferior quality.[87] American steel made from Salisbury iron was offered for file and spring manufacture,[88] and American blister steel sold at the rate of only 12¢ a pound as compared with 48¢ for German steel.[89] But New England arms makers were unenthusiastic about American steel. Steel makers were few, and their product unstandardized. Furthermore, much of the American steel was made from either Swedish or Russian iron,[90] and thus was indirectly subjected to the uncertainties of wartime shipping.

Despite the arms makers' strong preference for English and German steel the end of the war did not bring about the complete elimination of domestic steel in small arms manufacture. As late as 1818 a steel maker with whom the Springfield Armory had dealt during the war, confident of the excellence of his steel, still hoped for the Armory's renewed patronage. He wrote the Superintendent:

If you should send this steel to your workmen without letting them know where it was made I think they cannot tell it from English steel. By this way many of our best axe makers have been cheated out of their prejudice and now use my steel.[91]

He elicited from Lee only an admission that his steel was "of tolerable good quality."[92]

It proved all the more difficult for American steel makers to lure the New England small arms industry away from imported steel because of the competent salesmanship of foreign, especially German, producers. In 1824 the German firm of Halbach offered the Springfield Armory first quality German steel, drawn to any gage desired, warranted and delivered at Baltimore, Philadelphia, New York or Boston, for the average price of 14¢ a pound.[93] The following year Goddfrey Boker, an officer of the Prussian government, also solicited orders from the Armory, proposing to supply it with steel drawn to any desired size at 14¢ a pound, and with files at prices about 40% below those of the Armory's last contract.[94]

These offers were attractive in view of the fact that domestic undrawn steel of the same quality cost 15¢ a pound, and drawing it to the right size added 2¢ to its price.[95] Accordingly the Armory contacted for large quantities of steel with the two German suppliers, stipulating that the steel should be free of flaws, seams and cracks.[96] While Halbach's steel suffered some-what from these defects, and the deliveries of Boker's were delayed,[97] German steel proved very satisfactory, and continued to be used in large amounts by the Armory. Despite efforts by Boker to be constituted the Armory's sole supplier,[98] English steel was also used extensively there,[99] nor did the purchase of steel in specified sizes of rods completely eliminate at the arms plants the drawing of blister and German steel and the reworking of steel scrap.[100]

The dependence upon imported steel throughout the first thirty years of the nineteenth century was not due merely to prejudice on the part of New England arms makers. They would have preferred American steel, but even in the late 1820's its quality remained poor.[101] Lee probably spoke for the Valley arms industry as a whole when he gave the following verdict on American steel:

It is very desirable to effect the Manufacture of Steel from American Iron, but all experiments (so far as my knowledge extends) have hitherto failed of success; owing I presume to the peculiar texture and quality of the iron.[102]

The backward state of American steel making as well as the conservatism of mechanics and manufacturers was probably responsible for the failure to adopt steel for gun barrels at this time, although optimists foresaw extension in the use of steel, which occurred only many years later. In 1823 a mechanic of Troy, N.Y. patented a method for making cast steel from scrap and other iron.[103] His employer wrote Lee:

Perhaps even several parts of the musket & rifle might be furnished [of cast steel] in a rough state at considerable saving—& probably of a better quality—The barrels may be cast—& hammered subsequently on a rod or tool—and have, when bored or smoothed out, the strength & firmness of wrought steel—the ramrods may be made of *steel wire*—Implements may be afforded at moderate expense.—Anvils, swedges, hammers—& various other articles—Swords & bayonets may be cast & wrought. And I am inclined to think that Field artillery may be made lighter & better by a consequence of this discovery, which unites the compactness of steel with the toughness of iron.[104]

But even an institution as progressive as the Springfield Armory considered such reasoning visionary, and while it was conceded that cast steel rifle barrels might be feasible, the plan of using steel for musket barrels was not adopted.[105]

6. Stocks.

Black walnut of high quality was the only wood used for the stocks of military weapons.[106] Lee explained to a prospective supplier the requirements for timber from which stocks should be cut:

For your information I would mention that the walnut timber for stocks must be of a firm, tough kind, free from Sap and knots. Trees that grew in the forest and of large size are generally too soft and not of sufficient strength. The principal part of our stocks are taken from timber growing in the open field.[107]

The trees were felled in winter, when the sap was down and danger from worms at a minimum.[108] They were hauled over the snow to sawmills and the wood destined for United States guns cut to a pattern provided by the government and carefully seasoned.[109] Lee described the seasoning process as follows:

No arms should be stocked with timber that has not been cut from the plank three years and been placed in a dry place at least two years. Stocks should be very gradually seasoned for the first 6 or 12 months; Afterwards, they may be put in a dry place and should frequently (when the weather is suitable) be exposed to a free circulation of air. I think it would be advisable to instruct the inspectors on this subject, as some contractors have been in the habit of seasoning their stocks in a short time (by kiln drying) which injures the quality of the timber and renders it subject to be affected by the action of the atmosphere.[110]

The gun stock industry was centered in Pennsylvania and Maryland from the beginning of the nineteenth century. Prior to 1815 the stocks for the Springfield Armory were shipped from Philadelphia by the office of the Superintendent of Military Stores.[111] Later, contracts were made directly with the suppliers of stocks. Even when the walnut supplies in Pennsylvania and Maryland gave out and contractors had to search further afield for suitable trees, Philadelphia, Baltimore and Richmond remained the points from which stocks were shipped to New England.[112]

Stocks were bought in large quantities from contractors, who usually had three-year contracts. The size and duration of contracts depended in part on the insistence of the contractors, who felt that short term orders were unprofitable.[113] It was to the interest of the arms maker also to receive stocks in large quantities in order to allow for any additional seasoning required, as well as to protect himself against contingencies of shipping and supply. Where possible, stocks sufficient for several years' manufacture were kept on hand at arms plants. The Springfield Armory sometimes had a supply for four, five, or six years' production.[114]

Payment for stocks was contingent upon delivery and inspection at some place close to the arms plant, if not actually at it.[115] This policy continued despite the efforts of stock contractors to save shipping costs by arranging for delivery at Baltimore or some other southern city.[116] The following extract from a letter of 1819 from Lee to the Ordnance Department indicates the difficulties which would have resulted from inspections and delivery at any point other than the arms factory:

The loss in stocks when they are sawed from the plank when green, by springing and otherwise, is very great, for which reason I make my engagements to have the Contractor warrant every stock to work, and give 30 cents a piece delivered at Hartford (Conn.) This is much cheaper for the U.S. than to allow 27 cents and have them inspected in Philadelphia or Baltimore or any other place than the Armory. For in almost [every] instance we have condemned one fourth part of the stocks that have been received in that way.[117]

While gun stocks from the Pennsylvania-Maryland region were greatly preferred, the supplies of suitable walnut trees in these states dwindled so much that in 1827 the Springfield Armory found it necessary to increase the rigorousness of inspection of Maryland stocks in order to maintain their quality.[118] With growing frequency the stock suppliers asked to be allowed to fill contracts with walnut from the "Western Country" of New York and Ohio.[119] The water route of Lake Erie, the newly opened Erie Canal, and the Hudson River made this region accessible.[120] But the Springfield Armory resisted the introduction of western stocks, holding them to be of poor quality.[121] Nevertheless as time passed it became almost imperative to accept stocks from regions other than Pennsylvania and Maryland. One of the Armory's most reliable stock contractors was travelling in 1823 to Marietta, Ohio to collect walnut timber,[122] and by 1825 some stocks were being shipped by a contractor of Huron, Ohio.[123] Thus the source of supply was steadily pushed westward.

7. Coal.

Arms manufacture was almost completely dependent on charcoal until experiments in the late 1820's suddenly disclosed some of the potentialities of anthracite coal. As time went on anthracite coal greatly restricted the use of charcoal in the industry, except in such operations as case hardening, in which the "soft" iron parts of the lock were given hard, carbonized surfaces by heating with charcoal.

Charcoal was furnished on contract by numerous suppliers, many of whom were farmers. A large armory like the Springfield Armory might contract with a dozen or more, each supplying it with from 4,000 to 12,000 bushels a year.[124] Because of the number of suppliers and the large resources along the Connecticut River—which were such that as late as 1856 the Springfield Armory was receiving all its charcoal from villages within a twenty- or twenty-five-mile radius of Springfield[125]—the price of charcoal hardly fluctuated. Only occasionally did arms makers feel the pressure of rising prices of charcoal. The Master Armorer of Springfield complained in 1827:

The price of many articles have risen considerable this season,—oak & all hard wood has been selling all this winter at Two dollars per (two foot) cords, & pine at one dollar fifty cents per cord,—Hay at from 16 to 18 dollars per ton, Corn at seventy-five cents the bushel which makes the Farmers & Woodsmen etc. feel pretty stiff & independent.[126]

Bituminous coal was of limited use in early small arms manufacture. Mixed with charcoal, it was burnt in the Springfield Armory's forge where scrap iron was reworked.[127] In barrel welding the proportion of fuel used was three bushels of charcoal to one-fifth bushel of bituminous coal.[128] In 1800 a stock of only 5,000 bushels was considered a year's supply for the Armory.[129] Bituminous coal was contracted for at southern centers such as Richmond and Philadelphia. Occasionally a cargo of English coal came on the market,[130] presumably shipped as ballast rather than in an attempt to compete with the American product.

In 1828 the Springfield Armory began to experiment with welding barrels with Lehigh or anthracite coal from eastern Pennsylvania.[131] In the preceding year Armory welders working with different kinds of fuel had come to the conclusion that charcoal was the best, but the Master Armorer shrewdly observed, "I have no doubt but that the welders were inclined to favor the char more than the pit coal, as they prefer the use of it."[132] The experiments of 1828 with anthracite showed great promise. Of the first 139 barrels welded with a fire of Lehigh coal only five burst, and but six others were condemned for defects such as cross cracks and cinder holes. Lee, recounting this to Lemuel Pomeroy, estimated that one-third of the expense for fuel could be saved by the use of anthracite. He added with marked understatement, "my faith in the Lehigh is not shaken by the result [of the experiments]."[133]

A smaller quantity of Lehigh coal was needed to weld a barrel. Each of six welders at the Springfield Armory welded a set of twenty barrels with charcoal alone, twenty with Lehigh coal alone, and twenty with a mixture of the two. It was found that to weld a set required from forty-eight to fifty-two and one-half bushels of charcoal, from about eleven to slightly under sixteen bushels of Lehigh, or, when Lehigh and charcoal were mixed, from a little more than forty-five bushels of charcoal with about two of Lehigh to fifty-seven of charcoal and about three of Lehigh.[134]

Further encouragement came from a Rhode Island manufacturer, who discovered that a ton of Lehigh coal would heat six tons of iron—a saving of about fifty per cent in fuel cost.[135] A Ludlow, Mass. gun-barrel maker also worked with anthracite and found that its cost for drawing, scarfing, rolling and welding a barrel was only 19½¢, a saving of 8½¢ over the cost of these operations where charcoal was used.[136] Other arms makers kept close watch on these experiments,[137] and by December, 1828 a furnace had been put up at Millbury, Mass., for heating, drawing and rolling skelps with Lehigh coal. It was discovered there that when this coal was used only a three per cent loss by bursting resulted, while by the old method of welding nearly eleven per cent of all barrels burst and an even greater proportion suffered from other defects.[138] Thus anthracite broke charcoal's monopoly in the industry.

8. Miscellaneous Raw Materials.

Files were bought in great quantities for small arms manufacture. About three dollars a dozen was the average price of files throughout the first thirty years of the century, although this varied according to the quality, size and cut of the files, and with changes in the general price structure. For the specialized types of work necessary to finish the parts of a weapon many kinds of files were needed. Types regularly used were round, half-round, three square, square, flat, flat smooth, round smooth, flat rough, round rough, cast steel, pit saw, hand saw, three square rough, three square bastard, knife rough, knife bastard, bastard, second cut, and rasps.[139] Most files were imported from England, either on special orders filled in that country, or, probably more commonly as time went on, out of stock. Domestic files, however, were not entirely excluded from the industry. As late as 1815 opinion differed as to the comparative quality of domestic and imported files.[140] Arms makers would have welcomed American files of good quality,[141] and a few file makers in Connecticut and Rhode Island both made and repaired files.[142] But as was the case with steel, the American file industry was not sufficiently developed to compete seriously with the English.

Other tools such as planes, vises, anvils, and the chisels and gouges used for many years for finishing machine turned stocks, were imported from England.[143] Flints for firearms, emery for fine grinding, Turkey or English oil stone for whetting tools, buff leather, fire-sand, fire-clay and fire-brick also came from England.[144] Grindstones, the only significant import not English in origin, came from Nova Scotia, and ran in sizes of from two to three feet in diameter and four to six inches in thickness, to five and a half or six feet in diameter and a foot in thickness.[145] Miscellaneous metals such as copper, zinc, brass, and lead were easily acquired in any large city, as were moose-skin or buckskin for polishing and machinery belts. Old shoes were collected by the bushel from the countryside and burned with charcoal in case-hardening.[146] Boxes for packing arms were bought from local carpenters. For tempering and lubrication either whale oil or linseed oil, mostly the former, was used.[147]

An indication of the relative amounts of different raw materials used in producing small arms is given by the following statistics compiled by the Superintendent of the Springfield Armory in 1823. He based his figures on an annual production of 12,000 muskets, actually 2,000 less than the Armory produced in that year.

Amount of Raw Materials Necessary to Produce 12,000 Muskets a Year[148]

12,500 Rough Stocks	100,000 bus. Charcoal or 500 tons Pit Coal
120 tons Refined Iron	
12 tons Steel	2,000 bus. Old Shoes
2 tons Brass and Zinc	80 tons Grindstones
12,000 Files, Assorted	224 lbs. Candles
1 ton Emery, Assorted	224 lbs. Tallow
672 lbs. Band and Buff Leather	4 bbls. Tar
1,120 lbs. Woolen Rags	30 reams Sandpaper
112 lbs. Borax	150 cords Wood
500 gal. Sperm Oil	20 tons Sand (Fire)
100 gal. Linseed Oil	20 tons Clay (Fire)

CHAPTER VII

INTERCHANGEABILITY AND MACHINE TOOLS

I. The Introduction of Interchangeability

The possibility of achieving interchangeability in small arms, or uniformity of corresponding parts in different weapons, was early recognized, but years passed before it was widely accepted as a desirable end, and more years before a reasonable degree of uniformity was attained. Opposition to it was owing partly to conservatism, partly to honest difference of opinion, and partly to the realization that interchangeability could be achieved only at the cost of much money, time and effort. A reasonable degree of uniformity was not established until the contract system had been in existence for some years and contractors, anticipating future orders, could afford the expense involved in putting it into effect.

As early as 1785 Thomas Jefferson, while minister to France, became acquainted with the work of the French armorer, Le Blanc, who made corresponding parts of locks so nearly alike that smoothly working locks could be assembled at will from piles of parts. Jefferson failed in his attempt to induce Congress to bring Le Blanc to the United States to introduce his system in this country, because the full significance of Le Blanc's work was not realized.[1] Again, at the turn of the century when Eli Whitney set up interchangeability as a goal towards which to work in arms production, French and English ordnance officers were skeptical. They felt it would result only in prohibitively expensive arms.[2] Captain Decius Wadsworth, later able Chief of the Ordnance Department, manifestly failed to grasp the importance of interchangeability when he reported to the Secretary of the Treasury in 1800 that Whitney had in fact succeeded in his aim, but that he himself considered interchangeability pleasing to the imagination rather than practically valuable.[3] Whitney's scheme won little attention until he took ten specimens of every part of the musket to Washington and assembled them at random before some army officers and the Secretary of War.[4]*

* During the Civil War Whitney's son, Eli Whitney, Jr., himself a prominent arms maker, wrote P. C. Watson, Assistant Secretary of War, concerning the contribution of his father to American small arms manufacture. The younger Whitney hoped to receive preferential treatment on arms contracts on account of his father's inventions; nevertheless the extract from his letter here presented is a straightforward and unexaggerated account of his father's achievements:

There are some things connected with the history of the manufacture of arms at my Armory few at the present day are aware of.—The making [of] muskets on the uniformity or interchangeable System originated there, Viz. Drilling and filing by jigs, also the system of milling by irregular shaped cutters on which the whole system is based came from my Father's inventive mind. It is this interchangeable system that gives our arms their acknowledged superiority over

87

It was not until after the outbreak of the War of 1812—and probably owing to experience gained during it—that the War Department began to understand the value of interchangeability. The first official indication of its acceptance is found in a 20,000 pistol contract made with Simeon North in 1813, which stipulated that any part of any pistol made under it should fit any other pistol of the 20,000.[5] Five years later the Springfield Armory was ordered to adopt interchangeability.[6] But difference of opinion as to its value still persisted. In 1819 Lee wrote:

I can only inform you that my instructions are to make the muskets with that exact uniformity, that the several component parts will fit one musket as well as any other. Relative to the *practicability* of this course, experience must decide. With regard to the *utility* of the measure to the extent required by Government, the fidelity as well as the respect due to the authority from which I receive instructions and have the honor to hold my present station, forbid me to express an unfavorable opinion except it be to that authority when required, or when in my opinion the public interest makes it an indispensable duty. It now only remains for me strictly to observe my instructions, near as the circumstances will admit. My present impressions are, that this mode (of uniformity within the musket) must be entered into and pursued until experience (which is the most sure test) proves its practicability and utility, or the reverse.[7]

In the same year another ordnance officer, Major James Dalliba, reporting to the Chief of Ordnance on the Springfield Armory, held that the value of interchangeability in all arms parts was limited by the great expense and amount of time necessary to obtain it. He held that, whatever the degree of uniformity in small arms, major repairs would be made by experienced armorers, and not in the field; so that all that was required was interchangeability of the bayonets in particular, and secondly of the barrels, stocks and entire locks, but not of the parts of the locks.[9] By the late

Foreign arms. When he first began to manufacture on this plan it was understood by the English and French that our Government intended making their arms on the uniformity principle and they laughed at it as absurdity, and as a method calculated to *greatly increase* the *cost* of the arms, while the English gunsmiths said it was an impossibility, but my father's genius made it simple and cheap by his inventions for which he took out no patents, nor did he receive more than any one else for making muskets.

That simple and economical and beautiful method of polishing the outside of the gun barrel by machinery originated at my Armory, and no patent was taken out for that, tho it has saved thousands of dollars to Govt.—I ask in this matter of making muskets to be treated as well as others have been who had no such great claims to Govt. patronage, and ask nothing more than simple justice—for these great facts connected with the inauguration of the uniformity System, I think, are as great a claim in equity as could be preferred to, or entitled to consideration from the U. States Government. By this my Father has done as much for the manufacture of all military Small arms, as he did for the Country by the invention of the cotton gin. The latter an invention the great merit of which lies in its being now in universal use tho' invented in 1793 and to the fact that, tho there have been 300 patents taken out for supposed improvements in the Cotton Gin, it is virtually unimproved upon.[8]

1820's, however, the War Department fully accepted the value of inter-changeability. The Chief of Ordnance wrote in 1827 to the Secretary of War, in connection with the uniformity achieved in rifle making at Harper's Ferry:

This degree of perfection in the fabrication of small-arms has ever been considered an object of the highest importance in all national armories, and has been frequently attempted in the armories of Europe, but hitherto without success. And the attempt has been generally abandoned from the belief that the object was unattainable.[10]

From that time interchangeability has been a goal not only of American small arms manufacture but of the metal products industries generally. Perpetual refinements in methods of gaging and machine tool production have repeatedly caused older standards of practical interchangeability to be discarded in favor of more precise ones. Absolute interchangeability in factory production—that is, the manufacture of like parts truly identical in their dimensions—has never been attained; nor is it probable that it ever will be. This fact is generally recognized in engineering, as is shown by the establishment of specified tolerances or ranges of permissible varia-tions in dimensions of like parts. Nevertheless practical interchangeability, by which is meant the production of like parts which are sufficiently uniform to allow random assembly without impairment of the functioning of the complete mechanism, has long been established in small arms making.

II. Methods of Achieving Interchangeability

1. Pattern Weapons and Gages.

Early attempts were made to assure interchangeability by the use of pattern weapons and by inspection with gages, usually carried on after the arms were finished. To keep manufacturers to contract specifications the Chief of Ordnance recommended in 1815 that pattern arms be made and sent to the contractors to guide their work.[11] Finished arms made by these patterns were inspected in the manner described in the discussion of con-tract arms. As suitable methods of precision measurement had not yet been developed, specifications were of a qualitative kind. This held true even in the making of the pattern arms and inspection gages themselves, so that in 1821 duplicate gages were required to be as like one another "as con-venient for skillful and attentive workmen to conform to."[12] In 1827 con-tract arms of the same model made at different armories had a range of variation of 9 oz. in the weight of the barrel, which was on the average 4 lbs. 9 oz.; within one armory the range of variation was as much as 5½ oz. In view of the range of these variations the Ordnance Department decided to allow a deviation of 2 oz. either way from the model as lying within the requirements of the specifications.[13]

Variations from the pattern were not confined to contract arms. The two national armories found it exceedingly difficult to achieve and maintain interchangeability, either as between the two armories or within each armory.[14] In an effort at improvement arms made at each were checked with those made at the other.[15] As Lee pointed out while "contractors, and more particularly workmen run into error sometimes without any intention or even knowing that they do so, *even Uncle Sam's folks* are *not entirely* free from it."[16] It was considered a real achievement when in 1824 the Harper's Ferry Armory made bayonets which fitted barrels interchangeably.[17]

Except at the Springfield Armory the use of gages for anything but inspection of finished arms was apparently almost unknown in New England. Gaging during manufacture had reached a high state of development at Springfield by 1819, as shown by the following extract from the 1819 report of Major Dalliba:

In order to attain this grand object of uniformity of parts, the only method which can accomplish it has been adopted at Springfield, but it requires to be perfected, viz: making each part to fit a standard gauge. The master armorer has a set of standard patterns and gauges. The foremen of shops and branches and inspectors have each a set for the parts formed in their respective shops; and each workman has those that are required for the particular part at which he is at work. These are all made to correspond with the original set, and are tried by them occasionally, in order to discover any variation that may have taken place in using. They are made of hardened steel. The workman makes every similar piece to fit the same gauge, and, consequently, every similar piece must be nearly of the same size and form. If this method is continued, and the closest attention paid to it by the master workmen, inspectors, workmen, and superintendent, the desired object will finally be attained. The method practised at Springfield, of inspecting each part before the parts are put together, or before it goes to another workman, to be put through another process, has a great influence on the workmen; it does much towards improving the work generally and towards obtaining a uniformity of parts, and consequently a uniformity of muskets, and is undoubtedly the best possible method. If a part does not pass inspection, it goes back to the workman, either to be improved, or deducted from his wages. His interest compels him to do it well. It is on account of this method that the arms made at the national armories are, and will be, superior to those made on contract. In the latter case, the arm is finished before inspection, and, if a part is condemned, the whole piece, valued at $13 or $14, is condemned.[18]

Elsewhere, although continued effort was made to improve inspection gages,[19] there is no evidence of gages being used by arms makers in the first part of the nineteenth century during the manufacture of weapons. It was only in 1828 that Nathan Starr Jr., who was shifting from sword and rifle to musket production,[20] and who therefore was perhaps especially conscious of the need for accuracy in arms manufacture, asked to borrow a set of the

Springfield Armory's inspection and verifying instruments.[21] An identical request came from Lemuel Pomeroy the following year.[22] Lee granted Starr's request[23] and presumably Pomeroy's also, but he wrote Starr: "Col. Bomford [of the Ordnance Department] has not authorized me to furnish you with gauges, nor do I recollect that it has ever been done in a single instance."[24] The action of Starr and Pomeroy perhaps represented the first effort on the part of contractors to test the dimensions of the parts of their arms by gaging during manufacture and before inspection.

2. Occupational Specialization.

Another important factor in establishing interchangeability was occupational specialization, introduced in the first place because of shortage of skilled labor in the industry.[25] Whitney succeeded in avoiding the pitfalls of the contemporary English system of manufacture, whereby a workman was confined to one part of the weapon but carried out all operations on that part. Instead Whitney subdivided the work on a given part according to its nature, so that several workmen performed each only one or two operations on the part.[26] North, who with Whitney is generally recognized as having successfully introduced interchangeability in arms making,[27] as early as 1808 was having a worker make consecutively 2,000 similar parts. He found that in this way he could reduce the labor in making a part by at least one quarter, and in addition produce better quality arms.[28]

Contemporary observers realized that occupational specialization, while beneficial for the industry and in the short run for the workers, was damaging the independence of the armorer by reducing his general skill. Thus Major Dalliba commented:

By this arrangement, it will readily be perceived that each workman becomes an adept at his part. He works with greater facility, and *does the work much better* than one *could* who worked at all the parts. This is undoubtedly the best method for Government. The consequence however, to the workmen is, that not one of them becomes a finished armorer. If he is always employed at the Government factories, it is no matter for him; he is, in fact, the better for it, for he does more work, and gets more money; but if he wished to set up in business for himself, he has got no trade; he cannot make a fire-arm.[29]

The Springfield Armory Work Returns show rapid growth in occupational specialization between 1806 and 1830. The occupations listed in these records, of which the earliest date back to 1806, were counted for that year and for 1810 and the following years at five-year intervals, and appear in Table 1 of Appendix D. This table shows a decline in the number of men in any one occupation as specialization increased. Supervisory work, work classified only as "Day's Work," and work not directly connected with manufacture, such as packing arms, carpentry, masonry and shop tending, were excluded from this table. Workers engaged in day's work before 1820 were so numerous that one must suppose that many were actually making arms, but were performing such different operations that it was impossible to classify them more accurately. The earliest work returns show that filers and usually forgers spent part of their time on specific operations and part of it "jobbing," being paid by the day for the latter kind of work. In short, they were probably close to the skilled gunsmiths whose disappearance Major Dalliba deplored.

A ten-fold increase during a quarter century in the number of occupations at Springfield is shown in Table 1. The period of most rapid increase, between 1815 and 1820, occurred precisely at the time in which many processes were being mechanized for the first time. The contrast in types of occupation in 1806 with those in 1830 is interesting. In 1806 the eleven occupations directly concerned with gun manufacture, and excluding supervisory work, were welding barrels, helping to weld barrels, grinding barrels, boring barrels, polishing barrels, smooth-boring and cutting off barrels, drawing skelps, helping to draw skelps, polishing mountings, polishing locks, and forging butt plates, bands, guards and trigger plates. In January, 1830, there were twenty-three different occupations in filing alone, eighteen in forging—eight of which required full-time helpers—five occupations in grinding, three in fitting, four in finishing. In forging men spent their entire time working on one, or in some instances two, of the following parts and accessories: main springs, band springs, cocks, guard screws, side screws, butt plates, lock plates, batteries—or frizzens, the part of the lock against which the flint was struck—upper jaws, sears, guard bows, upper bands, middle and lower bands, tumbler screws, and wipers, screw drivers and lock screws, battery springs and battery screws, tang, cock and butt screws, and bayonets.

3. Swages and Jigs.

When the contractor received his pattern arm, he proceeded in his own way to reproduce it as nearly as he could. The barrel of a musket, rifle or pistol had a specified length, diameter, weight and bore, to which he conformed as closely as possible. All the other metal parts were reproduced by the use of swages and jigs, and with every change in model these had to be changed, causing a delay in production similar to the modern tooling up period.[30] A swage, or hand die for forging, was a tool with a hardened steel face, bearing the impression of a particular part. It was used in shaping that part from the iron or steel rods with which the worker was supplied.[31] The "work," or part of the weapon upon which the armorer was working, was held upon the swage, or the swage was held upon the work, which was forged by a sledge-hammer into the desired shape. Die forging was used in the industry after the War of 1812,[32] and probably for many years earlier. In Le Blanc's work in France it was an important means in achieving interchangeability, but was abandoned because arms parts were spoiled and cracked by improper swaging.[33]

Swages were made from the parts of the pattern weapon, doubtless by sand casting. Forged but unfinished parts were more valuable for this purpose, as filing and polishing altered the original shape of the forging.[34] Nevertheless contractors usually had to be content with making their swages from finished arms, allowing for the reduction in size which resulted from finishing. Here was one point at which deviations from the pattern slipped in. Another source of deviation was the constant use and consequent wearing away of the pattern arm in making swages from it.[35]

A forged part was taken in the "soft" or uncase-hardened state in which it came from the swage and hammer and if necessary put in a drilling jig, a plate or box which held the part and which contained holes so placed that by running a drill through the jig the hole or holes in the part would be drilled in their proper positions. Drilling jigs were probably in use from the beginning of small arms manufacturing.[36] After forging and drilling the part was clamped in a filing jig, which consisted of two hardened steel forms having the contours of the finished piece. Any excess metal on the part was filed off by hand.[37] Traditionally, Simeon North's son Selah invented the filing jig,[38] but Eli Whitney was using it almost as early as the Norths.[39]

When the parts had been filed in jigs they were assembled and tried for fit. They were then taken apart and after any necessary adjustments, were case-hardened in a mixture of charcoal and burnt leather, thus receiving a steel surface, and were then polished. It is reported that Simeon North in 1814 achieved such accuracy that his locks did not have to be assembled and fitted while "soft," but could be case-hardened immediately after filing.[40] This was probably accomplished by fitting every part to the same lock, an achievement on North's part which the Superintendents of the Springfield and Harper's Ferry Armories considered notable.[41] The common practice, however, was assembling parts in the soft state and filing to fit, since hardened parts could not be filed.

4. The Development of Machine Tools.

A natural development of employing swages and jigs was the application of power to their use. Mechanization was, with some exceptions, delayed until after the War of 1812, although Eli Whitney about the turn of the century had recognized the potentialities of water driven machines for forging, rolling, boring, grinding, and polishing.[42] These processes upon which inventors spent most effort, because most difficult to carry out by hand, were the ones first mechanized, so that up to 1830 invention was principally concerned with the successful mechanization of the boring, welding and turning of the gun barrel, and with the shaping of the gun stock.

A. Barrel Boring Machines.

Mechanization first took place in the boring of the interior of the welded barrel, which was carried out to give it a cylindrical bore of even diameter and a smooth surface. This was accomplished with a boring bit, often called a screw auger or nut bit. The auger was either a forged round rod with spiral grooves filed in it, or a forged flat rod twisted to form a spirally grooved rod; in either case it carried two cutters at one end. The barrel was slipped over the auger and moved as the cutters took off shavings of metal from the interior of the barrel. The spiral grooves on the rod discharged the metal shavings at the other end of the auger. The auger was turned by an endless screw driven by water, giving a slow, easy motion.[43] The carriage holding the barrel was moved by a hand turned crank operating on a rack, or toothed bar, and pinion gear.[44] Both barrel and bit were cooled by water.[45]

The screw auger, perhaps sometimes driven by hand alone, appeared almost simultaneously in several small arms plants, and was the subject of bitterly contested patent suits carried on for more than twenty years.[46] It was probably invented independently in more than one place. It seems to have been used in the United States in 1796 and in England somewhat earlier.[47] But James Greer was said to have invented it in 1797 and to have used it in a Philadelphia gun shop in 1798.[48] William Holmes claimed to have invented it in the Springfield Armory in 1798 or 1799.[49] It was used in 1799 by Eli Whitney, and at the Harper's Ferry Armory in 1807.[50] Daniel Pettibone of Philadelphia and Lemuel Pomeroy each claimed its invention.[51]

The fragmentary Census of Manufactures of 1810 listed as the sole type of gun machinery in the industry three boring machines or boring banks in Pennsylvania and three others in Virginia.[52] The 1820 Census of Manufacture shows that gun machinery outside New England for the most part consisted of boring machines. They were used in New York State, Pennsylvania, Virginia, Georgia, Tennessee and Ohio. In Virginia the machine took the form of a "horse auger," though it may be supposed that elsewhere water power was always used.[53]

B. Welding by Trip-Hammer.

Another laborious operation, that of welding barrels, was mechanized by the introduction of the tilt-hammer, or, as it was commonly called, the trip-hammer. The hammer was usually worked by cams attached to the shaft of a water wheel, which let the hammer fall at regular intervals, bending the barrel skelp around a mandrel.[54] Whitney, however, considered that driving the hammer with a belt was preferable to this method.[55] Four hammers were in some cases carried on one water wheel, two to weld the butt of the barrel and two to weld the upper part. The water wheel usually revolved continuously, but the hammers were so arranged as to be caught by a spring and fell only when a treadle operated. They might deliver as many as four hundred blows a minute.[56] The hammers had grooved faces forming dies, which shaped the skelps into barrels.[57]

In the Salisbury iron district the trip-hammer had been in common use from 1800 for forging round iron bars, scythes, hoes, and other tools.[58] In 1808 Aaron Broad, a worker at the Springfield Armory, rounded ramrods with a trip-hammer, instead of forging them by hand. Because Broad "from selfish motives . . . pursued this plan but a short time,"[59] the method as applied to ramrods was not developed further at the time. But in 1821 Charles Barstow claimed the invention of forging ramrods with concave dies in an ordinary trip-hammer.[60]

After these attempts no great ingenuity was required to apply the trip-hammer to barrel welding. Asa Waters, in whose Millbury armory a trip-hammer was used in 1809, patented the process in 1817.[61] The trip-hammer was probably used for welding barrels as early as 1809 in the musket and rifle factories of Pennsylvania,[62] and in 1810 it was certainly used at Canton, Mass.[63] A New England iron and steel maker, long familiar with the use of the trip-hammer for other purposes, remarked in connection with Waters's patent:

I should not think of gitting a patent for . . . applying a trip to welding a gun barel any moure than plating a scythe or a hoe it seems to me that a strange fanatism has opperated on sum people for gitting patents for such simple things.[64]

Although the Ordnance Department was skeptical of the validity of Waters's patent, barrel welding by trip-hammer, introduced in the Springfield Armory in 1815,[65] was so valuable an invention that the Department secured the right to use it in government and contractors' armories by giving Waters in 1818 a contract for 10,000 stands of arms.[66] Because of the heavier blows used barrels welded by trip-hammer were superior to those welded by hand.[67] The welder needed one striker or helper instead of the two required in hand welding.[68] The production of barrels per welder rose from six a day to fourteen or sixteen.[69] In addition, welding by trip-hammer was far less strenuous than hand welding, which undermined the health of the worker within a few years.[70]

C. Barrel Turning Machines.

Since the exterior of the barrel when it came from the welder was rough and not truly cylindrical, it was ground to its correct shape on a grindstone turned by water. This often left weak spots in the barrel where the bore was eccentric to the exterior of the barrel, making it liable to explode. Besides, grinding was a very slow process.[71] Just prior to 1820 several machines were invented to do away with hand grinding. Lee in 1818 counted no less than seven different kinds in operation in the United States.[72]

Most turning machines probably operated on the principle of the ordinary woodworking lathe, the barrel being held at its ends in chucks or vise-like holders and spun by the machine, while superfluous metal was trimmed from its surface by a chisel. The chisel was clamped to a rest which slid along ways as the barrel was turned. An exclusively wooden machine, as was soon discovered, was not sufficiently rigid to be successful in barrel turning.[73]

Whitney claimed that he had invented a turning machine as early as 1808, but that, although he felt it workable, he had not put it into operation since he feared the expense involved would be greater than the probable return would warrant.[74] But the mass of invention in barrel turning did not take place so early. One of the first successful machines was that invented by Sylvester Nash and introduced at the Harper's Ferry Armory in 1817.[75] Asa Waters took out a patent for a turning machine in 1818,[76] and in that year also Thomas Blanchard of Millbury completed a machine which would turn not only the round parts of the barrel but also the flat and oval portions near the breech.[77] This was particularly valuable for turning rifle barrels, which were frequently octagonal at the breech.[78] Blanchard's machine doubtless was based on the same principles as those on which his stocking machines, to be described later, worked, and changed from turning cylindrical to turning irregular forms.[79] It was used at Harper's Ferry by 1821 and at the Springfield Armory by 1823.[80]

The Springfield Armory was particularly dependent on a barrel turning machine invented in 1818 by Anthony Olney and Daniel Dana, which differed but slightly from several in operation in 1817.[81] This machine was capable of turning a barrel in twenty minutes, leaving it so well finished that it required very little grinding afterwards.[82] It saved over hand grinding eight cents on the direct cost of each barrel, and gave greater uniformity to the barrel, leaving it of an even thickness and thus less liable to explode. It could turn rifle and pistol barrels as well as musket barrels, and one man could tend two machines.[83] Lee considered this the best turning machine in the United States.

D. Stocking Machines.

The rough stock reached the arms worker sawed to a pattern, but its finishing was laborious and required great skill on the part of the stocker. He had to groove it for the barrel, which was deeply embedded in it, cut depressions for the bands which held barrel and stock together, and make recesses for the lock, sideplate, heel plate and other parts. Fitting the lock to the stock so that all parts worked smoothly was a delicate process. The stock as a whole had to conform to the dimensions of the pattern stock, and had to be carefully smoothed and oiled.[84]

The problem involved in mechanizing stocking was the turning of the irregularly shaped stock. This was met by more than one means. At John Hall's rifle works at Harper's Ferry gang saws were used. These were a set of circular saws on a spindle so arranged that the teeth broke the wood of the stock unevenly, which prevented splitting along the grain.[85] At Middletown, Conn., North was stocking by machine as early as 1816, perhaps with machinery designed by Selah Goodrich, of which we have no description.[86]

The outstanding development in stocking, however, was the work of one man, Thomas Blanchard of Millbury, Mass. His first stock turning machine, the forerunner of several variations, was made in 1818 and patented in 1820. Renewals of the patent, in 1834 and 1848, were granted in view of its great value to the industry.[87] Blanchard's machines were adapted to turning many kinds of irregular forms, such as shoe lasts, wheel spokes, and blocks for tackle, hats and wigs.[88]

Blanchard's stocking machine had a swinging frame in which the rough stock was hung and turned very slowly against a rapidly revolving disc-shaped cutting tool. A "former" or pattern of the finished stock, also hung in a swinging frame and revolving slowly, bore against a pattern wheel which pushed the frame carrying the rough stock against the cutting tool in accordance with the shape of the pattern stock.[89]

Blanchard installed a water-powered stock turning machine at Harper's Ferry in 1819, which made stocks that were nearly identical, and also reduced the direct cost of stocks by 25¢.[90] In the same year the Springfield Armory asked him to erect a machine there.[91] The Ordnance Department recognized the great value of this machine, in spite of the opposition of the Springfield stockers, who perhaps fearing their own displacement, pronounced the machine of little or no service.[92] In order "to bring the machinery to the most perfect state,"[93] the Department took the unusual step of having Blanchard work with his machine at the Springfield Armory and receive pay for the stocks turned, rather than royalties for the use of his machines. A contract was signed in 1822 by which the government agreed to furnish Blanchard with transportation, shop room, water privileges, the use of general machinery, etc., at the Armory, in return for which he promised to half-stock muskets—that is, perform half the stocking operations—at 37¢ apiece for one year.[94]

He remained at the Armory nearly five years, hiring as his help unskilled men and boys, much to the disapproval of the officers and other workmen.[95] From 1823 to 1827 inclusive he received more than $18,500 for stocking guns, part of which went to paying his workers.[96] In 1827 he sold eight machines to Harper's Ferry Armory for $1,600,[97] and for the two years following his payments from the Springfield Armory, totalling about $1,000, were made solely for the use of his machines.[98] Towards the end of 1829 his name disappeared from the Armory pay-roll.

Blanchard elaborated his invention as he went along. In 1820 he had made at least three separate stocking machines, one for turning stocks, one for cutting the recess for the lock, and one for jointing the faces of the stock.[99] By 1823 he had eight different machines,[100] and by 1827 fourteen, probably mostly operating on the original principle, and each performing one of the following operations: sawing off the stock to its proper length; facing the stock and sawing it lengthwise to its proper width; turning the stock; boring or cutting the bed or recess for the barrel; milling the bed for the breech of the barrel and the breech pin; cutting the bed for the tang of the breech plate; boring holes for the breech plate screws; gaging for the barrel; cutting for the tang of the breech pin; cutting the channel for the upper band; dressing or smoothing the stock for the bands and between the bands; cutting the bed for the lock plate; cutting the bed for the interior of the lock; boring the side and tang pin holes.[101] The increase in the numbers of these machines probably resulted in overspecialization so that some may not have repaid their cost. In addition, most armories could hardly have afforded investing the capital necessary to equip themselves with a complete set of stocking machines.

Other machines invented before 1830 were either of limited value or represented first steps only in the later mechanization of various processes, and are interesting chiefly from a historical viewpoint. Milling, which consisted of finishing forged parts with irregularly shaped cutters instead of by hand filing, was beginning to appear in the industry. North is supposed to have used a milling machine early in the century, but the important one of this period was made by Whitney before 1818.[102] This was a fixed spindle machine, with a work plate moved by a power screw feed driven by a worm gear.[103] Milling and drilling machines were used to a limited extent in arms making in the 1820's.[104] Rifling machines, worked by hand, had been in use for many years in Pennsylvania,[105] and one, perhaps power driven, used at Harper's Ferry in 1819, was probably invented by John Hall.[106] A machine for cutting bayonet sockets was introduced at the Springfield Armory in 1800,[107] and one for trimming butt plates, lock plates, guards, and for cutting out bands in 1818.[108] The latter operated with a lever raised by water, and like a stamping machine, struck parts out of rolled iron at one blow.[109]

Of considerable significance was a rolling mill for making barrel skelps, which replaced the trip-hammer for this purpose.[110] This method had long been in use in England, but was apparently an innovation in the Connecticut Valley.[111] Important developments of later years in connection with rolling were foreshadowed by 1829. At that time it was suggested at the Springfield Armory that barrels, ramrods and bayonet blades be rolled, rather than forged by trip-hammer, but this improvement was not adopted for more than twenty years.[112]

The introduction of steam power was, like barrel rolling, merely a subject of speculation at this time. As early as 1824 Lee had considered the feasibility of operating several trip-hammers with one water-wheel or steam-engine.[113] He wrote Whitney:

If the Armory is operated by steam power I have thought that four Engines might answer, viz. One for Drilling, Milling, turning, boring, polishing, etc. One for Grinding. One to operate 4 heavy trip hammers for drawing Scalps and Iron, welding and drawing Steel &c., and One to carry eight light hammers for welding barrels. For water power, with reaction Wheels . . . I propose two wheels for Drilling, Milling, turning, polishing &c. Two for grinding, One for boring and one wheel for two trip hammers—and One Bellow-wheel for all the hammers.[114]

But steam-power made little headway in the Valley industry before 1830, so that Lee in 1829 knew of no one capable of setting up a steam-engine at the Watertown Arsenal. He suggested that a man be sought in New York City for this purpose, adding: "It would require a person that is well acquainted with the nature of Steam power and the Engines operated by it, relative to which the Mechanics in New England have little or no experience."[115]

CHAPTER VIII

LABOR

1. Type of Workers.

Factory organization and mechanization brought as one result a change in the type of arms worker from one who was capable of making a complete weapon to one not necessarily less skillful, but whose skill was limited to one kind of work. Occupational specialization, as noted in the preceding chapter, was highly developed before 1820. Lee reported to the Ordnance Department in 1817: "A barrel welder or lock forger cannot without experience stock muskets. This is applicable to others."[1] Again, when discouraging a young man from entering arms manufacture in 1825, Lee warned his father:

Furthermore I think that some other trade would be more beneficial to him, as there are but very few in the Armory that work at all branches; and he would while employed at that business have to work as a journeyman,and although it might afford him a living yet it would not be a trade that he could set up and carry on, for himself under ordinary circumstances. A carpenter and joiner, Cabinet maker, or black or white smith, would be preferable in my opinion.[2]

Another change in arms labor occurred in the early 1820's, when increased mechanization brought about the development of a large body of semi-skilled workers who were either helpers of the highly skilled or machine tenders. This sharp division of the workers into two groups was reflected, as will be shown later, in very marked wage differences. An ordnance officer who made a study in the 1840's of the Springfield Armory, noted a decided diminution in the skill of the average arms worker after 1820.[3] Nevertheless, while the skill of many arms workers decreased below that of the old independent gunsmiths, arms making remained, with such occupations as printing and engraving, among the most highly skilled occupations in American industry.*

2. Springfield Armory Data as Representative of Labor Conditions in the Industry.

For information on arms labor it is necessary to rely chiefly on the Springfield Armory records, owing to the scantiness or absence of data on labor in other armories. The Springfield records seem fairly representative of the Valley industry as a whole. In the first place, the majority of

* In the nineteenth century women very rarely worked in small arms manufacture. Their work was limited to minor tasks, such as ornamenting the parts of arms. They were, however, widely employed in ammunition manufacture. Census figures which include women among the employees of small arms plants only show that some of these plants carried on ammunition as well as arms manufacture.

New England arms workers were concentrated at the Armory, as shown by the statistics presented in Table 4 of Appendix A. The Armory's data on labor are, in the second place, representative of the Valley industry as a whole, partly because in so limited a geographical area there was little opportunity for differentiation to develop, and partly because through the arms makers' cooperation conditions, wages and labor policies were deliberately standardized. The Springfield Armory's expressed determination was to keep its wages somewhat higher but still fairly in line with wages paid elsewhere in the industry. It seems reasonable to suppose, therefore, that, except for a few aspects peculiar to a government factory, which cannot be overlooked, the Springfield Armory records reflect with fair accuracy the state of labor in the Valley industry.

3. The System of Labor

Production in most Valley arms plants was apparently carried on under contract. Skilled armorers, who may be called "inside contractors" to distinguish them from the federal and the parts contractors, made written or oral contracts with the manufacturer, binding themselves to turn out a given number of parts at a fixed price, usually within a given period of time. While doing much of the work themselves, in addition they hired their own employees, and thus took over the supervisory functions usually delegated to foremen. The arms manufacturer furnished his inside contractors with materials, working space, machinery, heat, and perhaps with tools. In addition, he brought to the business his general managerial ability, and that of his partners, sons or other relatives. He might charge the contractor the material cost for faulty work turned in by him or by his employees, or a fixed amount for any part condemned.[4]

The Starrs apparently used inside contractors from the time of their first contract, made at the end of the eighteenth century.[5] They had separate contracts with different men for such processes as forging sword blades, finishing scabbards, punching and turning nuts, making sword guards, polishing swords and scabbards, and punching caps, guards and hoops.[6] These contracts commonly ran for a month and were probably renewed through oral agreement of the parties concerned. The Starrs usually required inside contractors to find their own board and to keep their tools in repair.[7] Occupations in which it was impracticable to use inside contractors included those of machinist, tool maker, pattern maker and shop tender.

Though the inside contracting system was used at the Harper's Ferry Armory,[8] at Springfield from the very beginning the modern relationship between employer and employees was maintained. The contract with Blanchard for stocking by machine is the only definite case of inside contracting at the Springfield Armory before 1830. A faint suggestion of the independence of the worker which was incidental to inside contracting existed at the Armory up to about 1815, when one worker paid another for helping him, although both were in the service of the Armory.[9]

The Armory's divergence from the general trend in respect to inside contracting was doubtless owing to its being a military establishment. Thus the workers were considered as in a sense soldiers responsible to their officers rather than as free employees. This is borne out by a suggestion of the Superintendent, made about 1800, that workers actually in the employ of the Armory be exempted from militia service, and from civil process for all debts or contracts, and that they be forced by legal process to fulfill their engagements at the Armory.[10] Only the first one of these suggestions was actually put into effect.

4. Labor Conditions.

The conditions of labor in small arms manufacture were more satisfactory than in many industries. While certain operations, such as forging, had to be carried on in the presence of great heat, this was no more than any blacksmith or metal worker might undergo, and the extensive use of the trip-hammer in the 1820's greatly reduced the heavy work in forging.[11] Bayonet forging, however, was throughout this period done by hand alone, and was decidedly damaging to the health of the worker.[12] The occupation most hazardous to health was hand finishing, since the grinding resulted in the worker's inhaling an excessive amount of particles of metal and emery dust. It was not until 1840 that Thomas Warner of the Springfield Armory invented machinery which eliminated hand finishing.[13]

Hours were shorter than those prevailing in industry. Springfield workers had a ten-hour day, so firmly established by custom that the Ordnance Department could not increase it. Elsewhere in the northern states mechanics usually worked twelve hours.[14] A day much longer than ten hours was probably uneconomical in small arms manufacture, as the work was of such a nature that it could not be well done by artificial light.[15] There was, however, no fixed stopping point in the working day. The Springfield Armory was sometimes open in the evening to accommodate those who wished to work late, although in peace time all-night work was not allowed.[16] The shops were heated in winter by fireplaces, until in the middle 1820's the Springfield Armory installed a hot air furnace similar to those used at the time in cotton factories.[17]

Several factors ameliorated the condition of the Springfield armorers, and some probably were adopted in private establishments. When, owing to a cut in appropriations or production large scale dismissals were necessary, the Armory made a practice of discharging the youngest men and those without families before the older and married workers.[18] It also tried to place its discharged employees with other arms makers.[19] Government workers, but not those in private factories, were exempt by law from all military duty.[20] They were not required to serve on juries, and those who lived on the grounds of the Armory were exempt from personal property and poll taxes. On the other hand they could not vote in local elections.[21] One privilege which Springfield armorers received for a time, and which may have existed in some private armories, was a system of relief, partly supported by the Armory. Lee, introducing the system in 1817, wrote that he planned a "permanent charity fund for the *temporary* relief of distressed armorers and their families, who by reason of sickness or other unavoidable misfortunes may be reduced to want." He added: "In order to increase the charity fund I shall calculate each individual workman to pay a moderate annual tax, say one dollar, and I am endeavoring to have the small forfeitures of the workmen applied to this object."[22]

Yet arms workers were subject to considerable hardships. A change in governmental policy might damage the prospects of workers of contract arms makers, and a cut in appropriations might drastically curtail the operations of the public armories. This might even go so far as to drive workers out of a particular factory.[23] Additional difficulties facing government arms workers were delays in wage payments, owing to the irregularity with which Congress voted appropriations, and the furnishing of funds in a medium which might be subject to heavy local discounts.[24] In the years directly following the War of 1812 such troubles were particularly acute. Lee wrote in 1815:

> Our workmen have some two weeks since received three months' pay which seems to give new life to the works. Their pay was in Treasury notes which caused some murmuring at first, but finally went down very well.[25]

Again, several months later he reported:

> Our workmen have almost seven months pay due. Many of them have large families to support and no other way but their daily labor, to obtain the means to carry them through this inclement season. Many of them have been compelled to sell their orders* at a discount of from six to 20%. By making this sacrifice they have sustained themselves and families to present time, with expectations that funds would soon arrive to pay the orders. The holders of them being disappointed in this: Orders will now hardly sell at any price. The armorers cannot subsist in this way, many of them must abandon the works and seek relief from their respective towns or find employment elsewhere for the purpose of obtaining immediate support.[26]

In spite of such disadvantages the workers at Springfield considered themselves in fortunate circumstances on account of the Armory's good wages and permanence.[27] The Armory had many more applicants for em-

---

* Apparently promissory notes issued by the Armory.

ployment than it could possibly use.[28] The desirability of Armory positions led to a peculiar development: the opportunity to work there became almost a tangible right, known as a "chance" or "privilege." Workers sought eagerly to acquire the privileges of those who left the Armory.[29] In 1825 Lee noted, "our complement of hands is more than full, with 40 or 50 hands hanging about, waiting for a chance."[30] Privileges were actually bought and sold. A worker who left the Armory sometimes sold his privilege for as much as $200, although in general the price was about $100.[31] In 1827 the heirs of a deceased arms worker, in an effort to realize on all his assets, offered his privilege for sale.[32] Although the practice of selling privileges was frowned upon by the officers of the Armory[33] it was not absolutely prohibited until 1833.[34]

5. Labor Relations.

The relations existing between small arms workers and employers in the Connecticut Valley were so far different from those in other industries that serious industrial disputes never developed prior to 1870. This was probably because neither worker nor employer was ever consistently so close to the margin of economic survival that struggles for a larger share of the industry's product became acute. A worker having acquired the necessary skill of an armorer was equipped to become a machinist, tool maker or blacksmith if he could not maintain himself in arms manufacture. The employer, on the other hand, partly because he failed to recognize all items of cost, could usually pay reasonable wages and yet make adequate profits. One evidence of continued industrial peace was the length of time workers remained at a given armory. Records of fifteen or twenty years' service with one employer are not unusual.[35] The struggle between capital and labor was never serious enough to result in the formation of a lasting union in the Valley small arms industry before 1870.

There were, however, some efforts made at labor organization. If one may interpret the word "cabal" as an early nineteenth century employer's definition of a union, one may suppose that Eli Whitney had had some experience with labor organization when he asked Lee to supply him with some workers, adding, "as for cabolling, grumbling, trouble making fellows, I do not want them—having enough such already."[36] The Springfield Armory in its early years set itself against any form of independent organization among its workers. An Armory regulation of 1816 stated:

All combinations against the officers or regulations of the Armory will be noticed by an immediate reduction of the wages of all concerned, or in such manner as in the opinion of the Superintendent circumstances may require.[37]

In that year also the officers of the Armory made the armorers sign a statement to the effect that they would work diligently at any occupation assigned them, giving a notice of sixty days if they wished to leave the Armory. Furthermore, they were required to promise to be faithful in discharging their duties, and to "accept of such pay and compensation as may be stipulated . . . by the superintendent."[38] As an additional means of keeping arms workers in subjection, Lee introduced the system, mentioned earlier in connection with the cooperative spirit which the contract system created among arms makers, of not employing armorers until they had completed their engagements with their last employers and had furnished certificates of good deportment from the armories where they had last worked.[39] To obtain employment a worker had to present an honorable discharge in writing.[40] Yet in spite of the apparent success of this method, workers did make use of the threat of going to other armories to force a rise in wages, nor did employers always honor their own agreement.[41]

Restrictions as to employment and discharge probably did much to stabilize the labor market within the industry, but arms manufacturers were occasionally troubled when other industries lured their workers away. Lee, always anxious to keep manufacturing costs at a minimum, was under such circumstances forced in 1822 to recommend wage increases. He wrote:

I find the rage for manufacturing cotton prevails to such a degree, and there is so great a call for first rate workmen, that I am apprehensive I shall lose some of our most valuable workmen except I am authorized to raise their wages according to circumstances. . . . They are sending for our machinists from Rhode Island and other places, and I have a few choice hands that are of great service to the establishment and such as I should be very sorry to part with, I am sure they cannot be retained without more wages; the additional pay will probably cost the government 250 or 300 dollars a year, but I believe this course will be the means of saving as many thousand.[42]

6. Wages.

A. Wage Policies.

Three tendencies may be distinguished in the wage policy of the Springfield Armory. In the first place, the officers attempted to keep wages in line with, but slightly above, wages at other armories and in other industries. Also, while reluctant to raise wages, they kept in view the cost of living, and if it rose sharply allowed wage increases. Finally for certain kinds of work an incentive wage might be applied to improve the quality of the product. One or more of these policies was probably pursued to a limited extent by the more progressive arms makers of the time.

The Ordnance Department endeavored to pay the workers at the government armories as well as or better than those of equal skill in private armories in the surrounding country.[43] Information concerning wage rates was continually exchanged among the Springfield Armory, the government arsenals and the contractors, and from this a "tariff" or scale of wage rates was worked out.[44] For this reason Springfield Armory wages—allowance being made for their being slightly higher and less fluctuating—may be considered fairly representative of those in the Valley arms industry. This makes less necessary an inquiry into wage differentials, which in any case cannot be made for this period in the absence of adequate data on wages in other armories. Nor, if such data existed, would wage differentials be easy to calculate, for, owing to varying degrees of mechanization, the processes of manufacture in different amories were probably not comparable.

Despite the close watch the officials of the Springfield Armory kept on wages, they tended continually to rise. Drastic reductions in all wages of 10 per cent, 15 per cent, and even, in 1820, of 25 per cent,[45] were made in an effort to equalize the Armory wages with those of other workers in armories and in analogous trades.[46] On the other hand considerable increases were granted, as for example in 1826, when 12 per cent was added to piece-rates.[47] The government required evidence that wages were out of line with those paid in the vicinity before making either general increases or reductions.[48]

Information concerning the cost of living was exchanged between the Armory and private arms makers,[49] and this was taken into account in making changes in wage rates.[50] A period of deflation gave the government an opportunity for cutting wages. Lee informed the Springfield armorers in 1820:

The great reduction which has already taken place in the necessaries of life, occasioned by a diminution of the circulating Medium requires some Reduction in the wages of the workmen at the National Armories. The fact is, that a Dollar purchases as much as a Dollar and a half was [sic] two or three years ago; And the prices of everything, labor among the rest, must be accommodated to the actual state of the Currency.[51]

When in 1829 the Springfield workers petitioned the Ordnance Department for a wage increase on the ground that the cost of living had increased, the Department denied it, stating that increased prices were only temporary and had not affected the wages paid by private manufacturers.[52]

The third objective of the Springfield Armory's wage policy, involving the use of incentive wages, was limited to work where a high quality product was particularly desirable. Incentive wages accordingly were used most widely in stocking and barrel welding. It is probable that other arms makers also found incentive wages valuable. Lee wrote in 1821:

We have for many years had three prices for stocking muskets, according to the skill and fidelity of the workmen; this plan has a good effect in stimulating them to perform their duty in the best manner. Their prices now vary from 82 to 89 cents.[53]

Even after stocking machinery was introduced, and there was a considerable reduction in costs, finishing the stock by hand was paid for at a higher rate than current machine production would have warranted, owing to the Armory's emphasis on quality. As Lee explained:

I allow them 50 cents per Stock for finishing, after the Stock is turned, barrels and locks let in, and bands fitted on, which is considered half the labor, though the operation by water, or half stocking, as we call it, costs the Government only about half that sum.[54]

Incentive wages were strongly entrenched in barrel welding. The Springfield Armory work returns throughout the first three decades of the century show two or more rates for welding barrels, although rarely they were all paid for at a single price. An extreme was reached in 1821, when the work returns for January show that welded barrels were paid for at six rates— 20c, 21c, 27c, 30c, 31c, and 37c.

B. Non-Money Wages and Other Sources of Workers' Income.

Apprentices at the Springfield Armory, probably typical of those in the Valley industry as a whole, were furnished with board, lodging, clothes and spending money.[55] At Harper's Ferry, and probably generally, apprentices were also entitled to "a certain portion of education," which was apparently of the most elementary kind.[56] The formal apprentice system was abandoned at Springfield by 1806, if not earlier.[57] It held out somewhat longer with private arms makers,[58] and continued in the Armory to the extent that sons of armorers entered the Armory, probably at a fairly early age.[59] Apprenticeship, implying the education of a boy in all aspects of arms making, was contrary to the trend toward occupational specialization. It was besides unsuited to factory production since semi-skilled work was more satisfactorily carried on by adult "strikers," or machine tenders.

Until 1814 each armorer at Springfield drew, as part of his wages, a ration and a half a day in kind. These rations consisted of such staples as flour, pork, beans, soap, candles, vinegar, salt and whiskey.[60] After 1814 the ration was converted to money wages.[61] The ration had a modest value which about 1805 varied between 14½ and 20¢.[62] While many of the workers lived on the public grounds, this was in no sense a form of remuneration, as only the officers, clerks and inspectors were allowed quarters rent-free.[63]

Farming eked out the incomes of some armorers throughout this period, but it was probably unimportant both as to the number of men who undertook it and the amount it added to income. The working day was so long that a gunsmith would have been hard put to it to find time and energy for farming. It is unlikely that armorers owned farms, unless there were able-bodied men in their families capable of managing them. During this whole period some armorers worked on farms during the summer months, particularly when low water curtailed manufacturing,[64] but they were almost certainly employed as farm hands, and relied on agricultural work merely as a temporary employment.

C. Piece and Time Rates.

The proportion of piece-work to time work in small arms manufacture bears a direct relation to the development of mechanization and factory organization. As the industry progressed more accurate measurements of the value of a given process could be arrived at, especially where machine production allowed labor to be paid for according to the number of identical units produced. Except in supervisory occupations and those concerned with the building and maintenance of the plant, and such indivisible jobs as those carried out by machinists and tool makers, there was a definite trend towards piece-rates at the Springfield Armory through the first thirty years of the nineteenth century. This was probably a reflection of what was taking place in all large armories in the Valley.

The wage system at the Springfield Armory was thoroughly revised in 1818,[65] resulting in a heavy increase in the proportion of piece-work payments. It is not to be supposed however that piece-work was non-existent prior to that year. On the contrary, piece-work predominated from as far back as 1806. Detailed work returns of the earliest years, if they existed, would probably show that piece-work was the most common basis of wage payment from the beginning of the Armory. Piece-workers by 1830, as shown in Table 2 of Appendix D had increased to ten times the number in 1806. Time workers increased only six times in this period. Certain of the time workers, such as foremen, shop tenders, and some maintenance workers varied but slightly in number in spite of the rapid growth of piece-workers.

The relation of piece-work to the reduction in skill of armorers through mechanization and plant organization did not escape the eye of Lieutenant-Colonel George Talcott, an Ordnance officer who examined the Armory in 1841, nor probably of the Armory officers in earlier years. Talcott observed:

Soon after the war, the system of *piece-work,* instead of *day-work,* was extensively introduced. Previous to this, an armorer was a very different kind of mechanic: the skill of the eye and the hand being highly valued and indispensable. A "lock-filer" filed up and fitted all the parts of a lock. The change of system caused each one to devote his skill and energies to the completion of some single part, and in time it was difficult to find many men who were able to file up all parts equally well; and whenever it became necessary to change men from one limb of a lock to another, in order to keep up a uniform supply of all parts, much difficulty occurred.[66]

The use of piece-work was a deliberate policy of the Ordnance Department. Major Dalliba's report, frequently mentioned in connection with technical changes at the Springfield Armory, shows great enthusiasm for this system:

The plan of having the work done by the piece is, undoubtedly, the best of all possible plans, provided there is a strict attention paid to the inspection of the several parts before they pass from one workman to another. It gives this advantage, that every man is paid according to his merit; it excites ambition and industry, and brings into operation and usefulness the otherwise dormant powers of the mind. It has a moral, good tendency upon the workmen, and at the same, or for less price, gives annually to the Government a much greater number of arms.[67]

D. The Course and Structure of Wages.

In order to examine the course and structure of wages, the writer has calculated both a simple mean of ungrouped data and a mode based on a five-dollar class interval from the Springfield Armory work returns and pay-roll books. January wages from 1802, when such data are first available, onward appear in Table 3 of Appendix D. Although in wage data skewing or weighting towards the higher values usually makes the simple mean less satisfactory than the mode, in this case it was found by comparing the mean and mode with the frequency tables of total January wages that the mean was the more representative of the two values for the 1802-1830 period. This is because all workers are included in the pay-roll figures from which the frequency distributions were made, even those who worked only a few hours or days in the month. The resulting low wages counterbalance the effect on the mean of the high wages at the other end of the scale.

Statistics showing the course of the cost of living in this period would be illuminating, but none have been compiled. To meet this problem the writer has worked out a crude index of Springfield Armory real wages by dividing a series of relative mean January wages by Cole's January index numbers of New York City wholesale commodity prices. A base period of 1824-1842 was used. In developing this index of real wages of Springfield armorers the writer has followed the method used by Harold G. Moulton for his index of real wages of all United States workers for the period 1801-1832.[68] To give a standard of comparison the relevant portion of Moulton's index has been adjusted to the base period 1824-1842 and plotted, together with the index of Springfield armorers' real wages, in Figure 1, Appendix D.

The correspondence of the curves of the two indices is remarkable, especially when allowance is made for the fact that data for a comparatively small group of workers, like the Springfield Armorers, are liable to be affected by extreme values and therefore to deviate widely from a general trend. This in part accounts for such peaks in Springfield real wages as occurred in 1824 and 1830. On the other hand, the resistance of armorers' real wages to the forces which pushed general real wages down in 1813 and 1814 is explained by the premium on the services of arms workers during the war.

The comparison between armorers' real and money wages is significant. While mean monthly money wages increased steadily throughout the entire twenty-nine-year period to more than double the original figure, mean monthly real wages were about tripled. In other words, the fall in the general price level of commodities was almost as important a factor in raising arms workers' real wages as was the rise in their money wages.

An examination of barrel production at the Springfield Armory may explain not only the surprising capacity of the curve of armorers' real wages to conform to that of the real wages of all United States workers, but also the means by which individual workers could and probably did adjust their earnings to meet changes in the cost of living. Barrel welders tended to produce a fixed quota of barrels every month with a regularity too great to be accounted for by chance, in view of the individual differences among the welders, absences from work, and the many forms of production delays. The high degree of uniformity normally occurring in the monthly production of individual barrel welders may best be illustrated by the table presented below.

This uniformity implies that some, perhaps even the majority of the Springfield workers, had considerable excess productive capacity which was not commonly put to use. When, however, there was cause for increased exertion, such as might arise from several days' absence or from a rise in

Barrel Production at the Springfield Armory, 1823*
(Total Production Before Proof)

Taken from the Springfield Armory Work Returns

Jan.	Feb.	Mar.	Apr.	May	June	July	Aug.	Sept.	Oct.	Nov.	Dec.
173	200	230	200	200	230	200	202	232	202	129	232
173	200	230	200	200	230	180	202	232	202	202	160
215	200	230	200	200	230	202	202	232	202	202	232
176	200	230	200	200	200	202	202	232	202	0	232
178	200	184	200	200	230	156	202	232	202	0	169
175	200	230	200	200	0	202	202	0	202	0	159

the cost of living, these men increased their output and thus managed to meet or exceed their production quota, as might be necessary. Assuming that similar conditions existed in other occupations at the Springfield

* The significance of this table lies in the uniformity of production within a given month, rather than in uniformity between months. There is no consistency of arrangement of workers as between months in this table, so that a given row does not represent the annual production of a specific barrel welder.

Armory, one can understand why, to a certain extent at least, wages had an elasticity which allowed them to adjust almost immediately to an increase in the cost of living. Wages fell when the cost of living dropped because substantial and sustained advances in monthly wages might cause the Armory official to reduce wage rates when a reduction in the cost of living warranted such procedure, or workers themselves might relax their efforts when they no longer felt the pinch of higher prices. Whether these conditions were peculiar to the Springfield Armory or prevailed in the Valley arms industry cannot be ascertained for lack of data.

Some knowledge of the structure of wages in arms manufacture may be obtained from examining monthly modal wages at Springfield. These appear in Table 3 and are plotted in Figure 1 of Appendix D. There is a strong tendency towards bimodality from 1808 onward, and, if allowance is made for accidental factors, it may be assumed that a certain degree of bimodality may have existed from the beginning. The presence of two modes in wage data usually indicates that two clearly differentiated types of workers are employed, in this case, highly skilled and semi-skilled, the latter group including helpers and machine-tenders. The difference in monthly wages of these two classes was roughly ten dollars throughout this period. Bimodality is one of the characteristic features of Springfield wages throughout the first seventy years of the nineteenth century.

The rise in the mean wage and the many changes brought about by mechanization failed in the period before 1830 to dislocate the structure of occupations at the Springfield Armory. Barring occasional cases where a worker through unusual effort earned far more than the average earned in his occupation, or, on the other hand, where undue absences cut pay, the different occupations retained their positions on the wage scale relative to one another throughout this whole period. A study of total monthly wages by occupation shows that for these thirty years the following occupations were most highly paid: work as foreman, cutting and drawing skelps, welding barrels, counterboring and milling barrels, drawing steel and iron, boring bayonets, breeching barrels and finishing muskets. Probably the three most highly paid occupations were welding barrels, drawing steel and iron, and cutting and drawing skelps. In the center of the wage scale were: helping draw skelps, helping weld barrels, grinding barrels, grinding bayonets and other work in grinding, stocking guns, some polishing and some forging work. Among the lowest paid occupations were polishing mountings, locks, and other polishing work, filing, some helpers' work, unclassified day's work, and shop tending.

7. The Productivity of Barrel Welders.

An estimate of the productivity of all small arms workers, even in a factory like the Springfield Armory where only one type of weapon was made, would be seriously complicated by the number of parts composing the complete firearm, by the many operations performed in making each part, and by the use of day's work in arms manufacture. For these reasons the writer has dealt only with the productivity of barrel welders as calculated from data found in the returns of work of the Springfield Armory. This group of workers was chosen because the barrel was a substantial item in manufacture, because unlike the parts of the lock the barrel was not subject to frequent or radical changes in design, and because barrel welding was usually paid for by the piece, which simplified the estimation of total production. Man-hour productivity figures were not calculated, as the writer believes that the records of the hours worked by Springfield armorers were too inaccurate to be relied upon. The average annual number of barrels produced per welder from 1806 to 1870 appears in Table 5 and Figure 2 of Appendix D.

Barrel production was sometimes suspended for a month or more because of insufficient water-power, temporary lack of funds, thoroughgoing changes in gun models, or changes in methods of manufacture. None of these factors reduced the productivity of the welders, so that only the months in which one or more welders worked were used in estimating average productivity. These calculations, however, make no allowance for time lost through the illness or absence of the worker, if such time amounted to one or more complete calendar months. The sum of the months all welders worked in a given year was divided by twelve to give a figure for the man-years worked in that year, from which all months in which welders did not work were excluded. This figure was divided into the Armory's total production for the same year, less the barrels condemned by inspectors. In this way annual figures for the average productivity of barrel welders were obtained.

In examining these figures the reader must keep in mind their limitations. In the first place, the barrels on which this estimate of productivity is based were not identical units, and so are not completely satisfactory as a means of measuring the productiveness of labor. The standards of the inspectors who accepted or rejected them varied from one inspector to the next, and no doubt with time those of an individual inspector changed. The use of incentive wages shows that marked differences in quality were recognized at the time the barrels were made, but the gradual rise in standards of quality passed unnoticed. This study of productivity makes no allowance for qualitative differences.

Nor is provision made in this estimate for changes in the number of hours worked. When Springfield welders worked longer than the usual ten hours a day their production of course increased. This affected productivity figures especially in war years, when workers tended to put in particularly long days. The writer believes, however, that in the long run excessive hours were cancelled out by absences and that both these factors had a negligible effect on productivity.

As each welder worked with one to three helpers, these figures represent the average productivity of the welding unit, rather than that of a single man. Barrels welded by the day were necessarily excluded from this study because of lack of data, but as piece-work was always used except for short periods during which experimental work was carried on, this omission is not significant. Where a barrel welder regularly worked at some other employment for more than eight days of the month, he was excluded from this estimate as tending to reduce unwarrantedly average productivity. This is perhaps not completely consistent with the writer's inclusion of men who were occasionally absent for part of a month but who otherwise devoted their whole time to barrel welding. Perhaps the most serious limitation of these figures arises from the fact that as the number of barrel welders employed at the Springfield Armory usually did not exceed ten or twelve, fairly large changes in productivity are not significant. It is also apparent that increases in productivity in other branches of arms manufacture did not necessarily follow the pattern of those in barrel welding.

The trip-hammer, introduced in 1815, resulted at first in no appreciable increase in the average number of barrels a welder produced annually. Table 5 and Figure 2 of Appendix D in fact show that a welder produced more barrels annually during the War of 1812 than in the year or two following the introduction of the trip-hammer. The longer hours prevailing in war-time, and no doubt a reduction of quality necessitated by the needs of the armed forces, offset the advantage gained by the use of the trip-hammer. Between 1815 and 1830 productivity increased steadily but only gradually. On the one hand, improvements in the technique of welding by trip-hammer no doubt raised average annual output in this period. On the other hand, workers must have exerted themselves to increase production in order to keep up with the rising cost of living. A steady but very gradual rise in productivity was characteristic of barrel welding until rolling replaced the trip-hammer in 1859 and 1860.

The effect of productivity changes on piece-rates is shown in Figure 2, Appendix D, in which piece-rates of barrel welders are plotted from data appearing in Table 6, Appendix D. Welders' helpers generally received one-half the amount that welders were paid per barrel. Prior to 1819 the Springfield Armory did not keep consistent records of rates of payment for piece-work. In 1820 piece-rates dropped while productivity rose, and in the ten years following piece-rates were stabilized at a lower level than those prevailing before 1820, while in the same period productivity remained steadily somewhat above its level in the first two decades of the century. In general, piece-rates fell when productivity rose, so that in time the labor cost of welding a barrel was greatly reduced. However, increased use of machine tools and higher standards of quality prevented a reduction in the cost of the finished weapon.

It must not be supposed that piece-rates necessarily fell proportionally to rises in productivity and that thus the financial position of welders remained stable or rather deteriorated with long run inflation. On the contrary, the high degree of sensitivity of average wages in reflecting changes in the general price structure indicates that productivity and piece-rates did not correspond to one another in their fluctuations, and that average monthly or annual earnings were adjusted to both short and long run inflationary trends. The order in which changes occurred in productivity, piece-rates and total average earnings seems to have been as follows: improved manufacturing methods steadily increased productivity; an appreciable rise in the cost of living forced workers to increase productivity still more by raising their normal quota of production; the Armory's officials responded to sustained increases in productivity and average earnings by reducing wage rates. These reductions were not so severe that average wages failed to rise steadily, so that over a period of years real wages were not adversely affected by inflation.

Part 3

INDUSTRIAL INDEPENDENCE
1831-1860

CHAPTER IX

THE NEW MANUFACTURERS

The thirty years between 1831 and 1860 brought a revolutionary change in the small arms industry. In this period it broke away from government domination and attained the independence characteristic of modern American manufacture. Earlier the industry had depended on the government for financial support, for patronage, and for direction in matters of technical improvement. But in these years all three forms of dependence came to an end. Arms makers acquired capital by the means other industries used, and broadened the base of the demand for their products to include many customers besides the government. The initiative in industrial progress passed from the government to the private manufacturers.

At this time the Springfield Armory lost its pre-eminent position in the industry, owing in part to more aggressive leadership among private arms makers, in part to a decline in the efficiency and enterprise of the Armory's personnel. In the first thirty years of the century the Ordnance Department, acting largely through the Armory, had pioneered in the fields of gun design, machine tool development and factory organization. But in the 1830's leadership in all these matters passed to the private arms makers. Thus, while the Springfield Armory continued to rate among the half-dozen most important arms factories in the country, its period of greatest usefulness came to an end.

1. *The Decline of the Contract System.*

The contract system, the channel through which contact between the industry and the government had been maintained, declined in importance as arms manufacture achieved independence. A few manufacturers it is true continued to rely almost exclusively on contracts, and the government extended the system to cover new types of arms. Contrary to the opinion of some authorities, contracting was never wholly dispensed with.[1] The Ames Manufacturing Co. of Chicopee had many contracts for swords, carbines and cannon.[2] Robbins, Kendall & Lawrence, later Robbins & Lawrence of Windsor, Vt. and Eli Whitney the younger made contract rifles.[3] The Colt Patent Fire Arms Manufacturing Co. of Hartford made revolvers, and the Massachusetts Arms Co. of Chicopee Falls made Maynard carbines for the government.[4] But no musket contracts were made after 1840,[5] and large scale contracting came to an end, except for a temporary revival during the Civil War.

Few arms makers in this period found it advisable to lean heavily on the contract system, since it was in constant danger of being discontinued.

The War Department chafed under the greater expense and the poorer quality of contract arms, the loss of prestige to the government armories, and the nuisance of inspection which the system entailed. On their side contractors were kept in a state of uncertainty as government policy veered about the question of continuing contracts. In 1834 a rumor started that the Ordnance Department planned to continue preferential treatment for faithful old contractors in renewals of orders.[6] A month later, however, the Secretary of War proposed that, on the expiration of existing contracts all small arms be procured on open purchase for the remainder of the year, and that thereafter no more arms from private armories be accepted by the government for the land service.[7] The protests of the contractors brought tempering of this drastic policy. The Ordnance Department later in 1834 advertised for large numbers of small arms to be made on contract.[8] The Chief of Ordnance attempted to pacify the contractors and at the same time to prepare them for any contingency:

It may be that the small arms herein required to be manufactured during the year 1835, will continue to be annually required during the next five or six years, tho nothing definite can now be stated in that regard, as it is possible that during the next following years, the States may require more of artillery and less of small arms than here-to-fore.[9]

The changes required for the manufacture of the new model musket of 1839 presented the contractors with an opportunity for improving their uncertain outlook. They indicated that without definite hope of future contracts they could not undertake the manufacture of the new model. Lemuel Pomeroy declared, "without some assurance of patronage for more than one or two years, it will be the height of folly for us to incur the great expense of change of tools and machinery."[10] The Ordnance Department saw the logic of this argument, and promised to supply the contractors with sufficient contracts to justify the conversion of machines and tools which the new model necessitated.[11]

Later the arms makers took the offensive in regard to the contract system. Apparently as the result of their pressure Congress in 1853 asked the Secretary of War whether it would not be economical and advisable to have all military weapons made on contract. The Secretary answered that with proper administration government arms could be supplied more cheaply than contract arms, and stressing the importance of what would now be termed the yardstick function, that production by the national armories was necessary for establishing and maintaining standards of quality and for determining proper prices for contract arms. The federal armories could obtain materials and labor on better terms on account of greater certainty of payment, while the fact that profits were not involved in government manufacture further lowered the cost of government made arms. Evidently overlooking some important items of cost, the Secretary stated that at a time when the average cost of a musket at the national armories was about $10.00, private muskets supplied under contract cost from $14.50 to $16.25. The Secretary believed that the pressure of competition with the national armories had forced down the price of contract rifles from $14.50 to $11.62½ between 1840 and 1853.[12]

In the matter of cost an exact comparison of contract and government made arms cannot be worked out because of the dubious means by which the government, and no doubt the contractors as well, determined costs. It seems certain that in quality many contract arms were inferior. Their greatest drawback, however, was their lack of practical interchangeability with government made arms.

With the decline of the contract system cooperation among arms makers, which had been a conspicuous characteristic of it, diminished, and in the early 1840's the industry abruptly lost much of its integrated quality. A high degree of cooperation had continued through the 1830's, during which the relation of the Springfield Armory to the contractors had been especially close. The Armory supplied them on occasion with necessary parts, for which return was made in money or other parts. It exchanged workers with the contractors and allowed its expert mechanics to visit the factories and lend advice. Workmen from other plants freely examined the Armory's tools and machinery, and in return the Armory occasionally took castings of valuable machines developed by the contractors.[13] While the regulations did not allow the Armory to make tools for others, it set baffled contractors on the road to acquiring tools by directing them to concerns competent to make them. The exchange of raw materials continued for some years.[14] The most common form of aid the Armory offered contractors for a nominal fee was rolling their iron to specified sizes in its rolling mill.[15] The prohibition in 1841 of this last service by the War Department because of the inconvenience to the Armory was symbolic of the end of cooperation between the Springfield Armory and the contractors.[16]

Cooperation between the two national armories naturally continued. Springfield supplied Harper's Ferry with Salisbury iron rolled at its mill at least until 1859.[17] It was not uncommon for the two armories to exchange gun parts or even work, in spite of the distance.[18] The Superintendents also consulted each other on technical matters.[19] This friendly relation extended to the state armories. In the fall of 1860 the State Armorer of Virginia wrote the Secretary of War that he wished to obtain "all the assistance we can from the national armories before our much honored and esteemed Secretary of War vacates his office, for I have no hopes of any assistance after a black Republican takes possession of the

War Department."[20] The Secretary of War permitted him to use the patterns and to make drawings of the machines and tools of both national armories—a favor which might have had serious consequences for the federal government in the ensuing months of war.[21]

The cooperative spirit among private manufacturers could not survive the keen competition of the new arms makers. An important aspect of this disappearance of cooperation was the decline of a united labor policy. The only continuing form of cooperation among private arms makers was in supporting one another against the government. This was particularly noticeable in the matter of the price of contract arms. This price, though theoretically and in general actually fixed by the government on the basis of earlier contract prices and of the cost of arms at the national armories, might be substantially affected by the refusal of manufacturers to accept contracts below a satisfactory level.[22]

2. The Disappearance of the Old Manufacturers.

The old arms factories active before 1830 were swept away with a completeness similar to the passing of a biological generation. Only two plants started before that year—the Springfield Armory and Whitney's armory—survived to the Civil War, while other early manufacturers in the Connecticut Valley disappeared in the 1830's and 1840's. The end of the old armories must have come in large part as the result of inadequate cost accounting, which allowed funds that should have covered renewal charges to be paid out as profits. Thus the productive capacities of arms factories were sucked dry, nothing finally being left to the manufacturers but impaired business credit and worn-out or obsolete equipment. The death or retirement of the original owner frequently was the signal for plant liquidation.

Then, too, success in arms making had always required a certain degree of flexibility whereby the business could accommodate itself to changes in demand and in arms designs. Simeon North made successively pistols, rifles and carbines; Robert Johnson, rifles, pistols and parts of muskets; Nathan Starr and his son, Nathan Jr., swords, rifles and muskets; the Whitney factory muskets and rifles.[23] But flexibility became more difficult to achieve as investment in machine tools became heavier. The high degree of mechanization necessary for the manufacture of practically interchangeable arms, coupled with the adoption of percussioning in the early 1940's apparently destroyed the Middletown small arms industry, as well as the businesses of Asa Waters of Millbury and Lemuel Pomeroy of Pittsfield. Pomeroy, in 1846 finding that the manufacture of the new percussion musket would have required an outlay of $30,000 for changes in his plant, gave up arms making.[24] Nathan Starr described the difficulties faced by a manufacturer in converting to newer types of arms when he wrote to the Chief of Ordnance:

With respect to making the pistols, carbines or rifles, you mention, I have to reply that as I am all prepared for muskets, I could not change on to either of the articles you name without incuring a similar expense to that I did on changing to muskets [from swords] about $15,000. and to do justice to the Gov't, as well as to myself, it would require 10 or 12 months preparation and a certainty of being continued for years. It is certain death to all contractors to change the articles manufactured so frequently, or not going steadily on from year to year. The machinery for manufacturing swords is now rusting on my hands. . . .[25]

Those arms makers who left the industry and were still in a position to carry on manufacture went into closely related fields. Pomeroy went into the iron industry,[26] and Elihu Starr, the son of Nathan Starr Jr., into plane iron manufacture.[27] The sons of Simeon North became makers of hardware.[28] The machinery from an armory which went out of business was sometimes purchased by another armory. In the 1840's after a contract for flintlock pistols had been finished the Waters armory at Millbury was dismantled and the machinery sold, later being used in the Palmetto Armory in South Carolina.[29]

3. The Rise of the New Manufacturers.

In the thirty years before the Civil War twenty important arms plants were established in the Connecticut Valley and five in the rest of New England.[30] In this period some of the firms were started which became the acknowledged leaders of the modern industry—Colt, Smith & Wesson, Winchester, and, in New York State, Remington. Some idea of the quantitative differences between these armories and those of the first three decades of the nineteenth century may be obtained from an examination of Table 4, Appendix A, which presents data collected from the Massachusetts and Connecticut state censuses and from the original schedules of the United States Census.

A. Representative Arms Makers.

Qualitative differences between the old and the new manufacturers may best be determined by a brief discussion of a few firms of this period. Nathan Starr the younger and Henry Aston, though both were active after 1830, were essentially of the older type of manufacturer. For the 1830-1860 period Robbins & Lawrence of Windsor, Vt. was typical of the successful, though short-lived firm, and the Colt Patent Fire Arms Manufacturing Co. and the Ames Manufacturing Co. of the highly successful, long-lived corporation.

Nathan Starr Jr. continued his father's business in the manner characteristic of arms making before 1830. He remained purely a contractor at at a time when the industry was shifting away from government patronage. His last contract was made in 1840,[31] and within the next few years his factory reached the limit of its productive life. It was doubtless burdened with worn-out and obsolete machinery and besides would have required heavy additional investment to allow for the manufacture of the percussion weapons introduced at this time. The older arms makers could not finance their plants from their private fortunes, and in these later years the government apparently did not make advances. Capital from other sources was attracted to the newer firms rather than to the old contractors. Starr therefore by 1845 gave up arms manufacture and the plant went into the hands of a firm headed by his son, for making plane irons.[32]

Another arms maker of the older type, Henry Aston of Middletown, made percussion pistols from about 1843 to 1852, and like Starr, was engaged exclusively in government contract work.[33] To improve his position Aston formed a partnership with three men, one of whom, John North, was a son of Simeon North. In 1851 Ira N. Johnson of Middletown was included in the partnership, probably because he could supply the firm with additional capital. The original partners assigned their interests in the pistol factory to Johnson in return for a cash settlement and a percentage of the profits. But complete dependence on government patronage and concentration on single-shot pistol manufacture at a time when revolvers were being widely and successfully developed, represented two forms of over-specialization which proved fatal to the firm of Henry Aston & Company. The firm failed in 1852, and Aston ceased arms manufacture.[34]

The Windsor, Vt. firm of Robbins & Lawrence stood part way between the old and the new manufacturers. Like the old arms firms it was of moderate size and counted heavily on government patronage, but like the new it worked its way into other fields of demand. As a firm it was outstanding for the many expert mechanics whom it trained and who later scattered throughout New England and played an important part in the development of arms manufacture and kindred industries, particularly the machine tool industry.

The forerunner of Robbins & Lawrence was N. Kendall & Company, one of several small custom gun shops in Windsor. Nicanor Kendall, inventor of a Kentucky squirrel rifle having a patent underhammer lock, in 1835 became connected, through marriage, with the National Hydraulic Company. The barrels of the Kendall rifles were made by Eliphalet Remington at Ilion, N.Y., other parts by convict labor at the Windsor Prison, and, where the work was difficult, by free mechanics. The guns were sold through the National Hydraulic Company's agents, who were scattered throughout the United States. Kendall rifles were especially popular among Texans, who received them through an agent in New Orleans and paid for them in Texas land. The guns were about half as expensive as government muskets.[35]

Richard S. Lawrence, who had long been interested in small arms, was hired by N. Kendall & Company in 1838, and in 1843 Kendall and Lawrence started a small custom gunshop in Windsor, while the manufacture of the rifle with underhammer lock passed to another arms maker.[36] The following year S. E. Robbins, a business man, foreseeing an opportunity to secure a government contract, went into partnership with Kendall and Lawrence, and the three took a three-year contract for a total of 10,000 rifles at $10.90 each. This contract lifted the firm from the gunsmithing trade into arms manufacture. The business was expanded and received a contract for 15,000 additional rifles. Kendall sold out to his partners in 1849.[37]

The firm of Robbins & Lawrence was for a time very successful. About thirty-eight per cent of its contract arms were rejected by the government as sub-standard, but these guns were sold to the California gold-seekers at the full contract price. Robbins & Lawrence received a contract for 5,000 Jennings rifles for Courtland C. Palmer about 1850, and two years later contracted to make 5,000 Sharps carbines at their Windsor plant and 15,000 Sharps rifles and carbines at a projected factory in Hartford. For the latter purpose the firm was advanced $40,000 by the Sharps Company. Robbins & Lawrence received also a contract from a commercial firm for 25,000 Minié rifles to be disposed of in England, and was promised contracts for 300,000 more. But in this last venture the arms firm overreached itself, for the promised contracts did not materialize, and in addition the partnership had become dangerously involved in railroad car manufacturing. It failed in 1855. Lawrence took charge of the new rifle and carbine factory at Hartford, which had been bought by the Sharps Company, and Robbins leased the Windsor plant and went into sewing machine production.[38]

Two firms representative of the new arms makers were the Colt Patent Fire Arms Manufacturing Co. of Hartford and the Ames Manufacturing Co. of Chicopee. In 1836 Samuel Colt patented his famous revolver,[39] and backed by New York and New Jersey money he set up a plant at Paterson, N.J. The firm became bankrupt in 1841, partly because the revolver was too complicated for production under the factory conditions of that time.[40] But providentially for Colt the Mexican War brought a demand for a thousand of the revolvers. He lacked a factory and therefore farmed out the parts as best he could, depending for the manufacture of the barrels, cylinders and certain castings on the armory of Eli Whitney Jr. He himself assembled the parts.[41] At this time he wrote a friend:

I am making arms on my own hook altogether on a borrowed capital. Have just furnished one thousand holster pistols for the First Regiment U. S. mounted rifles of a model agreed upon between the late Capt. Walker and myself. . . .

The government has ordered me to make a second thousand of these arms, varying a little from the Walker model, which together with a pocket gun which I am getting up for market will occupy me all winter with a force of from 40-50 hands which I have now employed. As said before, I am working on my own hook and have sole control and management of my business and intend to keep it as long as I live without being subject to the whims of a pack of dam fools and knaves styling themselves a board of directors, but yet I must creep before I walk, and am compelled to be mighty careful how I involve myself.[42]

This second venture of Colt's proved so successful that in 1854 the Colt Patent Fire Arms Manufacturing Co. of Hartford was incorporated, and became for its time the largest private armory in the world.[43] Colt had profited by his earlier experience and rather than secure outside capital, established himself as the main stockholder in the company. For the rest, the corporation was owned by its important employees.[44] It had an authorized capitalization of $1,000,000,[45] but not all the stock was at first issued. Colt is thought to have acquired some of the funds with which he started the company, during his early years as a popular lecturer on chemistry and a demonstrator of the effects of laughing gas.[46] It is, however, more probable that the profits of his first government orders were sufficient for launching his business. Eli Whitney Jr. estimated that on each of the first thousand revolvers Colt sold the government at $28 apiece, he made a profit of $10.[47]

Colt combined the qualities of a successful inventor with a remarkable degree of salesmanship. More than any other arms maker of his day he realized the importance of stimulating demand through aggressive sales promotion. With complete confidence in the merits of his revolver and untiring energy Colt himself directed the sales of his company. Even before he was securely established in business he found it to his advantage to make use of General John Mason, who acted as his agent and in return for a commission on every revolver sold acquired through influence orders from the War Department.[48]

Owing to the excellent management of the company by E. K. Root, its superintendent, Colt could devote himself to marketing. In 1840, before the Hartford company was formed, Colt considered it worth while to send to the Sultan of Muscat a few of the arms he had salvaged from the wreck of the earlier company.[49] From 1849 on he spent much of his time travelling in Europe, advertising his revolver.[50] He made it a practice to get introductions to heads of states, to whom he presented cases of beautifully finished weapons. Thus he became acquainted, for business purposes, with the King of Sardinia, the Sultan of Turkey, and the Prime Minister of England.[51]

The London Exposition offered the Colt Company, as well as other American arms makers, an excellent introduction to the European market. No corner of the world was so remote as to be neglected by Colt. On one occasion he sent revolvers to some English officers stationed at the Cape of Good Hope.[52] In 1854, as a result of Perry's expedition, he seems to have contemplated establishing business connections in China and Japan.[53]

In his concentration upon foreign markets Colt did not neglect domestic ones, although for the most part he left the exploitation of these to his agents. Unrest among the Indian tribes in Arizona and along the Mexican border during the late 1850's provided an opportunity for one of his agents to furnish United States troops with his revolvers.[54] Another agent spread the fame of his weapon in the northern and northwestern territories.[55] Colt solicited the patronage of the governors of the different states through printed circulars.[56]

A new development in marketing in the arms industry was the establishment by the Colt Company about 1859 of a widespread system of agents, or "allies."[57] Under the terms of a representative contract, the Colt Company arranged to keep an allied firm supplied with arms. In return for a five per cent commission the ally promised to sell other makes of revolving breech-loading arms only at retail prices, and forswore any interest in such arms. Monthly returns of all sales had to be made to the Colt Company, and cash prices were fixed at not less than ten per cent below the Colt Company's printed price list. In addition, the ally served as a financial aid for the Colt Company, for the contract stipulated that the latter could if it wished make drafts on the ally, payable in sixty to ninety days, to the extent of two-thirds of the net value of the arms held by the ally.[58]

The Ames Manufacturing Co., another example of the newer type of arms firm, was launched with capital provided by the Boston partnership of J. K. Mills & Co., a firm which poured capital into many kinds of enterprises. It developed at power sites on the Connecticut River three manufacturing towns, Chicopee, Chicopee Falls and Holyoke. The firm was a promoter of railroads, and was connected with cotton mills, machine shops and calico printing works.[59]

Edmund Dwight of Springfield, a prominent partner in J. K. Mills & Co., persuaded Nathan P. Ames Sr., who manufactured edge tools, to move from Chelmsford in northeastern Massachusetts to Chicopee. In 1834 the Ames Manufacturing Co. was organized. This company went into government sword and saber manufacture, a specialty which Nathan Starr had given up as unprofitable. In addition the Ames Company made cannon, cavalry accoutrements, and pistols for the federal armed services and for several state militias.[60] Other lines of manufacture of this versatile company were bells, bronze statuary, cotton machinery, gun machinery, solid cannon shot, water-wheels and mining machinery.[61] In time machinery became its most important product. Much of its gun machinery went to the Harper's Ferry Armory and to Europe.[62]

Like Colt, Nathan P. Ames Jr., who headed the Ames Company for many years, travelled widely for sales promotion on behalf of the company, while his brother James directed the company's production. The Ames Company concentrated on domestic trade, as far as small arms were concerned. Nathan Ames spent much of his time in New York, Philadelphia, Washington, and in different state capitals securing contracts for arms.[63] The company also sought some foreign patronage, and, like Colt, Nathan Ames did not underestimate the value of presentation weapons in this connection.[64]

B. Financing.

In the thirty years before the Civil War it was no longer necessary or even feasible for arms manufacturers to acquire their capital through government advances, and this means of financing apparently died out completely. What now became the most common means of financing arms manufacture was that used by Colt—the investment of the personal fortunes of the new entrepreneur and the plowing in of profits for expansion. Yet capital for small arms manufacture was more easily acquired at this time when the decline of the China trade forced merchant capitalists to seek other investment opportunities.[65] The Ames Company was dependent for financing on outside capital. Part of the company's stock was held by Edmund Dwight and James K. Mills,[66] and J. K. Mills & Co. had for many years an important position in the direction of the company's affairs. The Ames Papers show that in the three decades preceding the Civil War the Ames brothers kept J. K. Mills & Co. *au courant* on the most minute details of the business. No line of manufacture was undertaken or discontinued, no change in policy made, no technical innovation adopted, of which J. K. Mills & Co. was not informed. So subject was the Ames Company to the wishes of this firm that the former undertook what proved to be an unprofitable Navy contract to make Jenks carbines at the request of J. K. Mills & Co.[67] In fact, notwithstanding the independence of character for which the Ames brothers were known, one is almost led to believe that their company was nothing but another manifestation of the ubiquitous J. K. Mills & Co.

The Winchester Repeating Arms Co. of New Haven also acquired its capital from outside the industry. This company grew out of a series of arms enterprises which had been unsuccessful until Oliver Winchester, a prosperous New Haven shirt maker, brought his funds into the business. The original firm, the Volcanic Repeating Arms Co., was started by Horace Smith and Daniel Wesson at Norwich to make the Henry repeater, a weapon invented by B. Tyler Henry, whose work in connection with the metallic cartridge was discussed in Chapter II. The Volcanic Company became insolvent in 1857. Winchester bought it and reorganized it as the New Haven Arms Co., and in 1866 it was again reorganized as the Winchester Repeating Arms Co., with Winchester as president.[68]

Eliphalet Remington's arms factory at Ilion, N.Y., although it is outside the scope of this study, is worth noting, since its development is an example of expansion through the profits of real estate exploitation. Remington and his father had worked for two decades as small village gunsmiths. In 1828 Remington bought land on the new Erie Canal where a settlement, Remington's Corners, later renamed Ilion, sprang up. From 1835 to 1840 Remington continued as a gunsmith on a modest scale, in a shop equipped with only six machines. Suddenly he became prosperous, obviously as a result of soaring values of land along the canal. By 1855 he was able to complete the purchase of all the gun-finishing machinery of the Ames Company, and to assume the company's unfinished contract for several thousand Jenks carbines. Thus Remington entered the ranks of United State contractors. Aided by his three sons, he branched out into agricultural implement manufacture in 1856, while continuing his armory and employing over three hundred men. He put a pistol on the market and was rated during the Civil War as one of the most important government contractors.[69]

One factor in the rise of the new manufacturers was the development of the corporation. The benefits of the corporate form were indisputable: perpetuity, limited liability, ease of financing, and all those administrative and technical advantages which larger businesses possess as compared with smaller ones. Several large corporations were established in New England arms manufacture in the pre-war period, and while the typical form of business organization was the partnership rather than the corporation, the average size of arms firms was considerably increased.*

The arms maker who did not incorporate might face serious difficulties of financing. He could not hope to tap any but local sources of capital. His liability, in the case of failure, was unlimited, and not only his own fortune, but those of his partners might be lost. Moreover, merely local backing of an arms plant might prove hazardous. Thus the little partnership of Morrill, Mosman and Blair, an East Amherst concern, started in 1836 for the manufacture of cutlery and the "bowie-knife pistol," came to grief

---

* Satterlee and Gluckman, in *American Gun Makers,* list the following companies and corporations as being active before the Civil War:
  Albert, Douglas & Co., New London; Ames Manufacturing Co., Chicopee; Bristol Fire Arms Co., Providence; Burnside Rifle Co., Providence; Colt Patent Fire Arms Manufacturing Co., Hartford; Eagle Manufacturing Co., Mansfield, Conn.; Flagg & Co., Millbury, Mass.; Joslyn Fire Arms Co., Stonington, Conn.; N. Kendall & Co., later Robbins & Lawrence, Windsor, Vt.; H. C. Lombard & Co., Springfield; Massachusetts Arms Co., Chicopee Falls; Munson Morse & Co., New Haven; Maynard Gun Co., Chicopee Falls; New Haven Arms Co., New Haven; Savage Revolving Fire Arms Co., Middletown; Sharps Rifle Manufacturing Co., Hartford; Springfield Arms Co., Springfield; Union Arms Co., Hartford; Volcanic Repeating Fire Arms Co., New Haven.

when the panic of 1837 caused the failure of the firm which had endorsed its notes.[70]

C. Patent Arms and the Nature of Demand.

A peculiar feature of the arms firms of the three decades before the Civil War was their entire or partial dependence on patent arms. The Colt Company, for example, made Colt's revolver almost exclusively until the Civil War. Smith & Wesson likewise confined itself to making its famous revolver. The Sharps Rifle Manufacturing Co. of Hartford, as its name indicates, was set up to make that patented weapon. The Bristol Fire Arms Manufacturing Co. of Providence made Burnside rifles and carbines. Edwin Wesson of Hartford, between 1837 and 1849, and the Massachusetts Arms Co. in 1849, made revolvers under the Leavitt patent, later found to infringe Colt's.[71] James Warner, brother of a Master Armorer of the Springfield Armory and Superintendent of the Springfield Arms Co., patented a pistol manufactured by his company. The Worcester firm of Allen & Wheelock made Allen's patent pocket revolver as well as army and navy revolvers. H. S. North of North & Savage patented the Savage revolver in 1856. Allen & Forbes of Springfield made revolvers under Cochran's patent, C. R. Alsop and the Joslyn Arms Co. revolvers under Josyln's patent.[72]

This concentration on patent arms was reflected at the Springfield Armory. It is true that for the most part the Armory devoted itself to the manufacture of good standardized muskets in large quantities, and at the same time maintained standards of quality and cost for the contractors. But it was also the policy of the Ordnance Department to foster experimentation both by its own employees and by accredited independent inventors. The Armory spent much effort during the 1850's on the Maynard percussion primer and the Morse system of breech-loading. Christian Sharps, lacking in 1852 sufficient capital to equip a plant of his own, asked to be allowed to rent an unused portion of the Armory in which to make his patent arms.[73] Although this request was denied, two years later Lt. John C. Symmes received permission to use the Armory's facilities, paying for any expenses he incurred, to make a breech-loading rifle.[74] A revolver of John Brown the abolitionist was made at the Armory on an experimental basis shortly before the raid on Harper's Ferry. This revolver, despite Brown's extravagant claims, proved unsuccessful.[75]

The conditions which warranted the degree of specialization in which an arms concern now devoted itself to one type of weapon implied a radical change in the character of demand. It was largely private persons and foreign governments that constituted the buying public so far as patented arms were concerned, since the United States government and the states for the most part clung tenaciously to true and tried arms—flintlock and later percussion muskets and rifles, carbines and pistols. Before the 1850's only one patented arm, the early breech-loading rifle made by John Hall, was used in large numbers by the armed forces. An inventory made by the Ordnance Department in 1848 showed that besides this rifle only a few hundred unspecified patented weapons, including Jenks rifles and carbines and Colt revolvers and carbines, had been acquired by the government.[76] According to the records of the Colt Company up to and including 1857 about 18,000 rifles and revolvers had been sold to the War Department and about 20,000 to the Navy Department,[77] but in the two years 1856 and 1857 alone over 63,000 revolvers were sold to other customers.[78] Possibly some manufacturers secured sizable government orders for patent arms, but for the most part the government considered patented weapons merely as novelties. An Army board, convened at Westpoint in 1857 to pass on the value of breech-loading systems, opposed the adoption by the armed services of breech-loaders in their then imperfect state.[79]

While government demand for the new patent weapons was unresponsive, private demand was active. The domestic market was clear for American arms makers, as they were protected from foreign competition by the tariffs of 1842, 1846 and 1857, which applied duties ranging from fifteen to thirty per cent ad valorem to all types of small arms.[80] The demand in the West for Colt revolvers, Kendall rifles and Robbins & Lawrence rifles was growing.[81] In more established communities demand for sporting weapons was steady, if, indeed, it did not increase. The demand for the new patented arms, stimulated by sales promotion such as the Colt Company used, and by advertising which appeared at this time in the shape of detailed price lists mailed to stores,[82] probably grew at the expense of that for arms made in the small local gun shops. It is also likely that older arms were discarded more rapidly for improved types, and thus overall demand became more elastic.

The entrance of the Connecticut Valley arms industry into foreign trade at this time was spectacular. The Colt revolver was in the forefront of small arms exports. Thanks to the renown it acquired in the Mexican War, it was in great demand in Mexico.[83] In 1852, even before Colt built his great Hartford factory, he carried men and machinery to England and set up his London arms plant.[84] Although this was abandoned a few years later,[85] foreign demand for his revolver continued active. The English cavalry made large purchases of Colt revolvers in the 1850's.[86] During the Crimean War both Russia and Turkey were excellent customers of Colt, and Garibaldi's patriots were supplied with his revolvers.[87]

Nathan Ames, like Colt, took the rôle of travelling salesman, going to Europe in 1840, ostensibly to study arms factories but also with an eye to possible markets for the Ames Company's products.[88] The London Exposition of 1851 brought great publicity to American small arms. The fame of the Missouri rifle of Robbins & Lawrence became widespread.[89] As a result of the Exposition the Ames Company began exporting to Europe machine tools for gun manufacture, of which the first set shipped to England was alone valued at $44,000.[90]

While the United States government did not export arms, with what might seem naive helpfulness it aided certain countries to modernize their weapons. Possibly its comparative physical isolation gave this country a sense of being secure against European aggression. At any rate the Secretary of War in 1847 ordered that specimens of the various kinds of military small arms in use in this country be forwarded to the French Minister of War.[91] The British, Spanish and Prussian governments were presented with specimen rifles and muskets of American manufacture.[92] In 1857 an American manufacturer in manifest good faith planned to present one of the new government rifle-muskets to the government of Sweden.* The United States and Great Britain exchanged specimens of their new weapons in the middle 1850's.[93] Furthermore, the Ames Company was allowed to take drawings of the machinery of the Springfield Armory for the benefit of the British government, and in March, 1861, when the country was at the very brink of the Civil War, some officers of the Spanish government were authorized to examine arms manufacture at the Springfield Armory and to make drawings of its tools and machines.[94]

D. Costs.

The success of many of the arms firms established at this time was in part the result of a clearer understanding of the nature of costs. Possibly the rise of the corporation and the payment of dividends caused arms

---

* The following extract from a letter of Philos B. Tyler of the American Machine Works of Springfield to the Superintendent of the Springfield Armory is indicative of the candor of American manufacturers and government officials in regard to foreign interest in arms manufacture in this country:

Col. Ericsson is the Chief of the Government corps of engineers of Sweden, and during the past two years has made considerable inquiry in relation to the character, and mode of manufacture of small arms used by this government. I have communicated to him through Mr. Peytz who is with me, all the information I could from time to time. Col. Ericsson having learned that I proposed to visit Europe for my health, has sent me a pressing invitation to visit him in Sweden, which for many reasons I am desirous of doing, and particularly for the purpose of explaining to him more fully the complete and perfect system, which has been arrived at in our Government workshops, in the manufacture of small arms. And to enable me to do so more understandingly, I am desirous of exhibiting to him, and through him to his government, the beautiful and efficient musket rifle, now made at this Armory, both on account of its perfection as a small arm, and as a sample of the interchanging parts, and of the work done under one system of manufacture.

Believing my wish not inconsistent with the usages of our gov't in such cases I am induced to make this application to you for an arm for that purpose, and if supplied with one, I can either return it to you, or by authority of our government, present it through Col. Ericsson to his government as an act of courtesy from my own.[95]

manufacturers to become more aware of insurance and depreciation, items of cost which had usually been overlooked when capital had been acquired through government advances. In any case, a more highly developed conception of cost was now attained.

The federal report on manufactures, published in 1833, included in cost of general manufactures charges for wear and tear, replacement of machines, depreciation, insurance, commissions, bad debts and storage charges.[96] At the Springfield Armory an advanced understanding of cost was reached in 1837, when the classification of expenditures for "permanent improvements," "manufacture of arms," and "miscellaneous" was made, and deductions were allowed for work done for other government establishments, for unused stock, and the like. Interest at six per cent annually on $200,000 of capital, insurance at one-half of one per cent a year, and depreciation of two per cent annually on $130,000 were figured.[97]

In view of this competent analysis of costs the method of estimating costs used by the Armory in the late 1850's—and for an undetermined number of preceding years—was particularly inappropriate. This was simply to double the cost of labor on the musket, a device which automatically made it impossible to ascertain the effect of any change resulting from varying costs of raw materials, from mechanization, or from variations in the amount of total annual production. The Superintendent of the Armory blandly informed the Ordnance Department:

We suppose that if all the above excluded items [the arsenal costs] were charged to the arm and proper depreciation made on machinery and buildings, the entire cost of the musket would be nearly arrived at by doubling the cost of the labor upon the arm. This rule has been regarded for many years past, at this Armory, as affording a very near approximation to a correct result.[98]

Because of the absence of detailed records of private armories it is not possible to determine the amount or general course of costs in private small arms manufacture. The cost of muskets at the Springfield Armory during this period appears in Table 1, Appendix B. These figures, it may be recalled, have been calculated according to a method described in Chapter IV. In view of a marked decline in efficiency which occurred at the Springfield Armory at this time,[99] and of the great production of diverse patent arms by private manufacturers, Springfield cost figures for the pre-war period cannot be considered as so fully representative of the Connecticut Valley industry as were those of the thirty-year period ending in 1830. On their own account, however, these figures are of considerable interest.

Some of the Springfield cost figures in this period are out of line with the series as a whole. The large figures of $27.47 and $22.31 for 1840 and 1841 occurred during the tooling up period before the manufacture of the new percussion musket began. The Superintendent declared at this time that it was necessary for the workers practically to learn a new trade before they could produce the new weapon.[100] The complete change-over took from fifteen to eighteen months, a period sufficient to upset costs for two years.[101] The phenomenally high costs of $114.22 for 1856 and $50.58 for 1857 were the result of the change made during these years from smoothbore to rifled guns.[102]

Even with these extreme figures excluded, the Springfield Armory cost series shows a marked rise over that of the three decades before 1831. This was the result of secular increase in labor and material prices, as well as of a decline in the Armory's efficiency. Mechanization, however great its value in improving the quality of arms, failed in this case at least to bring a marked reduction in costs, and perhaps even increased them through added requirements for insurance and depreciation charges. Except in 1831 the cost of the Springfield musket was always well above the contract price of military weapons of the same model, as is shown by Table 1, Appendix B. This made contract arms unprofitable for all firms but those operating with very low costs, and hastened the decline of contract work in the industry.

CHAPTER X

RAW MATERIALS

1. *Transportation.*

The revolution in transportation which occurred in this period with the development of long distance canal and particularly railroad systems not only greatly simplified arms makers' supply problems but also affected the localization of the industry. It is significant that an important firm like Robbins & Lawrence developed in Windsor, Vt.—a town which had long possessed gunsmiths but no arms manufacture—only after railroad transportation had become feasible. By 1849 a continuous stretch of railroads ran between New Haven and Wells River, Vt., except for a distance of twenty miles between Bellows Falls and Brattleboro.[1] Worcester became a railroad center about 1840, at a time when its arms manufacture was rivalling that of the Connecticut Valley.[2]

Improved canal systems competed in the shipping of gunstocks and coal with ocean transportation. Canals were widely used not only in the Pennsylvania and Virginia coal districts—where they were apparently partly responsible for the marked decline in coal prices which occurred at this time[3]—but also in the long transportation routes to New England. The Delaware and Hudson Canal, using the Delaware River, connected Philadelphia and Kingston, N.Y., and was part of a protected water route going down the Hudson, through Long Island Sound and up the Connecticut.[4] An alternate route from Philadelphia ran up the Delaware River, through the Delaware and Raritan Canal, and along the Sound to the Connecticut. Transhipment was made at Hartford of materials destined for arms makers higher up the river.[5]

Railroads in the Connecticut Valley first sprang up in places where other means of transportation were unsatisfactory. Thus the first one joined Hartford and New Haven, points which deep water shipping, concentrating on long-haul traffic, had failed to connect. This railroad, the Hartford and New Haven, came into operation between these two cities in 1839, and in 1844 reached Springfield.[6] This brought serious competition to shipping on the river. In the very year the railroad began operating, steam-boats arranged to take freight from Hartford to New Haven, although earlier they had apparently limited themselves to the New York and Washington trade.[7]

Owing to the railroad New Haven grew as a commercial center for small arms manufacture, absorbing much of the import trade for the Valley industry formerly handled by Hartford, New York and Boston.[8] River transportation to Hartford, hitherto accepted perforce with all its limitations, no longer seemed desirable. The sailing packets ran, as always, only in the open season, and as late as 1842 steam-boat service remained irregular.[9] The railroads liberated the Valley arms industry from its dependence on the river.

The Western Railway, running from Worcester to Springfield and thence to Albany, was opened in 1841 between Worcester and Albany.[10] Probably through a branch line it linked the Salisbury iron region with the Connecticut Valley, and eliminated the cumbersome method of hauling iron by wagon to the Valley.[11] It also made possible the shipping of coal direct to the Valley from the Kingston terminal of the Delaware and Hudson Canal.[12] The Boston and Worcester, opened in 1835,[13] and the Western Railroad eliminated the long sea route for European imports, grindstones and whale oil from Boston around Cape Cod and along the coast. By 1849 much of the northern part of the Valley had been opened up by railroads, while the Valley's eastern edge was served by the New London, Willimantic and Palmer and the Amherst and Belchertown railroads, opened in the early 1850's.[14]

Information concerning freight rates on small arms materials is too scanty to allow of any comparison among different types of carriers or of much comparison in regard to short and long hauls. One fact, however, emerges—that a large part of the cost of transporting materials lay in the transfer from sea-going vessels to river boats above Hartford. Thus the Springfield Armory records show that in this period the cost of shipping stocks from Philadelphia to Hartford was from two to three and one-half cents apiece, while that of shipping them from Hartford to Springfield was two to two and one-half cents apiece.[15] Coal was carried from Philadelphia to Middletown at $2 a ton in 1833, but from Philadelphia to Springfield at $3 in the same year.[16] In 1857, when coal cost about $7 a ton in Springfield, the freight alone from Hartford to Springfield was $1.[17] Freight on steel in 1837 was 4¢ a hundredweight from Boston to Hartford, and 25¢ a hundredweight from Hartford to Springfield.[18] Freight on grindstones from Boston to Hartford was $2 to $3 a ton in the 1830's, while at the same time general freight was $2 to $3 a ton from Hartford to Springfield.[19] In 1837 the Superintendent of the Springfield Armory declared that freight rates from Hartford to Springfield had always been higher than those from New York to Hartford.[20] One may assume that rates were proportionally heavier on traffic going up the river to New Hampshire and Vermont.

2. Terms of Purchase and Means of Payment.

Problems facing the Springfield Armory in regard to the terms of purchase of, and means of payment for raw materials were probably typical in the Valley industry. The Armory continued to receive its materials on contract, a procedure almost essential where materials took a long time to prepare or ship. Terms of payment became less uniform. Instead of the three months' credit which had been almost universal before 1830, credit of widely varying periods of time became common. Credit ran as long as six months or even two years in grindstone purchases;[21] for six months in domestic iron purchases,[22] and for three, four or six months on European imports.[23] This showed a growing confidence on the part of merchants in the stability of the country's economy. Discounts for cash, ranging from two to five per cent, were common among importers who had to meet the complexities of changing rates of foreign exchange, but apparently were not widely used by suppliers of domestic materials.[24]

The means of payment depended on the location of the purchaser. The Springfield Armory paid for Salisbury iron in checks on a Springfield bank.[25] But Springfield bank notes were not always acceptable in other places. Therefore the Armory when paying for imports, coal and gun stocks used New York or Boston, and more rarely Philadelphia bank notes.[26] Checks on Boston or New York, payable in bank notes of those cities, were preferred to checks payable in bank notes of cities in the interior of the country.[27]

The Armory was reluctant to pay accounts held against it in specie.[28] In 1836, apparently fearing that the country's confused financial system might be easily disturbed, the Secretary of the Treasury warned the disbursing officers of the War Department to give notice through the Treasury to banks on which they planned to make large demands for specie payment before doing so.[29] The complexities of decentralized banking continued unabated throughout this period, hampering arms makers in all their financial dealings. As late as 1852, for example, the Armory was embarrassed in meeting its monthly pay-roll when the Springfield banks, paying out small silver change, discounted at four per cent the usually highly esteemed Boston bank notes.[30]

3. The Course of Prices.

Fragmentary evidence from the early federal and state censuses and from the Starr and Ames Papers indicates that the Springfield Armory data on raw materials continued in this period to be fairly representative of the Valley industry in regard to types, sources and prices of raw materials. At this time the prices the Armory paid for materials, which appear in Table 1 and Figure 1, Appendix C, became markedly more stable than they had been in the first thirty years of the century. They reflected to only a mild degree the influences which forced Cole's general commodity price index figure up in 1835, down in 1839, and up again in 1852.

Prices of charcoal and Salisbury iron, the chief raw materials produced locally, remained almost unchanging, partly as a result of the pressure the arms makers exerted on the producers. Imported iron, used extensively in the later years, was affected by changing conditions in a wider market, and consequently showed a different price curve. The fall in the price of coal in the early 1840's is attributable to improved transportation.

4. Iron.

The material which presented the most serious problems to arms makers was iron. It continued to be drawn largely from the Salisbury region, where thirty-five blast furnaces were built or rebuilt in the three decades preceding the Civil War.[31] It was the standard iron of the Valley industry, and was used by Eli Whitney the younger, Nathan Starr the younger, the Colt Company, and Robbins & Lawrence, as well as by the Springfield Armory.[32] The Harper's Ferry Armory also used it, presumably in preference to any iron obtainable closer at hand.[33]

But as the experience of the Springfield Armory in the period before 1830 had shown, Salisbury iron was by no means fully satisfactory. One crisis after another now occurred in the relations between the Armory and the iron producers. Either the suspicion that non-Salisbury pig was being incorporated in the wrought iron, or the generally poor quality sent the Armory caused the suspension of iron deliveries from time to time.[34] The iron masters for their part chafed under the system of government inspection, which they considered so severe that no iron made in the United States could stand it.[35] To this the Superintendent at Springfield responded, "that branch of our manufacture [iron refining] ought not to retrograde while every other is marching forward with rapid strides."[36]

As proof that the quality of Salisbury iron was steadily declining Superintendent John Robb in 1841 presented to the Ordnance Department figures showing the loss of barrels made from it in the preceding three years: 12.15 per cent, a justifiable loss, in 1837; 19.33 per cent in 1838, and 25.71 per cent in 1839. This, he believed, was the result of carelessness in iron manufacture.[37] The reputation of Salisbury iron became so bad that in 1853 a Congressional committee started to investigate it, on the basis of the testimony of certain inspectors who claimed that its quality had deteriorated in the last twelve years.[38] In defense, the iron masters attributed the loss in gun barrels to the severity of inspection, to the method of welding barrels by rolling, and to the use of anthracite coal in welding.[39] One firm tried to improve its iron by fagotting, that is, by piling five or six iron bars on one another and welding them together.[40] Another guaranteed to make good losses in barrels, aside from those resulting from rifling the barrel, which exceeded 25 or 28 per cent.[41]

But arms makers were so dissatisfied with Salisbury iron that they continued throughout this period the investigation of iron from other sources. Iron from Huntingdon, Cumberland and Mifflin Counties in central Pennsylvania, from New Jersey, and from Albany and Rockland County in New York was tested at the Springfield Armory.[42] But iron from these sources proved to be either of inferior quality or too expensive. The Armory's plan of refining its own iron from the Salisbury pig was also found to be impractical.[43] Therefore it began using imported gun barrel iron on a large scale in 1841.[44] It was followed in this by Nathan Starr and probably by other Valley arms makers.

The Armory tested Swedish, Norwegian, English and Belgian irons. Except for the Belgian, which was inexpensive but of poor quality, most of them were well above the standard price of Salisbury iron, owing in part to duties, which ran from about $17 to $27 a ton.[45] The use of imported iron did not completely resolve the Armory's problems. A reputable importer admitted that Swedish and Norwegian irons, which were the best that Europe could produce, might not respond well to being worked in anthracite fires.[46] In 1849 the Master Armorer at Springfield conceded that the Armory preferred Salisbury iron to all others and for the most part used it rather than imported iron.[47]

The Armory held in fact an ambivalent attitude towards Salisbury iron. It insisted that this iron was very poor, yet better than any other to be had, and regularly took it as the standard by which it judged other irons.[48] The Armory's policy seems to have been to praise Salisbury iron when dealing with importers and foreign iron when dealing with the Salisbury firms in an effort to raise the standards of each group. At last the Salisbury iron masters became desperate because of the apparent preference for foreign iron and appealed in 1855 to the Secretary of War to direct the officers of the federal armories to discontinue the purchase of Norway iron. They declared that imported iron was more expensive than domestic, and that foreign influence had been brought to bear on the federal armories to insure its use.[49] The Superintendent at Springfield promptly replied to these charges:

In reference to the declaration that the Salisbury iron, formerly known as the Livingston iron has an established reputation as being the best gun iron in the world, I have to invite the attention of the Hon. Sec. of War to the statement of the condemnations of gun barrels, accurately prepared from the books of this armory, for nearly five years last past, which proves conclusively, that the condemnations or losses for bad metal have been more than 25% greater from Salisbury than from the foreign iron which has been used in this armory, and that the cost to the govt. of each barrel made from American iron has exceeded the cost of those made from the foreign iron, by six cents two mills and a fraction, amounting to upwards of $12.00 per ton. Besides it has been the opinion of our mechanics that the barrels made from foreign iron are even more reliable for service, being finer grained, taking a higher polish and therefore less liable to rust and deteriorate in damp climates. In reference to the use of the Salisbury iron by individual contractors for the manufacture of muskets and rifles for the use of the govt. I can only say that we have no definite knowledge upon that subject.

The complainants represent lastly that foreign influence has been brought to bear on the officers of said Armories at Springfield and Harper's Ferry, so that for the last few years Norway iron has taken the place of the Salisbury iron almost entirely. I deem it is sufficient answer to this allegation to refer you to the table herewith submitted, which proves that for nearly five years past, up to the present moment, about 5/6 of the whole number of muskets fabricated at this armory have been made from the Salisbury iron. That is since July 1, 1850, there have been manufactured from foreign iron only 17,146 gun barrels against 92,718 from American iron, in the same period at this Armory.

I consider it due to my predecessors in the superintendency of this Armory to say that I believe they have ever desired to encourage the use of the American iron in the manufacture of guns, and have ordered foreign iron only occasionally, that they might compare the quality and perfect the manufacture of American iron by apprising our manufacturers of the comparative merits of the foreign article, with the view of securing increased care and improved quality at home. The files in your dept. we think as well as the records of this armory will show that repeated complaints have been made by former Superintendents of the bad quality of American iron, and that the necessity for improvement therein or a resort to the foreign article has been insisted upon.

As the reputation of our armories is to be sustained only by the manufacture of the best muskets or rifles in the world, I should deem it an unfortunate embarrassment to have a positive order to purchase only iron of a particular description, thereby giving us no opportunity for the exercise of judgment in the choice of our material and subjecting us to the payment of such prices as a combination of a few interested manufacturers might force upon us. It will give me great pleasure to cooperate in the encouragement of the manufacture of American Gun iron, by a continuance of orders to the Salisbury ironmasters, so far as it can be done consistently with the production of a suitable and acceptable arm for the government.

(I think the complaints that have arisen have proceeded mainly from the fact, that private manufacturers have diverted the business of making guns for the government so much from the national armories that the consumption of iron at these establishments has been materially lessened, and if the entire business of supplying our armories with iron had been given to the Salisbury manufacturers our demand would have been insufficient to meet their wishes.)[50]

Shortly before the Civil War a serious blow was dealt the Salisbury iron industry, when the introduction of barrel rolling machinery from England brought a complete change in the arms makers' demand for iron. For welding barrels by rolling only iron which had been cut into barrel plates of specified dimensions could be used.[51] These plates were made exclusively in England of the famous "Marshall" brand of wrought iron.[52] As the Springfield Armory had for several years bought only barrel iron, reworking the scraps from barrel manufacture for locks and mountings,[53] barrel rolling brought to an abrupt end the Armory's need for Salisbury or any other domestic iron.

5. Steel.

American gun makers became at this time more confirmed than ever in their dependence on steel of foreign manufacture. Despite the Springfield Armory's clearly expressed policy of encouraging American producers of raw materials, it was reluctant to use domestic steel. Occasionally on request its officials tested American steel, but they would not accept it, however highly the Armory's own mechanics recommended it. Thus American cast steel made by a firm in Jersey City was tried out in 1850, but although several of the Armory's technicians declared it equal for certain tools to the best imported English brands, the Superintendent made no attempt to use it.[54] A similar instance occurred eight years later, when domestic steel from a New York concern was tested and held by the foreman of the Armory's forging department to be the best steel yet found for welding. Nevertheless the Armory's management failed to follow up this lead.[55]

This steady opposition to domestic steel had developed as a result of its uneven or poor quality. The Colt Company favored English steel because it was better refined and more homogeneous.[56] One American steel manufacturer's explanation of the poor reputation of domestic steel—that it was owing to the widespread policy of turning unsalable iron into steel[57]—seems improbable in view of the effort expended by domestic steel makers to secure the patronage of the arms industry. Nor can one believe that it was wholly owing to the use of inferior iron, for such iron as that of the Salisbury region was, at its best, superior to most imported iron. The more probable cause of the poor quality of American steel was the failure of smelters, partly because of higher labor costs and perhaps partly because of ignorance of the technique of steel making, to take the care in refining steel which foreign manufacturers took.

As in the period before 1830, three types of steel, German, cast and shear, were used in small arms manufacture. In time, however, cast steel drove out the other forms. German steel, of which the most famous brand was the Halbach, from Remscheid in the Ruhr,[58] was used extensively for bayonets. But in the early 1840's it was entirely superseded in musket manufacture by English double—that is, twice refined—shear steel.[59] Double shear steel was in its turn driven out by cast steel about 1845. Cast steel was used exclusively by the Ames Company for sword blades, and by the Colt Company for revolver barrels and cylinders. It was notable for its compactness, hardness, elasticity and freedom from flaws.[60] The best steel for tools and dies was English cast steel made from Swedish Dannemora iron.[61]

The introduction of steel gun barrels at this time marked an important advance in the small arms industry. These barrels were made by drilling solid bars of cast steel, since welding from flat plates left a weak seam in a steel barrel which made it liable to explode.[62] Steel was apparently first considered for barrel manufacture on a large scale in 1845, when the Navy Department decided to have the Ames Company substitute cast steel barrels for iron ones on its Jenks carbine contract. Nathan Ames considered this a needless and wasteful innovation. He believed the use of steel would require changes in the proportions of the barrel, and these in turn changes in machinery, which he held unwarranted by the size of the contract. He was besides convinced that iron barrels would more than outlast all the other parts of the gun, so that the longer life of steel barrels was immaterial. Finally, he feared that the steel barrel of a gun when the latter was discharged would vibrate excessively, and that thus undue strain would be put on the breech, where the barrel's dimensions were smallest.[63] So opposed was Ames to the use of steel barrels that he gave up the carbine contract to Remington.[64]

But the disapproval of steel barrels by one arms maker was offset by the strong advocacy of others. As a result apparently of the insistence of Eli Whitney Jr. an Ordnance board investigated the possibilities of steel in 1848 and recommended "the propriety of using cast steel instead of iron for rifle barrels."[65] The board recorded:

The cost of materials for a barrel of iron is about 72 cents; for a barrel of steel $1.70. In the workmanship of steel barrels there is a saving which must nearly compensate for the greater cost of material. Boring steel barrels is less expensive than reaming iron ones, because the machines for drilling feed themselves and one man may attend to several. All the steel barrels nearly would pass inspection, and consequently no loss. Of iron barrels there is a very considerable loss in manufacturing.

From these circumstances it is believed that cast-steel barrels do not cost more than iron ones, but as a change would require new machines for boring, etc., an allowance as asked by Mr. Whitney on, say, 2,000 barrels, to complete his contract for iron barrels, might very justly be made.

The board would recommend the adoption of cast-steel barrels for rifles; which, from experiments, are shown to possess superior strength, smoothness, and stiffness to iron.[66]

In the same year Simeon North received permission from the Ordnance Department to make cast steel barrels on a contract for carbines. His first steel-barreled arms were delivered before the end of the year, and thenceforth he made no more iron barrels.[67] In 1852 J. D. Johnson of

Middletown was authorized to make steel pistol barrels on a government contract.[68] The Colt Company from its founding made all its revolver barrels of steel, although in the Civil War it reverted to iron barrels for the military muskets it produced.[69] The Springfield Armory did not follow the general trend, but clung tenaciously to iron barrels throughout the Civil War.

Aside from its use in barrels, steel was required for bayonets, ramrods, springs and cones, and sometimes for hammers and batteries. Early experiments with all-steel tumblers were not satisfactory,[70] and the Springfield Armory's attempt in 1840 and 1841 to make screws of steel proved unsuccessful except in the case of flint screws.[71] The advantages of steel were numerous. Even manufacturers who at first opposed its use for barrels admitted that, if properly handled, steel might be more economical than iron, and that it was certainly superior in taking threads and grooves.[72] The loss in manufacturing steel barrels was less and their durability greater. But the great difficulty in obtaining satisfactory gun barrel iron was as compelling a reason for using steel barrels as their technical superiority.

It is noteworthy that steel did not immediately drive iron out of barrel manufacture. Conservatism in part accounted for this. Then, too, the fact that iron barrels could be expected to outlast other parts made the use of steel less imperative. These two reasons may not fully explain the reluctance of some arms makers to accept steel barrels. It is significant that Colt, who made them from the outset, was a new manufacturer, able to invest from the start in machines appropriate to their production. Whitney received government aid in adapting his plant to making steel barrels. An important factor in the delay in conversion must have been that the expense of the necessary alterations of machinery was greater than the anticipated gain.

6. *Other Raw Materials.*

The supply of gun stocks of high quality, a serious problem prior to 1830, after that date became adequate. Tough, field grown walnut was now obtainable in ample quantities, partly because the wood was cut more economically than formerly, but chiefly because improved transportation opened up new areas to the stock collectors. Pennsylvania remained the source of supply of most stocks, with Philadelphia the center of the stock trade. Occasionally collectors from New York State, North Carolina, Missouri, Ohio, and even Michigan tried to break into the Pennsylvania monopoly, but only those from North Carolina and Ohio met with any measure of success. Ohio stocks, however, were in disfavor because of their softness,[73] and Pennsylvania stocks kept an undisputed superiority. Pennsylvania even supplied some English arms makers with stocks on terms very favorable to the producers.[74] Since the seasoning of rough stocks took several years attempts were made in this period at "steam-boiling," which was supposed to hasten natural drying by removing the sap. Experimentation at the Springfield Armory, however, proved that this process was unsatisfactory.[75]

Charcoal, in spite of the competition of anthracite in other processes in arms manufacture, continued to be purchased in large amounts for annealing.[76] Years of arms manufacture on the Connecticut River had not greatly depleted the chestnut forests along its banks, and as late as 1860 the Armory was still supplied with charcoal from Monson, Stafford, Wilbraham and other near-by villages.[77] With transportation costs negligible, the abundance of chestnut and the large numbers of producers kept charcoal at a stable and nominal price.

Until steam replaced water-power Virginia or bituminous coal was used primarily for heating, as it contained too many impurities for arms manufacture. The Springfield Armory usually purchased bituminous coal by the bushel, and even in the 1850's consumed not more than fifty tons a year.[78] The superiority of anthracite coal to charcoal in welding had been clearly demonstrated by experimentation, and doubtless it replaced charcoal for this purpose throughout the industry. A serious drawback to its use was that it remained for many years very expensive, running from about $10 to $13 delivered at the Springfield Armory. In the early 1840's a sharp decline in price set in as a result of reduced transportation costs, so that coal sold in Springfield for about $6 or $7 a ton.

Files, the most important tools of small arms manufacture, continued to be imported from England in large quantities, although it was recognized that the increased accuracy of machine tools substantially reduced the number required.[79] A sharp decline after 1840 in the number and size of orders for files may be noted in the Springfield Armory records. In this period the file cutters of Sheffield, which was the center of the industry, were banded together to stabilize prices and prevent cutthroat competition among themselves, as is clear from references in the correspondence of the Springfield Armory to "the usual and well known Sheffield List,"[80] below which Sheffield files could not be bought. Added to this minimum price were the rate of exchange, insurance, freight costs, duties, and commissions—additional charges which were far from unimportant, being reckoned in 1841 as 45 per cent of the cost of the files in pounds sterling.[81]

American file makers sought unsuccessfully to establish their product in the small arms industry. Nathan Starr operated in 1849 a file cutting machine which he claimed cut files that armorers and experienced file cutters pronounced more accurately cut than and superior to any files they had seen.[82] The Springfield Armory tested, but did not use, his files,[83] and later Starr admitted that they were more expensive than English files. He declared:

I have for a long time tried to find out their [English files'] cost of importation in N. York, but there are so many British agents paid for putting down all manufacturing establishments in this country, they will deceive you in every way, and to my certain knowledge obstruct the sale in every possible way.[84]

Domestic production of files of sufficiently high quality for small arms manufacture could not compete with importation. The American producer must have had to import his steel from England, whereby he lost an initial advantage. File cutting by machine was probably only partially satisfactory, and high labor costs curtailed the manufacture of good handmade files. Finally, the increasing precision of machine tools reduced the demand for files in most of the metal products industries.

CHAPTER XI

INTERCHANGEABILITY AND MACHINE TOOLS

I. Advances in Interchangeability

Time and again arms manufacturers thought that they had achieved practical interchangeability only later to find, as advances in precision measurement occurred, that the standards which they had established fell short of newer requirements for interchangeability. Thus practical interchangeability—or, simply, interchangeability, as it was then called—meant one thing to Eli Whitney the elder and quite a different thing to his son. This substitution of higher standards for lower ones as knowledge and technical skill increased explains why production of interchangeable weapons remained the central problem in arms manufacture long after practical interchangeability had been achieved.

The evolution of standards of interchangeability may to a certain extent be traced chronologically. One set of standards was replaced by a more highly developed set partly because more refined methods of precision measurement made arms makers aware of the limitations of earlier standards, and partly because the trend towards substitution of machine production for hand labor substantially increased uniformity. It is notable that the standard was altered the moment improvements in production and precision measurement occurred.

One level of interchangeability was achieved in 1827, when the parts of John Hall's rifles, made by machines at Harper's Ferry, were considered so uniform that they required no marking but could be assembled at random.[1] Higher standards of interchangeability were developed a few years later. By these standards arms of government manufacture, which earlier had been considered uniform, were held to be far from interchangeable in their parts. A comparison of these arms, made in 1831, showed that while the Springfield Armory's muskets were superior to the Harper's Ferry Armory's rifles in interchangeability, smoothly working weapons usually could not be assembled at random even from the parts made at Springfield. The Master Armorer of that armory reported:

> The comparative uniformity of the musket was much nearer than any which I have before examined. Some of the barrels would shift in the stocks and make a tolerable good fit. The locks were much nearer alike than formerly, and could be shifted in several of the component parts.[2]

By 1835, however, arms makers had succeeded in producing guns measuring up to contemporary standards of interchangeability. Such was the degree of practical uniformity then achieved that the Ordnance Department was again able to assemble arms at random from heaps of parts to its complete satisfaction.[3] This was in large part the result of improvements in lock-forging which were so great at the Springfield Armory that in 1835 only three-fourths or four-fifths of the filing formerly required was necessary.[4] Since much variation crept into manufacture through hand filing, this greatly increased the possibilities of attaining practical interchangeability. A Congressman reported at this time:

The system of machining is reduced to such perfection that every part of a musket is made with such nice precision and accuracy that every screw or spring made for a given part or purpose will fit every musket or pistol that is made in each of our factories.[5]

A new standard of interchangeability was developed in the early 1840's. To meet this requirement the Springfield Armory in 1842 acquired a set of weights and measures standardized by Ferdinand Hassler, head of the Bureau of Weights and Measures of the Treasury Department, to aid in making model percussion arms.[6] At the Whitney Armory a limited degree of interchangeability according to the newest standard was secured by dividing parts into groups of ten and making the parts within each group interchangeable.[7] At the Springfield Armory Thomas Warner, the Master Armorer, in 1840 obtained uniformity on the new level by extending the use of milling machines, by jig filing, and by careful inspection between operations. Because of this care it was unnecessary to assemble locks soft and file them to fit before hardening.[8] In 1842 Albert Eames resorted to an essentially old method of achieving uniformity when he used a fine set of gages and jigs to produce for the Ames Company parts of Jenks carbines and pistols which were considered interchangeable.[9]

Hardly had this level of uniformity been attained when more highly refined standards again made it necessary for arms makers to increase the accuracy of their manufacture. From 1844 to 1849 at least the Springfield Armory, incapable of achieving throughout its production the higher degree of interchangeability now recognized as desirable, reverted to the method used earlier at the Whitney Armory and limited itself to assembling locks in the soft state in sets of ten and marking them before hardening.[10] About 1851 the Providence firm of Brown & Sharpe introduced to New England industry the vernier caliper, reading to one-thousandth of an inch.[11] Perhaps as a result of this the range of known variation in the dimensions of gun parts became so evident that the Colt Company in effect gave up for the time being attempts at securing interchangeability in favor of "tailoring" the parts of its arms. In 1856 the parts of Colt revolvers were assembled and each piece of an individual weapon numbered. After this they received their final finishing and were assembled according to their numbers.[12] Thus each weapon was unique, as was the case with all arms in the period before interchangeability had been introduced. The adoption of this method of manufacture by the Colt Company, which was perhaps the most progressive of the Valley arms makers in technical matters, indicates its acceptance of the fact that with the best manufacturing methods of which it was then capable it could not produce arms which in view of its knowledge of precision measurement, it could consider truly interchangeable.

Standards of inspection were raised in conformity with increasing refinements in interchangeability, although inspection methods ran in general along the same lines as formerly. Sixty-eight different gages were used in the early 1840's for inspecting contract muskets.[13] Connecticut Valley arms contractors were still furnished with model weapons to work from, but by the 1840's at least they commonly used in the manufacture of their arms gages made by the Springfield Armory.[14] In the 1850's the Colt Company supplied its own inspectors with very fine sets of gages.[15] Barrels, swords and bayonets were proved by the same methods used earlier.[16] For contract inspection of such parts as hammers no better means had yet been found than breaking them to examine the steel of which they were made. Up to ten per cent of these parts might be broken for inspection. If they were defective breakage was paid for by the contractor, but if they were satisfactory it was paid for by the government.[17] The best means of inspecting springs was by snapping the lock repeatedly.[18]

II. Developments in Machine Tools

1. The Machine Tool Industry.

Mechanization aided the development of higher standards of interchangeability in the thirty years preceding the Civil War chiefly through the progress made in forging parts, and in finishing them with milling machines and turret lathes. This period which, for originality and ingenuity of thought in tool building has probably not since been equalled, certainly not surpassed, marked the emergence of machine tool manufacture as an independent industry. The industry owed its development to the adoption of steam as a source of power, to exceedingly active foreign demand for small arms and the machinery with which to make them, and particularly to the presence of a school of highly inventive machine tool builders.

The first peak of activity in machine tool production was reached about 1845. At this time Nathan P. Ames, a leader in the field, wrote that not for several years had good tool builders been so much in demand.[19] So great was the capacity for absorbing machines of American industry as a whole, and of small arms manufacture in particular, that firms could now afford to specialize in building steam-engines, machinery or machine tools. Many centers of machine tool manufacture sprang up in the more heavily industrialized parts of the country. The records of the Springfield Armory show that during this period the Armory dealt witth steam-engine companies in Albany, Boston, South Bridgewater, Providence, New York City and Pittsburgh; with machinery makers in Springfield and Holyoke; and with machine tool builders at Windsor, Vt., Nashua, N.H., Providence, Windsor Locks and Windham, Conn., New York City, Waterford, N.Y., and Philadelphia.*

Steam-power was widely accepted by American industry several years before the peak in machine tool production was reached. In 1831 the demand for steam-engines in the country as a whole exceeded all previous experience. Every engine manufacturer had more orders than he could fill.[20] But in the small arms industry, although steam offered a more dependable source of power than water, and widened the choice of location of factories, serious difficulties stood in the way of its adoption. Engines were still in an experimental stage and liable to failures which were not inherent in steam-power itself. Yet each setback tended to damage the outlook for steam. An attempt to introduce it at the Springfield Armory in 1830, for example, was crippled by so minor a matter as frozen valves.[21] Further, early steam-engines were not powerful. A large plant like the Springfield Armory considered buying one which could generate only fifteen horsepower.[22] Engines were in addition almost prohibitively expensive. In 1833 one of twenty horsepower cost about $13,000.[23] The Springfield Superintendent stated two years later, "the advantages that would be derived from the use of an Engine is [sic] not considered of sufficient importance to justify the expenditure necessary to its erection etc."[24] Conservatism also hindered the introduction of steam. As late as 1855 in discussing the motive power for a rifling machine, a Springfield Superintendent concluded, "Steam power is thought to be impracticable."[25]

Wherever established arms makers did accept steam, it was at first rated far below its potentialities and was used only for running light machinery, for blasts for forging fires, for steaming stocks, for heating shops, and for pumping out gravel and mud which interfered with the operation of the water-wheels.[26] The Springfield Armory found that steam could replace water-power in driving tilt-hammers, but made use of it for this purpose only experimentally.[27] Although the Armory used steam to a

---

* The names and locations of these manufacturers were:
Steam-engines: Many & Ward, Albany; Lazell & Perking Co., South Bridgewater; Clark's Patent Steam & Fire Regulator Co., New York City; William Wade, Pittsburgh; Cyril Babcock, agent of Babbitt's Fan Blower, Providence; Ethan Earle, Boston.
Machinery: American Machine Works, Springfield Tool Co. and Bemis & Co., Springfield; Hadley Falls Co., Holyoke.
Machine Tools: Robbins & Lawrence of Hartford and Windsor, Vt.; Gage, Warner & Whitney, Nashua, N.H.; Fairbanks, Bancroft & Co., Providence; White & West, Windsor Locks; Weaver, Windham, Conn.; Gage & Campbell, Waterford, N.Y.; New York Screw Co., and Stevens Brothers & Co., New York City; Merrick & Towne and Philos B. Tyler, Philadelphia.

considerable extent it grossly undervalued its utility except so far as stand-by power was concerned. The Commanding Officer* wrote in 1845:

> The steam Engine has been kept in active operation during the year. One particular instance of the utility of steam power at this establishment is essentially felt in its being so constantly available at all times during working hours entirely unaffected by the frosts of the winter or the drought of summer by both of which our operations by water are often seriously interrupted and very considerably so by the drought of the present season. Another may be named in the blast and facilities it furnishes for forging at these shops by which the anthracite coal can be used which is found to be a cheaper fuel than charcoal. The exhaust steam is conducted through the departments of the shops in pipes and is a safe and effectual method of warming the rooms whereby stores and fuel are saved.[28]

The unwillingness of established arms makers to rely to any great extent on steam is not surprising in view of its experimental state, the heavy initial expense of installing it, and the widespread and justified satisfaction with water-power. But the case of arms makers just entering the field was quite different. Since they were building their factories from the ground up they could install steam without undergoing the sacrifice required of established manufacturers in changing to steam. Colt depended on steam as early as 1855. His factory used in that year a beam engine with a seven-foot stroke and a thirty-foot flywheel, of two hundred and fifty horsepower.[29]

Interchangeability in small arms, popularly known at the time as the "American System," was introduced to many European countries in the 1850's.[31] This opened a new market for small arms and also for the machines for making them, and gave added stimulus to the machine tool industry. In America mechanization of gun manufacture had advanced in many respects far beyond that of the European industry. Although barrel rolling was brought to America from England, and French and Belgian rifling machines had advanced so far by 1856 as to be worthy of investigation by the United States Ordnance Department,[32] yet in the development of many and probably of most arms machines America was ahead of Europe. Thus Colt, opening his London revolver factory in 1853, found England so retarded in the machine tool industry that he was forced to take both men and machines with him from the United States.[33]

English armories, both private and public, were particularly important buyers of American gun machinery.[34] J. H. Burton of the Ames Company

---

* Until 1841 the Springfield Armory was in charge of a civilian Superintendent appointed by the War Department. The Department, in an effort to increase the Armory's efficiency, in 1841 replaced the Superintendent with a military Commandant or Commanding Officer. In 1854 the Armory came again under a civilian Superintendent, but from 1861 to the present a Commanding Officer has always been in charge of the Armory.[30]

made drawings for the use of the British government of American machine tools, including those at Springfield.[35] The British government bought $40,000 worth of stocking machinery alone from the Ames Company.[36] The Aaron Whitney Machine Co. of Woodstock, Vt. made for the British a complete set of machine tools for the manufacture of the Enfield rifle.[37] Colt drop-hammers were used extensively in English armories for forging the smaller parts of locks.[38] Within the next fifteen or twenty years almost every other European government also acquired large quantities of American gun machinery as they raced to replace their outmoded arms with interchangeable weapons.[39]

A factor which contributed heavily to the growth of the machine tool industry in this period was the development of what might well be called a school of inventors and gifted master mechanics. In the Connecticut Valley the most famous of these were Cyrus Buckland and Thomas Warner of the Springfield Armory, E. K. Root of the Collins Company, later Superintendent of the Colt Company, Frederick W. Howe, H. D. Stone and R. S. Lawrence of Robbins & Lawrence, Albert Eames and William Ball of Chicopee, and James H. Burton of the Harper's Ferry Armory and the Ames Manufacturing Co. Many of these men were separated from one another geographically; yet they were stimulated by one another's work and achieved a sort of cooperation similar to that which had so greatly aided invention among the gun manufacturers of the first thirty years of the century. For the most part they were closely connected with gun making, either as highly paid employees in armories or as independent workers in arms centers. Many of the future leaders of the machine tool industry received their training in armories under these men. This is perhaps the best evidence of the great debt the machine tool industry owes to small arms manufacture.

The inside contracting system played a vital rôle in the development of this school of master tool builders.[40] Since inside contractors were paid by the piece and hired their own labor, they benefited directly from increases in production or reductions in labor cost brought about by mechanization. Charles H. Fitch, special agent for the Bureau of the Census, studied in 1880 the development of interchangeability in several industries and concluded that invention of the special machine tools used in the small arms, sewing machine and related industries was the result of the system of contract labor. He commented:

It is to their [the inside contractors'] interest and profit to increase the productiveness as largely as possible, and to the devices of this class, in the development of minor details to secure the greatest result from the smallest outlay, the improvement in productive efficiency in this and in kindred manufactures is largely due. The system of employing head machinists by piece-work or contract may almost be esteemed as a germinant principle in the development of special machinery and a higher productive efficiency in the manufacture. . . .[41]

2. Forging.

Forging, while not strictly classified under machine tool manufacture, was integrally connected with the development of interchangeability and therefore cannot be overlooked in any discussion of small arms manufacture. Advances in forging were made on the one hand through improved methods of securing the dies and on the other through innovations in hammering. Barrel welding, a special type of forging, was revolutionized by the introduction of rolling machinery.

At this time more accurate forging was secured by the use of the "jumper" and "sow block." The upper die was fastened in a stock or jumper, which guided it over the lower die so that the work would not be spoiled by inaccurate judgment in placing the upper die upon the lower die. The lower die was fastened in the heavy cast-iron sow block, which held it securely under the blows of the hammer.[42] This method of die-forging was apparently used by Albert Eames in 1842 at Chicopee when he forged pistol parts with two sets of dies and heavy hand sledge-hammers.[43]

The tilt-hammer, formerly limited to barrel welding, was extended in the 1840's to bayonet forging.[44] But in other forging operations the hand sledge-hammer was replaced by the drop-hammer, rather than the tilt-hammer, as the force of the blow of the former was greater and also more easily adjustable. Although the Valley arms industry became famous for drop-forging the process was earliest established at Harper's Ferry, where Hall in 1827 used drops lifted by an endless chain rigged over pulleys and driven by a crank. A hook on the drop was caught in the chain and the drop was lifted between a set of ways. A lever disengaged the drop so that it fell and struck the dies containing the work.[45]

Different methods of raising the drop developed in New England. Albert Eames in the middle 1840's used a leather strap wound around a cylinder. Possibly the direction of rotation of the cylinder could be reversed, or the drop disengaged from the strap in the same manner as that by which Hall's drop was disengaged from the chain. E. K. Root, who established die-forging on its present basis,[46] developed two types of drop-hammers which were far superior to the chain and strap drops. In Root's screw drop a large vertical screw lifted the hammer—or hammers, if it was a compound drop-hammer. The hammers were stopped and detached by dogs and springs. This method of forging was slow and Root's crank drop, invented about 1850, replaced the screw drop. A crank at the top of a frame raised a vertical column, thus lifting a set of vertical notched rods. Opposite each moving rod was a stationary notched rod set in the frame, and each hammer moved between a stationary and a moving rod. Two puppet bolts, worked by flat springs, were set in each hammer, one bolt coming in contact with the stationary notched rod and the other with the moving one. As the central column was raised by the crank the moving rods rose, and the puppet bolts with a jogging motion lifted the drops notch by notch. When the drops had reached the point desired by the forger a mechanical device pushed the puppet bolts back from the notches and allowed the drops to fall.[47]

Through Root's inventions the Colt factory became in the 1850's the greatest center of drop-forging in New England. Reputedly all parts forged at Colt's were swaged into shape at a single blow,[48] but it was probably more usual to block out a part first and finish it in different dies with additional blows.[49] Drop-hammers were built in sizes ranging from pony drops, for forging small gun components, to large drops which were so satisfactory that the steam-hammer, used at the time in England for heavy forging, was not introduced into the Valley arms industry.[50]

Welding barrels by rolling, instead of under the tilt-hammer, was foreshadowed in experiments many years before it was put into practical operation. Nearly a quarter of a century intervened between this period of experimentation and the adoption of barrel rolling in America. This long delay was partly owing to the introduction of steel barrels, which were drilled from solid bars instead of being welded from flat sheets, and partly owing to the great expense of barrel rolling machinery. To some extent the delay may be attributed to the death of Superintendent Lee of the Springfield Armory, whose keen imagination had been the moving force behind early experimentation in barrel rolling.

Barrel rolling consisted in passing a curved iron barrel plate through a series of rollers which bent it around a rod or mandrel. The plate was forced into the form of a cylinder, the lap was welded through the pressure of the rollers, and the mandrel which had prevented the barrel from collapsing was withdrawn. In 1831 Lee confided his plan for rolling barrels to the Superintendent of the Harper's Ferry Armory:

I have in progress a plan for welding musket and rifle Barrels by rolling, which if successful will materially reduce the expense of that heavy and important part of the Arm. When I first commenced on this work, I had never heard that barrels were welded by this method. But a few days since, an Englishman by the name of Aston, called here and offered to put the plan into operation, and he would receive for compensation the saving of the expense. But being [not] altogether pleased with the man, and believing that I could effect the object without his aid, I declined his offer.[51]

It was through Henry Burden of Troy, N.Y., a manufacturer of machinery and castings with whom the Springfield Armory had business relations of long standing, that the experiments were carried out. In 1831 Burden wrote Lee:

I have at length tried to roll your gun-barrels and find the experiment exceeds my most sanguine expectations. I find no difficulty in the rollers taking the barrel off the rod. Anything further I have not tested, as you know everything else can easily be effected.[52]

Although Burden wished to put the new process into operation,[53] Lee's illness prevented for the time any further development of barrel rolling. But at the end of 1832 he arranged with Burden to make a lathe for turning the grooves in the rollers.[54] Because a spiral lap would be less liable to burst open than a straight one, Burden suggested that the barrels be twisted. He thought this would reduce the danger of bursting from around twelve per cent to a mere two per cent.[55] But just when the experiments seemed most promising Lee's death in 1833 brought them to an end.

Welding barrels by rolling was only a step further in the direction already taken in rolling the skelps from which the barrels were welded. Yet, although the Springfield Armory continued rolling its iron and steel into skelps and rods,[56] it took no further interest in rolling barrels. In 1841 Joseph C. Vaughn of Oswego, N.Y. claimed to have invented a barrel rolling machine which would turn out tapered barrels, smooth both within and without. He had worked with Burden on Lee's machine, and had great hopes of his own, especially as a similar machine, recently patented in England, had proved fairly successful.[57] But since at Springfield no one in authority partook of Lee's adventurous spirit Vaughn's efforts to have his machine tested there failed.

A decade later, in 1850, the Armory, using rollers made by James T. Ames, renewed its experiments in rolling barrels, but without success.[58] A few years later word came that the new armory at Enfield, England, used rolled barrels exclusively.[59] The Springfield authorities conceded that in this case foreign experience was worth profiting by. An agreement was made between the Ordnance Department and James T. Ames in 1856, by which the latter undertook to procure from England for the Springfield Armory rolling machinery and fifty tons of iron suitable to be used in it.[60] The machinery was to be furnished at the lowest price possible, and Ames was to be paid reasonable expenses.[61] Ames in 1858 brought over under contract an expert barrel welder, William Onions of Birmingham, England, under whose direction barrel rolling was introduced at the Springfield Armory.[62]

The method proved an immediate success. Of the first hundred barrels rolled, only one was found to be defective when proved. The experts at the Armory prophesied that there would be an even smaller loss as time went on.[63] A few months after the installation of the machinery had been made the Superintendent declared that it had met his most sanguine expectations, that it saved about fifty per cent of the cost of welding, and resulted in less condemned work.[64] Two thousand barrels had been rolled by the middle of January, 1859, and the Superintendent believed that more than the entire cost of the machinery could be recouped each year.[65] By the following April all the barrels made at the Springfield Armory were welded by rolling.[66] Shortly afterwards the process was introduced at the Harper's Ferry Armory.[67]

3. Milling and Profiling Machines.

The development of power driven milling machines was of immense value to the small arms industry, for it greatly reduced the hand filing formerly necessary for finishing gun parts after forging, and at the same time increased the interchangeability of these parts. Milling machines used irregularly shaped cutters which acted as formers of the work, or part being finished. These cutters ran at high speed, shaving off particles from the work piece, which was fed slowly against them.[68]

Millers were in use before 1830, particularly for making the Hall rifle at Harper's Ferry. But these were hand driven machines, and the adoption of power came only later. It was largely the application of power to milling and drilling which made it possible for the Middletown contractors in the 1830's to mill, drill and edge the component parts of Hall rifles at about $4.00 less a stand than it cost the government using Hall's machines.[69]

The steady elaboration of milling machines in this period demonstrates the value of pooled knowledge in the development of machine tools. A milling machine capable of milling bands, breech plates, guards, and of turning the breeches of barrels was in operation at Middletown in 1834 and was copied at the Springfield Armory.[70] Thomas Warner, borrowing from another Middletown machine working in 1835, made a machine for finishing lock plates of a uniform thickness.[71] At Waters's armory in Millbury a machine for milling the irregular edges of lock plates was built at about the same time. This was also introduced at Springfield, and in 1840, no doubt inspired in part by these machines, Warner made outstanding improvements in millers. His machines had the cutter placed on a horizontal shaft or spindle, adjustable in vertical slides, a principle used in milling machine design for many years thereafter. At first five machines were built at the Springfield Armory, with power screw feed for steady cutting and disengaging gear to stop the milling process without stopping the machine. Since these machines could finish all parts of the bayonet they eliminated grinding.[72]

With Warner's machines the cost of milling by the piece dropped in 1841 from ten to about two cents,[73] but more significant was the substitution of finishing by machine for a dangerous hand process. Warner was liberally praised by the Chief of Ordnance, who reported to the Secretary of War, "the construction of an entire set of machinery for *finishing* in *all its parts,* and thereby dispensing with the *process of grinding,* so ruinous to the health of man, deserves an award of a medal of gold from the friends of humanity. Thomas Warner, the present master-armorer, is entitled to all the credit of these invaluable improvements, and merits the consideration of the Government for his ingenuity and devotion to the interests of the armory."[74]

Although the value of Warner's improvements must have been evident to all the industry, it was not until about 1850 that millers were regularly manufactured for the trade.[75] Two principles of great significance to modern milling were applied in the 1850's. A universal milling machine, made by Robbins & Lawrence in 1855,[76] differed from ordinary millers in that the table on which the work was held could be tipped at an angle, thus increasing the versatility of the machine.[77] Two years later the index milling machine was in use.[78] This machine carried an index or dividing head, a device by which the circumference of a cylindrical piece could be divided into equal parts as it was machined. It was valuable for cutting flutes on reamers, for making milling cutters and gears, and for any other work in which it was necessary to have evenly spaced cuts made in the work piece.[79]

Profiling machines, also called jigging or edging machines, were developed to mill surfaces which were too intricate for milling machines to reach. Some of these machines could hardly be distinguished from millers. The essential difference between the two classes of machines was that profilers machined according to templates or formers, while millers depended for cutting on intricately cut rotary milling tools which acted as formers. Millers could therefore machine only those surfaces which were curved in one plane, while profilers could handle all types of closed curves, whether in one plane or more. Physically, the two classes of machines differed in that the cutter of the profiler was usually on a light spindle in a movable frame, while that of the milling machine was on a very heavy spindle in heavy and rigid bearings. In consequence the cut of profiling machines was less steady and smooth than that of millers.[80]

Profilers, using templates, were derived in part from stocking machines. As late as 1845 side plates, lock plates and other irregularly shaped parts of arms were put on stocking machines for finishing. The results were so rough that hand filing was required after such machining. Yet, since stocking machines could be used for profiling it is not surprising that metal working profilers were not introduced until the late 1840's, where hand powered millers had been in use for many years. F. W. Howe, a pioneer in profiling, invented in 1848 a profiling machine with steadier feed. By shifting the cutters, a preliminary or roughing cut and a final or finishing cut could be given without removing the part that was being machined.[81] At the Springfield Armory a metal-profiling machine was apparently first developed in 1849.[82] Another profiler, invented by E. K. Root sometime before 1857, derived its power from a vertical spindle around which were set four spindles bearing the cutters. The cutters could be shifted about at will and lowered into position for working.[83]

4. Turret Lathes.

Of all metal working lathes the turret lathe was the most important in small arms manufacture, for, together with improvements in forging and milling, it was vital in raising standards of interchangeability.[84] Metal working lathes as a class differed from millers in that in millers the tool revolved rapidly as the work was fed on to it, while in lathes the work piece revolved rapidly as the tool was fed into it.[85] The turret lathe developed from the chucking lathe, which carried a cluster of tools set in a tool stock. In the chucking lathe both tool stock and work piece were fixed on a horizontal axis. The tool stock could be "chucked" or rotated when the operator wished to change the type of machining operation. Thus with a chucking lathe a series of operations could be performed on a work piece without removing it from the lathe.

When the tool stock of a chucking lathe was fixed on a vertical, instead of a horizontal axis, the machine became a turret lathe, one of the most widely used machines in metal working today. Tools projected from the turret which was rotated by hand as each machining operation was completed. The development of turret lathes was the work of more than one man. Root, Howe and other machine tool builders had used similar machines, although only those of Howe had turrets on a vertical axis, when Robbins & Lawrence first built turret lathes commercially in 1854.[86] As early as 1852 Root invented a double turret lathe, in which both ends of a part were machined simultaneously as it revolved horizontally between two turrets.[87]

5. Mechanization of Rifling and Barrel Finishing.

With changes in gun design the development of rifling machines held the concentrated attention of machine tool builders. The first rifling machines operated by means of a rod of square cross section, twisted to give the desired spiral, and bearing a block through which a hole had been cut so that it could turn about the rod.[88] The cutters were so fixed on this block that as the block spun slowly along the rod, the cutters chiselled the rifling grooves in the barrel. The rod bearing the cutters was held stationary, and the barrel was moved along upon it and over the cutters.[89] In the early 1830's Hall used such machines at Harper's Ferry,[90] and in 1836 the Superintendent there declared that a rifling machine—probably Hall's— was capable of rifling eleven barrels a day.[91] Decreasing grooves were cut apparently either by reducing the pressure on the barrel or by regulating the length of the cutting strokes.

Rifling machines were developed in several places independently and on different principles. Some were built in Philadelphia before 1840. William Ball of Chicopee made one for Whitney's armory about 1842. It is supposed that a machine with expanding cutters was used at Frankford Arsenal in 1853. In the same year Howe at Windsor designed a rifling machine capable of rifling a hundred pistol barrels a day. In the next year Stone built at Windsor for the English government a machine which could cut three grooves at once.[92] By 1857 Colt's plant was using rifling machines which had perhaps been built there.[93]

The most advanced type of rifling machine was invented about 1855 by Cyrus Buckland, master machinist at the Springfield Armory. Through the use of expanding cutters this machine was capable of cutting grooves of even or decreasing depth.[94] Small oblong plates, on the faces of which were the cutters, were so set with flat springs on a tubular rod that a second rod inside the tubular one would force them outward as the inner rod was pushed forward by ratchet action.[95] The machine was so much improved within a year that it could rifle a barrel in twenty-five minutes.[96] One man could tend two machines, and the rifling was considered superior to that which the painstaking Belgians achieved.[97]

Boring barrels by machine had been so well developed before 1831 that, aside from slight modifications, little radical change was made in boring machines, in the pre-war period. Indeed, so slight were the improvements that in 1857 the Springfield Armory was using the same kind of bit for boring barrels that it had used in 1807.[98] Howe about 1850 made a four-spindle machine capable of boring four barrels at once, of a type widely adopted in later years.[99]

Greater changes occurred in machines for turning the outside of the barrel. Dana and Olney's turning lathe was rapidly superseded by improved types. The Springfield Armory reported in 1832 that Pomeroy was the only gun maker it knew who still used Dana and Olney's machines.[100] Increasingly accurate and close-working turning machines reduced the grinding of barrels—a hazardous occupation—to a simple finishing process.[101] Turning lathes became highly specialized. Some, for example, were capable of turning certain parts of the barrel only, such as the breech or muzzle.[102] Nevertheless they could be substituted for stocking machines, as both worked on the principle of turning to a former. Thus as late as 1852 the Ordnance Department ordered a turning lathe which, with a change of tools, could be used for wood as well as for iron.[103]

Drilling steel barrels was alternative to welding iron barrels, although later, steel barrels were both drilled and rolled.[104] Drilled barrels had the advantage of requiring less subsequent boring and reaming.[105] As early as 1832 a barrel drilling machine was used at the Watertown Arsenal. In this the barrel lay horizontally and, by means of hand levers, was forced forward against drills of different lengths placed in the headstock of the machine. There was considerable difficulty in keeping the drill in the center of a horizontal barrel, and the machine could not make use of weights acted on by gravity to force the drills into the barrel. In 1846 Albert Eames, working on a machine for Remington for drilling the steel barrels of Jenks carbines, introduced a vertical four-spindle drill, in which heavy weights at the top of the machine pressed the drills into the barrel. E. K. Root made a similar machine, with vertical spindles surrounding a center, and finally horizontal drills became obsolete.[106] By 1857 Ames was making commercially these drilling machines, or, as they were generally called, drill presses.[107]

6. Stocking Machinery.

Stocking machinery, highly developed by Blanchard prior to 1830, was, like boring and turning machines, elaborated and perfected rather than radically altered in the thirty years before the Civil War. While Blanchard's machinery was the type most generally employed, other tool builders made machines operating on different principles. In the early 1840's an apparent improvement, of which Samuel D. Sizer of Middletown claimed to be the inventor, was applied at the Springfield Armory. It consisted of bits or cutters eccentrically attached to a spindle, so that the diameter of the cut could be increased or decreased by turning the spindle.[108] In practice, however, this innovation proved either unworkable or useless, and the Armory returned to the Blanchard machines.[109] Hall's saw gang, consisting of a set of circular saws on a spindle, was still used at Harper's Ferry as late as 1844.[110] In Windsor, Vt. gun stocks after 1849 were roughed out by a band saw and then "slabbed" off by a special revolving planing machine.[111]

It was especially for stocking machinery that American tool builders earned foreign recognition. As early as 1840 an Englishman attempted to secure drawings of Blanchard's machines,[112] although European demand for the machines only became widespread a decade later. In the 1850's machine tool companies such as the Ames Company, the American Machine Company of Springfield and Robbins & Lawrence did considerable business with foreign countries in stocking machinery alone. In 1850 the Chief of Ordnance advised that some of the Springfield stocking machines be sent to London for the Exposition of 1851.[113] As a result of the London Exposition the Ames Company was awarded a contract to make Blanchard's stocking machinery for the English government, and by 1855 the company was deeply engaged in the manufacture of these machines as improved by Cyrus Buckland.[114] The company was credited with supplying several foreign governments with stocking machinery, including Russia and Spain. In Vermont Robbins & Lawrence made Blanchard stocking machines for the prosecution of the Crimean War.[115]

7. Other Machine Tools.

In this period punch presses and shearing machines were used for shaping some small parts and for cutting metal.[116] The numerous screw holes and recesses in the parts of small arms, as well as the cylinders of revolvers were drilled and finished mechanically. In drilling, parts were clamped in jigs and drilled in multi-spindled drill presses, which were in use by the later 1850's.[117]

In one branch of manufacture, screw making, the industry suffered greatly from over-specialization of machine tools, a condition which was all the more conspicuous in view of the versatility of chucking and turret lathes. Until shortly before the Civil War many processes in screw making were carried out on separate machines. In the middle 1830's the Springfield Armory used a machine invented there by Allen Foster, perhaps as early as 1821 or 1823, which could cut the threads of lock screws only.[118] A machine for swaging or forging small screws and pins was invented by Samuel Sizer in 1834.[119] A one- or two-spindle screw cutting machine was in use at Springfield in 1839. It was said to have reduced by three-fourths the cost of cutting breech plate and guard plate screws.[120] In 1856 a machine for making the breech pin screw and tapping the breech of the barrel was developed at the Armory.[121] As late as 1857 machines were made for the single operation of slitting screw heads, or of cutting screws.[122] Long-delayed progress in screw making occurred in 1858 when Stone's turret lathe was applied to screw making. It was capable of gaging, turning, threading, stamping, pointing and cutting off the screw. The turret lathe quickly drove out the over-specialized screw making machines.[123]

The polishing of gun parts was in general done with emery or leather polishing wheels. For the barrels a special machine with a perpendicular movement was developed at Springfield in the early 1830's.[124] Twenty years later the machine used there polished thirty barrels at a time. The barrels were arranged in six sets, or banks, operated independently. Five sets made a rotary motion while the sixth was given a straight finishing stroke.[125] Wooden jaws, fed with a paste of oil and emery, were pressed against the moving barrels.[126]

The extent of arms makers' investments in machine tools cannot be determined quantitatively for lack of data. In the case of the Springfield Armory the money devoted to machine tools was a small fraction of total annual expenditures. The Armory spent a total of about $77,000 for machines from 1820 to June, 1841.[127] The annual expense fell in 1831 to slightly over $300, not much more than enough to pay for a single machine. In these two decades total annual expenditure at the Armory ranged from about $129,000 to about $226,000.[128] But the Armory cannot be considered truly representative of the industry in this respect, since it suffered a serious decline in efficiency during the 1830's as a result of poor management.[129] Even before this decline set in private arms makers, as government officials acknowledged, had taken the lead in the development of some machines.[130]

The Colt Company veered to the other extreme in its extensive use and production of machine tools. In 1853 Colt boasted that his machines had become almost autonomous, capable of performing their work under the guidance of women and children, and that hand labor was required only in the finishing department.[131] So great was the degree to which machinery had replaced hand labor in the Colt factory that wages were said to be only twenty per cent of so-called "manufacturing costs," a term which excluded the cost of materials and overhead.* If full costs of manufacture had been figured the proportion attributable to wages would have been even smaller.

* Manufacturing costs at the Colt Company were broken down by a contemporary observer as follows:

Machine tender's wages, 10 per cent; wages of workers in assembling, finishing and ornamentation, 10 per cent; costs of machinery, 80 per cent. This obviously leaves out of account the cost of raw materials and all overhead charges, except, perhaps, depreciation on machinery.[132]

CHAPTER XII

LABOR

1. Type of Workers.

The skill of the average arms worker continued to decline as a result of increased mechanization and improved factory organization. The majority of armorers became machine tenders, but nevertheless remained among the most highly skilled and highly paid of American industrial workers. These men were described by a contemporary observer as a mixture of gunsmith and "machinist"[1]—as machine tenders were sometimes called— who received good wages but who could never look forward to achieving the position and skill of the old time armorers.

The development of machine tools was clearly recognized at the time as a factor of major importance in the reduction of skill, although it was only in the southern branch of the arms industry that it made practical the substitution of boys for adult workers. Talcott wrote in 1841:

Machines for performing work (that was formerly done by the skill of the eye and the hand) have been gradually introduced from time to time, until at length the machines perform nearly all the work, leaving the workman nothing to do but to fix the article in a proper position, apply the necessary oil, and set the machine in motion. A great part of the severe hand-labor is thus dispensed with. The machines are usually so constructed as to stop when the work is done without the aid of the overseer. In this way a man can attend two or more machines. The excellence of this mode of working is fully exemplified at Hall's rifle-works at Harper's Ferry, where the machines are generally attended by *boys* and *young men,* who place and replace the pieces to be wrought, and only a *few men* are required to keep the machines in good order. In this way the skill of the armorer is but little needed; his "occupation's gone." A boy does just as well as a man. Indeed, from possessing greater activity of body, he does better.[2]

With the highly skilled, versatile armorer relegated to the small gun shop the apprenticeship system in arms making virtually disappeared. Where it continued apprentices were trained as all-around machinists, not as armorers. Otherwise boys entered the industry as learners rather than as apprentices, since most of them could look forward only to positions as machine tenders.

Mechanization menaced the tenure of the older workers. Even at the Springfield Armory, where it was traditional that the armorers served the government for life,[3] increased use of machine tools made more dispensable the special skills of the older workers. Yet they struggled against displacement. Superintendent Robb declared in 1838 that the idea prevailed among the workers that they had a vested right to employment at the Armory after their period of usefulness was past. He doubtless felt he acted with commendable boldness when he adopted the plan of giving a year's notice of discharge to workers who were nearing seventy.[4]

2. The System of Labor.

Inside contracting continued as the system of employment typical of the industry. The Colt Company had regularly as many as a score or two of contractors. Each contractor might employ from one to forty men, or he might do all his work himself or let it out on sub-contract.[5] Limits were, however, set on the contractor's independence. Tools and materials were furnished by the employer, for which the contractor was responsible, and work had to be done in regular factory hours.[6] Since the system naturally lent itself to the exploitation of the unskilled workers by the contractors it became necessary for the management of the Colt Company to set up a minimum scale of wages for the employees of contractors, and to restrict discharges to those granted with the approval of the general managers of the factory.[7] It was also necessary for the company to employ inspectors to examine the work the contractors turned in.

In contrast to this system, at the Springfield Armory workers continued to be directly employed. They were supervised by foremen and assistant foremen or assistant master armorers and the quality of their work was checked by inspectors. Materials and tools were furnished by the government and the workers were each credited at the end of the month with all work which had been passed by the inspectors.[8] The cost of parts spoiled by the workers was deducted from their monthly wages.[9] Barrel welders alone were charged a fixed condemnation rate, one dollar for every barrel condemned, regardless of the stage at which the inspector discovered the defect.[10]

The Springfield Armory resisted the introduction of the inside contracting system, fearing conflicting loyalties rather than inferior workmanship, since the types of workers employed and the form of inspection used were the same under both systems. The employment of so-called apprentices by the highly skilled Springfield Armory workers was in its effect the same as inside contracting, and was expressly forbidden by the Chief of Ordnance in 1838:

The Practise of allowing master workmen at the ordnance establishments to engage apprentices, being considered injurious to the public interests, the Commanding Officers and Superintendents of those establishments are hereby directed to discontinue it on the expiration of the indentures of such apprentices as may be actually employed.[11]

But inside contracting continued to dominate the industry, since for most employers it was superior to the direct employment of workers. Where an arms plant was sufficiently mechanized, a limited number of highly skilled men to adjust or repair the machines and to lay out and oversee the work could be supplemented by boys and other unskilled workers as machine tenders. Much of the supervision could safely be passed on to the inside contractor, for it was to his immediate disadvantage if parts made by his workers failed to pass inspection. On the other hand, it was not the weight of tradition alone which prevented the Springfield Armory and the government arsenals from converting to the inside contracting system. Since there was no chance of advancement for more than a few of the unskilled workers of the inside contractors, their loyalty to any particular armory could not have been great, and a high labor turnover could be expected wherever generous wages were not to be had. To assure a sufficient labor force at all times under the inside contracting system would have required a flexibility in wage scales which the Ordnance Department would have found difficulty in achieving. Then, too, the workers at the Springfield Armory, at least, exercised a considerable amount of political power in the administration of the Armory, being capable in an emergency of going over the heads of their immediate superiors to the Secretary of War or even the President, and the majority would probably have resisted strenuously the imposition of the inside contracting system.

3. Labor Conditions.

The working day continued to be shorter in arms making than in other industries. In the Connecticut Valley the twelve-hour day was common in other occupations in the 1830's and doubtless throughout the pre-war period.[12] But the Colt plant and the Springfield Armory, the two largest arms factories in New England, worked on a ten-hour day.[13] The season determined the actual length of the working day in the industry. At the Springfield Armory it was eleven and a half hours long in June and eight in December.[14]

While a maximum was set on hours by enlightened self-interest, or, in the case of the Springfield Armory and the federal arsenals, by government regulation,[15] there was no minimum below which they might not drop as a result of managerial inefficiency. The Springfield Armory, after making a splendid record under Roswell Lee, in 1833 was put under the superintendence of John Robb, a political appointee, and lapsed into a state of demoralization which continued until 1841.[16] A change of Superintendents was then made following an examination by a board of officers appointed by the War Department.[17] The board was particularly shocked by the irregularity of working hours. It recorded:

It was a matter of surprise to the board to find that no regular hours were established for labor. Every mechanic, working by the piece, is permitted to go to his work any hour he chooses, and to leave off at his pleasure. In some instances the machinery at the water-shops has been kept running for the accommodation of a single mechanic; and in most of the visits of the board, though made in hours usually devoted to labor, these shops were found nearly deserted. The reading of newspapers during the ordinary hours of labor appears to be so common a practice as not to be deemed improper; for, in several instances, the reading was continued even during the inspection of the board.

The practice of commencing and leaving off work at irregular hours, by those who are employed by the piece, is, in the opinion of the board, attended with serious evils. It leads to great irregularity in the hours of labor, and operates as a strong motive to despatch the work of the day in the shortest time possible, often to the injury of the work itself, and not infrequently to that of the health of the mechanic.

It also tends to the injury of the machinery, which is often suffered to run beyond its proper speed, and to the destruction of the tools, which are furnished and repaired by the Government. In all the private establishments which were visited by the board, the hours of labor are fixed by regulation, and are observed by those who work by the piece as well as those who work by the day.[18]

Many years later, rumor had it that the Springfield armorers worked in summer only in the early morning and the late afternoon, occupying the rest of the day with extended siestas.[19] The *Springfield Republican,* looking back over nearly sixty years to this period, asserted as known fact:

Some of the men owned farms outside and would come in early in the morning, do their day's work, and then go back and put in most of the day in the hayfield. A man would sometimes do two months' work in one, go away for a month's vacation, and on his return turn in his work and draw his pay.[20]

A detailed study of the actual hours of work at the Armory made in 1842 showed that for three months of the previous year hours had run from about three and a half to slightly over ten a day, the average being slightly under seven hours.[21] Talcott reported that most Armory employees worked only five to seven hours a day, and not even all the day workers put in ten hours a day.[22]

The irregularity of working hours at the Springfield Armory strikingly parallels the situation in modern bituminous coal mining. Here, wherever improved methods of organization of production and the extensive use of machinery have not brought it under control, a system of "indiscipline" has prevailed, under which the miners have worked or stayed away from work as they chose. This freedom of the miners is based on the fact that they, like most small arms workers of the nineteenth century, have been piece-workers, and in a sense independent contractors.[23]

In other conditions, as in hours, armorers remained a favored class of workers. Colt's men in the 1850's worked in steam-heated, gas-lighted, ventilated rooms with sixteen-foot ceilings and running water.[24] Elsewhere arms workers had little to complain of. The introduction of steam-power provided an inexpensive and clean source of heat for factories. Compared with many industries the work was pleasant, and it was carried on completely under shelter. Developments in drop-forging greatly lightened the physical labor involved. Mechanical milling and profiling replaced much of the hand filing and grinding, and reduced the hazards to health accompanying these operations.

Yet despite the generally excellent conditions of labor in the industry, armorers frequently had cause for anxiety. The complex interdependence in factory production sometimes resulted in bottlenecks where key workers, behind in their own work, threw others into temporary or partial unemployment.[25] Also in government arsenals and armories workers continued to suffer periodically from shortages of funds voted to the War Department. Reduced appropriations forced the discharge of some Springfield armorers in 1833, of almost all the armorers at both national armories in 1842, and of many in 1853.[26] As late as 1855 the Ordnance Department ordered the Springfield Armory closed down because of a change in model.[27] The workers of government contractors suffered from the uncertainty of renewal of contracts.[28] Finally, rapid mechanization brought the risk of technological unemployment.[29]

4. Labor Relations.

A. The Bargaining Power of the Workers.

Armorers remained a peculiarly independent group of workers, yet with little tendency toward labor organization. They failed to develop lasting unions because of their generally favorable circumstances and, in the case of government armorers, because of their political power, which reduced the relative importance of economic action. Reference in the records to strikes in the industry are therefore exceedingly rare, and are lacking as far as the Connecticut Valley is concerned. In 1832 the stockers of Marine T. Wickham of Philadelphia struck in an effort to raise their wages from about one dollar to two dollars and twenty cents a day.[30] The whole working force at Harper's Ferry in 1842 "broke off from discontent with the regulations."[31] This strike lasted hardly more than one week.[32] In each case it is improbable that anything more than a most ephemeral union was formed.

Though uninterested in organization, the Springfield armorers at times showed considerable independence of spirit. Inspectors, by the nature of their work, were regarded by the other employees with such hostility that in 1834 an Armory regulation was issued requiring workers to respect the official character of the inspectors. This regulation, which might besides have acted as a deterrent to the formation of a trade union, stated in part:

"All combinations formed for the purpose of disparaging them, [the inspectors] or any other officer or for impeding the progress of the work will subject the delinquents to dismission from the armory."[33] The Springfield workers did not hesitate to acquaint the Armory officials with their feelings. "I regret to observe," Commanding Officer J. W. Ripley wrote of them in 1853, "if not a spirit of insubordination, at least a feeling of restlessness or feverishness."[34]

The political power of the Springfield armorers was phenomenal among workers in any industry. This power must have been a source of irritation to the Ordnance Department, and its existence was stoutly denied. Talcott maintained in his report to the Secretary of War in 1841: "The armorers, as a body, have never been noted for much interference with politics since the last war."[35] Yet in the same report he described in detail the extent of their political pressure, which was exerted in particular throughout the 1830's and in the early 1840's:

The prices of labor had again advanced here in 1832 so much, that a revision was deemed proper, as it was alleged that they were very unequal. A board was formed, and a careful examination made, by which it appeared that a reduction would be just. A tariff of prices was formed. The matter was then taken out of the hands of the Colonel of Ordnance by the Secretary of War, in consequence of the clamors of the workmen. He had committees of them calling upon and in frequent correspondence with him, and he finally yielded the point. The next year, 1833, he sent General Wool to Springfield, with a *carte blanche*, to adjust the prices of labor, and the farce ended in his giving them a small *increase* of wages.[36]

Although the Ordnance Department had established the policy of paying the Springfield armorers more than the going rate of wages for mechanics in similar work,[37] their desire for higher wages seemed insatiable. In 1836 another wage increase was obtained, estimated by Talcott as amounting to ten or twelve per cent.[38] Pressure continued and further increases were granted, until in 1841 the Ordnance Department finally balked and cut wages.[39] Talcott, summing up the situation, made an earnest plea for taking labor relations out of politics by giving a governmental commission power to determine wages and for the rest, placing authority over the workers completely in the hands of the Superintendent. In this connection he commented:

A manufactory carried on by private individuals or a corporation, and managed as the armory has been, would have become insolvent and broken up long since. It cannot perhaps be expected that a national establishment should be managed with quite as much skill and economy as a private concern, but there may be a much nearer approximation than has been witnessed. In a private manufactory, the judgment and will of the owner is the law which governs the operations, and his interest is found to comport with strict justice to the men. In a public establishment, the superintendent must have a large portion of the power that pertains to the owner of a private concern. The Government must confide in his judgment and sustain him in his efforts at reform.

The difficulty of finding good armorers no longer exists; they abound in every machine-shop and manufactory throughout the country. The skill of the eye and the hand, acquired by practice alone, is no longer indispensable; and if every operative was at once discharged from the Springfield Armory, their places could be supplied with competent hands in a week. With the proper number of able and honest inspectors of work, the product of the armory would be placed on the best possible footing in one month. The most ample justice should be accorded to operative mechanics; and those now employed at Springfield are good men, well able to judge of their present position and of the measure of justice that may be extended to them. They are too sensible of their great privileges to lightly part with them. Any just course in relation to their wages will meet the acquiescence of all who are worth keeping, and the Government will demand only a reasonable return for the money paid out. A commission of disinterested individuals can determine what that return should be, and fix the compensation of the operatives at a fair and liberal rate. Such a course is called for by every principle of justice between the Government and the workmen, and though last, not least, between the Government and private manufacturing establishments; for the genius of our institutions does not admit of a privileged class, built up in the midst of a manufacturing population, to become the object of desire to all and the envy of those who cannot participate in its profits.[40]

The board of officers examining the condition of the Armory had made a comparative study of an ax factory at Collinsville, Conn., the armories at New Haven, Middletown, Millbury and Pittsfield, and several large foundries in New York City.[41] A month after Talcott had made his report, this board came to the conclusion that Springfield Armory wages were nearly fifty per cent higher than those paid for equivalent work in private plants. It recommended a reduction in wages which would still leave those at the Armory above private wages.[42] The board declared that there had been "great looseness" in the management of the Armory, and suggested as a further improvement to efficiency that very old workers be discharged.[43] As a result of the investigations and recommendations of the board a military Commanding Officer replaced the civilian Superintendent in 1841, and the workers were brought suddenly to account. Following what the supporters of civilian management considered the principles of the "most despotic monarchies of Europe,"[44] the Commanding Officer, Major J. W. Ripley, carried out a drastic reorganization of the Armory. His enemies declared that he drove out or degraded the "free and independent mechanics" of the establishment,[45] but the Armory was at last whipped into a condition of reasonable efficiency.

B. Labor Policies.

The most clearly defined labor policies of arms makers revolved about the problems of employment and discharge. Prominent among these was the suppression of labor stealing. From early years the gentlemen's agreement among the manufacturers not to lure away one another's workers had been implemented by written notices of honorable discharge as a prerequisite to the employment of workers by reputable arms makers.[46] Thus the freedom of the worker as well as that of the employer was still limited in the matter of employment. While this system perhaps regulated resignations, there was no means by which it forced the employer to give reasonable notice of discharge. The worker also suffered from the fact that, even if he had not broken a contract, he might be adjudged unemployable by other arms makers. For example, a certain armorer declared that he had no contract with his former employer; yet Superintendent Robb at Springfield maintained that he would not employ him if he were "under any obligation . . . either moral or legal" to his former employer.[47]

Fortunately for the arms workers employers did not by any means always abide by the gentlemen's agreement. Inflexible as the arms makers might be on the terms on which they honorably discharged workers, they were liberal enough in interpreting the rule when applying it to men they wanted to hire. In 1836 the Master Armorer of Springfield, in flagrant violation of the rule, sent a foreman to Millbury to entice away the best workers from the Waters Armory. When complaint was made to Superintendent Robb of the Springfield Armory, he retorted that it was the constitutional right of a day or piece worker, if not under contract, to change his place of employment at will.[48]

The gentlemen's agreement, which had never functioned with complete success, apparently broke down in the late 1830's with the decline in the general cooperative spirit of the older manufacturers and the appearance of the more highly competitive new arms makers. By the early 1850's a worker could leave the Springfield Armory at will, and the Armory could discharge him without notice.[49] After 1835 complaints of labor stealing became more frequent and no further attempts were made to invoke the gentlemen's agreement. Private armories charged that with the high wages paid at Springfield, only apprentices, and there were few of these, could be depended upon for not being drawn off to work there.[50] Even after the downward revision of wages made by the Ordnance Department in 1842 Springfield continued to lure workers from other factories.[51] Such was the reputation of the Armory's wages that in 1849 a forger was drawn there from as far away as Pennsylvania.[52]

The trend in diversion of labor gradually swung in the other direction, however, as new arms concerns arose in which great emphasis was laid on machine tool construction. Private arms makers were willing to pay generously for the services of good mechanics, and became a constant drain on the Springfield Armory's supply of experts. The Superintendent of the Armory complained in 1860:

It is with regret that I am compelled to part with one after another of our most promising young men for the reason that our limited appropriations forbid me . . . to extend any special inducements to retain them.[53]

It was not until the early 1830's that another policy affecting employment, that prohibiting the sale of chances of work, was finally put into effect at the Springfield Armory. The sale of chances was stamped out only by the strict enforcement of the rule that the price paid for a chance and the names of the workers involved in each sale be reported to the management.[54] Even as late as 1834 a worker claimed that he had a just reason for employment at the Armory because of having had two brothers who at death had left their chances to others.[55]

When a reduction of the working force of the Springfield Armory became necessary an effort was made to discharge workers with a view to the best interests of the individual men, and not exclusively according to the Armory's own economic needs. Thus, when the Secretary of War in 1832 ordered a cut in the number of employees at the Armory the reduction was made not only on the ground that the Armory was suffering from a superfluity of workers, but also because it was considered unjust to the armorers themselves to continue to employ all of them without furnishing them with a sufficient supply of work to keep them constantly occupied.[56] The men who were discharged might have found such solicitude distasteful, but there could be no doubt of the kind intentions of the Armory officials when the following January the discharges were suspended until April, owing to the "inclement season of the year which might occasion great inconvenience to the workmen discharged."[57]

Further evidence of the Armory's humane policy was the Ordnance Department's regulation of 1833 concerning the order of discharge. The first men who were to be let go were the intemperate; next, the single men who had been employed the shortest time at the Armory and who were least acquainted with the work; next, the married men of the same description.[58] A trade union could hardly have improved upon such a system of seniority. Attempts were occasionally made by arms manufacturers to find openings in other plants for men displaced by technological changes.[59] There is evidence that the cost of living continued to be taken into consideration, at least at Springfield, when wage rates were fixed.[60] True paternalism developed in some armories. Colt built four-family houses, fitted with gas and running water, for his workers. He added a social center, dedicated to the "sovereignty of labor,"[61] where his employees could have lectures, debates, concerts and dances.[62] The federal government encouraged invention by granting free patents to its armorers, although it retained the right to use any invention made in its arsenals and armories.[63]

5. *Wages.*

A. Wage Policies.

It was the expressed intention of the Ordnance Department, reiterated throughout this period, that Springfield Armory wages should be governed by those paid in private armories.[64] An elaborate effort to equalize wages paid in private and government armories was begun in 1832, when a board of officers inspected Springfield with this purpose in mind. The board divided the Armory workers into six classes according to the degree of skill and intelligence necessary for each occupation, and established for each group a standard wage for a ten-hour day, capable of being earned by a workman of average skill and energy.[65] From information obtained from the Superintendent, Master Armorer and inspectors, from questioning the workmen, and from examining the Armory's pay-roll the board made recommendations as to appropriate piece-rates and the number of pieces which should constitute a good day's work.[66] A comparison was made with wages in factories making cotton machinery and other machinery. Under the schedule of wages which the board recommended the labor cost of muskets would be reduced nearly to what it had been in 1821, yet the board held that Armory workers would still receive higher wages than similar workers in private factories. Through this wage differential the board hoped that the Armory might be able to acquire and retain superior workers.[67]

Another effort to keep Springfield wages proportional to those paid elsewhere was made in 1836 when the Superintendent asked the Ordnance Department to grant a large increase in wages, amounting to as much as twelve per cent for piece-workers. He believed that even such a rise in wages would be "but a small proportion to the increased price of provisions, the advance in the price of all kinds of labor in this part of the country, and the improved quality of the work."[68] Industrial expansion at this time was luring workers westward. The nearby Ames Manufacturing Co. was forced to raise wages ten to twenty per cent, and even so could not be sure of retaining first rate workmen.[69] In view of this situation the Ordnance Department authorized an increase.[70] By 1841 Springfield wages had risen far above the level of those paid elsewhere in the industry. As has been mentioned, the board which examined the Armory in that year found that, if the "perfection of the machinery" were taken into account, Springfield wages were about fifty per cent above those paid in private plants for similar work.[71]

On the whole, however, wages at the Springfield Armory in the thirty years before the Civil War were fairly representative of those in the entire Connecticut Valley, not only because a large proportion of the Valley's armorers were employed there, and because the government to some extent regulated Springfield wages by those paid in private arms making, but also because, as will be noted later, the Springfield workers themselves kept their wages from appearing excessive by working below their capacity. To be sure, considerable differences existed between the Armory's wages and those paid in private arms plants. The most obvious one was the result of the Ordnance Department's efforts to pay somewhat above the general rate. Springfield wages were uncharacteristic of those in the industry in so far as they were subject to political pressure from the Armory's employees. The relative financial security of the Armory, as a government factory, and its production of one type of weapon for which the demand was steady, made it unique among New England armories. Nevertheless its wage data probably give a fairly accurate picture of the condition of wages in the entire Valley industry.

B. Other Sources of Income; Piece and Day Work; Wages of Different Occupations.

By the 1830's all but a very few armorers were completely dependent on their wages. While in earlier years farm work had provided a few extra dollars for Springfield armorers who were temporarily unoccupied, it had never been more than a minor source of supplementary income. Of the 261 men employed at the Springfield Armory in 1833 only 31 had farm employment. The efforts of these few were concentrated in the haying and harvest seasons.[72] The Master Armorer reported of these workers that "very few, if any, of them, can with propriety be denominated farmers."[73] Farming as an auxiliary occupation became negligible at this time chiefly because steam, either as the main source of power or of stand-by power in arms plants, removed the likelihood of seasonal unemployment.

Table 2, Appendix D shows at five-year intervals the number of piece and day workers and of men who worked under both systems at the Springfield Armory. The majority of workers were paid by the piece, and it was in the number of piece-workers that the sharp decline in employment of the later 1850's took place. The presence of foremen and inspectors in the group paid by the day partly accounts for the stability of the figures for day workers. For the rest, day workers were mostly highly skilled jobbers in filing, forging, machine and tool making, and in the production of experimental arms. They were essential to any production, and therefore would be among the last men to be discharged.

At the Springfield Armory differences among average wages in different occupations continued to be very marked. Most piece-workers were poorly or moderately paid, while the day workers fell at the two extremes of the pay-roll. Some, such as watchmen, shop tenders and laborers, received the lowest wages paid, while jobbers, foremen, assistant foremen and inspectors received the highest. In the upward trend of wages over these thirty years, with a few exceptions each occupation remained in the same position relative to the others. Classification of occupations at the Colt factory, where the lower grades of workers were machine tenders and the highly skilled men finished and assembled arms, was in general parallel with the classification of the Springfield Armory.[74]

Poorly paid occupations at Springfield were shop tending, polishing, fitting barrels and locks into stocks, helpers' work, and up to about 1845 most filing. In that year filing came to rank as a moderately well paid job, owing to the introduction of milling machines which displaced much hand filing. The tenders of these machines had to have a considerable degree of skill, and therefore these men rose in earning capacity relative to the other workers. At the same time there was a complete revolution in hand filing, which now was used only in experimental work or in finishing, and was done by the highly paid filing jobbers. Helpers were extensively used and continued to receive low wages. Most forging required the services of helpers.

Moderately paid occupations included forging by trip-hammer, boring, filing, straightening, proving, tapping and breeching the barrel, grinding bayonets, and stocking. Other occupations in this class were turning, forging, some filing work, milling, drilling, fitting, annealing, edging, jigging, and tempering. Day workers such as machinists and some tool makers also fell in this group. Highly paid workers were the foremen and inspectors, proof masters, bayonet borers, barrel welders, stockers, and assemblers and finishers of guns. Rolling iron to specific sizes and filing, forging, grinding and milling by the day were highly paid. Until the 1850's tool making and pattern making were also among the highest paid occupations, but by 1855 workers in these fields fell into the class of moderately paid employees. This change reflected an increase in the number of well trained machinists rather than contraction in the industry's demand for them.[75]

C. Wage Differentials.

The meager data on wage differentials of this period show a fairly close relation among day rates paid by New England armories. Piece-rates, on the other hand, apparently differed widely among factories.[76] This is to be expected since piece-rates were particularly dependent on factory organization and mechanization of production, and no two factories were alike in these respects. A few data on comparative monthly wages in New England arms manufacture and in the allied occupations of gunsmithing and machinists' work appear in Table 7, Appendix D. They indicate that the mean wages paid at Springfield were fairly representative of those paid in the Valley industry as a whole.

Springfield Armory mean wages in 1832 were, however, considerably below the average of the Middletown armories. This may be accounted for by a short period of great activity in machine tool building which apparently occurred at this time in the Middletown rifle factories. Machinists' wages in other industries in the Valley were well above the average of arms workers' wages, but probably not materially higher than those paid arms factory machinists. In 1845 mean and modal wages at the Armory were about equivalent in range to the wages paid by the near-by Ames Company.

The mean monthly wage at Springfield in 1850 was about $9 below that of the newly established Colt Company. This was doubtless owing in part to a difference in the stage of development of the two factories. The bulk of the Springfield Armory's workers were production workers, in general moderately paid men. Highly paid machinists, tool and pattern makers were used by the Colt Company to build up its phyiscal plant. The difference between these two establishments, each the largest arms factory in its respective state, affected the average monthly wages of arms workers in Massachusetts and Connecticut as a whole.

By 1860 mean wages in Massachusetts arms manufacture had risen sharply. Springfield Armory wages kept pace with those paid elsewhere in the state except at the Smith & Wesson factory. This newly organized firm was probably in the same condition of plant development that the Colt Company had been in a decade earlier. The drop of average monthly Connecticut wages in 1860 below those of Massachusetts may be explained by an increase in the proportion of production workers at the Colt Company.

D. The Course and Structure of Wages at Springfield.

Between 1831 and 1860 United States real wages, as shown in Table 3 and Figure 1 of Appendix D, moved steadily upward. Only in one period, from 1835 to 1839, did they seriously lose ground. Springfield armorers' real wages continued to parallel the real wages of other workers, while showing the wide deviations characteristic of the wages of a small group. The money wages of Springfield workers rose appreciably towards the end of this period.

In 1831 and 1832 Springfield armorers suffered a substantial reduction in real wages. As has been mentioned earlier in the chapter, the Secretary of War responded to pressure from the workers and in 1832 appointed a board of officers to investigate wages at the Armory.[77] As a result a schedule of wage rates was adopted which the Ordnance Department considered above those existing in private armories,[78] but which failed to satisfy the workers. The schedule was suspended soon after it had been applied,[79] a new investigation was made and another schedule was drawn up in 1833.[80] This gave the workers a general wage increase, which was reflected in a rise in real wages in 1833 and 1834. But real wages fell again in 1835 and

1836. In the latter year the workers, supported by the Superintendent, obtained a ten or twelve per cent increase in wages on the ground of general inflation.[81] Another increase was authorized in the middle of 1837,[82] and real wages rose in 1838, only to decline sharply the following year.

The armorers' real wages were at their highest peak in a decade when the Armory was investigated in 1841. Wage rates also were very high. The examining board reported that rates were such that a worker could be absent for as much as two weeks in a month and still receive adequate wages. Again, a worker might be absent an entire month and receive wages for work done on his behalf by another worker, who himself received good wages. The board stated:

It appears that an opinion prevails among the workmen that their monthly earnings ought not to appear too large on the payroll; and, to avoid such a result, work is transferred from one to another, or kept back at the end of the month; and this has been done with the knowledge of the inspectors, though in direct violation of the regulations of the armory. These facts show a general looseness in the management of the armory, which could not exist in a private, and ought not to be permitted in a public establishment.[83]

The overhauling of wage rates which followed the board's examination did not in the long run prevent Armory real wages from keeping pace with real wages elsewhere.

The Springfield Armory, in its efforts to equalize its workers' wages with those paid elsewhere and to make allowance for changes in the cost of living, found it simple enough to raise wages rates but difficult to reduce them. Talcott commented in 1841:

A change in the form or models of parts affords a favorable opportunity for the operatives to press an increase of their wages. The late change of model has been thus used to some extent. There are likewise periods in the general business of the country when labor and provisions advance in price. Such times are always seized on to increase their wages. When a revulsion takes place and prices elsewhere sink to their former level, it is no easy matter to reduce the wages of armorers. We have witnessed this state of things several times during the last twenty-five years.[84]

While Talcott recognized the power of the workers to meet an increase in the cost of living by forcing up wage rates, he probably failed to realize that such an increase could be met in part through greater exertion on the part of the workers. The work records of barrel welders at the Springfield Armory show that the monthly production quotas discussed in Chapter VIII continued in force, and that therefore all barrel welders in normal circumstances did not work up to their full productive capacity. A rise in the cost of living forced them to exert themselves to maintain their real wages, while a fall allowed them to relax their efforts. In so far as barrel welding was in this respect representative of other occupations in arms manufacture, the workers could, within limits, avoid reductions in their real incomes.

Arms wages at Springfield continued to show marked bimodality, owing to the presence of one class of highly skilled, highly paid workers and of another of machine tenders and helpers. This bimodality is depicted in Figure 1, Appendix D. The distance between high and low wages varied. In 1848, for example, there was a $10 gap between the two values, which by 1858 had increased to $34. This last figure is partly explained, as are the high means of the later 1850's, by a tapering off of employment at the Armory which began in 1856. This was owing to preparations for the manufacture of the new percussion rifle-musket.[85] As employment dropped the proportion of moderately paid production workers to highly paid pattern makers and machinists fell, and consequently the figure for mean wages rose.

6. The Productivity of Barrel Welders.

With gradual improvement of the process of welding barrels by trip-hammer the average annual production of barrel welders at the Springfield Armory rose steadily between 1831 and 1857, while at the same time piece-rates for barrel welding fell. As may be seen from Table 5 and Figure 2 of Appendix D annual production of about 5,000 barrels per man was achieved in 1857. Production dropped sharply in 1859 owing to experimental work in barrel rolling, but the following year it rose to more than 12,000. Even so it was not until the Civil War that the potentialities of barrel rolling were completely demonstrated.

PART 4

EXPANSION AND ADJUSTMENT
1861-1870

CHAPTER XIII

THE CIVIL WAR

The spring of 1861 found the federal government totally unprepared to furnish its armies with small arms on anything like the scale necessary for waging a civil war. This was in large part the result of earlier governmental policy. Independence from the contract arms system, which the War Department had sought in an effort to raise the quality of military weapons, reacted unfavorably on immediate expansion of production of standard arms by private manufacturers. Pre-war government policy had emphasized experimentation leading towards the adoption of breech-loading arms, rather than production at the federal armories and arsenals. This delayed unduly the expansion of production of government made weapons.

Nor were these the only difficulties which the federal government faced in equipping its troops with arms. At the close of 1859 Secretary of War John B. Floyd had ordered shipped to five southern arsenals 65,000 percussion muskets and 40,000 flintlocks converted to percussion.[1] Secretary of War Simon Cameron was convinced this action had been taken in preparation for the rebellion.[2] It seriously affected the Union armies in the first few months of the war.[3]

Another blow was the loss at the beginning of the war of the Harper's Ferry Armory. The arsenal attached to the Armory, which at the time contained about 15,000 stands of arms, was burned by federal troops in April, 1861, to prevent it from falling into the hands of Confederate soldiers.[4] But the machinery of the Armory was carried off by the Confederacy and installed at Fayetteville, N.C.[5] This left the North but one government armory equipped for the complete manufacture of small arms.

Perilous though the position of the federal government was in regard to supplies of small arms, that of the Confederacy at the outbreak of the war was even more difficult. It cannot be stated categorically that the South bought the bulk of its weapons from Europe, since the records of the Confederate Chief of Ordnance, the one certain source of information on this matter, are as yet unavailable.* But small arms manufacture in the South was carried on to a limited extent only. A decade earlier the machinery of the old Waters Armory at Millbury, Mass. had been shipped to South Carolina, and it was later known to be at the Palmetto Armory at Columbia, S.C. By 1861 much of this machinery was probably obsolete or worn-out, and the Palmetto Armory concentrated during the war on cannon, cannon ball, and Minié rifle ball manufacture, and probably altered

---

* These records were left to the Library of Congress with the stipulation that they be not opened for a considerable number of years.[6]

flintlock muskets to percussion.[6] The machinery at the Palmetto Armory and that taken from Harper's Ferry doubtless constituted the greater part of the Confederacy's supply of gun-making equipment at the beginning of the war.

Since the South had lagged so far behind the North in its industries it was at a disadvantage which became increasingly greater as time went on. Factory production of small arms on anything like the scale required could not be established on short notice. More than five months passed after the war opened before armories in the Confederacy began delivering small arms.[7] Tens of thousands of Southerners, according to Jefferson Davis, had to be refused admission to the army because of shortage of arms.[9] It was only at the end of 1863 that Davis believed that the Confederacy would soon become mostly independent of foreign supplies.[10] A year later, however, the Confederate Chief of Ordnance estimated that northern armories were turning out 5,000 stands of arms a day, while the daily output of the South did not average 100.[11]

1. Methods of Meeting the Needs of the Union Armies.

Although the Northern small arms industry won the race in production, it did so only by employing every device to increase its capacity. The Springfield Armory, the federal arsenals and existing private armories were expanded to the utmost. New arms makers who came into the field found almost unlimited governmental work. Firms from other industries flocked into arms making, concentrating on manufacture of gun parts. Yet even with the greatly increased productive capacity which was thus built up it was nevertheless necessary for the Ordnance Department in the first years of the war to depend heavily on importation of foreign arms. At first the government had to accept many weapons clearly recognized as inferior in quality, and it was not until 1862 that the War Department felt in a position to limit its imports to small arms of the first quality only.[12]

A comparison of government purchases of foreign and of domestic small arms from April, 1861 to June 30, 1862 is given in the table on the following page. The figures for foreign purchases for this period represent the heaviest imports of small arms. Nearly four times as many were bought abroad in these fifteen months as were made in private American armories at the same time. The qualitative superiority of the American, however, in part made up for this. Foreign purchases were concentrated on the older types of arms—muskets, rifles and edge weapons. Domestic production far surpassed imports in carbines, pistols and revolvers. Many of the carbines were the new multi-shot patent arms.

Of foreign countries supplying the federal government with 10,000 or more of one type of weapon in this period, England specialized in Enfield rifles, Prussia in muskets, Austria and Belgium in muskets and rifles, France in revolvers and rifles, Bohemia in carbines. Many firearms were bought from unspecified foreign sources, and no country of origin was listed by the Ordnance Department for swords and sabers. It is probable that England, Prussia, Belgium and France manufactured most of the edge weapons.[14]

Private arms makers relied on Europe for aid in filling their early contracts with the federal government. Immediately after the war broke out Colt informed the Secretaries of War and of the Navy that he could fill a contract of from 100,000 to 500,000 rifle-muskets.[15] But since his plant had been confined to revolver manufacture he himself could not make rifle-muskets. He therefore contracted with English and Belgian manufacturers

Table 1

Government Purchases of American and Foreign Small Arms,
April, 1861 to June 30, 1862.[13]

	American Arms	Foreign Arms
Muskets and Rifles	30,788	726,705
Carbines	31,210	11,113
Revolvers and Pistols	88,584	15,254
Swords, Sabers, and Cavalry Lances	74,123	173,010
Totals	224,705	926,082

for barrels and locks. Like the parts of other contract arms, these had to be approved by Ordnance Department inspectors who were stationed in Europe.[16]

Of necessity many arms bought abroad at the beginning of the war were of foreign pattern, the best available at the prices the War Department could afford to pay. The manufacture of spare parts and appendages for the repair of these arms fell to the Springfield Armory, loaded down though it was with other work. Demands for these parts poured in constantly from the various arsenals where repairs were made, and probably continued as long as the foreign arms remained serviceable.[17] The inconvenience of making and maintaining supplies of spare parts of foreign arms of several types must have been considerable, while at the same time mutinies occurred among Union soldiers who could not be armed with Springfield rifle-muskets.[18] To overcome these problems the Ordnance Department, by the fall of 1862 if not earlier, began contracting with foreign manufacturers and importers for arms altered in certain respects to conform to the regulation Springfield rifle-musket.[19] There is no evidence, so far as the writer knows, to show that the entire Springfield gun was ever made abroad.

European countries were especially qualified at this time to supply the

United States with arms. Just prior to the Civil War they had equipped themselves with machine tools of both European and American manufacture, and their small arms industries were in an active condition. They did not suffer the acute shortages of skilled labor which hampered both the Union and the Confederacy throughout the war. Good raw materials were available to European arms makers, while raiders and blockades made them scarce and expensive in America.

The Ordnance Department, owing in part to its dependence on the good will of foreign governments, continued cordial relations with them. Even considerations of national security did not prevent technical information on small arms from passing out of the country. A French officer, visiting the United States in 1863 to examine arms production, was, on the order of the Chief of Ordnance, freely supplied by the Springfield Armory with specimens of the different parts of the government rifle-musket and with information on manufacturing techniques.[20] A rifle-musket of the newest pattern was presented in 1864 to the Swiss Government.[21] In the last months of the war the Minister from Denmark was authorized to attend meetings of a military board investigating breech-loading arms.[22]

While large scale importation of arms by the Union continued for some time, filling the gap between domestic production and the needs of the armed forces, the American industry expanded steadily. It showed rapid development along three lines—temporary conversion of plants in other industries to parts manufacture, increased output of existing plants, and entry of new enterprises into the field.

The numerous manufacturers of small arms parts played an important rôle in the early part of the war, increasing production at a time when much of the effort of the industry proper was concentrated on plant expansion. Scores of firms not equipped for the manufacture of complete arms were fully qualified for making one or more specific parts for the government arms contractors. Since these parts were made on contract a subcontracting system became an established feature of the arms industry throughout the war. An arms contractor usually made the more important parts of the gun at his own plant, letting out minor parts to his subcontractors. But this was by no means universal. A Connecticut contractor, for example, had his barrels made by a Norwich firm, his locks in West Chelsea, and the other parts of the gun in his own plant at Greeneville.[23]

No manufacturer depended more heavily on the parts contracting system than did the Springfield Armory.* As it was the expectation of the

* The Springfield Armory Correspondence lists many firms engaged, or prepared to engage in parts manufacture for the Armory. Their names and locations, and the parts they were capable of making, are as follows:
Barrels: New Haven Arms Co., New Haven; Bridgeport Armory, Bridgeport; Fairmount Rifle Works, Philadelphia; William Muir & Co., Windsor Locks; Bay State

Ordnance Department that the Armory would take up any slack in arms production, it found itself burdened with making parts for foreign arms, with supplying parts to contractors, and with inspection work on all kinds of ordnance, while at the same time it was expected to meet constantly increasing production goals. With all these requirements the Armory found the parts contractors invaluable. Except for stocks, it at times put out all parts of the Springfield rifle to sub-contractors scattered throughout New England, New York, New Jersey and Pennsylvania. The Armory may have ceased altogether making some minor parts.[24] Thus some of the production formally attributed to the Armory was in fact the work of these makers of parts which were assembled at Springfield.

The parts manufacturers came from many different industries. They might be makers of machines or tools, or even of locomotives. Manufacturers of solar compasses, of rules and levels, and of bells, became parts contractors.[25] Some contractors of complete arms also made parts, although this was the exception rather than the rule. The bulk of arms production was handled by the regular armories, but the elasticity vital to wartime requirements was given the industry by the parts contractors, large or small, who collectively contributed to a productive capacity beyond that which the armories alone could have attained. The system in effect pre-

---

Hardware Co., Northampton; O. F. Burt, Windsor Locks; Cooper Hewitt & Co., Newark; L. & A. Coes, Worcester; Whitney Armory, New Haven.

Bayonets: Collins Co., Collinsville, Conn.; A. Waters & Co., Millbury; W. H. Harrington, Millbury; Norwich Arms Co., Norwich; Harvey Waters, Northbridge, Mass.; Ridgeway & Reiffe, Germantown, Pa.; Alfred Jenks & Son, Philadelphia; Wetherby Tool Co., Millbury.

Locks and Parts of Locks: Alrood, Bridgeport; Samuel Norris, Middletown and Providence.

Gun Tips: W. & E. Fitch, New Haven; Arcade Iron Works, Worcester.

Rear Sights: Henry A. Chapin & Co., Bridgeport.

Guards: Wm. M. Hawes & Co., Fall River.

Ramrods: J. Pierce, Lowell; Andrew Moody, Lowell Machine Shop, Lowell.

Guard and Butt Plates: A. Merredy's Sons, West Troy, N.Y.

Bands: Amoskeg Manufacturing Co., Manchester, N.H.

Main Springs: D. Schuburth, Providence; C. B. Hoad, Watertown, N.Y.; F. Reed, Canton; C. A. Newell, Middletown.

Tompions or Gun Stoppers: Stanley Rule & Level Co., New Britain; G. H. Mix & Co., New York City; R. & G. Cushman, Pawtucket; J B. Jastian, Providence; R. Kingsley, Springfield, Mass.; J. Parkman Blake, New York City.

Percussion Caps: American Flask and Cap Co., Waterbury, Conn.

Appendages:

Screw Drivers: O. B. North & Co., New Britain and New Haven; A. W. Crossman, Warren, Mass.; Dwight, Chapin & Co., Bridgeport; Arthur H. Jackson, Middletown; George Holmes & Bros., Keene, N.Y.

Spring Vises: Cotrell & Babcock, Westerly, R.I.

Punches: Fay & Mason, West Warren, Mass.

Swivel Vises: Charles Parker, Meriden.

Screws: American Screw Co., Providence; W. Coleman & Sons, Providence.

Miscellaneous Appendages and Parts: Trenton Locomotive & Machine Manufacturing Co., Trenton; W. S. Schoener & Co., Bridgeport; W. & E. Gurley, Troy, N.Y.; Welch, Braun & Co., Norfolk, Conn.

sented the regular arms makers with auxiliary factory space and managerial ability, raw material stocks and channels of supply, skilled labor and, probably most important, additional machine tools. While imports of foreign arms backed up the Union armies at the outset of the war, the parts makers supported the small arms industry proper until it had built up its plant for production on a wartime scale.

The expansion of existing small arms plants got under way gradually. The efforts of the arms makers were divided between the necessity for making immediate deliveries of weapons and for increasing productive capacity. Production for the war years of the two largest New England arms plants, the Springfield Armory and the Colt Company, appears in the following table. Despite the immense effort exerted by the Springfield Armory it was not until 1864 that it reached its productive peak. Even the Colt Company, which was mechanically the best equipped plant in New England at the outbreak of the war, did not reach its peak of production until 1863.*

Table 2

Civil War Production of the Springfield Armory and the Colt Company.[26]

	1861	1862	1863	1864	1865
Springfield Armory					
Muskets, Rifles and					
Carbines	13,803	102,410	217,784	276,200	195,341
Colt Company					
Revolvers	69,655	111,676	136,579	10,406	58,701
Rifles	3,193	2,287	1,213	——	——
Muskets	——	8,500	49,844	46,201	9,435
Total of Colt Company	72,848	122,463	187,636	56,607	68,136

The struggles of the Springfield Armory to attain the production goals set for it by the Ordnance Department are worth following in detail. On the eve of the war the Ordnance Department frankly admitted that neither the Springfield nor the Harper's Ferry Armory had been working up to capacity, owing to insufficient appropriations and to the diversions of the Armories' efforts to non-manufacturing activities.[29] In February, 1861, the Department, expecting the outbreak of war, ordered Springfield to increase its working force so that 1,200 rifle-muskets a month, or 14,400 a

---

* The importance of these figures for the Connecticut Valley arms industry and for arms manufacture as a whole is indicated by the fact that from the time it began manufacture in the 1840's to the end of the Civil War the Colt company sold about 850,000 revolvers, while all other American firms had sold only about 250,000 revolvers in the same period. About one-third of the Colt arms had been sold abroad.[27] The total output at the Springfield Armory of manufactured and assembled arms from 1861 to 1865 inclusive was 815,139 rifle-muskets, as compared with the 643,439 rifle-muskets contracted for and delivered during the war by all private arms makers in the Union.[28]

year, could be produced.[30] This goal was revised upward in May to 100,000 a year,[31] and in June to 120,000 a year.[32] One of the Department's production experts recommended that the Armory make 5,000 barrels a month, that the number of workers in key positions be increased, that night work be instituted, and that small parts be put out to allow the greatest possible expansion in stock and barrel production.[33]

Most of these suggestions were carried out, but even so production lagged. Owing to the quiescent state of the Armory at the beginning of the year, and to the Armory's efforts to enlarge the plant, actual annual production for 1861 was only 13,801 arms. Not discouraged by this failure to attain the goal in the first year of the war, the Ordnance Department continued to set, and the Armory officials accepted, production quotas which greatly surpassed output. For 1862 the capacity of the Armory was said to be at least 200,000 rifle-muskets,[34] but only a little more than half that number, 102,410, were produced. For the next year the Ordnance Department hoped that 24,000 guns would be turned out every month—a figure greater than the total pre-war annual production of both federal Armories.[35] This estimate would amount to 288,000 for the year of 1863, but only 217,784 were produced. During the next year 276,200 arms were made at Springfield, but production fell in 1865 to 195,341.[36]

The Springfield Armory was not alone in failing to attain the production expected of it. Private plants presented on the whole a poorer showing. One authority notes that of the total 1,525,000 Springfield rifle-muskets contracted for during the war, only 643,439, or less than one half, were actually delivered.[37] Yet in 1863, when the Springfield Armory was supposed to be capable of producing 288,000 a year, the total annual production of small arms contractors was estimated at about 700,000.[38]

Detailed data relating to wartime expansion of other armories are scarce. The Norwich Arms Co. made 1,200 rifle-muskets, 3,000 bayonets and 2,000 locks a week, besides rifles and carbines. Parker, Snow & Co. of Meriden produced about 100 Springfield muskets a day. The arms industry of Middletown revived temporarily owing in large part to Remington's being so overloaded with government contracts that it transferred some of them to the Savage Revolving Fire Arms Co. of Middletown. At Hartford Sharps employed during the war about 450 men and produced about 30,000 rifles annually. The Ames Company's body of armorers increased to 800 men, who made nearly 300,000 swords a year. The Massachusetts Arms Co. of Chicopee Falls employed 300 workers upon manufacture of the Maynard rifle. The Clement Hawkes Manufacturing Co. of Northampton developed during the war from a small hoe shop to a parts making concern with a capital of $100,000, with a working force in 1866 of 230 men. E. G. Lamson & Co. of Windsor, Vt. employed about 400 men.[39]

Many new concerns sprang up in the arms industry. The list of firms in the industry in Appendix A shows that nineteen new arms plants appeared in the Valley, while twenty survived from earlier years. These figures do not include firms that were not primarily arms concerns. Boston, Providence, Worcester, Springfield, Hartford and New Haven remained the centers of the New England industry. Meriden, Conn. developed into an important though smaller center, and Middletown and Windsor, Vt. were temporarily very active in small arms production.

As a result of the work of the parts manufacturers, of expansion of existing arms plants, and of the appearance of new firms, the Connecticut Valley contributed a large portion of the arms manufactured for the Union armies. Of the 643,439 Springfield rifle-muskets delivered on war contracts, 309,520, or about half, came from the Valley, including the region as far east as Norwich. About two-thirds of the total, or 436,002, came from New England as a whole.[40] The Springfield Armory's production accounted for 815,139 rifle-muskets in the total number made during the war. In addition, Colt made 387,017 revolvers and 6,693 rifles. Smith & Wesson's revolvers, though not adopted by the government, were so popular with army and navy officers that there were orders on the company's books for all its possible production for two years ahead.[41] Winchester's Henry repeating rifle with rim-fire copper cartridge, first manufactured in 1860, although considered a sporting gun, was used in large quantities by state troops. This rifle failed of adoption by the federal government, but was pronounced by one authority the best military rifle of its time.[42]

2. Costs.

Unit costs during the war were greatly affected by the heavy investments in plant which took place at this time. Table 1, Appendix B shows that average annual cost at Springfield dropped steadily during the war years, rising only when production was being brought to a halt at the close of the war. Contemporary cost estimates for the Armory are very rare, but in 1861 the Ordnance Department listed the cost of the rifle-musket with its appendages at $13.93, a figure much below the $26.25 derived by the writer from Armory statistics.[43] The Department did not explain the method by which it arrived at its figure. In 1876 it looked over its records and reckoned the average cost of the rifle-muskets made in the course of the war at $11.70. This included all costs of labor, materials, direct supervision, inspection, condemnation of defective parts, six per cent interest on the plant, and depreciation on tools, fixtures, machinery, buildings, etc. No item for fire and accident insurance was included, since the Armory maintained a fire engine and watchmen.[44] Table 1 shows a much higher average—$17.70—for the cost of the rifle-musket in the Civil War period.

Nothing can be ascertained concerning wartime profits, nor can the cost of privately made arms be satisfactorily determined, because of the absence of data. The price of arms was certainly high enough to allow considerable profits, or contractors would not have long continued in the industry. At some time between 1849 and 1870, and quite possibly during the war, the Ames Manufacturing Co. is said to have paid on four occasions a fifty per cent dividend on its capital of $250,000 and at another time a seventy-five per cent dividend.[45]

The price of Springfield rifle-muskets ranged from $18 or $19 for small contractors to $20 for guns made by holders of contracts of from 20,000 to 50,000 arms. In the beginning of 1864 the price was generally $18 or $19.[46] Patented cavalry carbines were bought by the government at $30 each, and Colt revolvers at $25.[47] The Ordnance Department later estimated that the average cost of all contract arms over the war period was $20, with inspection costs amounting to a dollar extra.[48]

3. Type of Arms, Contract Arms and Inspection Problems.

The enormous requirements of the army forced an admitted reduction of government standards, and almost any type of rifle or musket, provided it took .58 caliber ammunition and was serviceable, was acceptable for the use of the armed forces.[49] The government led the way in the down-grading of arms, a policy essential for the whole industry if the needs of the army were to be met. As late as the middle of 1864 government made arms were divided at the direction of the Secretary of War into two grades according to quality. Both grades were issued to the troops. Gun parts which had been rejected for the highest grade of arms because of defective material, if they were nevertheless "serviceable," were ordered assembled into second grade arms. These parts included "dirty" or cinder-marked barrels, stocks from which the sap had not been completely removed, or which contained small cracks or knots, and component parts with slight seams or cinder marks. Condemnations were ordered made with great circumspection, to save all possible parts. It was prohibited for a time to sell metal parts from the War Department's stores of condemned ordnance.[50]

While no specific evidence appears that the terms of government contracts ever allowed manufacturers to supply second-grade arms, in their case as in that of the Springfield Armory there was a reduction in the rigidity of inspection. Parts contractors for the Armory openly and regularly supplied it with second class, as well as with first class parts.[51] The Colt Company, which made large quantities of Springfield rifle-muskets, also manufactured second class parts.[52]

The circumstances which allowed the acceptance of a poorer quality of arms also resulted in the acceptance by the government of guns not of the regular pattern, but workable and meeting certain minimum requirements. In this way a large number of heterogeneous weapons were acquired. Sporting rifles and the old Hall breech-loaders were used.[53] Quantities of parts were made to keep in service muskets of the model of 1822, altered to percussion locks.[54] Between January 1, 1861, and June 30, 1866, the government bought, mainly for the cavalry, nineteen different types of American made breech-loading arms, totalling 396,856 weapons. These were mostly Burnside, Gallagher, Joslyn, Merrill, Maynard, Remington, Sharps, Smith, Spencer and Starr rifles and carbines.[55]

Possibly the purchase of the new breech-loaders stood for the government in lieu of experimentation of its own, for in the first two years of the war, when production goals of the muzzle-loading Springfield were still far from attained, the Ordnance Department seemed deaf to suggestions for improvements in types of arms. It is true that it showed considerable interest in the Colt Company's modification of the standard military musket in the summer of 1861.[56] But it apparently did not investigate an improved Prussian needle gun—a bolt action breech-loading weapon, so called because of the type of firing pin it used—which was said by its American promoter to be capable of firing five times as fast as any muzzle-loading gun.[57] Nor was any interest displayed in the English Enfield rifle.[58] The Pettingill pistol met with a lukewarm reception in 1862, when Captain A. B. Dyer, Commanding Officer at Springfield, stated that it was as unlikely to get out of order as any revolving pistol he had seen, and another Ordnance officer suggested that the manufacturer be given an order, to encourage its development.[59]

By 1863, however, when the immediate needs of the army promised to be sufficiently met by the increased capacity of the industry, more attention was paid to experimentation. The government tested the efficiency of several breech-loading carbines, among them the Ballard, Joslyn, and Sharps and Hawkins arms.[60] The only specifications required of the arms under examination was that they should be of .50 caliber, with twenty-two inch barrels and a weight of six to eight pounds.[61]

This revival of interest in new types of arms culminated in the appointment by the War Department of a board of officers convening early in January of 1865 to examine and recommend for government adoption a suitable breech-loading device for muskets and carbines, and a repeater or magazine carbine.[62] Inventors and owners of patented arms were requested to furnish model arms and sealed proposals of the terms on which they would transfer their rights to the government.[63] So desirous was the Department of acquiring a practical breech-loading mechanism that the board was willing to examine any type of breech-loading gun, whether completed or not, whether rifled or not, and whatever its caliber and weight.[64] The Commanding Officer of the Springfield Armory explained the Board's point of view to an applicant as follows:

The point to which their [the applicants'] attention is chiefly directed, is the mechanism of closing the breech, the working of these parts under all the various circumstances of actual service. The Board is desirous of getting the strongest, simplest and most perfect breech loading arrangement that can be found.[65]

The end of the war cut short for the time the government's interest in this matter, although some investigation in breech-loading arms continued.

Inspection problems, enormously multiplied by the war, as far as the Connecticut Valley was concerned were thrown on the Springfield Armory. The Armory's jurisdiction was extended to cover heavy ordnance and miscellaneous military supplies such as gun caissons, cavalry equipment, and accoutrements.[66] While the office of Inspector of Contract Arms for this area was established at Watervliet or New York City, the Armory was frequently called on to send out its inspectors to aid in this work.

The official attitude towards inspection reflected the same spirit as that shown in the classification of government made arms into two grades. It had been the rule to reject work when condemnations exceeded ten per cent of the lot examined,[67] and inspectors who passed parts later found to be defective were charged their full money value.[68] Yet when certain gun components were badly needed, an inspector might be ordered to re-examine previously condemned work, and if it was serviceable, remove the condemnation stamps.[69]

Apparently in an effort to stimulate production contractors were given for their arms a price in part dependent on the number they supplied. If they contracted for a large number they received a higher price per weapon than did the smaller contractors.[70] Failure of delivery, unless caused by some action of the Ordnance Department, was met with forfeiture of the right to make any further deliveries.[71] To increase the number of arms at its command the government prohibited the export of small arms from the United States, a measure which occasionally resulted in some hardship to a manufacturer temporarily lacking a government contract.[72]

Even with the best possible planning, maladjustments in the rate of production of various parts of arms within a plant and among factories could not have failed to exist. Not infrequently large numbers of weapons could not be completed for lack of a specific part. To diminish such losses in production the Ordnance Department authorized the Springfield Armory to acquire and issue spare parts on contract, and also to buy and sell them outright to contractors at cost.[73] In fact the Armory was ordered in 1862 to be prepared to supply whatever parts contractors might need to hasten the completion of their contracts.[74]

4. Raw Materials.

Prices paid during the war for the main raw materials of arms manufacture by the Springfield Armory appear in Appendix C, together with data concerning quarterly wholesale prices of ninety-two commodities as given in Wesley C. Mitchell's *Gold, Prices and Wages Under the Greenback Standard.*[75] Mitchell's material is based in part on the Aldrich Report to the Senate Committee on Finance made in 1893. His figures are unweighted and have 1860 as the base year. The data are presented as deciles or ten equal divisions of relative price ranges within each quarter. For the purposes of this study Mitchell's fifth decile or median was taken as a successor to Cole's index figure which ends in 1861, although as the two figures were arrived at by different statistical methods they are not strictly comparable.

The correspondence between Mitchell's wholesale commodity price curve and the course of prices of small arms raw materials is striking, and might have been even closer had it been possible to collect quarterly figures for prices of small arms materials. Charcoal prices alone were independent of the general trend. The prices of steel, musket stocks, coal and both domestic and imported wrought iron rose sharply during the war, paralleling the rise in Mitchell's general wholesale price figure. A deviation from this pattern occurred in 1863 in the May price of imported iron. This, however, related to a single delivery of iron and was not representative of a general trend. If this particular item is omitted the curve follows closely that of domestic iron as well as the general wholesale price curve.

It is to be noted that changes in the general wholesale price curve lagged by as much as a year behind changes in iron and coal prices. A rapid rise in iron and coal prices had set in by 1862, but did not begin in wholesale prices generally till the last quarter of 1862. By March and April, 1865, imported iron and coal had dropped from their wartime peaks, but a comparable drop in general wholesale prices did not occur until the middle of 1865. Perhaps iron anticipated changes in general wholesale prices because dealers depended to a large extent on importation and were therefore immediately affected by fluctuations in the rate of exchange. The extensive use of coal in all industry made its price extremely sensitive to inflationary and deflationary trends, which did not show up immediately in the less sensitive, because more widely diversified, index figure for general wholesale prices.

Much of the wartime price rise in the raw materials of arms manufacture was purely inflationary and independent of shortages in stocks. This is borne out by the average quarterly prices of gold in greenbacks collected by Mitchell for the period 1862-1870,[76] which are plotted in Figure 1 of Appendix C. This curve shows in a more extreme form the fluctuations of the general wholesale price index and of the price curves of several of the raw materials of small arms manufacture.

The uncertainties of the war disrupted long established customs in the supplying of raw materials to the small arms industry. Dealers became less willing to let accounts run for the usual three or four months' credit period, and the practice was developed of giving a four or five per cent discount for cash or payment within thirty days of delivery.[77] Various methods were used by importers to protect themselves against inflation. One was the demand for cash payment,[78] although as the currency was devaluated this proved increasingly unsatisfactory. One English importer required that payment be made in approved sterling bills at three days' sight in London,[79] but this method was unusual, owing doubtless to its inconvenience to the purchaser. Commonly payment in gold or its equivalent in currency was demanded.[80] This method was refined to the point where it was customary for the dealer to quote a fixed price to which would be added the current premium on gold on the day the goods were delivered.[81]

The Springfield Armory's difficulties in paying for raw materials during the war may have been representative of those under which the small arms industry generally suffered. At first the Armory was authorized by the United States Treasury to pay its accounts by check on the deposits of the War Department, in United States notes or in coin.[82] But by the beginning of 1862, as the premium on gold rose, the Treasury restricted payment of coin to interest on the public debt.[83] This made it necessary for the Armory to pay its accounts with approved certificates of inspection of the goods purchased, on which the receiver could collect in Washington, generally exchanging them for certificates of indebtedness issued by the government. The certificates of inspection were not welcomed by the Armory's creditors and were regularly subjected to a considerable discount.[84] The federal certificates of indebtedness themselves were less favorably received than drafts on New York or Boston banks.[85]

The Civil War threatened iron imports and caused domestic iron to retrieve a part of the position it had formerly held in small arms manufacture. The introduction of barrel rolling machinery, together with the decline in quality of the Salisbury ore, had made the Armory dependent on English iron imported in shapes suitable for rolling into barrels, and to a limited extent on Norway iron for use in component parts manufacture.[86] But with the outbreak of war it became obvious to the Ordnance Department that England might stop iron shipments, and intensive efforts were therefore made to find an American substitute.[87] The Department experimented with many irons refined in New England and Pennsylvania, but all proved unsatisfactory.[88]* For a time the Springfield Armory was

* In its efforts to secure a high quality American iron the Armory occasionally came across iron manufacturers who showed an intense hostility to the English suppliers. A Pennsylvania iron master whose iron, after trial, had been rejected by the Springfield Armory, wrote indignantly:

The report of your Foreman would be to me *simply ridiculous* if my 34 years' experience of the Bar Iron manufactured from pig metal made here with cold blast, backed by the voluntary testimonials of many of the best iron makers

190

forced to borrow iron from other arms makers whenever imports fell off.[89]

At last in the fall of 1862 the Secretary of War became convinced that Cooper, Hewitt & Co., owners of the Trenton Iron Co. of Trenton, N.J., a firm which was one of the largest importers of English iron for the Springfield Armory, could produce a domestic gun barrel iron of high quality. The following extract from a letter from P. H. Watson, Assistant Secretary of War, to Captain Dyer, Commanding Officer of Springfield, presents the War Department's stand on the problem of an adequate supply of iron:

On learning that Mr. Hewitt was about going to Europe to procure an additional supply of gun barrel iron, of the Marshall brand, the Secretary of War sent for him to come to Washington, and after a full discussion of the subject, decided it to be better to defer his visit to Europe, and any further orders for foreign gun-barrel iron, until the result is known of a full and complete trial of the Trenton iron, which it is understood you have recently undertaken.

If a supply of iron can be had in this country which is equal in all its essential qualities to the Marshall iron, and inferior only in freedom from specs, and a high silvery lustre when polished, we may well dispense with these merely ornamental qualities for the sake of rendering ourselves independent of foreign nations for the supply of an article so important as gun-barrel iron. Moreover if it is probable that such an article can be

---

of the Country did not warrant me in saying it is as I firmly believe entitled to a few more appelations.

The result is just what I or any other loyal American Manufacturer who gives his sons to defend the life of the nation, and his treasure to aid it, has a right to expect from the Ordnance Department of the Army. Its proclivities are confessed to be foreign and must crush American competition . . . [The Ordnance Department] is so very certain to condemn American iron although it may stand five times the charges and wear of the pet Marshall British iron. . . . So long as the head of the Bureau is Anti-American, no workman dare counteract his Foreign traducers without fear of dismissal. I have had enough experience practically to laugh your Foreman's assertion for which he ought to blush scarlet, to scorn.[90]

On the other hand, attempts to find another serviceable type of imported iron to eke out the limited supply of Marshall iron were unavailing and were in one instance at least balked by the jealousy of their trade secrets on the part of other arms manufacturers. Thus some Windsor Locks manufacturers who discovered an excellent type of gun barrel iron, really a soft steel, were unwilling to have their discovery made public. Joel Farist & Co. of the Hartford Cast Steel Works of Windsor Locks wrote Captain Dyer concerning the experiments of these manufacturers:

. . . out of the six samples they find two brands good ones, one especially so, far superior to the Marshall brand in their estimation, but whether this one brand is the Soli brand or not, we are not able to inform you, because they say it has cost them some $1500 to obtain the fact, that such an iron is manufactured that is superior to the Marshall brand, and at a less price per ton, but they offered to put us in possession of all the facts belonging to this brand of iron, on condition that it was only to be used for the benefit of ourselves in our business of steel making.—This brand of iron they think so much of is made under the *Besemer Patent* we were shown a barrel unpolished, and also shown a piece cut off the end of a barrel polished, and afterwards submitted to the action of acids, and we must confess in our judgment it is a superior article it had the appearance of small squares distinctly marked out showing the marks of the pile as welded together, it is called an iron but we think it better named as gun metal.[91]

procured at home, it is the plain duty of the Government to encourage its production, and to use it to the exclusion of the foreign article.

The Secretary of War is highly gratified to learn that you have so opportunely undertaken a series of experiments to determine whether Trenton iron can be used to fabricate gun barrels, and he desires you to prosecute the experiments to completion without delay, and report the result to this Department.

He further desires that in conducting experiments and estimating results, you will seek mainly to develop the useful qualities of the iron, treating freedom from specs, silvery lustre, susceptibility of high polish, and other merely ornamental qualities as entitled to little or no consideration, provided the essential useful qualities of sufficient tenacity, evenness of texture, easy welding and proper hardness and density are present.

The Secretary of War is the more desirous that a full trial should now be made of the Trenton iron because he is convinced that the daily experience of Cooper Hewitt & Co., their liberal expenditure of means, and the enterprise, science and skill which they command, stimulated by their high public spirit and patriotism, will soon overcome every obstacle to the production of American gun-barrel iron, of a quality equal, if not superior, to any now made by any foreign nation.[92]

The Secretary of War requested Cooper, Hewitt & Co. to make 2,000 tons of their iron and deliver it to the Armory as fast as possible. If the company could surpass the minimum requirements, and furnish iron free from specks, with a high, silvery luster, and capable of the fine finish of the Marshall iron, it would be granted a price equal to that paid for the English iron.[93]

Once this arrangement had been made, the War Department threw caution to the winds and in the fall of 1863 instructed the Springfield Armory to cancel all orders for foreign gun barrel iron.[94] Two other events added to the finality of this step. One was the outbreak of the Schleswig War, which brought a sharp increase in prices of European raw materials.[95] The other was the imposition of the tariff of 1864, under which Congress clapped on a fifty per cent increase in the duty on imported iron.[96] While this was calculated to improve the domestic iron industry it left the arms makers with no alternative to the use of American iron.

As might have been foreseen, it was not long before the War Department had cause to regret its wholehearted adoption of domestic iron. As early as February 1864 the uneven quality of the Trenton iron was being noised about among arms makers.[97] At the very time that imports of iron were being discontinued by the Springfield Armory the Commanding Officer complained to the Chief of Ordnance that the Trenton gun barrel iron was uneven in quality, although iron for other gun parts made by the same company remained satisfactory.[98] The Remington Company, another user of the Trenton iron, found inspection losses on contract barrels so great as to make it necessary either to abandon this iron or ask that the inspection be made less rigorous.[99] It is not improbable that the measure of security granted the Trenton Iron Co. by the War Department's contract and by the increased tariff had seriously interfered with its incentive to manufacture superior iron.

Nevertheless, in spite of the fact that unfavorable reports on the Trenton iron were received up to the end of 1864,[100] the Springfield Armory depended completely upon it, continuing to use it until well after the close of the war.[101] While the persistence of offers of foreign iron in the Armory's correspondence indicates that some entered the country throughout this period, the Civil War reinstated domestic iron in the Connecticut Valley small arms industry.

No such progress was made in developing a domestic source of supply of steel, nor was the use of steel in the gun extended. Steel continued to be among the most crucial and problematical of imported materials. Not only was the rate of exchange unfavorable to American buyers, but a new tariff applied in the summer of 1862 further raised the price of steel.[102] This was followed in the spring of 1864, as with iron, by a fifty per cent increase in duty.[103] England continued to be almost the sole source of steel, although German manufacturers solicited the gun makers' patronage.[104]

Domestic steel makers, however, persisted in their efforts to force their way into the industry. It was the firm belief of one American steel manufacturer that steel of a quality fit for rifle barrels could be made in this country, despite what he considered the great prejudice against it.[105] New Jersey and Pennsylvania steels were tested at the Springfield Armory, but while there was apparently no definite opposition to them, they were used there to only a negligible extent.[106]

The policy of the War Department towards domestic iron blocked progress in the wider use of steel in small arms, as the following extract from a letter from the Commanding Officer at the Springfield Armory to a steel importer shows:

We are now endeavoring to encourage the manufacture of American iron, suitable for gun barrels, in order that we may be independent of foreign nations for our supplies for this purpose, and we entertain the hope that American enterprises will soon afford us an iron equal to that brought from foreign parts. Until we have proved the futility of such efforts I do not propose to make any trials of other materials with a view to adopting them, unless they are of domestic manufacture. However I shall be glad to try some of your steel barrels and if you will furnish me with 500 barrels or tubes for making musket barrels, I will give you the price indicated in your letter.[107]

The Department's stand, while laudable from the point of view of achieving independence of foreign supplies, adversely affected the technical development of small arms in the course of the war.

The provision of sufficient anthracite coal presented another problem to arms makers. "There is quite a scramble for coal," one dealer commented in 1862, and this probably was typical of conditions throughout the war.[108] The price of coal becomes at this time exceedingly difficult to estimate since the dealers tended, as the war continued, to quote prices at certain shipping points only, rather than at places of delivery. This indicates that freight rates were undependable and that dealers preferred to have transportation costs transferred directly to the consumer.

Charcoal prices at this time are also difficult to ascertain. This was partly owing to the substitution of anthracite coal in much of the forging work and of other materials for case-hardening. Old shoes and leather scraps continued to be used for case-hardening.[109] A new product, "leather coal," made from partly burned leather, now appeared on the market.[110] Also a mixture of leather and crushed bone was burned and used for case-hardening.[111]

Musket stocks from Pennsylvania continued to be preferred to those from other regions, although the acute needs of arms makers caused Michigan, Illinois and Indiana to join New York, Pennsylvania and Ohio in the production of stocks.[112] One supplier in Cincinnati declared that more black walnut was cut in the three states of Ohio, Indiana and Illinois than in all the rest of the United States.[113] Yet Philadelphia remained the acknowledged center of the industry, although not all stocks shipped from that city originated in Pennsylvania. Many stocks from the West, admittedly of a poorer grade than genuine Pennsylvania stocks,[114] were shipped to Philadelphia, via Albany, worked up by the mills there and reshipped to the arms makers in New England and elsewhere.

While increasingly close work by machine tools reduced hand filing, as late as 1862 it was estimated at the Springfield Armory that 6,328 dozen files of various sizes and cuts were necessary for making 100,000 riflemuskets.[115] The Armory proceeded to lay in a large stock of English files, and by carefully husbanding them found it had on hand at the war's end more than 360,000—a number which Armory officials estimated was sufficient for more than twenty years of peace-time production.[116] Domestic file production increased during the war. It was carried on in Boston, Lawrence, Pawtucket and Newark, N.J.[117] R. Hoe & Co. of New York, printing press manufacturers, made files as well as machine tools.[118] Probably most of the domestic files were machine cut,[119] a fact which reduced their accuracy as well as their cost.

5. Interchangeability and Machine Tools.

The concentration of wartime production on a few types of standard weapons had a beneficial effect on the interchangeability of parts of these arms. The development of an extensive parts contracting system and the Springfield Armory's ability to supply contractors with specific parts, indicate that practical interchangeability had been achieved. Parts made in one factory could now be expected to fit reasonably well parts made in other factories. It was only with the Civil War that uniformity among the products of different arms plants became widespread.

The best means of assuring the general adherence of contractors to over-all specifications continued to be the use of model or pattern arms. Early in the war twelve pattern rifle-muskets were made for the contractors,[120] and in January, 1862, the Springfield Armory was directed to supply a perfect model arm to any manufacturer presenting a government contract.[121] Gages had become a recognizable item in the cost of arms. One manufacturer offered to make gages for testing the parts of the United States rifle-musket at $1,800 a set.[122] Gages of closer tolerance were used, although no radical changes in precision measurement were made. The Springfield Armory played a leading rôle in precision work, a fact of which the Ordnance Department was proud.[123] The Armory aided contractors with their specification problems, and even allowed them to use its tools and machinery to make their gages and patterns.[124]

Wartime expansion in the machine tool industry took place on a scale comparable to that in small arms in New England, New York, New Jersey and Pennsylvania.* Although not so many factories were equipped to make machine tools for gun manufacture as were prepared to make arms or their parts, concerns in such industries as watch-making, locomotive manufacture, and iron founding branched into the production of machine tools for small arms. In addition, several armories followed the example of the Colt Company and turned in part to machine tool manufacture.

Nevertheless throughout the war machine tools of any type were exceedingly hard to procure. Armories specializing in their manufacture as a sideline were in a very favorable position, and probably no large armory was incapable of making, certainly none was incapable of repairing and improving, some kinds of machines. But many had no facilities for the heavy operations of machine manufacture, such as casting, even if the

* Machine tool makers with whom the Springfield Armory dealt during the Civil War included the following:

The American Machine Works, Springfield; Pratt and Whitney, Hartford; Ames Manufacturing Co., Chicopee; Massachusetts Arms Co., Chicopee Falls; George Compton, Wood Light & Co., Sheperd Lathe Co., T. F. Taft, W. A. Wheeler, Bull & Williams, Worcester; American Watch Co., Waltham; Lowell Machine Shop, Lowell; John C. Whiten, Holyoke; Lamson, Goodnow & Yale, Windsor, Vt.; George W. Davis, Nashua, N.H.; Spencer Repeating Rifle Co., Boston; Parker Snow & Co. and N. C. Stiles Co., West Meriden; Birmingham Iron Foundry, Birmingham, Conn.; A. T. Cheney, Stafford Springs, Conn.; George S. Lincoln & Co., Woodruff & Beach Iron Works, and Colt Patent Fire Arms Manufacturing Co., Hartford; C. B. Rogers & Co., Norwich, Conn.; Pacific Iron Co. and Henry A. Chapin & Co., Bridgeport; J. Brown & Sharpe, Providence; R. Hoe & Co., Stover Machine Co., New York; Powers Rifling Machinery Co., and Trenton Locomotive and Machine Manufacturing Co., Trenton, N.J.; William A. Sellers & Co., Alfred Jenks & Son (Bridesburg Machine Works), Bement & Dougherty, Morris Tasker & Co. (Pascal Iron Works), Philadelphia.

required skilled labor could have been used for it without hampering arms production.

One aid to hard-pressed arms makers was the second-hand market in machines, brought about by plant failures, which occurred even at the height of the war. The opportunities here, however, were at the best limited, since second-hand machine tools were sometimes held for sale in a block, which prevented the manufacturer from buying those of which he had need.[125] Arms makers tried to overcome the machine shortage by borrowing or exchange between two armories. This practice, however, implied each armory's having an over-supply of machines desired by the other, and this was not common.[126]

The drafting of skilled workers delayed production in machine tool plants.[127] Delivery was at the best uncertain, and usually very slow. It might take two, three, or even six months to fill orders. A firm sometimes refused to accept orders.[128] Occasionally a given type of machine was so much in the experimental stage that the effort and expense of making it proved more than it was worth.[129] Yet hard-pressed arms makers could hardly have been expected to calculate probable costs accurately before placing their orders. Consequently financial loss occurred in connection with machine tool purchases.

No system of standardization had been found whereby the prices and quality of machines could be in some degree correlated. Such standardization would have been difficult to achieve, partly because of the difference in production of the various tool plants, partly because of the experimental stage in which many machines remained, and partly because of fluctuations in labor and material costs. But the lack of standardization made it possible for machine tools to be sold at grossly inflated prices.[130]

An example of the problems arising from this situation concerned fourteen rifling machines made by R. Hoe & Co. for the Springfield Armory in 1862. The Hoe Company presented a bill averaging about $2,400 for each machine, where two other manufacturers had charged $550 and $600 for such a machine, and the Armory itself had made some rifling machines at a cost of less than $1,000 each. The Commanding Officer, whose indignation was increased by the fact that the machines had been made from drawings and patterns the Armory itself had supplied, refused to accept the Hoe Company's bill. The initial blame in the matter rested with the Commanding Officer himself, for he had failed to set the price he would pay when authorizing J. T. Ames to negotiate for the machines. Ames, also, failed to specify the price. The Armory at first tried to shift the responsibility for this mismanagement to Ames, then agreed with the Hoe Company to submit the matter to arbitration. The arbitrators fixed the price of each rifling machine at $1,850, which was much below the price Hoe had asked, but still almost twice the cost of one of the next most expensive machines.[131]

Machine tool development in small arms during the war consisted more in the perfecting and elaboration of existing types of machines than in the invention of new ones. This was to be expected since machine tool builders were occupied with constructing machines of established kinds to meet the acute demand. The most notable improvement was the rolling of bayonet blades, which replaced the process of welding them by trip-hammer. Harvey Waters of Northbridge, Mass. derived this invention from the rolling of scythe blades, which he had done before the war. A heated steel rod was passed successively through six grooves of increasing length cut on the faces of two large, continuously revolving rollers. Waters estimated that four blades could be thus pressed into shape in a minute, and considered a day's work of the machine to be 1,500 blades.[132] Rolling greatly decreased the number of operations connected with making a bayonet blade, which in 1862, before the introduction of the machine, amounted to thirteen at the Springfield Armory.[133] Waters proposed to build and put in operation bayonet rolling machinery at the Armory, but, possibly because the process was still in the experimental stage, it was not until 1864 that a Connecticut firm, at a cost of $2,000, finished the machinery.[134] Waters himself continued rolling bayonets at his plant at Northbridge at least as late as 1864. The process had been introduced by that time at Remington's and at the Norwich Arms Co.[135]

Other important machines introduced in the war were broaches, also called drifting machines, for cutting irregular holes by forcing into the work a tapered tool with a file-like surface; and slotting machines, also called splining or mortising machines, which, through intermittent movement of the tool and the work, cut and gradually enlarged recesses or holes that could not be handled by milling or profiling machines.[136] These machines solved some of the most complicated problems of small arms manufacture, but they were not widely used until after the Civil War.[137] Machines for cutting the thread of the breech screw—one of the most difficult operations in gun making when done by hand—came into use at this time.[138]

The drop-hammer was thoroughly exploited by the Colt Company and at the Springfield Armory.[139] The Providence Tool Co. introduced in 1861 lead center bearings for turning barrels, which increased the smoothness of the operation and made barrels much more nearly cylindrical.[140] On the other hand, the war emergency caused some retrogression in techniques, especially where this resulted in lower cost. The Colt Company had been outstanding among New England arms makers in the use of drilled steel barrels for its revolvers. Ten days after the fall of Fort Sumter the company sent an agent to England to purchase barrel rolling machinery similar to that used at Springfield. The company reverted to iron barrels for its Springfield rifle-musket made on government contract.[141]

6. Labor.

Throughout the war the small arms industry was faced with an acute shortage of skilled labor. Its needs were far above peace-time labor requirements, and army enlistments and the draft, unrestricted by any public policy of deferment of essential workers, cut sharply into the supply of qualified workers. By July, 1863 the Springfield Armory had lost through the draft twenty-nine men from its forging department alone,[142] for not even the Springfield workers were exempt from military service. If they had been, it would have been on the basis of government employment rather than of essential work. But for a time the misconception prevailed that these workers could escape the draft, and men were tempted to leave other plants and flock to the Armory. An official of the Colt Company complained to the Commanding Officer at Springfield in 1862:

We are at this moment suffering serious inconvenience in consequence of a large number of men enlisting, others having to escape being drafted and many of our best men are applying to us daily for a certificate from us which will ensure their employment in your works.[143]

The parts contracting system only slightly alleviated the shortage of skilled labor by tapping the labor reserves of factories in other industries. Another partially effective expedient for meeting the labor shortage was extension of the inside contracting system. The Springfield Armory in the first months of the war attempted to increase the efficiency of its skilled labor by the use of contractors placed at critical points of production. This method had been initiated in barrel rolling in July, 1859, when William Onions, the master barrel roller, provided himself with two or three helpers whom he paid. It was extended in May, 1861 to other departments, until at last about sixteen master workmen were each paid several hundred dollars a month for work in which they were aided by helpers employed by them rather than by the Armory. Each master workman might have from one to eighteen helpers, although the usual number was two or three. The master workmen were not perhaps under specific contract with the Armory to turn in a fixed number of parts a month, yet for all practical purposes they were the equivalent of the contractors so characteristic of the industry. This system was used temporarily at Springfield in welding, grinding, boring and sighting barrels, in milling and turning bayonets, and in all sorts of forging; that is, with the exception of stocking—where the Armory was well equipped with excellent machines—in the most highly skilled occupations, where bottlenecks in production were likely to develop. A reflection of the Armory's swing into its full wartime pace was the discontinuance of the contract system in all occupations except barrel rolling at the end of August, 1862.[144]

Occupational specialization made more effective the work of men of limited skill Owing to the Springfield Armory's efforts to confine each man to one type of work the number of occupations in arms manufacture, exclusive of supervisory work, rose from 113 in January, 1860 to 390 in January, 1865 (Table 1, Appendix D). In the preceding forty years occupational specialization at the Armory had been limited by the number of workers employed; the number of occupations increased as employment rose, and fell with reductions in employment, regularly maintaining an average of about two or three men per occupation. At the height of the Civil War employment had risen to such an extent that despite the great increase in number of occupations there were on the average nearly six men working in each occupation.

Overtime work allowed a more complete use of the capacities of skilled workers as well as of plant facilities. Gas lighting was introduced at the Springfield Armory to permit night work in key departments, such as barrel welding and stocking.[145] Workers alternated on day and night shifts every month.[146] Night work continued at the Armory throughout the war,[147] but it is questionable if it added very much in the long run to total output. Until the last year of the war the Armory shops were dimly lit, owing to a faulty understanding of the needs of the plant. Gas lighting made the shops warm and the air bad, and the workers found night work a severe strain.[148] Spoilage rates must therefore have run high. The Colt Company's night workers at about this time were said to produce only about half of what the day workers produced because of the higher rate of spoilage and the heavy breakage of tools.[149]

No expedient could do much to relieve the shortage of skilled workers in the industry. The old habit of labor stealing, which had practically disappeared during the preceding twenty years, sprang up again. To combat this the gentlemen's agreement calling for written discharges was reinstated among arms makers,[150] but its terms were frequently violated.* The Springfield Armory itself, although officially deploring the practice, was not above accepting workers who had not received discharges from other arms makers.[152] On the other hand, the relatively abundant supply of skilled workers at the Armory was a source of continual temptation to other manufacturers with contract deadlines to meet. Some contractors, visiting the Armory shops on matters of business, took occasion to lure the workers there to their own plants. The Commanding Officer at times required con-

* Labor stealing on a limited scale only might severely damage an arms maker where much of the organization of a factory revolved about a few key workers. Thus one Springfield employer, threatened with the loss of a single planer who was being lured away by higher wages, complained that not only would the departure of so experienced a worker be an immediate loss to him, but that his successor might throw away hundreds of dollars worth of tools which the man in question had had made to "suit his own peculiar mode of doing things."[151]

tractors who had to go into the shops to agree beforehand not to employ any of the workmen there without his consent.[153]

Competitive bidding for labor moved men from one plant to another, and from that plant to a third, or perhaps back to the original factory. In response to a protest of the Springfield Armory Smith & Wesson declared in 1863:

We regret to learn that any unpleasant feeling exists on your part in reference to our hiring men from the Armory, and we feel confident that if you are in possession of the facts in the matter and will consider them for a moment, no such feeling can exist. It was not until after we had suffered great inconvenience from our men's leaving us to go to the Armory (of which fact we had sent word to the Master Armorer by Mr. Bush with a request that he would consider us in this respect) that we hired a single man from the Armory and then not with the slightest desire to retaliate but simply as a matter of necessity, and in proof of this would say, that among all the men that we have hired from the Armory, only two of them (we believe) were men who had not previously *left us* to go to the Armory.[154]

To reduce labor turnover the Springfield Armory required its employees to give two weeks' notice of their desire to leave, and limited hirings and firings to those ordered by the Commanding Officer.[155] The Armory also threatened covetous contractors with action by the government.[156] The private arms makers, on the other hand, had nothing but the moral strength of the gentlemen's agreement to protect themselves from labor stealing. The only effective limits to labor mobility were, on one side, the employer's unwillingness to pay wages above a certain level, on the other, the worker's dislike of constantly changing his residence, or his valuing long-time security higher than temporary wage increases.

The labor market for skilled workers remained tight throughout the war. As late as the spring of 1864 J. T. Ames complained of the difficulty of getting and holding good machinists.[157] It is true that in the summer of 1862 and again in the winter of 1864 the Springfield Armory received many applications for employment which it would not even consider. "I have fifty applications for every vacancy," the Commanding Officer wrote to an applicant in December, 1864,[158] and to another, two weeks later: "Applications for employment here are very numerous, & any vacancy may be filled at once from the twenty to forty applicants that apply daily."[159] But this superfluity of workers represented not skilled armorers but semi-skilled men, or those from other industries who hoped to escape the draft by entering the supposedly protecting walls of the Armory. At the very time when it boasted of the numerous applicants for its positions the Armory was searching desperately for skilled workers. It was in great need of stockers, finishers and tool makers at the end of 1864 and in the early months of 1865.[160] It sought workers as far away as New York and Philadelphia through the New York and Frankford Arsenals.[161] So acute was the shortage of highly skilled armorers that a firm specializing in importing raw materials for arms manufacture found it worth while to bring to America some highly skilled Swedish mechanics, paying them ten dollars each and their transportation.[162]

The strategic position of the arms workers on the one hand prevented the development of labor organization, and on the other brought about a sharp upward thrust in the general wage level. A rare case of organized action on the part of arms workers occurred in the spring of 1862, when the Commanding Officer at Springfield noted:

Our barrel rollers talk of making a strike, and if they attempt it, I shall replace them and to change all of them at the same time will cause some delay.[163]

The Armory thwarted this impending strike by securing a supply of ready rolled barrels, and by arranging with New York and Philadelphia firms for the employment of additional barrel welders.[164]

One manufacturer in 1863 described as a "commotion among the laboring classes" what was probably rather a general ill-defined restlessness of labor, born of wartime conditions.[165] In an effort to stabilize wages in different factories arms makers exchanged information concerning specific wage rates.[166] But little could be done to control the general advance in wages. Total earnings were increased not only by higher rates but also by the introduction of time and a half pay for night and Sunday work. Although the Armory officials at first tried to carry on night work with no increase in rates,[167] later all work carried on outside the usual hours was paid at time and a half rates at the Springfield Armory, in the Philadelphia region, and doubtless in the arms industry generally.[168] Even learners at the Springfield Armory received $1.25 a day,[169] a good wage prior to the war. Wages were so high at the Armory in 1862 that they attracted the attention of the Commissioner of Internal Revenue, but there is no indication that arms workers were ever actually subject to the wartime income tax.[170]

The Springfield Armory real wage index, plotted in Figure 1 of Appendix D, stops in 1861, since this is the year in which Cole's index of commodity wholesale prices in New York ends. However, some conclusions concerning the course of Springfield real wages during the war may be drawn from Moulton's index, from Wesley Mitchell's cost of living index, and from the figures of money wages at the Armory. The median values of Mitchell's annual cost of living index for the eastern United States, with 1860 as a base year, have been plotted in Figure 1 of Appendix D.[171]

If Springfield armorers' real wages continued to follow general real wages as closely during the Civil War as they had in previous years, it may be assumed that from 1861 to 1864 they dropped rapidly, descending more gradually between 1864 and 1865. Mitchell's cost of living index gives a rough mirror image of the curve of United States real wages. The cost of living index rose abruptly until 1864 and more gradually afterwards. Arms workers' mean money wages began a sharp ascent between 1861 and 1862, but leveled off in 1863 and 1864, at a time when the cost of living was rising rapidly. By 1865 mean money wages reached their highest point in the first seventy years of the nineteenth century. But their failure to rise appreciably in the middle of the war, which was the very time when the cost of living was rising most rapidly, makes it certain that armorers suffered a serious reduction in real wages.

During the war both the monthly mean wages of all Springfield workers and the monthly modal wages of the highly skilled increased by about $30. This was close to a sixty per cent increase in wages of the highly skilled workers. The rise in modal wages of the semi-skilled was much less marked. The Civil War in fact permanently widened the gap between the modal wages of these two groups, probably because the war emergency brought about improved factory organization as a result of which a somewhat poorer grade of labor than formerly required could be satisfactorily employed.

The productivity of barrel welders at the Springfield Armory shot up as rolling replaced the trip-hammer. In 1861 the average number of barrels rolled was about 20,000, nearly four times the peak of annual production with the trip-hammer (Table 5, Appendix D). Average annual production remained about 20,000 in 1862, but rose the following year and in 1864 approached 25,000. In the five months in which barrels were made in 1865 production lagged as the war neared its end. As output rose piece-rates for barrel rolling dropped sharply (Table 6, Appendix D). About ten or eleven cents was paid for rolling a barrel in 1861 and 1862, and only four and a half cents in the last three years of the war.

One effect of the war was to awaken arms makers to a keener sense of the financial loss involved in the incomplete utilization of the workers' time, and of raw materials and machinery. At the Springfield Armory workers absent without leave three times in one month were discharged.[172] Bookkeeping was increased to such an extent that most departments of the Armory were for the first time each supplied with a special clerk. The foremen were ordered to keep books of requisitions and of property consumed by the workers. Above a fixed percentage of allowable wastage, spoiled material was charged against the worker.[173] Oil, files and other tools used by piece-workers had to be bought by them from the Armory.[174] Tools or machines broken or damaged through carelessness or incompetence were repaired at the worker's expense.[175] In short, the war awakened the Springfield Armory to something like a modern understanding of plant efficiency.

CHAPTER XIV

POST-WAR ADJUSTMENT AND DEVELOPMENT

The Civil War left small arms manufacture not only with a productive capacity far greater than that necessary to satisfy peace-time demand, but also in a situation where production of arms at high cost was almost inevitable. Increased capitalization during the war demanded a very large increase in the volume of production to keep overhead costs at reasonable levels. High overhead costs resulted in part from improved standards of interchangeability, and from the introduction of breech-loading single- and multi-shot weapons, which were more expensive to make than the old muzzle-loading arms. In addition, the industry suffered from high direct costs. Raw material prices, if not above pre-war levels, were not appreciably below them. Labor continued a large item in the direct cost of a weapon.

In the half decade between the close of the Civil War and 1870 the small arms industry, by one means or another, resolved these problems, so that it could function efficiently in a peaceful economy. These few years of post-war adjustment are especially interesting because they highlight an ever present although frequently unrecognized aspect of small arms manufacture—that, by the very nature of the industry the unit cost of the product increases with time, subject to a limited extent only to reductions brought about by mass production. Firearms made over a period of time have never been truly identical. Newer arms, because of their increased intricacy of design and because they conform to more advanced standards of performance and of interchangeability of parts, have always been more expensive to make than earlier models. Mass production of arms reduces their unit cost, but cannot be carried on in the absence of machine tools, and these represent a form of investment on which the charges become oppressive when a large output is not maintained. A large volume of production of small arms has been limited by a government demand which was such that the industry could not meet all its costs in time of peace, by a foreign demand for military weapons which lasted only until foreign mass production was achieved, and by a civilian demand which has been somewhat inelastic and which in addition has frequently called for variety not entirely compatible with mass production. These conditions existed from the beginning of small arms manufacture, but they became particularly acute with the contraction of the industry in the years following the Civil War. Arms makers were forced at this time into diversification of production to maintain themselves, and since then, during peace, diversified production has been characteristic of the industry.

I. Costs

1. Overhead Costs.

Overhead costs in small arms manufacture were particularly heavy in the period following the Civil War. Capital in the entire industry rose from $2,500,000 in 1860 to $4,000,000 in 1870.[1] Certain Connecticut Valley small arms firms showed sharp increases in capitalization at this time. The capital of Smith & Wesson was more than quadrupled from 1860 to 1870, and that of Eli Whitney Jr.'s firm increased by more than fifty per cent. Winchester's capital in 1870 was eight times the size of the capital of its predecessor, the New Haven Arms Co., in 1860. The J. Stevens Arms Co. of Chicopee, with a capital of $30,000, was a war-fostered company. The Ames Company, on the other hand, had no larger a capitalization in 1870 than in 1850, and the capital of Colt and particularly of the Sharps Company was greatly reduced between 1860 and 1870.[2]

Part of small arms capital in 1870 no doubt represented paper assets only—the result of war-inflated prices of plant sites, building material and factory equipment. Part of it represented investments which had been necessary to meet the wartime demand for small arms, but which left the industry with an excessive productive capacity for peace-time demand. Part of this capital represented essential investment in expensive machine tools and equipment necessary to produce the more complicated and more highly perfected breech-loading single- and multi-shot arms.

The influence of overhead costs on unit costs at the Springfield Armory in the post-war period is shown in the cost series made by the writer and appearing in Table 1, Appendix B. In 1866 production at the Armory was drastically curtailed, and cost allocation among comparatively few units forced the average cost of the gun to almost $350. Production picked up in the next two years so that unit costs became fairly reasonable, but in 1869, when the Armory was converting two hundred rifle-muskets a day to breech-loaders,[3] production of new guns fell off and unit cost shot up.

Contemporary cost figures worked out by the Ordnance Department appear in the same table. Their uniformly moderate size leads to the conclusion that much overhead cost was not taken into account. This is in striking contrast to the care taken by Springfield Armory officials in the determination of direct costs. At this time no operation of any importance was undertaken without a painstaking preliminary determination of direct cost. Not only were direct costs carefully estimated on arms made at the Armory, but also on weapons of private manufacturers which the Ordnance Department planned to purchase.[4] There was in addition some awareness of overhead costs. Armory officials clearly recognized the nature of the cost involved in tooling up for the manufacture of new weapons or parts.[5] The belief of Major James G. Benton, Commanding Officer at the Armory, that a hundred guns a day was the smallest number which the Armory could make economically,[6] implies that he recognized the effect of overhead cost on unit cost.

Yet when it came to the actual allocation of costs, overhead costs were given a nominal valuation—usually being considered equal to direct labor costs—regardless of the number of weapons produced. For example, a detailed cost estimate of the Remington navy rifle made in 1870 at the Springfield Armory gave the total cost of the gun as $14.45. Figures were carefully worked out for the cost of materials, oil, coal, labor, assembling, proving and inspecting of the rifle. All other items of cost were accounted for by adding an amount equal to the direct labor cost—in this case $5.43.[7] This method of estimating overhead costs was apparently based upon some production norm which had perhaps never been attained at the Springfield Armory.

Increasingly high standards of interchangeability, as well as the development of more complicated types of arms with higher performance requirements, operated to keep overhead costs high. Reductions in tolerances and particularly the use of the micrometer caliper, introduced to the small arms industry in 1867 by Brown & Sharpe of Providence,[8]* stimulated the refinement of standards of interchangeability. Investment in machine tools continued to be an important factor making for heavy overhead costs. The Springfield Armory estimated at this time that to make a hundred rifles a day, as determined by actual practice, an investment of $177,700 in machines alone was required.[9] Remington, a very efficient firm, calculated that to make one or two hundred Remington breech-loading systems a day cost $30,000 to $35,000 in tools, machines, gages and fixtures.[10] This excluded the very considerable cost of machines for making barrels and stocks. Charles H. Fitch estimated in the early 1880's that the cost of machines in small arms manufacture, exclusive of engines and boilers, averaged from $300 to $350 per employee, with tools and fixtures adding half as much more to this amount.[11]

Invention increased necessary machine tool investment, on the one hand through mechanization of processes formerly carried on by hand. In the post-war period only one operation in small arms manufacture—the "truing" or straightening of the barrel—remained completely unmechanized.**

* The micrometer caliper worked on the principle of a screw with a thread of fixed pitch turning in a nut. When an object was placed within the caliper and the screw tightened the size of the object could be measured on a scale based on the number of turns made by the screw.[12]

** "Truing by shade" was the method used at this time. The workman looked through the barrel at a horizontal line in a framed glass or on a window pane, and noted the lines of reflection in the bore of the barrel. Where these deviated from the straight line he carefully hammered the barrel to straighten it. This process was made more difficult by the reduction in the bore of small arms. It was so laborious a technique that as late as 1880 the straightening of forty or fifty barrels was considered a fair day's work.[13]

On the other hand, invention increased the machine investment of existing armories by rendering obsolete earlier types of machines, not yet completely worn-out. Rolling barrels from drilled steel tubes became the standard method used in making barrels for military firearms, and replaced the process of rolling barrels from iron plates.[14] Rolling machinery for making steel barrels also drove out barrel boring machines, since the drilled steel barrels did not require boring.[15] In forging, the plank drop-hammer gradually replaced the earlier crank drop and screw drop. The plank drop was superior to other hammers in that the weight was attached to a vertical wooden plank which could be grasped at any point by two cast-iron rolls, one of which had its bearings in a movable yoke. This made it possible to adjust with comparative ease the force of the hammer blows of the plank drop.[16] For heavy forging the steam-hammer in some instances replaced the heavier drop-hammers.[17]

2. *Material Costs.*

The material cost of Springfield weapons remained at about one-half of the labor cost.[18] Most raw material prices continued close to their pre-war levels, or in some cases rose above them.[19] Prices of gun stocks found in the Springfield Armory records appear to have remained at their pre-war level only because in the post-war period the Springfield Armory data refer to resales of part of the Armory's large supply of gun stocks to other arms makers, rather than to purchases in the open market. The price of charcoal rose very sharply at this time, but against this must be set the great reduction in its use. After the war anthracite replaced charcoal in much case-hardening and annealing work.[20] Anthracite coal prices were near their pre-war level, as was the case with the prices of iron and imported steel.

Of special importance was the price of steel, since in the years following the Civil War steel replaced iron in many parts of the gun. A comparison of the two metals in connection with total unit cost of the gun cannot be made for lack of data on rates of waste in manufacture. At this time steel, either cast or decarbonized, was universally adopted for barrels.[21] The best steel for gun manufacture was imported, principally from England and to a limited extent from Westphalia.[22] Although the cost of steel barrels, including their machining, was slightly greater than the cost of iron barrels, this was more than offset by the higher quality and greater durability of steel barrels, and by the superiority of the rifling which they could take.[23]

For component parts steel cut steadily, though less spectacularly, into the industry's demand for iron. The Springfield Armory records show in this period reduced purchases of component iron and increased purchases of component steel. The Armory experimented with a so-called "homogeneous" iron, really a soft steel intermediate in composition between wrought iron and cast steel.[24] Steel was now used in the breech systems of guns, and for hammers, triggers, sights and pins, as well as for springs, bayonets and ramrods.[25]

3. Labor.

Labor continued to represent about two-thirds of the direct cost of weapons made at the Springfield Armory.[26] A considerable part of the labor cost covered charges for the services of men who worked by the day rather than by the piece. In a sense this represents overhead labor cost rather than direct labor cost, although as it would not have continued if the Armory had been completely closed down, in the narrowest definition of the term it was not truly an item in overhead cost. That this type of cost was a very important item in total labor cost may be gathered from the fact that the Ordnance Department attempted in the post-war years to institute an eight-hour day at all government establishments for the purpose of economy, rather than to improve the conditions of the workers. The War Department believed that the Springfield armorers, of whom over forty per cent worked by the day, while another twenty per cent worked both by the day and piece in 1870,[27] would produce as much in eight as in ten hours.[28] But shorter hours were strongly opposed by the workers, and the innovation resulted only in wearisome recalculations of pay rates by the federal authorities, and in the development of greater antagonism on the part of the Springfield workers than the Ordnance Department had ever encountered. The plan was a failure, and in the early 1880's the government tacitly admitted defeat by returning to the ten-hour day, which prevailed throughout the industry.[29]

The eight-hour day was established at the Springfield Armory by a federal law of 1868.[30] At first it hardly affected total average earnings since Major Benton, apparently failing to realize fully the relation of shorter hours to lower labor costs, paid time workers the same wages for eight hours as they had previously received for ten.[31] He reasoned thus:

With the piece workmen the decision of the Secretary of War [to reduce wages proportionately to the reduction in hours] will make but little difference as they have managed under the old tariff to make quite as much per day under the eight as under the ten-hour system, while I believe that the day workers have worked harder and more faithfully under the eight than under the ten-hour system. I am not of course prepared to say that they have accomplished fully as much for the Government.[32]

The War Department's intention of reducing daily wages by reducing hours threw the day workers into a degree of concerted action unusual in the history of the Armory. A committee of day workers visited other government establishments where the eight-hour day was in effect, and declared that the Springfield armorers alone were singled out for discrimination in connection with wage payments.[33] In protest of the government's action the day workers refused for several months to draw their wages.[34]

The law was referred to the Attorney General for clarification, and he affirmed the decision of the Secretary of War that the workers be paid for eight hours only. Benton had no alternative to making out the pay-rolls at the reduced hours. Many of the men accepted their pay under protest, on the ground that it did not represent a full return for the services rendered.[35] The piece-workers, through increased efficiency, managed to do the same amount of work, and therefore received the same wages for eight hours as they had for ten. Day workers who did not wish a reduction in total earnings were forced to work ten hours a day, and since the two types of employees often worked side by side in the shops, the shorter hours of the piece-workers aggravated the discontent.[36]

Owing presumably to political pressure the President in 1869 proclaimed that wages would not be reduced under the eight-hour law.[37] Later, on the advice of the Attorney General, the government compensated day workers with back pay.[38] The eight-hour day was unofficially repudiated in 1884 when, by special agreement, the Springfield workers signed up for a ten-hour day in spite of the law. All claims to back wages were paid at the same time.[39]

The eight-hour day had proved unenforceable because the workers resisted any substantial reduction in total earnings. It did not reduce the labor cost of arms, probably because whatever potential value it had in this respect was offset by the resentment of the workers. Benton declared that on the whole less work was done under the eight- than under the ten-hour system, and that only those piece-workers whose rates of pay had remained unchanged continued to do as much work as formerly.[40]

The high overhead costs of small arms manufacture were well recognized at the time, and were occasionally somewhat modified by arms firms through the exercise of ingenuity in production methods. The Remington Company, for example, was successful for some years after the Civil War in keeping unit costs at a minimum. It curtailed investment in equipment by using less highly specialized machine tools than those commonly found in large armories, and by introducing makeshift mechanical devices instead of elaborate ones. It ran machines beyond their capacity, a practice which, though apparently uneconomical, was probably in fact justified in view of the high obsolescence rate on such machine tools. This firm reduced standards of workmanship except in essential points. It used inside contracting, a system of labor which not only allowed the employment of very poorly paid workers, but also reduced to a minimum the form of overhead labor cost from which the Springfield Armory suffered at this time. The Springfield Armory in 1871 sent a foreman to study the Remington factory. The following extracts from his report to the Commanding Officer describe the methods by which Remington modified conditions of high cost:

Assembling. In assembling the arm they are particular on a few points only. They never alter the chamber or butt of barrel after it is screwed into the system; these points having previously been verified. Whatever adjusting is necessary between the butt of barrel and cam of hammer is done by grinding off the friction surface of breech block. . . . They prove the arm after the system is assembled, before applying the stock. They use a butt stock, which they slip on each one without fastening. This process provides against liability to injure the stock, as well as saves time, if it should be found necessary to readjust any part of the system.

Remarks. In looking over the works of Remington & Co. it is easily seen how they accomplish so much, with such limited facilities. In the first place, the work is all contracted to a few men. These men make their own tools and fixtures, furnish oil, emery, glue, buff leather, waste, or rags etc. for doing the work, and cleaning the machinery, hire and pay their own help, employing good mechanics only so far as it is necessary to assist them in making tools, keeping them in repair, and in doing such work as cannot be entrusted to cheaper help; a large proportion of their help being lads, from twelve to twenty years old. These boys with a little experience, can operate the machines and produce as much work as good mechanics. Then again these contractors are good mechanics, and are always studying to make improvements, by which they can simplify the operations, and produce more work, thus increasing their profits. In starting the milling of the frame, they had the same trouble that we found in getting power enough to drive the mills for the purpose of cutting out the inside. But instead of increasing the size and width of the pullies, they reversed the cone pulley on the counter shaft over the machine, thereby running two belts over the two larger grades of the cone they increased the power sufficiently to overcome the difficulty. I mention this as one of the many operations that might be cited, showing the simplicity with which they accomplish an object, and save expense. On their musket work as I said before, they are not particular except on a few working points. The general workmanship is rough and will not compare favorably with ours. They do but little filing, polishing the parts as they come from the milling and profiling machines, without removing the burrs. In milling and profiling the parts, they, in most cases force their machines beyond their capacity to do good work.[41]

II. Means of Adjustment to Peace

1. Plant Liquidation and Consolidation.

The problems of cost facing the industry in the post-war period in many instances brought about the liquidation of firms. The list of arms makers in Appendix A shows that from the end of the Civil War to 1870 inclusive twenty-seven New England firms disappeared. Of these eighteen were located in the Connecticut Valley. In the same period only eight New England arms manufacturers are listed as having begun business. Three of these were in the Valley.

As far as a given firm was concerned, consolidation might be tantamount to liquidation not only because of the loss of identity involved, but also because a firm's physical assets might cease to be used for small arms production. Consolidation however was an uncommon form of adjustment. It was likely to burden one firm with heavy additional costs incidental to the purchase of the other. Winchester alone was outstanding for its absorptive propensities. It bought the American Repeating Rifle Co. of Boston, formerly the Fogerty Rifle Co., in 1869, the Spencer Repeating Rifle Co. in 1870, the Adirondack Arms Co. in 1874, and the Whitney Arms Co. in 1888. The first two companies were purchased mainly to reduce competition. Winchester moved their machinery to New Haven and left their patents undeveloped.[42]

2. Contract Work and Government Purchases of Arms.

At the end of the Civil War the government would have completely abandoned the contract arms system except that the substitution of breech-loading for muzzle-loading arms was effected more expeditiously through the use of contractors. The parts contracting system and the manufacture of standard military arms on contract were discontinued. The replacement of muzzle-loading by breech-loading arms took place with great rapidity. By 1869 all the United States infantry, heavy artillery, and engineers were equipped with breech-loading Springfield rifles.[43]

The War Department used the breech-loading system developed by Erskine Allin, Master Armorer at the Springfield Armory, while the Navy Department adopted the Remington breech-loading system.[44] For this reason the Remington Company found itself in a strategic position in which it furnished the Navy with breech-systems for converting muzzle-loading arms at a price of $7.00 each.[45] The Colt Company transformed its revolvers to breech-loaders for the War Department for $3.50 per weapon.[46] These were the only firms which received government contracts in the post-war period for altering arms to breech-loaders.

Changes in ammunition offered another type of contract work. The Ames Manufacturing Co. and the Sharps Rifle Co. altered the Sharps breech-loading carbines, which the government had purchased in large numbers during the war, to take metallic ammunition. The change was made at a price of $4.50 per carbine, and at the rate of 2,500 arms per month.[47] The Sharps Company alone undertook to alter 30,000.[48] A comparatively simple type of alteration adapted government-owned Joslyn carbines to take center-fire instead of rim-fire metallic ammunition.[49]

A few firms received contracts or orders for patent arms. The War Department in 1868 adopted the Spencer carbine, made by the Spencer Repeating Rifle Co. of Boston.[50] The cavalry was armed exclusively with Sharps carbines, later considered by the Ordnance Department to be superior to the Spencer carbine.[51] A small but steady government demand called for Colt army revolvers, and, from 1866 onward, for the new Gatling machine gun, the manufacture of which was under the control of the Colt Company.[52] Some Smith & Wesson revolvers were also bought by the Ordnance Department.[53] The Ames Company continued to supply the government with sabers and bayonets.[54]

3. Manufacture of Sporting Arms.

Another means of adjusting to peace was through the production of sporting arms. This was a satisfactory solution for the small firm which could not hope to attain the quantity production necessary for foreign or United States government contracts, and which was not burdened with heavy capitalization. The manufacture of derringer, pepper-box and pocket pistols, sporting revolvers, target and sporting rifles, double and single barrel shotguns and patent arms of various types supported many arms makers in the years following the Civil War.[55] It may be assumed that manufacturers of this time not specifically designated in published lists of arms makers as producers of military weapons made only sporting arms. On the other hand it is significant that firms which manufactured military arms usually made sporting weapons as well. Remington was an exception, for its foreign trade was so heavy that it was not until the 1880's that the company paid much attention to civilian demand at home.[56] In the postwar period the Springfield Armory was the only armory in the Connecticut Valley restricted to the manufacture of military small arms.

The training in the use of small arms which a large proportion of the population had gained in the war probably increased public interest in sporting arms. A significant demand was from the western states and territories. Credit in the post-war development of the West has been claimed for the Colt revolver and the Winchester rifle.[57] These weapons were not competitive with each other; rather, each stimulated the demand for the other since they used interchangeable ammunition.[58]

4. Foreign Demand.

Active foreign demand offered a profitable, though transient, method of adjustment for the industry. The Ames Company supplied the French government with 100,000 sabers during the Franco-Prussian War, and the Turkish government with 236,000 in its war with Russia.[59] Smith & Wesson exhibited revolvers in the Paris Exposition of 1867, and as a result received large contracts from China, France, Great Britain, Japan, Russia, Spain and several South American countries.[60] This company contracted with the Russian government in 1870 for the production of 20,000 revolvers.[61] In the same year Winchester agreed to supply Turkey with 15,000 Winchester repeating rifles and 5,000 carbines. This contract had profitable ramifications, for by 1873 the company had a Turkish contract for 2,000,000 blank metallic drill cartridges and 50,000,000 Snyder rifle cartridges.[62] From the end of the Civil War to 1880 Winchester sold many arms abroad, chiefly to Australia, China, France, Japan, the South African Republics, Spain and Turkey. This firm also shipped much cartridge-making machinery to the Spanish and Turkish governments.[63]

The Colt Company's arms were eagerly sought by foreign governments. Between 1866 and 1867 an officer of the company noted efforts to purchase its arms by Egypt, England, Canada, France, Russia, Spain and Switzerland. Russia took especially large orders of Colt weapons. The company did not overlook the possibility of marketing its new Gatling gun in South America.[64] Pratt & Whitney, a machine tool company which was a direct offshoot of the Colt Company, made large quantities of gun machinery for European armories. Francis Pratt went repeatedly to Europe to take orders for gun machinery, receiving heavy orders from Germany during the Franco-Prussian War.[65] Even in the depression of 1873 Pratt & Whitney was fully occupied with foreign orders.[66]

The Providence Tool Co. in 1867 was engaged in making breech-loading arms for the Swiss government,[67] and in 1870 Martini-Henry rifles for Turkey.[68] Later it made Peabody rifles for Canada, Cuba, France, Mexico and Rumania.[69] The Peabody Rifle Co. of Providence furnished Turkey in 1870 with Peabody rifles.[70]

Although Remington lay outside the Connecticut Valley its post-war development is worth noting. It was a family-owned concern, incorporated in 1865 with a capitalization of $1,000,000, the plant and stock being valued at $1,500,000.[71] The post-war Remington breech-loader, designed by John Rider, was responsible for many of the company's foreign orders.[72] Samuel Remington, an owner of the firm, went to live in Europe as sales agent.[73] By 1870 the Remington Company had sold rifles, carbines and pistols to Denmark, Egypt, France, Japan, Rome, Spain and Sweden to the extent of nearly 385,000 stands of arms.[74] During seven months beginning in the fall of 1870 Remington shipped about 155,000 arms to France. Such was the urgency of this order that 1,300 to 1,400 workers were regularly employed at the factory, which ran twenty hours a day.[75] In 1870 Remington supplied Greece with weapons while at precisely the same time three or four New England firms were selling arms to Turkey.[76] Remington also made large quantities of metallic cartridges at Bridgeport for both Russia and Turkey, then on the verge of war with each other.[77] The company sold gun machinery to Denmark and Sweden in 1867, and in 1869 supplied Egypt with machinery for equipping an armory at Alexandria.[78]

The United States government itself became involved in foreign sales. The end of the war had left on its hands large quantities of weapons in various states of disrepair, and of new parts of arms. It disposed of the latter by selling them to American firms, which assembled them into complete weapons and resold them.[79] Many of the government's second-hand muzzle-loading guns were of comparatively little value to it in view of the adoption of breech-loading weapons. In 1869 at least 60,000 government-owned Enfield rifles were cleaned and repaired at the Springfield Armory and sold to the Turkish government.[80] 125,000 Springfield rifle-muskets had been sold by the government by the end of July, 1869.[81] Some of these presumably went to the frontier and to the states' militias, but it is not improbable that the majority were sold to dealers who shipped them abroad, or were perhaps sold directly to foreign countries. There was a demand in Germany for thousands of Springfield rifle-muskets which had been converted to breech-loaders.[82] The Turkish government was even hopeful of buying from the United States government machines and other equipment with which it could make two hundred Springfield muzzle-loading rifle-muskets a day.[83]

The federal government continued its policy of freely supplying foreign governments with information on weapons, no doubt partly in an effort to stimulate foreign demand. It is true that A. B. Dyer, Chief of Ordnance, disapproved of sending specimens of the new Springfield breech-loading rifle abroad with a view to its being adopted by foreign governments.[84] Nevertheless, in 1866 the Springfield Armory was directed to prepare 3,000 cartridges for the Russian government; two of the new Springfield breech-loaders, one of the Allin system and one an improvement on the Allin system, and 2,000 cartridges for the Danish government; and a new breech-loader with ammunition for the Swedish government.[85] Samples of the new government arms were also sent to the governments of Italy, Costa Rica and New Granada.[86]

The Swiss government sent an army officer to the United States in 1867 to investigate breech-loading arms, as Switzerland was preparing against a possible continental war. The Swiss consul general wrote the Commanding Officer of Springfield that any suggestions on breech-loading arms which the latter might have he felt confident would not be withheld from the officers of a "Sister Republic." He stated:

You have seen and experimented so much that we know nothing of, that to save us from going over the same ground you have, will alone be a most invaluable service.[87]

The United States obliged foreign governments in yet another way, by undertaking the inspection of private arms being made on foreign contract.[88] The foreign governments concerned paid the expenses of inspection, but the United States rendered them a valuable service in keeping these weapons up to the standards required by the federal government itself.[89]

5. Diversified Production.

Foreign demand, though of prime importance to the American small arms industry in the post-war period, could be depended upon only as long as other countries remained too retarded economically and technologically to produce arms in sufficient quantities to meet their military needs. Those American arms makers who shipped gun machinery abroad hastened the eventual independence of foreign countries. Sooner or later, therefore, the entire industry had to find some other means of adjusting to a peace-time economy. That which proved most satisfactory, with the high overhead costs established in the industry, was diversification of production. The industry was prepared to make metal products requiring a degree of accuracy in manufacture similar to that used for small arms—specifically, ammunition, sewing machines, small tools, machines and machinery, and later typewriters, bicycles and motorcycles.

Although Winchester produced $75,000 worth of cartridges in 1870 as compared with $300,000 of guns,[90] it is said that it was the company's ammunition business which enabled it to weather the lean years following the war.[91] The Ames Manufacturing Co. made a few swords on government contract as late as 1870,[92] but it was listed in that year by the United States Census of Manufactures as producing no small arms, but machinery and iron and brass castings.[93] As early as 1865 the Windsor Manufacturing Co., successor to Lamson, Goodnow & Yale, was making in addition to small arms, sewing machines, needles, saw milling equipment, rock drills, mining machinery and gun machinery.[94] The Providence Tool Co., another Civil War contractor, turned in part to sewing machine manufacture.[95] J. Stevens & Co. of Chicopee, a maker of sporting arms, put out in 1870 $20,000 worth of pistols and about $12,000 worth of calipers, dividers, levels, trusses and screws.[96] The Sharps Rifle Co. of Hartford in 1871 sold most of its plant to the Weed Sewing Machine Co.[97]

An outstanding example of the damaging effects of high costs in small arms manufacture, even in the presence of diversified production, is the post-war history of the Remington Company. Apparently as a result of a decline in foreign orders the company turned to the manufacture of sewing machines, cotton gins, farm implements, typewriters and other products. Its most successful project was the manufacture of the Remington typewriter. The company sold its interests in this typewriter to acquire enough money to reestablish its sporting arms business, but was unsuccessful and went into receivership in 1886. Two years later a large interest in the company was purchased by Hartley & Graham, a New York firm dealing in small arms. Through this firm Remington became connected with the Union Metallic Cartridge Co., a very successful Bridgeport company. Remington and the Union Metallic Cartridge Co. continued linked together through the interests of the Hartley family until both companies were purchased by Du Pont in 1934.[98]

A clear idea of the trend of peace-time adjustments of the industry may be gained by following the careers of certain of the outstanding mechanics and designers of this time. Frederick Howe, machine tool builder of Robbins & Lawrence, who worked later for North & Savage in Middletown, and for the Providence Tool Co., moved to Bridgeport in 1865 to work with Elias Howe on the latter's sewing machine. In 1869 he became associated with the Brown & Sharpe Manufacturing Co. and built milling machines.[99]

Charles Billings, who had worked at Colt's and Remington's in the Civil War, spent the years 1865-1868 at Hartford as the superintendent of the Weed Sewing Machine Co. For a few years thereafter he was associated with Christopher Spencer in working on the Roper gun at Hartford, but in 1872 the two men turned to drop-forging. Billings & Spencer became one of the pioneer firms in the die-forging of complicated shapes.[100] Sylvester Roper of the short-lived Roper Repeating Arms Co. of Amherst, went into the Hartford Machine Screw Co.[101] Francis Pratt and Amos Whitney, originally connected with the Colt Company, set up a plant for building machine tools in 1865 and four years later the Pratt & Whitney Company was formed.[102]

George A. Fairfield, a machinery contractor at Colt's in the late 1850's, turned to sewing machine improvements in 1865. He organized quantity production at the Weed Sewing Machine Co., becoming the company's president in 1876. Through Spencer he became interested in the development of Spencer's automatic screw machine. Out of this the Hartford Machine Screw Co. was developed in 1876. With the reduction in the demand for sewing machines which occurred about 1880 Fairfield encouraged the establishment of the Pope Manufacturing Co. in Hartford. This company was located in the plant of the Weed Sewing Machine Co., and produced bicycles and motorcycles.[103]

In the few years which followed the Civil War the small arms industry thus acquired a highly significant characteristic—that of diversified production. That this was essential to the economic health of the industry had been repeatedly demonstrated by the difficulties firms encountered in meeting for any length of time their full costs through the production of small arms alone. At first government patronage and an incomplete understanding of the elements of cost, and later heavy foreign demand prevented this fact from becoming fully apparent to arms makers. But the straits into which the industry was thrown as the result of wartime expansion followed by the practical evaporation of domestic demand at the close of the Civil War—tempered only by a surely declining foreign demand—emphasized the fundamental dilemma of the industry.

This dilemma was bound up with the nature of the demand for and the cost of small arms. On the one hand, American demand has never been so steady that a great volume of production could be absorbed for any length of time. On the other hand, heavy investment and the use of a considerable amount of highly skilled labor have been essential for factory production of small arms of generally acceptable design and quality. The resulting heavy overhead costs could be met satisfactorily only through distribution over a large volume of production, and this has been impossible to achieve in the absence of a steady demand. Manufacture of products requiring little extra investment and a similar type of labor, which could share overhead costs by eliciting other types of demand, possibly more elastic ones, has been the only satisfactory solution of this central problem of the small arms industry.

Conclusion

Basically, the economic problems of small arms manufacture in the Connecticut Valley have revolved about two peculiarities of the industry —its heavy overhead costs and the inelasticity of demand for small arms. These characteristics have accounted for much of its economic instability.

Small arms manufacture, quantitatively insignificant in American industry as a whole, has played a vital rôle in the development of machine tools, of precision measurement, and of interchangeability. Yet, so long as it restricted itself to the production of small arms alone, the industry never fully profited for a long period from the system of mass production to the development of which it has so heavily contributed. On the contrary, the narrow demand for small arms has made more oppressive the overhead costs arising from the methods of production essential for making interchangeable weapons.

The industry was brought into existence by the federal government only at the expense of great effort. The heavy investment required even for early nineteenth century arms manufacture necessitated continued government support in the form of advances on contracts and promises of future patronage. But the low price of contract arms, together with an inadequate understanding of the nature of cost, prevented the industry from becoming prosperous during the first thirty years of the century. With a new generation of arms makers in the three decades before the Civil War came not only the end of government domination, but also the discovery of foreign markets for small arms. Of great significance was the industry's manufacture of machine tools for sale, an important step towards diversified production.

The Civil War brought temporary profits to the industry, but overexpansion as well, so that the post-war period of readjustment was particularly difficult. Foreign markets became of prime importance, but their value lasted only so long as foreign countries delayed in developing their own small arms industries. The alternative means of survival was diversification of production—the manufacture of sewing machines, bicycles, motorcycles, motors, tools and other metal products—and this has been the line of development which in general the industry has since taken.

The future of small arms manufacture may perhaps be predicted with fair accuracy from the nature of the industry, and from its history both before 1870 and since that date. Heavy machine tool investment and highly skilled labor promise to continue to be necessary to the factory production of small arms. Normal demand for guns has shown no clear tendency towards expansion. In these circumstances diversified production of goods capable of eliciting more responsive types of demand has been the only means of abating the pressure of overhead costs. It seems probable that this will continue to be the means by which small arms manufacture will approach economic stability.

APPENDIX A

TABLE 1

Statistics of Small Arms Manufacture Derived from the United States Censuses of Manufactures, 1850–1940. Rounded Figures. See notes following Table 3

Census Year	Percentage Arms Workers Are of All U. S. Workers	Percentage Arms Capital Is of All U. S. Capital	Percentage Arms Value of Product Is of All U. S. Value of Product	Percentage Arms Value Added by Manufacture Is of All U. S. Value Added	Average Annual Wages of All U.S. Industry	Average Annual Wages of Arms Manufacture
1850	.16	.11	.10	.17	$ 247	$ 335
1860	.16	.25	.12	.11	289	431
1870	.16	.19	.13	.26	378	755
1880	.18	.29	.11	.20	347	699
1890	.06	.07	.03	.06	484	616
1900	.08	.07	.04	.07	437	567
1910	.09	.07	.04	.08	518	653
1920	.12	.12	.05	.09	1,158	1,181
1930	.08	—	.03	.06	1,315	1,347
1940	.06	—	.03	.06	1,153	1,369

TABLE 2

Statistics of the Small Arms Industry Selected from the United States Censuses of Manufactures, 1850–1940. See notes following Table 3

Census Year	All U. S. Arms Workers	All U. S. Arms Capital	All U. S. Arms Value of Product	All U. S. Arms Value Added by Manufacture
1850	1,547	$ 577,509	$ 1,073,014	$ 803,341
1860	2,056	2,512,781	2,362,681	985,768
1870	3,297	4,016,902	5,482,258	4,481,259
1880	4,862	8,115,489	5,736,936	3,877,910
1890	2,759	4,672,424	2,922,514	2,436,568
1900	4,482	6,916,231	5,444,659	4,139,238
1910	6,002	13,033,000	8,058,499	6,489,765
1920	11,287	51,917,782	30,181,370	22,567,586
1930	6,838	—	21,970,367	17,853,268
1940	5,001	—	17,711,651	14,659,095

TABLE 3

Concentration of Small Arms Manufacture in New England: Percentage Figures Based on the United States Censuses of Manufactures, 1850–1940. See below, Notes 1 and 2

Census Year	Percentage of U. S. Arms Workers Located in New England	Percentage of U. S. Arms Capital Located in New England	Percentage of U. S. Arms Value of Product Located in New England
1850	34.07	37.17	35.69
1860	55.20	82.07	65.07
1870*	67.45	62.49	60.66
1880	84.06	88.32	80.53
1890†	84.52	80.74	81.11
1900‡	61.29	68.79	62.54
1910§	67.14	88.24	82.86
1920	60.37	68.32	71.48
1930	68.31	—	72.39
1940	71.89	—	72.74

* Data compiled from the Compendium of the 1870 Census, as they were not tabulated separately in the 1870 Census of Manufactures.

† Excludes one arms establishment in New Hampshire, as the census does not publish regional statistics which might reveal confidential information. This establishment appears in the general statistics, and, therefore, in Tables 1 and 2.

‡ Excludes one establishment in Maine for the same reason.

§ Regional, but not general statistics for small arms for this year were lumped together with those for ammunition manufacture. They have been separated according to a method worked out by the writer and described in detail in the notes following this table.

Notes on Tables 1, 2 and 3

1. United States Armories.

The Census Bureau apparently does not include in the Censuses of Manufactures data on the three federal armories—the Springfield Armory, the Harper's Ferry Armory (destroyed in the Civil War), and the Rock Island Arsenal—with sufficient regularity to take them into account in these general and derived statistics. Material on the Springfield Armory, at least, was collected by the enumerators for the earlier Censuses, but was not published.

2. Notes on Statistics of New England Small Arms Manufacture in 1910. (Table 3).

As regional statistics for small arms were lumped with those for ammunition in 1915 proportions between arms statistics alone and arms and ammunition statistics were calculated by the writer for 1900 and 1920, and the mid-points of the differences of the respective proportions were taken as probable proportions for the two types of statistics in 1910. The statistics were calculated separately for Connecticut and Massachusetts—the only New England states listed in the regional figures for small arms manufacture—because the degree of importance of small arms in the combined figures for arms and ammunition were very different in the two states. The steps by which detailed statistics for 1910 were calculated are worked out below.

Statistics for 1900

	Small Arms Manufacture	Small Arms and Ammunition Manufacture	Per Cent Small Arms Is of Small Arms and Ammunition Manufacture
Capital			
Conn.	$ 2,825,000	$ 7,606,000	37.14
Mass.	1,933,000	1,933,000	100.00
Number of workers			
Conn.	1,444	5,278	27.36
Mass.	1,603	1,603	100.00
Value of Product			
Conn.	$ 1,477,000	$11,301,000	13.07
Mass.	1,928,000	1,928,000	100.00

(No ammunition manufacture in Massachusetts in 1910)

Statistics for 1920

	Small Arms Manufacture	Small Arms and Ammunition Manufacture	Per Cent Small Arms Is of Small Arms and Ammunition Manufacture
Capital			
Conn.	$30,174,424	$74,364,002	40.58
Mass.	5,294,048	12,422,117	42.62
Number of Workers			
Conn.	4,561	17,050	26.75
Mass.	2,253	4,702	47.92
Value of Product			
Conn.	$15,928,706	$55,925,651	28.48
Mass.	5,644,510	11,605,900	48.63

Derived Statistics for 1910*

	Small Arms Manufacture	Small Arms and Ammunition Manufacture	Per Cent Small Arms Is of Small Arms and Ammunition Manufacture
Capital			
Conn.	$ 8,425,000	$21,681,000	38.86
Mass.	3,076,000	4,313,000	71.31
Number of Workers			
Conn.	2,309	8,533	27.05
Mass.	1,721	2,327	73.96
Value of Product			
Conn.	$ 4,144,000	$19,946,000	20.78
Mass.	2,533,000	3,408,000	74.31

* Italic figures are calculated from the percentages and the statistics of small arms and ammunition manufacture for 1910. Percentages for 1910 are the mid-points between the corresponding percentages of 1900 and 1920.

TABLE 4

Data on Connecticut Valley Small Arms Manufacturers Selected from the United States Censuses of Manufactures of 1810 and 1822, from the Reports of the Federal Census Enumerators, and from Other Sources. (Complete list of Sources follows Table)

Census Year and Name of Firm or Manufacturer	Capital	Number of Workers	Annual Wages	Quantity and Type of Product	Value of Product
Connecticut—New Haven County					
1810					
Eli Whitney	$ —	—	$ —	2,000 guns	$ 26,000
1822					
Eli Whitney	50,000	53	15,000	—	26,000
1832					
1839					
1850					
Eli Whitney Jr.	50,000	80	28,800	3,400 guns, v. $44,200; machinery, v. $2,000	46,000
1860					
Eli Whitney Jr.	50,000	70	29,900	4,500 pistols, 1,500 rifles	—
New Haven Arms Co. (later Winchester)	50,000	138	39,000	guns and pistols	25,000
Frank D. Bliss	8,000	16	9,600	3,000 pistols	18,000
Thomas J. Stafford	6,000	9	4,800	automatic pistols	15,000
1870					
Eli Whitney Jr.	76,000	86	67,765	11,318 revolvers and double and single guns; gun parts	80,106
Winchester	400,000	205	213,000	15,000 guns, v. $300,000; 7,000,000 cartridges, v. $75,000	375,000
Connecticut—Middlesex County					
1810					
Simeon North*	—	—	—	1,000 guns	10,750
1822					
R. and J. Johnson	30,000	30	9,000	rifles	17,000
Simeon North	75,000	60	20,000	pistols	40,000
Nathan Starr	50,000	15	7,500	swords	15,000
1832					
Johnsons, Starr and North	106,200†	90	average wage $1.50 a day	5,000 muskets and rifles	60,000
1839					
Simeon North*	50,000	60	—	carbines, muskets and pistols	—
1850					
North & Savage	50,000	30	18,720	1,500 guns	26,250
H. Scovil Estate	1,200	3	780	1,000 pistol barrels	2,600
1860					
John D. Couch	500	3	1,200	800 pistols, v. $1,600; miscellaneous products, v. $400	2,000
1870					
Connecticut—Hartford County					
1810					
Unknown firm or firms	—	—	—	1,400 guns	12,000
1820					
1832					
1850					
Colt	60,000	150	84,000	9,000 pistols	150,000
Ezra Clark	1,500	19	6,840	rifles	1,500
1860					
Colt	1,250,000	369	184,560	45,000 firearms, v. $575,000; machinery, v. $25,000	600,000
Sharps Rifle Co.	500,000	300	144,000	10,000 firearms, v. $300,000; machinery, v. $25,000	315,000
1870					
Colt	1,200,000	1,060	750,000	12,000 pistols, v. $120,000; 30,000 guns, v. $660,000; 100 cannon, v. $150,000; 200 machines, v. $600,000	1,530,000
Sharps Rifle Co.	125,000	250	96,000	30,000 rifles	600,000
Roper Sporting Arms Co.	12,000	4	1,350‡	500 rifles	5,000
Massachusetts—Hampden County					
1810					
Springfield Armory	—	—	—	11,240 muskets	134,000
1822					
1832					
1845					
Springfield Armory	727,000	250	—	12,000 muskets	144,000
Two unnamed firms	25,200	49		5,100 pistols, rifles, carbines, fowling pieces	45,800

TABLE 4—*Continued*

Census Year and Name of Firm or Manufacturer	Capital	Number of Workers	Annual Wages	Quantity and Type of Product	Value of Product
1850					
Springfield Armory	886,700	320	161,000	10,155 muskets and muske-toons and appendages	291,000
Ames Mfg. Co.	250,000	159	72,000	50 cannon, v.	17,000
				2,800 swords, v.	15,410
				machinery	
					32,410
Massachusetts Arms Co.	35,000	30	12,000	revolvers, v.	4,500
				machinery, v.	12,500
					17,000
1860					
Ames Mfg. Co.	—	200	108,000	—	245,000
Massachusetts Arms Co.	70,000	75	262,500	firearms and machinery	112,000
J. Warner	12,000	24	7,600	3,000 pistols	27,000
Smith & Wesson	40,000	57	38,832	8,400 firearms	75,600
				ammunition	12,000
					87,600
1870					
Ames Mfg. Co.	250,000	—	—	machinery, v.	300,000
				iron castings, v.	60,000
				brass castings, v.	10,000
				jobbing & repairing	50,000
					420,000
Smith & Wesson	170,000	187	172,000	6,000 revolvers v.	500,000
J. Stevens	30,000	58	20,000	7,000 pistols, v.	20,000
				5,000 calipers and dividers, v.	2,500
				4,000 levels, v.	8,000
				1,000 trusses, v.	1,000
				40,000 screws, v.	350
				jobbing	500
					32,350
Massachusetts—Berkshire County					
1810					
Lemuel Pomeroy	—	—	—	1,800 muskets	20,000
1822					
Lemuel Pomeroy	30,000	35	12,000	2,000 muskets	—
1832					
Lemuel Pomeroy	35,000	34	$1.12½ per day	2,200 muskets	26,400
1845					
Pomeroy and a gunsmith	30,500	33	—	1,500 muskets; 10 rifles; 20 fowling pieces; 10 pistols	23,100

* This manufacturer unnamed in the original data, but clearly North.
† Includes $1,200 listed as investment in machinery or tools.
‡ Wages paid for ten months. This company was in poor condition.

List of Sources for Table 4

Tench Coxe, *A Statement of the Arts and Manufactures of the United States of America for the Year 1810,* Tabular Statement, Parts I and II.
Digest of Accounts of Manufacturing Establishments in the United States and of their Manufactures, 1822.
Louis McLane, *Documents Relative to the Manufactures of the United States, Collected and transmitted to the House of Representatives, in compliance with a resolution of Jan. 19, 1832, by the Secretary of the Treasury.*
R. R. Hinman, *Statistical Tables and Abstracts of Conditions and Products of certain Branches of Industry in Connecticut, November 1, 1838 to February 1, 1839, prepared from the Returns of the Assessors.*
John G. Palfrey, *Statistics of the Condition and Products of Certain Branches of Industry in Massachusetts, for the year ending April 1, 1845.*
Federal Census Enumerators' reports for Hartford, Middlesex and New Haven Counties, Connecticut and for Hampden County, Massachusetts, for the Censuses of Manufactures of 1850, 1860 and 1870.

A List of New England Small Arms Manufacturers and Gunsmiths, 1770–1870

See notes at end of Table

* indicates an arms manufacturer

*Albertson, Douglas & Co., New London, Conn., about 1840–1860.
Alden, E. B., Claremont, N.H., 1863–1868.
Allen, Amasa, Walpole, N.H., 1799–1801. Associated with Samuel Grant and Joseph Bernard in 1798 on a federal musket contract.

Allen, Brown & Luther, Worcester, Mass., 1852.

Allen, C. B., Springfield, Mass., 1836–1841. Includes Allen & Falls.

*Allen & Thurber, Grafton, Mass., 1832–1842; Norwich, Conn., 1842–47; Worcester, Mass., 1847–1856; Allen & Wheelock, Worcester, 1856–1865; continued in Worcester after Ethan Allen's death as Forehand & Wadsworth, 1871–1890; total business 1832–1890.

Alsop, C. R., Middletown, Conn., 1859–1866.

*American Arms Co., Chicopee Falls, Mass., in Civil War.

*American Arms Co., Boston, Mass., about 1870–1893.

*American Nut & Arms Co., Boston, Mass., 1868–1870.

Ames, David, Bridgewater, Mass., 1790.

Ames, John, Bridgewater, Mass., 1798.

Ames, Nathaniel, Boston, Mass., 1800.

*Ames Manufacturing Co., Chicopee, Mass., 1832–1880's.

Andrus & Osborn, Canton, Conn., in Civil War.

*Aston, Henry, Middletown, Conn., about 1843–1852.

Aston, William, Middletown, Mass., about 1854.

Austin, Thomas, Charlton, Mass., Committee of Safety, (i.e., Revolution).

Babcock, Moses, Charlton, Mass., 1777–1781.

*Bacon Arms Co., Norwich, Conn., 1852–1888.

Baggett, Elijah, Attleboro, Mass., contractor of 1798.

Bailey, Nathan, New London, Conn., 1776–1779.

Baldwin, Elihu, Branford, Conn., Committee of Safety.

*Ballard Arms Co., Worcester, Mass., Civil War.

*Ballard & Fairbanks, Worcester, Mass., 1870.

*Ball & Williams, Worcester, Mass., 1861–1866.

Barnes, Thomas, North Brookfield, Mass., active to 1800.

Barret, Samuel, Concord, Mass., 1775 and later.

Barstow, J. and C. C. Exeter, N. H. Contractors of 1808.

Bartlett, Asher and Pliny, Springfield, Mass. Contractors of 1808.

*Bay State Arms Co., Uxbridge, Mass., about 1870–1875.

Beckley, Elias, near Berlin, Conn., flintlock period, died 1816; son, Elias Jr. carried on business, died 1828.

Bell, Josiah, Walpole, N. H., 1799–1801.

Bemis, Edmund, Boston, Mass., active 1746–1785.

*Beutter Bros., New Haven, later Meriden, Conn., before and after 1850.

Bidwell, Oliver, Hartford, active 1756–1810.

Bisbee, D. H., Norway, Me., 1835–1860.

Bishop, Henry, Boston, Mass., before and after 1847.

Bishop, William, Boston, Mass., 1818–1860.

Blackman, Elijah, Middletown, Conn., Committee of Safety.

Blaisdel, Jonathan, Amesbury, Mass., Committee of Safety.

Bliss, New Haven, about 1856–1863; probably the same as Bliss & Goodyear.

Boardlear, Samuel, Boston, Mass., 1796.

*Boyd Breech-loading Arms Co., Boston, Mass., 1870–1872.

*Brand Arms Co., Norwich, Conn., 1866–1875.

*Bristol Fire Arms Co., Bristol, Conn., 1855–1859.

Brown, Elisha, Providence, R. I., active 1799–1801.

*Brown Manufacturing Co., Newburyport, Mass., 1869–1873. Took over Merrimac Arms & Manufacturing Co.

*Buckland, E. S. & Co., Springfield, Mass., 1866–1868.

Buell, Elisha, Hebron, Conn., 1776; probably the same Elisha Buell of Marlborough Conn., 1797 to 1808 at least.

Buell, Enos, son of Elisha, succeeded father about 1825–1850.

Burnham, Elisha, Hartford, cleaned and repaired guns for Connecticut, 1777, accounts rendered 1781.

*Burnside Rifle Co., Providence, R. I., organized 1860 by creditors of Bristol Fire Arms Co., made government arms up to 1865.

Chase, Anson, Enfield, Mass., before 1830; Hartford, 1830–1834; later New London, Conn.

Chipman, Darius, Rutland, Vt., active 1798–1801; Contractor associated with Royal Crofts, Thomas Hooker and John Smith.

Chipman, Samuel, Vergennes, Vt., associated with Thomas Towsey in contract of 1798.

Clark, Carlos, Windsor, Vt., 1856–1868.

Clark, Ezra, Hartford, Conn., 1850.

Clark, Joseph, Danbury, Conn., contractor of 1798.

Clement, W. T., associated with W. S. Norris in Springfield in Civil War.

Cobb, Nathan and Henry, Norwich, Conn., contractors of 1798.

Coleman, H., Boston, Mass., before and after 1847.

Collier, Elisha, Boston, Mass., 1807–1812.

Colt Patent Fire Arms Manufacturing Co., Hartford, Conn., 1848 to present.

Connecticut Arms Co., Norfolk, Conn., about 1864.

Continental Arms Co., Norwich, Conn., 1866–1867.

Copeland, T., Worcester, Mass., about 1860.

Cowles and Smith, Chicopee, Mass.; 1868, W. L. Cowles, Chicopee, 1870.

Cummings, Charles, A., Worcester, Mass., 1866–1869, later Cummings & Lane, Worcester, 1869–1871.

Curtis, Jesse, Waterbury, Conn., associated with Thomas Fancher in work for Committee of Safety.

Darlington, Barton and Benjamin, Bellingham, Mass., and Woonsocket, R.I., 1836.

Davenport, W. H., Firearms Co., Norwich, Conn., about 1855–1910.

Davis, N. R., & Sons, Assonet, Mass., established 1853.

Denslow & Chase, Hartford, Conn., about 1847.

Dewarson, R., Boston, Mass., before and after 1847.

Dewey, Samuel, Hebron, Conn., 1775–1776.

Dickenson, E. L., Springfield, Mass., 1870.

Dike, Bridgewater, Mass., 1775.

Dwight, H. D., Belchertown, Mass., before and after 1847.

Eagle Manufacturing Co., Mansfield, Conn., Civil War.

Earl, Thomas, Leicester, Mass., 1770–1776.

Eaton, J., Boston, Mass., before and after 1847.

Eggers, Samuel, New Bedford, about 1840–1865.

Elliot, Matthew and Nathan, Kent, Conn., contractors of 1798.

Eli, Martin, Springfield, Mass., about 1770–1775.

Emmes, Nathaniel, Boston, Mass., 1796–1825.

Fairbanks, A. B., Boston, Mass., before 1841. Died 1841.

Falley, Richard, Montgomery and Westfield, Mass., active 1774–1801 and later.

Flagg, B. & Co., Millbury, Mass., 1849.

Fogerty Repeating Rifle Co., Boston, Mass., about 1867; changed to American Repeating Rifle Co.; sold to Winchester 1869.

French, Blake and Kingsley, Canton, Mass., contractors of 1808.

Gibbs, Tiffany & Co., Sturbridge, Mass., about 1820–1850.

Gilbert, Daniel, North Brookfield, Mass., 1798–1808.

Goodwin, Jonathan, Lebanon, Conn., Committee of Safety.

Greene Rifle Works, Worcester, Mass., 1864.

Groot, Henry, Pittsfield, Mass., 1866–1868.

Hall, John, Yarmoth, Me., until 1816; later at Harper's Ferry, Va.

Hall, Samuel, East Haddam, Conn., Committee of Safety.

Hall, Thomas, Carlotta, Vt., Committee of Safety.

Hanks, Uriah, Mansfield, Conn., Committee of Safety.

Harrington, Luke, Sutton, Mass., before and after 1832.

Harris, Luke, Sutton, Mass., 1832.

Harwood, Nathaniel, Brookfield, Mass., about 1825–1840.

Hill, Thomas, Carlotta, Vt., 1790–1810.

Hilliard, D. H., Cornish, N. H., about 1860–1880.

Holden, C. B., Worcester, Mass., about 1864–1868 and later.

Hopkins & Allen, Norwich, Conn., 1868–1915.

Howard Bros., Whitneyville and New Haven, Conn., 1866–1869.

Hulett, Phineas, Shaftbury, Vt., 1840–1865.

Huntington, Gurden, Walpole, N. H., contractor associated with J. Livinston, Josiah Bellows, David Stone, 1799–1801.

Huntington, Hezekiah, Windham, Conn., Committee of Safety, 1775–1778.

Hurd, Jacob, Boston, Mass., 1816–1825.

*Jenks, Stephen, North Providence, and Pawtucket, R. I.; active about 1770–1814 and after; worked with Hosea Humphreys in 1798.

*Johnson, R. and J. D., Middletown, Conn., active 1820–1854.

*Johnson & Smith, Middletown, Conn., 1866–1868.

Johnson, William, Worcester, Mass., 1787.

Jones, Amos, Colchester, Conn., 1774–1777.

*Joslyn Fire Arms Co., Stonington, Conn., about 1858–1865.

*Kellogg Bros., New Haven, Conn., 1850–1890.

*Kendall, N. & Co., Windsor, Vt., 1835–1843; Robbins, Kendall & Lawrence, 1844–1847; Robbins & Lawrence, 1847–1855; Lamson, Goodnow & Yale, 1855–1864; E. G. Lamson & Co., 1864–1867.

Kingsley, Adam, Bridgewater, Mass., contractor associated with J. Perkins in 1798.

Lamerson & Furman, Windsor, Vt., about 1841.

Lamson, J., Bennington, Vt., Civil War.

Lane & Read, Boston, Mass., 1826–1836.

Langdon, W. C., Boston, Mass., 1857–1868.

Langdon, W. G., Boston, Mass., Civil War.

Lautz, Becket & Minet, Boston, Mass., 1868.

Lawrey, David, Wethersfield, Conn., 1777.

Leonard, A. and Sons, Saxons River, Vt., about 1840–1860.

Leonard, Eliphalet, Easton, Mass.; Committee of Safety; also before and after 1800; his son, Jonathan, started a gun forge at Stoughton, Mass., later Canton, in 1798; business of son and father about 1775–1820.

Leonard, Charles, son of Jonathan, Canton, Mass.; associated with R. Leonard, as contractors of 1808.

Lewis, Joseph, Groton, Conn., 1780.

*Lindsay, J. P., Manufacturing Co., New Haven, Conn., 1864–1869.

*Lombard, H. C. & Co., Springfield, Mass., 1860–1861 and later.

*Lovell Arms Co., Grover & Lovell, J. P. Lovell & Co., Boston, Mass., total business 1844–1887.

*Lowell Arms Co., Lowell, Mass., about 1864–1868; formerly Rollin White Co.

Mansville, Cyrus, New Haven, Conn., 1866–1867.

Mason, William, Taunton, Mass., Civil War.

*Massachusetts Arms Co., Chicopee Falls, Mass., 1850–1880.

*Maynard Gun Co., Chicopee Falls, Mass., 1857 to early Civil War.

McCartney, Robert, Boston, Mass., 1805–1815.

McKenny & Bean, Biddeford, Me., 1866–1871.

*Meriden Fire Arms Co., Meriden, Conn., Civil War.

*Meriden Manufacturing Co., Meriden, Conn., Civil War.

*Merrimac Arms and Manufacturing Co., Newburyport, Mass., 1867–1869.

Merritt, Allan, East Randolph, Mass., about 1855.

Merritt, John, Boston, Mass., before 1789 and after 1798.

Miller, S. C., New Haven, Conn., 1855.

Miller, W. D., Pittsfield, Mass., about 1850.

Moore, William, Windsor, Conn., 1860.

Morgan & Clapp, New Haven, Conn., 1864–1866.

Morgan, Lucius, New Haven, Conn., 1858–1877.

Morrill, Mosman and Blair, East Amherst, Mass., 1836–1838.

Morse, Thomas, Lancaster, N.H., about 1866–1890.

Mowry, Norwich, Conn., Civil War.

*Muir, W. & Co., Windsor Locks, Conn., Civil War.

Mulloy, N. P., Worcester, Mass., 1869–1871.

Munson, Morse & Co., New Haven, Conn., 1856–1862.

Newton, P. S., Hartford, Conn., 1870.

Nichols, Jonathan, Vergennes, Vt., contractor of 1798.

North & Couch, Middletown, Conn., about 1860.

*North, H. S., Middletown, Conn., 1852.

*North, Simeon, Middletown, Conn., 1799–1852.

*North & Savage, Middletown, Conn., 1850–1859.

*Norwich Arms Co., Norwich, Conn., Civil War.

Orr, Hugh, Bridgewater, Mass., about 1737–1798.

Osborn, Lott, Waterbury, Conn., 1776–1777.

Osborne, H., Springfield, Mass., before and after 1812–1821.

Page, John, Preston, Conn., Revolution.

*Parker, Snow & Co., Meriden, Conn., Civil War and before and after 1868.

Peck, Abijah, Hartford, Conn., contractor of 1798.

Perkins, James, Luke and Rufus, Bridgewater, Mass., 1799–1812.

Phelps, Jedediah, Lebanon, Conn., Committee of Safety.

Phelps, Silas, Lebanon, Conn., 1770–1777.

*Plants Manufacturing Co., New Haven, Conn. about 1863.

*Pomeroy, Lemuel, Northampton and Pittsfield, Mass., (mostly the latter), 1790–1845.

*Pomeroy, Seth, Northampton, Mass., 1770–1777 and earlier.

*Pond, L. W., Worcester, Mass., before 1863 to about 1870.

Prescott, E. A., Worcester, Mass., 1860–1874.

*Providence Tool Co., Providence, R.I., about 1850–1917.

Putnam, Enoch, Granby, Mass., Committee of Safety.

Quinby, Denis, Northfield, Vt., 1864–1868.

Rhodes, William, Providence, R. I., associated with William Tyler as contractor of 1798.

Richardson, Joel, Boston, Mass., 1816–1825.

Riggs, B., Bellows Falls, Vt., before and after 1850.

Ripley Bros., Windsor, Vt. 1835.

*Roper Repeating Rifle Co., Amherst, Mass., later Hartford, Conn., about 1867–1875.

Rowe, A. H., Hartford, Conn., 1864.

*Savage Revolving Fire Arms Co., Middletown, Conn., about 1860–1864.

Schaefer, William, Boston, Mass., 1853–1870.

Schenkl, J. P., Boston, Mass., 1850–1854.

Schubarth, C. D., Providence, R. I., Civil War.

Seabury, J. & Co., Southbridge, Mass., 1861.

Sever, Joseph and Shubabel, Framingham, Mass., Committee of Safety.

Seward, Benjamin, Boston, Mass., 1796–1803.

*Sharps Rifle Manufacturing Co., Hartford, later Bridgeport, Conn., 1848–1881.

Slocum, Harding, Worcester, Mass., 1820 and later.

Smart, Eugene, Dover, N. H., about 1865–1890.

Smith, Jeremiah, Lime Rock, R. I., 1770.

Smith, Major & Son, Westville, New Haven, Conn., 1866–1868.

*Smith & Wesson, 1855 to present, Springfield, Mass.

*Snow & Co., New Haven, Conn., 1869.

Speed, Robert, Boston, Mass., 1820–1840.

Spencer, Dwight, West Hartford, Conn., 1860.

Spencer, Martin, Greenfield, Mass., before and after 1830.

*Spencer Repeating Rifle Co., Boston, Mass., about 1861–1869.

Springfield Armory, Springfield, Mass., 1794 to present.

*Springfield Arms Co., Springfield, Mass., 1850–1869. Run by James Warner, later under his own name.

Stafford, T. J., New Haven, Conn., 1860–1861.

*Starr, Nathan Sr. and Jr., Middletown, Conn., 1798–1845.

*Stevens, J. & Co., J. Stevens Arms Co., Chicopee Falls, Mass., 1864 to present.

Stillman, Amos & Co., Farmington, Conn., contractors of 1798, in business to 1812, at least.

226

Stocking & Co., Worcester, Mass., 1849–1852.
Story, Asa, Windsor, Vt., 1835.
Tonks, Joseph, Boston, Mass., before and after 1860.
*Union Arms Co., Hartford, Conn., 1857–1861 and later.
Varney, David M., Burlington, Vt., before and after 1850.
Wallach, Moses A., Boston, Mass., 1800–1825.
Walters, A., Millbury, Mass., 1837.
Ware, Joseph, and John Morse, Worcester, Mass., 1825–1833 and later.
Ware & Wheelock, Worcester, Mass., 1825 and after.
Washburn, Nathan, Worcester, Mass., Civil War.
Waters, Asa, Sutton, Mass., 1776.
*Waters, Asa & Co., Millbury, Mass., including the later members of the Waters family the business ran from about 1798–1841.
Watson, Jonathan, Chester, N. H., before and after 1800.
Welch, Brown & Co., Norfolk, Conn., Civil War.
Welton, Ard, Waterbury, Conn., before and after 1773–1801.
Wesson & Prescott, Northboro, Mass., 1849.
Wesson, Stevens & Miller, Hartford, Conn., 1837–1849.
Whall, William, Boston, Mass., 1813–1819.
Wheeler, A. G., Farmington, Me., 1867–1868.
White, Horace, Springfield, Mass., Committee of Safety.
Whitmore, Andrew, Somerville, Mass., 1868.
Whitmore, D., Cambridge, Mass., 1860.
Whitmore, H. G., Boston, Mass., 1853 and later.
Whitmore, Nathan, Marshfield, Mass., about 1825–1880.
*Whitney Armory, New Haven, 1798–1888; run by Eli Whitney Sr., P. and E. W. Blake, Edwards R. Goodrich, Eli Whitney, Jr.
Whittemore, Amos, Boston, Mass., about 1775–1785.
*Winchester Repeating Arms Co., New Haven, Conn., 1857 to present; included in these dates are its predecessors the Volcanic Arms Co., Henry Repeating Arms Co. and New Haven Arms Co.
*Windsor Manufacturing Co., Windsor, Vt., 1867–1868.
Wood, John, Roxbury, Mass., Committee of Safety.
Wood, John, Boston, Mass., 1800.
Wood, Luke, Sutton, Mass., 1808.
Wrisley, Loren, Norway, Me., 1834 and later.

Notes

This list is based on the following sources:

Arcadi Gluckman, *United States Martial Pistols and Revolvers.*
James E. Hicks, *Notes on United States Ordnance*, 2 volumes.
H. B. C. Pollard, *A History of Firearms.*
L. D. Satterlee and Arcadi Gluckman, *American Gun Makers.*
Charles W. Sawyer, *Firearms in American History*, 3 volumes.
Charles W. Sawyer, *United States Single Shot Martial Pistols.*
Enumerators' Reports of the United States Census of Manufactures, for Hartford, Middlesex and New Haven Counties, Conn., and for Hampden County, Mass., 1850, 1860, 1870.
Springfield Armory Records.

This list of small arms makers is subject to the following limitations:

1. The representativeness of this list is doubtful because it is weighted in favor of the gunsmiths who worked for the Committees of Safety during the Revolution, and of the federal contractors, of whom public records of one sort or another have been preserved. On the other hand, it is improbable that important gunsmiths or manufacturers were excluded from public work, and so this list probably represents the important members of the trade and industry.

2. The dates given in this list are obviously approximate in some cases, and in others fragmentary. Arms makers listed in the references used as being active in some general period of time, as for example the flintlock period, have been excluded from this list for lack of more specific data. Where there is conflict among the sources primary data or more recently published material have been used in preference to secondary data or material published earlier.

3. In some cases it has been difficult to differentiate between gunsmiths and arms manufacturers. Where government contractors were involved the size of the contracts has been of importance in this matter. Indications of mechanized production and the employment of ten or more workers have been other criteria used in determining whether an arms maker should be classed as a gunsmith or manufacturer.

4. Some of the lists of arms makers include inventors as well as makers of small arms. Inventors have been excluded from this list if they did not actually make arms; the makers of parts of arms and those concerns in other fields which went only temporarily into arms production during the Civil War have also been excluded.

Representative Federal Small Arms Contract, 1822

(Source: Miscellaneous Incoming Letters, 1822, Springfield Armory Records)

This agreement, made this _____ day of _____ One thousand eight hundred and twenty two. Between George Bomford Lieut. Col. of artillery on Ordnance Duty, in the service of the United States, acting with the consent and under the direction of the Honbl. John C. Calhoun Secretary of War, of the one part; and Marine T. Wickham of Philadelphia of the State of Pennsylvania of the other part Witnesseth—

1st. That the said Marine T. Wickham shall manufacture and deliver for the Military Service of the United States, Five thousand stands of Arms, with Bayonets and Ramrods complete; at the rate of two thousand stands in each year, for two and a half years, commencing with the first day of January in the year one thousand eight hundred and twenty two.—The Arms to be manufactured, shall in all their parts, conform in model or form, and be equal in workmanship and quality, to the pattern or standard Musket, to be furnished by the Ordnance Department.—

2nd. It is agreed, that the Arms shall be proved and inspected, by an Officer or person, appointed by the Ordnance Department for that purpose; and in the manner prescribed by the regulations, which are or may be established by the Ordnance Department.—It is understood, however, that no methods of proof or inspection, more rigorous than those established for, and practised at the National Armouries of the United States; shall be at any time established. The arms are to be proved and inspected at or near Philadelphia; and in parcels consisting each of not less than two hundred and fifty stands. The expense of proof and inspection to be defrayed by the United States.

3rd. It is further agreed that the price of the Arms to be manufactured, shall be as follows—Viz. For each musket complete; including Bayonet, Ramrod and flint, including also, the proportion of Screw Drivers, Ball Screws, and Spring Vises, stated in the fourth article of this agreement; the price shall be Twelve Dollars.—Subject however to the following proviso that if during the period prescribed for the existence of this agreement, there be any new agreement made by the Ordnance Department for the manufacture of Arms, in which the price for Similar Arms, shall be greater, or less, than the price stipulated in this article; then the price herein stipulated shall be so modified as to conform and be equal to the price stipulated in such new Agreement.—The new price shall not take effect, upon any arms delivered under this agreement, within the period of four months, from and after the commencement of the new agreement; nor until at least two hundred and fifty stands complete shall have been delivered under the latter, nor until four months previous notice shall have been given of the change.—It is understood, that if the United States shall make an agreement for the manufacture of Arms, at any place South or West, of the place where Arms are now manufactured, under contract, for the United States; an additional allowance, equal to the cost of transporting Arms from the one place to the other, may be made in such agreement, without thereby augmenting the allowance stipulated in this Agreement.

4th. It is agreed, that the said Arms shall be safely and properly packed for transportation, in good and sufficient boxes, and in the manner which is or may be prescribed by the regulations of the Ordnance Department and Practiced at the National Armouries; each box to contain twenty muskets complete, twenty Screw Drivers, two ball screws, and two Spring vises; and the said arms, when so packed, shall be delivered at the United States Arsenal near Frankford, Pennsylvania. A reasonable price is to be allowed by the United States, to the said Marine T. Wickham for the packing boxes, and for transporting the arms to the Arsenal.

5th. It is agreed, that the arms manufactured and delivered under this agreement, shall be paid for on the delivery of each parcel, consisting of not less than two hundred and fifty stands complete; at the price stipulated in the third article; and to the full amount of the parcel delivered, not exceeding, in any one year, the number specified in the first article. The vouchers upon which payment will be made, will be a certificate of the person appointed to inspect the arms, and the receipt of the person to whom they were delivered, for the service of the United States.

6th. It is agreed, that if the United States should alter or modify, the pattern or model musket, or establish a model or pattern, at the National Armouries, differing in any respect from that upon which this agreement is founded; then the arms to be hereafter manufactured under this agreement, shall be made conformable thereto, if it be required by the Ordnance Department.—Provided however, that the said Marine T. Wickham shall be allowed a reasonable compensation, for any extra expense occasioned by such alteration.— And provided also, that the amount of such compensation shall be agreed upon and established before any alteration is made. No deviation from the established pattern will at any time be made, unless expressly directed, in writing by the Ordnance Department.

7th. It is agreed that the United States possess and reserve the right to declare this agreement null and void; whenever the said Marine T. Wickham shall fail to deliver, in any one year, the number of arms stipulated in the first article.

8th. It is expressly conditioned that no member of Congress is or shall be admitted to any share or part of this contract or agreement or to any benefit to arise thereupon.

In witness whereof, the parties aforesaid have hereunto set their hands, and affixed their seals, the day and year first above written.

Seal

Witness Present

Seal

TABLE 1

Costs and Prices of the Springfield Musket and Breech-Loading Rifle, 1798–1870

Contract price, Ordnance Department estimates of costs of privately made and publicly made arms, the writer's estimate of costs of publicly made arms. See explanatory note following Table.

Year	Contract Price of Springfield Weapon	Ordnance Department Estimate of Cost of Springfield Weapon in Private Armories	Ordnance Department Estimate of Cost of Springfield Weapon at Springfield Armory	Alternative Ordnance Department Estimate of Cost of Springfield Weapon at Springfield Armory	Writer's Estimate of Cost of Springfield Weapon at Springfield Armory
1798	$13.40				$ 16.28
1799				$ 9.29	17.82
1800			$12.06		13.42
1801					15.17
1802					7.00
1803					6.70
1804					11.73
1805			12.06		12.13
1806					18.31
1807	10.75				8.48
1808	10.75				13.14
1809	10.75				14.45
1810	10.75		12.06		13.16
1811	13.00				10.07
1812	14.25				13.46
1813					16.07
1814	14.25				10.93
1815	14.00		12.06		18.81
1816	14.00				21.57
1817	14.00	$13.56	12.50		12.21
1818	14.00		12.40		12.94
1819	13.00⎱ 14.00⎰		13.21	12.40	14.02
1820	13.00⎱ 14.00⎰			10.85⎱ 12.18⎰	12.99
1821	12.25⎱ 14.00⎰		12.51	10.00	13.41
1822	12.25⎱ 14.00⎰		12.40	11.35⎱ 11.50⎰	13.66
1823	12.25	14.00	12.23	11.45	13.05
1824	12.25	12.25	12.23	11.27	12.38
1825	12.25	12.25	12.23	10.50	12.01
1826	12.25	12.25	12.23	10.47	11.59
1827	12.25	12.25	12.23	10.49	11.63
1828	12.25	12.25	12.23	10.50⎱ 10.54⎰	11.98
1829	12.25	12.25	12.23	10.02	11.24
1830	12.25	12.25	11.12	10.80⎱ 10.98⎰	11.77

TABLE 1—*Continued*

Year	Contract Price of Springfield Weapon	Ordnance Department Estimate of Cost of Springfield Weapon in Private Armories	Ordnance Department Estimate of Cost of Springfield Weapon at Springfield Armory	Alternative Ordnance Department Estimate of Cost of Springfield Weapon at Springfield Armory	Writer's Estimate of Cost of Springfield Weapon at Springfield Armory
1831	12.25	12.25	11.26	11.44	11.80
1832	12.25	12.25	11.64	11.66	13.91
1833	12.25		11.80	12.39⎱ 12.70⎰	15.68
1834	12.25			11.05	13.53
1835	12.25			10.93	12.44
1836	12.25			11.07	13.52
1837	12.25		13.00	11.69	15.38
1838	12.25		11.69	11.84	13.64
1839	12.25			11.79	14.38
1840	12.25		17.44	17.44	27.47
1841	12.50		13.00		22.31
1842			12.78		17.56
1843			12.78		19.88
1844					17.42
1845					15.15
1846			13.00		14.20
1847			13.00		15.46
1848					13.09
1849			13.00*		14.41
1850					11.47
1851					12.33
1852			13.00		12.60
1853			13.00		15.38
1854			13.00		17.05
1855			13.00*		20.93
1856					114.22
1857					50.58
1858			13.22		23.13
1859					24.28
1860			14.04		26.37
1861	20.00⎱ 25.00⎰		average of Civil War		26.25
1862	18.00⎱ 20.00⎰				20.28
1863	18.00⎱ 20.00⎰		11.70		16.86
1864	18.00⎫ 19.00⎬ 20.00⎭				14.44
1865	19.00			14.12	21.30
1866			14.31†– 18.70‡–		348.12
1867			18.00		30.73

TABLE 1—*Continued*

Year	Contract Price of Springfield Weapon	Ordnance Department Estimate of Cost of Springfield Weapon in Private Armories	Ordnance Department Estimate of Cost of Springfield Weapon at Springfield Armory	Alternative Ordnance Department Estimate of Cost of Springfield Weapon at Springfield Armory	Writer's Estimate of Cost of Springfield Weapon at Springfield Armory
1868		22.39§	22.48‖	14.12¶	17.69
1869			21.18		136.28
1870		14.45**	18.90††	19.66‡‡– 12.00§§–	10.14

* $13.59 with appendages.
* $13.25 with appendages.
† Altered breech-loader—$10.69 unaltered.
‡ Breech-loader model 1866.
§ Muzzle-Loading Springfield altered by Remington system at Springfield Armory.
‖ Converted breech-loader.
¶ Muzzle-loader.
** Cost of Remington Navy Rifle made at Springfield Armory.
‡‡ Model 1868 (new breech-loader).
‡‡ Converted breech-loader.
§§ Muzzle-loader, "value of."

Note on Table 1

This table is based on the following sources:

James G. Benton, *Total Expenditure of Money and Fabrication of Arms, Equipments &c. at the National Armory, Springfield, Mass.*

James E. Hicks, *Nathan Starr.*

James E. Hicks, *Notes on United States Ordnance,* 2 volumes.

American State Papers, Class V, Military Affairs, 7 volumes.

Ordnance Reports, Vol. I, II, III.

Springfield Armory Records.

The titles of the first two columns of this table are self-explanatory. The third and fourth columns contain data on the costs of the Springfield weapon at the Springfield Armory collected from the records of the Armory and of the Ordnance Department. Where two series were found each was retained as a unit and the one containing on the whole lower costs was placed in the fourth column of this table. In general the fourth column of this table represents direct costs, in some cases with supervisory costs added, while the third column seems to include, at least occasionally, some allowance for overhead costs. Sometimes additional cost figures were worked out by the Armory officials or the Ordnance Department, and these have been included. The records usually fail to explain any discrepancies. The fifth column of this table contains an estimate of costs at the Springfield Armory calculated by the writer according to a method described in Chapter IV. The material on which this estimate is based is found in James G. Benton, *Total Expenditure of Money and Fabrication of Arms, Equipments, &c. at the National Armory. Springfield, Mass.*, Abstracts A and F.

The costs of appendages were included in the price of contract arms and in the writer's cost figures, but the Ordnance Department figures for costs, both of privately made arms and government made arms, are not consistent in this matter. Sometimes appendages seem to have been included, and other times excluded from costs.

The first two columns indicate that the Ordnance Department may have confused cost and price from 1824 to 1832.

The following statistics, taken from the Springfield Armory Records, show the relative importance of labor and material costs. Wages always remained a large item in the direct cost of the Springfield musket and breech-loading rifle; it was regularly about twice the cost of raw materials. Just what "contingencies"—a term frequently used in Springfield Armory cost estimates—included cannot be determined.

Year	Labor Cost of Weapon	Cost of Materials, Coal, Files, and Repair of Tools	Contingencies, Loss, Wear and Tear of Machines	Total
1818	$6.57	$3.58	$2.25	$12.40
1820				
before a reduction in wages	6.35	3.83	2.00	12.18
after two reductions in wages	5.67	3.57	1.61	10.85
1821	5.01	3.57	1.42	10.00
1829	5.11	3.39	—	8.50
1873	6.73	3.23	—	9.96

TABLE 2

Annual Production at the Springfield Armory, 1795–1870

Source: James G. Benton, *Total Expenditure of Money and Fabrication of Arms, Equipments &c. at the National Armory, Springfield, Mass.*, Abstract F.

Year	Muskets, Rifles and Carbines*	Year	Muskets, Rifles and Carbines
1795	245	1833	12,400
1796	838	1834	14,000
1797	1,028	1835	13,000
1798	1,044	1836	13,500
1799	4,595	1837	14,500
1800	4,862	1838	15,000
1801	3,205	1839	10,000
1802	4,358	1840	5,967
1803	4,775	1841	10,700
1804	3,566	1842	9,720
1805	3,535	1843	4,690
1806	2,018	1844	7,656
1807	5,692	1845	12,107
1808	5,870	1846	14,265
1809	7,670	1847	14,504
1810	10,302	1848	15,975
1811	12,140	1849	16,237
1812	10,140	1850	20,171
1813	6,920	1851	23,000
1814	9,585	1852	21,800
1815	7,279	1853	17,000
1816	7,199	1854	13,000
1817	13,015	1855	9,505
1818	13,000	1856	2,721
1819	12,250	1857	5,031
1820	13,200	1858	11,198
1821	13,000	1859	13,002
1822	13,200	1860	9,601
1823	14,000	1861	13,803
1824	14,000	1862	102,410
1825	15,000	1863	217,784
1826	15,500	1864	276,200
1827	14,500	1865	195,341
1828	15,500	1866	2,405
1829	16,500	1867	25,695
1830	16,500	1868	27,848
1831	16,500	1869	2,201
1832	13,600	1870	46,229

* A negligible number of carbines were made at the Springfield Armory, and no rifles until the breech-loading rifle replaced the muzzle-loading rifle-musket.

TABLE 1

Prices of the Main Raw Materials of Small Arms Manufacture. 1800–1870

Data collected from the Springfield Armory Records. See note following Table.

Year	Wrought Iron, Domestic, per Long Ton	Wrought Iron, Imported, per Long Ton	Steel Blister, per Pound	Steel Cast, per Pound	Steel German, per Pound	Steel Double Shear, per Pound
1800	$120	$	¢	¢	¢	¢
1801						
1802						
1803						
1804						
1805						
1806						
1807						
1808						
1809						
1810	pre-war price					
1811	140					
1812			19–27		44	
1813				47	43–48	
1814	160		12½	75A*	23A*	
1815	200, cut to 170		12½–22A*	30	22	
1816	160		12½A*	25A*	13½–16A*	
1817	170					
1818	160					
1819	150		17	24		
1820	160		17	24		
1821	140			18A	16½	
1822			14–16	20–25	12–15½	
1823	130		14			
1824	120B§		12¾–14		13¾–15	
1825	140		13½–14		13½	
1826	140A*		14–17½	19	13	
1827			14–15½	14¼–23A	12½–14	
1828			12½–12¾	16½–19	13–14½	
1829	140				13½	
1830	140	80–90			11A	21
1831	140			18¾A	10–14A	22
1832	140			18–19½A	13½	
1833	140				13½	19½–20
1834	140			16A		16½–22
1835					11½–12½	18
1836				18	11½	16¾–19
1837	160 to Oct., 145 afterward			17	11½–12	17
1838	145 to June			16½	12	
1839	140			16½–17A	12	
1840	140					
1841				17A		

Table 1—*Continued*

Year	Wrought Iron, Domestic, per Long Ton	Wrought Iron, Imported, per Long Ton	Steel Blister, per Pound	Steel Cast, per Pound	Steel German, per Pound	Steel Double Shear, per Pound
1842	140					17–18A
1843	140 (200 exp.)‖	110–120A		18½A		
1844				17½A		17½–18
1845		124			13½A	
1846						
1847						
1848				16A		
1849	140	190A				
1850	140	190				
1851		190				
1852	140	190				
1853	150	200A		13		
1854	160	200				
1855	160					
1856		200		16		
1857		180–185				
1858		200				
1859	150A	110–130				
1860		200		16		
1861	180	200		15–19		
1862	180	200		17–23¶		
1863		225–310**		18A		
1864	280 Mar. 425 Oct.	280 Mar.		15½ Mar. 25 June		
1865		225 Mar.		26½ Mar.		
1866				20		
1867				21*		
1868						
1869				8½g††		
1870				7½gA†† 10A		

* A represents price asked by dealer, used in absence of actual price.
§ B represents price offered by purchaser, used in absence of actual price.
‖ Used experimentally.
¶ 18½ Jan.; 17 Aug.; 21–23 Dec.
** 225 Jan.; 310 May; 235 Nov.
†† Price in gold.

TABLE 1—*Continued*

Year	Char-coal, per Bushel	Coal, Anthracite, per Long Ton	Coal, Bituminous, per Bushel*	Musket Stocks Apiece	Whale Oil, per Gallon†	Grind-stones per Short Ton
1800	¢3–4.3	$	¢33⅓A	¢	¢	$
1801	3–4.1		50A			
1802	3.3–3.5					
1803	3.3–3.5					
1804	4–4.1		50			
1805						
1806						
1807						
1808						
1809						
1810						
1811						
1812						
1813			37½	40		
1814				40		
1815				25		
1816			47		$1.08–$2.00	40
1817			30–34	30		
1818			34A	32		
1819				30	$1.30A	
1820	5–6			30A		28
1821			28A	30–33		
1822			28	25	75	20A
1823			25	25	62½–67	
1824				28		
1825	6		40	28		
1826	6		36½	29A		18A
1827	6–6½A		37A	28	67–80	
1828	6		42	25–28	32–60A	
1829	5½–6		25	25	39–63A	
1830		8.50A		28	67	
1831		8.88A‡			80–95A	19
1832	6	9.95	35A	28H§	92	
1833				26H§		
1834					78–98A	
1835	6½			25	90–98A	15–20
1836	6½–8	13.50		25–26½	86–95	
1837	8	14.50		26½	90–$1.00	15, 18H§
1838	8	10–12A		26½		
1839	7½			26½–32		16A
1840				28		
1841	6½	10.50	37½	28	$1.00	17A
1842	6½	10.00A	36A	25		11A NY‖
1843	6½	7.75	35–36A	24		
1844	6½	7.75A	35A			
1845	6½			24		16
1846	6½			24B		
1847	6½			28		
1848	6½			28		

TABLE 1—*Continued*

Year	Char-coal, per Bushel	Coal, Anthracite, per Long Ton	Coal, Bituminous, per Bushel*	Musket Stocks Apiece	Whale Oil, per Gallon	Grind-stones per Short Ton
1849	6½			28		
1850	6½	6.75		28		
1851	6½			28		16
1852	8			28		
1853	8			28		
1854				28		
1855	8			28		
1856	8			26		
1857		6.75		26		
1858				26		
1859	8			25		
1860	8			25	$1.42	
1861	8–10	6.25–7.75A 7.12A		28 Nov. 30 Dec.	$1.45–1.47	18A T.¶
1862		7.85	7.40A NH**	28–33††	$1.48–1.50A	
1863			12.00	34–37½		
1864		17.94–18.83‡‡		35–45§§	$1.79–2.30	
1865		11.30 Apr.		35B	$2.20–2.35A	
1866		10.75A			$2.25–2.65A	
1867		8.65–9.40Ad ||||	9.65Ad		$1.50–2.70A	
1868			9.25–10.25Ad	30***	$2.25–2.30A	10AO¶¶
1869	15	8.75–9.25A 11.90Ad ||||	8.00–9.15A	30***		11O¶¶
1870	15	8.64–9.15Ad || ||	8.30–9.60Ad	30***		

* Bituminous coal bought by the bushel up to 1844; by 1862 bought by the long ton.
† Whale oil used up to 1841; replaced by sperm oil by 1860.
‡ $1.50 added to Hartford price of coal as approximate cost of transportation to Springfield.
§ Price at Hartford.
|| Price at New York.
¶ Price at Troy, N.Y.
** Price at New Haven.
†† 33 Jan.; 28 Feb.; 32½ May.
‡‡ Probably anthracite coal.
§§ 38 Mar.; 35 July; 45 Nov.
|||| d indicates price of goods delivered at Springfield Armory.
¶¶ O indicates price in Ohio.
*** Indicates price at which Armory sold stocks to other arms makers; the Armory bought no stocks in the post-war period.

Notes on Table 1 and Figure 1

Springfield Armory Prices.

Prices quoted from 1800 to 1830 inclusive on charcoal and iron are prices paid for goods delivered at the Springfield Armory. Prices of other materials purchased in this period are Hartford prices unless otherwise indicated. For the period 1831–1870, except

FIGURE 1. APPENDIX C. PRICES OF RAW MATERIALS OF SMALL ARMS MANUFACTURE, COLE'S AND MITCHELL'S COMMODITY PRICE INDICES, AND THE PREMIUM ON GOLD, 1800-1870.

(SEE TABLE 1. APPENDIX C.)

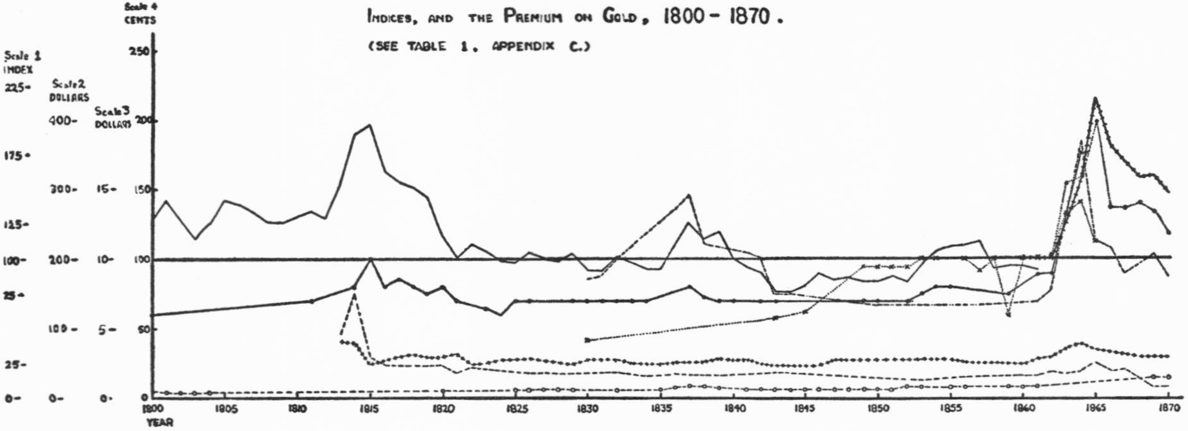

COLE'S INDEX OF JANUARY WHOLESALE COMMODITY PRICES IN NEW YORK CITY. BASE: 1824-1842. (Scale 1)
MITCHELL'S INDEX OF JANUARY WHOLESALE PRICES OF 92 COMMODITIES. BASE: 1860. (Scale 1)
AVERAGE PRICE OF GOLD IN GREENBACKS, FIRST QUARTER, 1862-1870. (MITCHELL'S FIGURES)(fixed in Dollars on Scale 1).

WROUGHT IRON, DOMESTIC - DOLLARS PER TON (Scale 2)
"   "   , FOREIGN   "   "   (")
STEEL, CAST - CENTS PER POUND (Scale 4)
CHARCOAL - CENTS PER BUSHEL (Scale 4)
COAL, ANTHRACITE - DOLLARS PER TON (Scale 3)
MUSKET STOCKS - CENTS APIECE (Scale 4)

(Average Prices for Raw Materials are Given)

where otherwise indicated, prices are for goods delivered at the Armory. However, coal prices usually were Springfield prices, rather than prices for delivery at the Armory.

In the absence of actual prices the writer has used the prices asked by dealers and offered by the Springfield Armory. These seem to have been fairly close to the level of actual prices. The symbol A following a price represents the price asked by the dealer; the symbol B the price offered by the purchaser.

The iron prices used in this table cover iron of the highest quality used in arms manufacture, usually called barrel iron. Bituminous coal was bought by the Springfield Armory by the bushel until some time in the 1840's or 1850's. Following the introduction of steampower it was bought by the ton. The oil used during much of this period was whale oil, but later sperm oil, and to a less extent lard oil replaced whale oil.

Cole's Index.

The principal wholesale price index plotted in Figure 1 of this appendix is found in Arthur H. Cole, *Wholesale Commodity Prices in the United States*, 135–136, Appendix B, Table 45; "All-Commodity Index of Wholesale Prices with Variable Group Weights at New York, Monthly, 1797–1861." January figures only have been plotted because the Springfield Armory material on prices is too scanty to have warranted the use of monthly figures. There are from about 110 to 140 price series in Cole's index. This index was used rather than an alternative index Cole developed which had constant group weights, since Cole considers the former more representative of price changes over a long period of time. See Cole, *op. cit.*, 3–21, 135–136.

Mitchell's Indices.

The second wholesale price index plotted in Figure 1 of this appendix has been taken from Wesley C. Mitchell, *Gold, Prices, and Wages Under the Greenback Standard*, Table 4: "Relative wholesale prices of 92 commodities: by quarters, 1860–1880." The material in this table is based on data from *Wholesale Prices, Wages, and Transportation*, a report made in 1893 by Mr. Aldrich of the Senate Committee on Finance. The material in this table is not weighted. Mitchell uses instead of a single index figure for a given quarter a series of figures, each representing a decile or tenth of the range of price variations for that quarter. The fifth decile, or median, appears in Figure 1 of this appendix.

The series for the average price of gold in greenbacks in Figure 1 has been taken from Table 2: "Lowest, average, and highest price of gold in greenbacks, and of greenbacks in gold, by months, quarters, and years: 1862–1878," of the same reference. Only the average quarterly prices of gold have been plotted. See Mitchell, *op. cit.*, 4–13, 18–24, 63–69.

APPENDIX D

TABLE 1

The Growth of Occupational Specialization Among Production Workers at the Springfield Armory, 1806–1870*

Source: Springfield Armory Work Returns for January

Year	Number of Occupations	Number of Workers in Each Occupation†
1806	11	5
1810	20	10
1815	34	6
1820	86	3
1825	100	3
1830	98	3
1835	99	2
1840	97	2
1845	118	2
1850	151	2
1855	84	2
1860	113	2
1865	390	6
1870	211	3

* In this appendix the phrase "production workers," unless otherwise indicated, excludes the following persons employed at the Springfield Armory:

Officers, office staff, Master Armorer, Assistant Master Armorers (equivalent to foremen), foremen, assistant foremen, inspectors, carpenters, masons, watchmen, shoptenders, laborers and arsenal workers.

† Figures rounded to nearest whole number.

TABLE 2

Piece and Time Work of Production Workers, Assistant Master Armorers, Foremen, Assistant Foremen and Inspectors at the Springfield Armory, 1806–1870*

Source: Springfield Armory Work Returns for January

Year	Men Paid by the Piece	Men Paid by the Day or Month	Men Paid under Both Systems
1806	16	11	3
1810	55	17	11
1815	56	29	6
1820	134	58	60
1825	161	62	40
1830	160	65	49
1835	153	56	36
1842†	137	39	46
1845	126	57	36
1850	229	76	43
1855	69	58	44
1865	1,235	1,083	281
1870	272	231	129

*† See next page for footnotes to table 2.

TABLE 3

Mean and Modal Monthly Money Wages of Springfield Armory Production Workers, 1802–1870; Real Wage Index of Springfield Armory Production Workers, 1802–1861; Moulton's Index of Average Real Wages in the United States, with Shifted Base, 1802–1870

See note following Table

Year	Mean Wage	Modal Wage	Armorers' Real Wage Index Base: 1824–1842	Moulton's Real Wage Index Base: 1824–1842
1802	$16.12*	$12.68*	34*	54
1803	14.27	15.78	34	57
1804	17.24	13.57	38	62
1805	15.51	17.11	30	67
1806	17.39	17.18	34	66
1807	20.23	18.12	42	71
1808	20.49	{17.37 / 26.25	44	65
1809	18.98	17.33	41	73
1810	22.07	17.69	47	65
1811	23.35	18.12	48	60
1812	20.33	17.59	43	68
1813	22.05	17.87	40	58
1814	29.35	{22.98 / 31.86†	43	44
1815	30.40	27.75	43	57
1816	33.71	37.21	57	70
1817	35.84	{27.73 / 42.73†	64	71
1818	39.53	{42.17 / 51.58	72	68
1819	38.43	37.36	74	72
1820	33.71	27.65	80	82
1821	33.06	32.50	90	93
1822	30.49	33.22	76	83
1823	33.26	{32.12† / 41.89	88	100
1824	38.25	42.37	106	98
1825	35.65	{27.79 / 41.86	100	94

* March statistics used because none could be found for January or February.
† Slightly larger mode—otherwise the two modal classes are equal in size.

Footnotes to Table 2

* The figures in this table do not correspond with the figures for employment at the Springfield Armory in Table 4, not only because supervisory workers were included in this table but also because some arsenal workers have been inadvertently included. This is due to the fact that this table is based on the Springfield Armory Work Returns, which do not always differentiate between arsenal work and production work. Table 4, on the other hand, is based on the Pay-Roll Books, and includes only those workers listed under the heading "Manufacture of Arms." For most purposes the figures in Table 4 should be relied on in preference to those in this table. Since arsenal workers were paid by the day, this table somewhat overestimated the number of workers paid under this system.

† Owing to a clerical error, figures for 1840 and 1841 were not collected.

TABLE 3—*Continued*

Year	Mean Wage	Modal Wage	Armorers' Real Wage Index Base 1824–1842	Moulton's Real Wage Index Base 1824–1842
1826	37.12	27.50	98	85
1827	34.73	{28.33† / 42.93}	96	100
1828	34.28	32.31	96	96
1829	39.44	46.86	106	97
1830	41.36	32.83	124	103
1831	32.63	40.09	98	102
1832	33.17	32.46	90	104
1833	34.79	32.67	99	105
1834	37.01	46.92	110	117
1835	31.64	31.66	94	99
1836	31.76	32.76	80	89
1837	37.78	{37.29 / 52.53}	83	89
1838	43.21	51.87	104	93
1839	33.49	42.43	77	92
1840	36.29	36.95	100	111
1841	41.69	47.50	122	108
1842	35.14	42.01	107	120
1843	28.09	36.28	100	123
1844	29.42	33.08	105	123
1845	34.13	42.88	117	126
1846	37.60	{33.22 / 47.57}	116	125
1847	34.76	37.50	113	124
1848	38.00	{37.46 / 47.42}	122	131
1849	37.42	43.00	123	135
1850	37.84	47.22	124	134
1851	43.07	46.19	135	129
1852	45.32	47.61	149	133
1853	41.45	47.40	117	128
1854	45.28	{37.50 / 47.56}	118	127
1855	48.33	{32.73 / 51.92}	122	130
1856	52.58	{23.74 / 47.91}	132	130
1857	45.81	51.40	112	134
1858	49.78	{18.61 / 52.54}	146	148
1859	49.48	49.27	142	151
1860	49.01	44.08	142	152
1861	47.61	51.45	141	150
1862	62.18	{37.50 / 62.34}		132
1863	59.44	73.00		119
1864	60.11	{37.64 / 72.57}		106

TABLE 3—*Continued*

Year	Mean Wage	Modal Wage	Armorers' Real Wage Index Base: 1824–1842	Moulton's Real Wage Index Base: 1824–1842
1865	78.42	$\begin{cases}43.05\\82.49\end{cases}$		104
1866	71.71	$\begin{cases}47.56\\82.72\end{cases}$		125
1867	72.00	$\begin{cases}48.06‡\\83.32\end{cases}$		144
1868	68.51	$\begin{cases}51.70\\81.55\end{cases}$		156
1869	65.91	76.18		171
1870	70.53	76.90		187

‡ Ten-dollar class interval used because there were two modal classes side by side.

Notes on Table 3 and Figure 1

The Mean Wage of Springfield Armorers.

This is the simple arithmetic mean of ungrouped monthly wages of production workers. It is based on the Springfield Armory's January pay-rolls.

The Modal Wage of Springfield Armorers.

This is calculated from a five-dollar class interval of monthly wages of production workers. It is based on the Springfield Armory's January pay-rolls.

The Index of Springfield Armorers' Real Wages.

In developing this index the writer has followed the method used by Harold G. Moulton in his calculation of real wages of all workers in the United States. A series of relative wages of Springfield armorers, with 1824–1842 as a base period, was calculated from mean January wages of production workers at the Armory. These relatives were divided by Cole's index numbers of wholesale prices of commodities in New York and the resulting quotients multiplied by 100 to give a crude measure of the real wages of Springfield armorers. See Cole, *op. cit.*, 3–21, 135–136, and Moulton, *op. cit.*, 181–183.

Moulton's Index of United States Real Wages.

This index covers the period 1801–1932, with 1926 as the base year. It was arrived at by dividing an index of money wages by an index of wholesale prices. For purposes of comparison with armorers' real wages the writer shifted the base to 1824–1842, by dividing the series by the average index number of the 1824–1842 period. See Moulton, *op. cit.*, 181–183.

Mitchell's Cost of Living Index.

The cost of living index plotted in Figure 1 of this appendix is found in Wesley C. Mitchell, *Gold, Prices and Wages Under the Greenback Standard*, Table 28: "Relative cost of living in Eastern and Western States: by years, 1860–1880." Mitchell weighted his retail prices with the detailed statistics of expenditures of 2,567 families published in the eighteenth Annual Report of the Commissioner of Labor, and with statistics from the Aldrich Report. He makes use of deciles rather than a single series of index numbers. The median figures for the cost of living in the eastern United States only have been used in Figure 1. See Mitchell, *op. cit.*, 83–89.

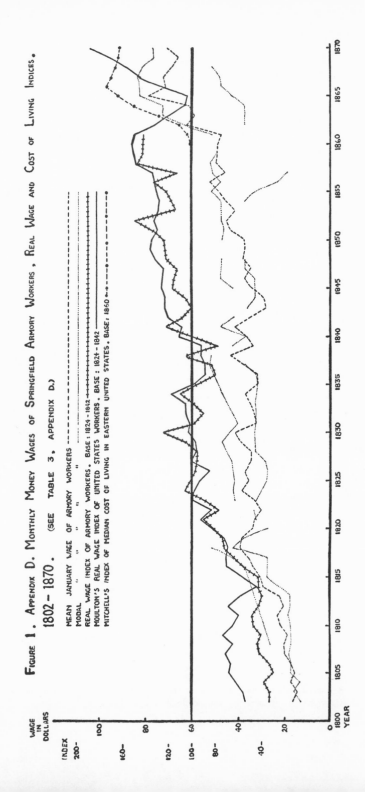

FIGURE 1. APPENDIX D. MONTHLY MONEY WAGES OF SPRINGFIELD ARMORY WORKERS, REAL WAGE AND COST OF LIVING INDICES. 1802 – 1870. (SEE TABLE 3, APPENDIX D.)

MEAN JANUARY WAGE OF ARMORY WORKERS --------
MODAL " " " " " ....
REAL WAGE INDEX OF ARMORY WORKERS. BASE: 1824-1842 +++++++++++
MOULTON'S REAL WAGE INDEX OF UNITED STATES WORKERS. BASE: 1824-1842
MITCHELL'S INDEX OF MEDIAN COST OF LIVING IN EASTERN UNITED STATES, BASE: 1860 -●--●--●--

TABLE 4

Employment of Production Workers at the Springfield Armory, 1802–1870

Source: Springfield Armory Pay-Roll for January

Year	Number Employed	Year	Number Employed	Year	Number Employed
1802	66*	1825	247	1848	245
1803	75	1826	244	1849	232
1804	76	1827	245	1850	334
1805	72	1828	247	1851	334
1806	58	1829	247	1852	288
1807	95	1830	250	1853	239
1808	105	1831	260	1854	166
1809	133	1832	266	1855	135
1810	204	1833	263	1856	158
1811	206	1834	251	1857	243
1812	219	1835	229	1858	240
1813	233	1836	231	1859	241
1814	225	1837	268	1860	182
1815	203	1838	252	1861	227
1816	236	1839	242	1862	1,309
1817	231	1840	238	1863	2,203
1818	231	1841	231	1864	2,467
1819	231	1842	226	1865	2,298
1820	236	1843	123	1866	723
1821	244	1844	165	1867	885
1822	247	1845	218	1868	562
1823	245	1846	234	1869	267
1824	244	1847	261	1870	571

* March statistics used because none could be found for January or February.

FIGURE 2, APPENDIX D. PRODUCTIVITY AND PIECE RATES OF SPRINGFIELD ARMORY BARREL WELDERS, 1806-1870.
(SEE TABLES 5 AND 6, APPENDIX D.)

AVERAGE NUMBER OF BARRELS WELDED ANNUALLY PER MAN ————
PIECE RATE FOR WELDING BARRELS ♦–––♦

TABLE 5

Productivity of Barrel Welders at the Springfield Armory, 1806–1870

Source: Springfield Armory Work Returns

See note following Table

Year	Average Number of Barrels Welded Annually per Man, Rounded to Nearest Whole Number	Year	Average Number of Barrels Welded Annually per Man, Rounded to Nearest Whole Number
1806	1,200	1839	2,420
1807	1,565	1840	2,207
1808	1,454	1841	2,537
1809	1,267	1842	2,984
1810	1,319	1843	3,791
1811	1,485	1844	3,975
1812	1,495	1845	3,501
1813	1,117	1846	3,988
1814	1,050	1847	4,780
1815	1,118	1848	4,368
1816	1,087	1849	3,882
1817	1,249	1850	4,079
1818	1,357	1851	3,700
1819	1,654	1852	4,178
1820	1,939	1853	3,828
1821	1,851	1854	4,198
1822	1,873	1855	3,632
1823	2,208	1856	4,825
1824	2,407	1857	5,403
1825	2,397	1858	4,767
1826	2,137	1859	1,231
1827	2,494	1860	12,615
1828	2,378	1861	20,180
1829	2,153	1862	20,430
1830	1,856	1863	24,620
1831	1,824	1864	24,959
1832	2,209	1865	22,669
1833	2,157	1866	—
1834	2,378	1867	—
1835	2,444	1868	—
1836	2,237	1869	20,995
1837	2,471	1870	25,077
1838	2,338		

Note on Table 5

These figures were arrived at by the following method:

The sum of the months all barrel welders worked in a given year was divided by twelve to give the man-years worked. All months in which welders did not work were excluded. The total annual barrel production of these men for this year, less barrels condemned on inspection, was divided by the number of man-years worked. Barrel welders who regularly worked in some other occupation for more than eight days in the month were excluded from these figures, as were the barrels they produced. Welders who spent all of their working time on barrels, but who were absent for part of a month, were included. See Chapter **VIII**.

TABLE 6

Piece-Rates for Barrel Welding at the Springfield Armory, 1806–1870

Source: Springfield Armory Work Returns

Year	Piece Rate	Year	Piece Rate	Year	Piece Rate
1806	¢21, 25	1829	18, 26.4*	1848	13
1807	28	1830	18, 26.4*	1849	13
1808		1831	18, 26.4*	1850	12
1809		1832	18, 26.4*	1851	12
1810		1833	23.8, 25, 26.4	1852	12
1811			⎧ 20, 22.6, 23.8,	1853	12
1812		1834	⎨ 25, 26.4,	1854	12
1813			⎬ 27.6, 28.8,	1855	14
1814			⎩ 30, 32, 35	1856	14
1815		1835	12, 14, 18, 20	1857	13
1816			22.6, 25,	1858	13
1817	35		26.4	1859	13
1818		1836	25	1860	11.75
1819	25, 32, 35, 42	1837	27	1861	10.50, 11.75
1820	22.5, 31	1838	27	1862	4.25, 4.5,
1821	20, 21, 27, 30,	1839	27		10.5
	31, 37	1840	27	1863	4.5
1822	26.4, 31	1841	20, 27	1864	4.5
1823	18, 26.4	1842	17.5, 20	1865	4.5
1824	18, 26.4	1843	15, 17.5	1866†	—
1825	18, 26.4*	1844	13	1867†	—
1826	26.4	1845	13	1868†	—
1827	18, 26.4*	1846	13	1869	2.8
1828	18, 26.4*	1847	13	1870	2.8

* The most commonly used piece-rate in this year.
† No barrels welded in this year.

TABLE 7

Average Monthly Wages of Small Arms Workers and Machinists in the Connecticut River Valley, 1822–1870

Complete list of Sources follows Table

	Connecticut				Massachusetts			
Year	New Haven	Middle-town	Hartford	Average for State	Springfield (m =mean; md =mode)	Chicopee	Long-Meadow	Average for State
1822	$23.58 Whitney	$25.00 Johnson 27.78 North 41.67 Starr	$	$	$33.71m 27.65md Spfd. Armory			
1832		39.00 at all armories			33.71m 32.46md Spfd. Armory 39.00–50.00 for machinists in two cotton factories	39.00–52.00 machinists in joiners' tools factory		
1845					34.13m 42.88md Spfd. Armory	32.50–45.50 Ames		
1850	30.00 Whitney	52.00 North & Savage 21.66 Scovil Estate	46.66 Colt 30.00 E. Clark	40.44	37.84m 42.88md Spfd. Armory	38.00 Ames 33.50 Mass. Arms Co.		29.21
1860	34.00 Whitney 23.55* N.H. Arms Co. 50.00 Bliss 44.44 Stafford	33.33 J. D. Couch	41.64 Colt 40.00 Sharps	37.50	49.01m 44.08md Spfd. 75.00 Smith & Wesson	45.00 Ames 46.66 Mass. Arms Co.	33.33 J. Warner	42.50
1870	65.66 Whitney 86.59 Winchester		58.96 Colt 32.00 Sharps 33.75 Roper	57.29	70.53m 76.90md Spfd. Armory 76.64 Smith & Wesson	28.73 J. Stevens†		69.77

* Over two-thirds of employees women.
† Half of employees women.

Note on Table 7

This table is based on the following sources:

Digest of Accounts of Manufacturing Establishments in the United States and of Their Manufactures, 1822.

Louis McLane, *Documents Relative to the Manufactures of the United States, Collected and transmitted to the House of Representatives, in compliance with a resolution of Jan. 19, 1832, by the Secretary of the Treasury.*

John G. Palfrey, *Statistics of the Condition and Products of Certain Branches of Industry in Massachusetts, for the year ending April 1, 1845.*

Federal Census Enumerators' reports for Hartford, Middlesex and New Haven Counties, Connecticut, and for Hampden County, Massachusetts, for the Censuses of Manufactures of 1850, 1860 and 1870.

Ames Papers.

Springfield Armory Records.

Table 3, Appendix D.

BIBLIOGRAPHY

A. PRIMARY SOURCES

1. Unpublished Manuscript Material.

The Springfield Armory Records. These consist of a large quantity of letters, returns of work, pay-roll books, records of experiments, estimates of cost, and records of expenditures, from 1798 on. The pay-roll books begin in 1802, the returns of work in 1806, and the correspondence becomes especially detailed in 1815. The completeness of these records is no doubt owing to the Armory's position as a public institution. The material is in excellent condition. It has been removed from the Springfield Armory, where the writer examined it, and is now in the National Archives, Washington, D.C. These records are by far the most important source of information on small arms manufacture in the Connecticut Valley.

The Ames Papers. These consist of a much smaller collection of records of the Ames Manufacturing Co. of Chicopee, Mass. Their content is similar in general character to that of the Springfield Armory Records, but the Ames Papers are less detailed and far less illuminating. The writer could discover no data concerning profits or costs, nor any wage data of particular value. The Ames Papers begin in the early 1830's and run throughout the period under study. They were at the time the material for this study was collected, in the possession of the descendants of J. T. and N. P. Ames, but their whereabouts is at present not known to the writer.

The Starr Papers. These consist of correspondence, diaries, day books and miscellaneous business records of Nathan Starr, Sr. and Jr. and E. W. N. Starr, a family of arms makers of Middletown, Conn. The material runs from 1799 to about 1849. It parallels closely the Springfield Armory Records, but, like the Ames Papers, lacks much valuable detail. Here, too, there is no information concerning the profits of these arms makers. The Starr Papers are in possession of the Middlesex County Historical Society, Middletown, Conn.

The Henry Aston Papers. These consist of a small amount of correspondence between Henry Aston, his partners, and the War Department, from 1845 to 1852. They are of value for comparison rather than of first importance to this study. They are in the possession of the Middlesex County Historical Society, Middletown, Conn.

The Colt Papers. These consist of correspondence of Samuel Colt and of officers of the Colt Company; a diary of one of the directors; newspaper clippings and articles concerning the company. This material is preserved in the Arthur L. Ulrich Museum of the Colt Company in Hartford. It runs from about 1840 on. The Colt Papers in the possession of the Connecticut Historical Society, Hartford, were not examined by the writer, as they were not accessible during the war.

Codicil of Will and Inventory of Estate of Eli Whitney, Sr. The codicil of Eli Whitney Sr.'s will, Jan. 7, 1825, and the inventory of his estate, May 14, 1827, are in the Connecticut State Library at Hartford, Conn. They are particularly valuable in regard to contemporary concepts of cost.

2. Government Documents.

Connecticut, *Statistical Tables and Abstracts of Conditions and Products of certain Branches of Industry in Connecticut, November 1, 1838 to February 1, 1839,* prepared from the returns of the assessors by R. R. Hinman, Secretary of State, April, 1839. (Manuscript). State House, Hartford, Conn.

Massachusetts, *Statistics of the Condition and Products of Certain Branches of Industry in Massachusetts, for the year ending April 1, 1845,* prepared from the returns of the assessors, by John G. Palfrey, Secretary of the Commonwealth, Dutton & Wentworth, Boston, 1846.

United States, *American State Papers, Class III, Finance,* Vol. 11, Gales and Seaton, Washington, 1832, and *Class V, Military Affairs,* Vols. I-VII, Gales and Seaton, Washington, 1832-1861.

United States, *A Collection of Annual Reports and Other Important Papers, Relating to the Ordnance Department, taken from the records of the office of the Chief of Ordnance, from Public Documents, and from Other Sources,* edited by Stephen V. Benet, Government Printing Office, Washington, 1878. Vols. I-III. Referred to in this study as *Ordnance Reports.*

United States, *A Statement of the Arts and Manufactures of the United States of America, for the year 1810,* edited by Tench Coxe, A. Cornman, Philadelphia, 1814.

United States, *Digest of Manufacturing Establishments in the United States, 1822,* printed as Document No. 662, 17 Cong., 2d Session, *American State Papers, Class III, Finance,* Vol. IV.

United States, *Documents Relative to the Manufactures in the United States collected and transmitted to the House of Representatives by the Secretary of the Treasury,* Duff Green, Washington, 1833, 2 Vols.

United States, *Message of the President of the United States, containing a Digest of the Statistics of Manufactures according to the Returns of the Seventh Census.* Executive Documents of the Senate of the United States, 35 Congress, 2nd Session, Document No. 39, 1850.

United States, *Manufactures of the United States in 1860,* Government Printing Office, Washington, 1865.

United States, *A Compendium of the Ninth Census, 1870,* Government Printing Office, Washington, 1872.

United States, *Report on the Manufactures of the United States at the Tenth Census, 1880,* Government Printing Office, Washington, 1883.

United States, *Report on Manufacturing Industries in the United States* at the Eleventh Census, 1890, Government Printing Office, Washington, 1895. Part. I.

United States, *Twelfth Census of the United States, Taken in the Year 1900, Manufactures,* Part I, United States Printing Office, Washington, 1902.

United States, *Thirteenth Census of the United States, 1910,* Vol. VIII and X, *Manufactures,* Government Printing Office, Washington, 1913.

United States, *Fourteenth Census of the United States, 1920,* Vols. VIII and X, *Manufactures,* Government Printing Office, Washington, 1923.

United States, *Fifteenth Census of the United States, Manufactures: 1929,* Vols. I and II, United States Government Printing Office, Washington, 1933.

United States, *Sixteenth Census of the United States: 1940, Manufactures, 1939,* Parts I and II, United States Government Printing Office, Washington, 1942.

United States, Federal Census of Manufactures Enumerators' Reports for Hartford, Middlesex and New Haven Counties, Conn.; and for Hampden County, Mass., for 1850, 1860 and 1870.

3. Newspaper Files.

The files of the *Hampshire Gazette* of Northampton, Mass., and of the *Springfield Republican* of Springfield, Mass., for the first seventy years of the nineteenth century, have been of considerable value to this study. They were examined in the Forbes Library, Northampton, Mass.

B. Secondary Sources

Alden, J. Deane, *Proceedings at the Dedication of Charter Oak Hall.* Case, Tiffany, Hartford, 1856.

Barnard, Henry, *Armsmear,* Alvord, New York, 1866.

Benton, James G., *The Fabrication of Small Arms for the United States Service,* Government Printing Office, Washington, 1878.

Benton, James G., *Total Expenditure of Money and Fabrication of Arms, Equipments, &c. at the National Armory, Springfield, Mass.,* privately published, Springfield, 1880.

Bishop, J. Leander, *A History of American Manufactures from 1608 to 1860,* 3rd edition, Edward Young & Co., Philadelphia, 1868. 3 Vols.

Blake, William P., *History of the Town of Hamden, Connecticut,* Price, Lee & Co., New Haven, 1888.

Byrn, Edward W., *The Progress of Invention in the Nineteenth Century,* Munn & Co., New York, 1900.

Carpenter and Morehouse, (editors), *The History of the Town of Amherst, Massachusetts,* Carpenter and Morehouse, 1896.

Chapin, Charles W., *Sketches of the Old Inhabitants and Other Citizens of Old Springfield of the Present Century,* Springfield Printing and Binding Co., Springfield, 1893.

Clark, Victor S., *History of Manufactures in the United States,* McGraw-Hill Book Company, New York, 1929. 3 Vols.

Cole, Arthur Harrison, *Wholesale Commodity Prices in the United States 1700-1861,* Harvard University Press, Cambridge, 1938.

Colt, Samuel, *On the Application of Machinery to the Manufacture of Rotating Chambered-Breech Fire-Arms,* excerpt minutes of proceedings of the Institution of Civil Engineers, Vol. XI, William Clowes & Son, London, 1853.

Dillin, John G. W., *The Kentucky Rifle,* National Rifle Association of America, Washington, 1924.

Elstmer Publishing Co., editor, *Inland Massachusetts Illustrated,* Springfield, Mass., 1890.

Field, David D., *Centennial Address,* William B. Casey, Middletown, Conn., 1853.

Fitch, Charles H., *Report on the Manufacture of Hardware, Cutlery and Edge- Tools,* Extra Census Bulletin, Government Printing Office, Washington, 1883.

Fitch, Charles H., *Report on the Manufactures of Interchangeable Mechanism*, Extra Census Bulletin, Government Printing Office, Washington, 1883.

Fuller, Claud E., *Springfield Muzzle-Loading Shoulder Arms*, Francis Bannerman, New York, 1930.

Fuller, Grace, "An Introduction to the History of Connecticut as a Manufacturing State," *Smith College Studies in History*, Northampton, Mass., 1915.

Gluckman, Arcadi, *United States Martial Pistols and Revolvers*, Otto Ulbrich Co., Buffalo, 1939.

Goddard, Calvin, "The Development of Small Arms," *Encyclopaedia Britannica*, Encyclopaedia Britannica Co., Ltd., London, 1941.

Goodrich, Carter, *The Miner's Freedom*, Marshall Jones Co., Boston, 1925.

Green, Constance McLaughlin, *History of the Springfield Armory*, in process.

Hacker, Louis M., *The Triumph of American Capitalism*, Simon and Schuster, New York, 1940.

Herbert D. Hall Foundation, *The Machine Tool Primer*, Newark, N. J., 1943.

Hart, Harold G., "The Colt Revolver in the Arthur L. Ulrich Museum," *Hobbies*, July and August, 1944.

Haven, Charles T., and Frank A. Belden, *A History of the Colt Revolver*, William Morrow & Co., New York, 1940.

Hicks, James E., *Nathan Starr*, privately published, 1940.

Hicks, James E., *Notes on United States Ordnance*, privately published, 1940. 2 Vols.

Hubbard, Guy, *Windsor Industrial History*, mimeograph, copyright 1922.

Jany, Curt, *Geschichte der Königlich Preussischen Armee bis zum Jahre 1807*. K. Siegismund, Berlin, 1928-1937. 5 Vols.

Keith, Herbert C., and Charles Rufus Harte, "The Early Iron Industry of Connecticut," reprinted from the *51st Annual Report of the Society of Civil Engineers, Inc.*, Mack & Noel, New Haven, 1935.

Kistler, Thelma, "The Rise of Railroads in the Connecticut River Valley," *Smith College Studies in History*, Northampton, Mass., Oct. 1937-July 1938.

Kling, C., compiler, *Geschichte der Bekleidung, Bewaffnung und Ausrüstung des Königlich Preussischen Heeres*, Prussian Ministry of War, Weimar, 1902. 2 Vols.

Martin, Margaret E., "Merchants and Trade in the Connecticut River Valley, 1750-1820," *Smith College Studies in History*, Northampton, Mass., Oct. 1938-July 1939.

Miller, Clifford A., "Springfield Arms, 1794-1939," reprinted from *Army Ordnance*, July-August, 1939, the Army Ordnance Association, Washington.

Mitchell, Wesley, *Gold, Prices and Wages Under the Greenback Standard*, University of California, Berkeley, 1908.

Moore, Frank, *The Rebellion Record*, G. P. Putnam and D. Van Nostrand, New York, 1862-1866. 9 Vols.

Mordecai, Alfred, *Military Commission to Europe in 1855 and 1856*, House of Representatives, Executive Documents, 36th Congress, 2nd Session, Washington, George Bowman, 1861.

Moulton, Harold G., *Income and Economic Progress*, The Brookings Institution, Washington, 1935.

North, S. N. D. and Ralph H. North, *Simeon North, First Official Pistol Maker of the United States*, the Rumford Press, Concord, N. H., 1913.

Norton, Charles B., *American Breech-Loading Small Arms*, F. W. Christern, New York, 1872.

Norton, Charles B., *American Inventions and Improvements in Breech-Loading Small Arms*, Chapin & Gould, Springfield, Mass., 1880.

Olmsted, Denison, *Memoir of Eli Whitney, Esq.*, reprint from the *American Journal of Science*, 1832, Durrie and Peck, New Haven, 1846.

Pease, John C., and John M. Niles, *A Gazetteer of the States of Connecticut and Rhode Island*, William S. Marsh, Hartford, 1819.

Pollard, H. B. C., *A History of Firearms*, Houghton Mifflin Company, Boston and New York, 1926.

Pomeroy, Albert, A., *History and Genealogy of the Pomeroy Family*, privately published, 1912.

Remington Arms Company, Inc., *A New Chapter in an Old Story*, Remington Arms-Union Metallic Cartridge Co., New York, 1912.

Roe, Joseph Wickham, *Connecticut Inventors*, Tercentenary Commission of the State of Connecticut, Yale University Press, 1934.

Roe, Joseph Wickham, *English and American Tool Builders*, Yale University Press, New Haven, 1916.

Rohan, Jack, *Yankee Arms Maker*, Harper & Brothers, New York, 1835.

Satterlee, L. D. and Arcadi Gluckman, *American Gun Makers*, Otto Ulbrich Co., Inc., Buffalo, 1940.

Sawyer, Charles Winthrop, *Firearms in American History*, privately published, Boston, 1910. 3 Vols.

Sawyer, Charles Winthrop, *United States Single Shot Martial Pistols*, Arms Co., Boston, 1913.

Sharpe, Philip B., *The Rifle in America*, William Morrow & Co., New York, 1938.

Stearns, Charles, *The National Armories*, 2nd edition, G. W. Wilson, Springfield, Mass., 1852.

Waters, Asa Holmes, *Biographical Sketch of Thomas Blanchard and his inventions*, Lucius Goddard, Worcester, Mass., 1878.

Whittlesey, Derwent S., *A History of the Springfield Armory*, copyrighted M.S., 1920.

Winchester Repeating Arms Co., *Interesting Facts on Winchester Repeating Arms Co.*, typescript by company, no date.

Works Progress Administration, *Springfield, Massachusetts*, 1941.

REFERENCES

CHAPTER I

1. Charles H. Fitch, *Report on the Manufactures of Interchangeable Mechanism,* 4.
2. Joseph W. Roe, *English and American Tool Builders,* 5, 131.
3. Roe, *ibid.,* 136.
4. Fitch, *op. cit.,* 4.
5. Fitch, *ibid.,* 6.
6. Fitch, *ibid.,* 68.
7. Fitch, *ibid.,* 69.
8. Fitch, *ibid.,* 60.
9. Fitch, *ibid.,* 35; Roe, *op. cit.,* 144.
10. Fitch, *op. cit.,* 47-48.
11. Roe, *op. cit.,* 120.
12. Roe, *Connecticut Inventors,* 13.
13. Fitch, *op. cit.,* 5.

CHAPTER II

1. John G. W. Dillin, *The Kentucky Rifle,* 6; Charles B. Norton, *American Breech-Loading Small Arms,* 10.
2. Calvin Goddard, "The Development of Small Arms," *Encyclopaedia Britannica,* 1941; James E. Hicks, *Notes on United States Ordnance,* I, 11.
3. Dillin, *op. cit.,* 25, 46-103.
4. Dillin, *op. cit.,* 25.
5. Dillin, *op. cit.,* 26, 99, 102, 103.
6. Charles W. Sawyer, *Firearms in American History,* I, 80.
7. Hicks, *op. cit.,* I, 14.
8. Hicks, *op. cit.,* II, 11-17.
9. Sawyer, *op. cit.,* I, 118.
10. Norton, *op. cit.,* 10; Sawyer, *op. cit.,* I, 33-34.
11. Dillin, *op. cit.,* 4; Sawyer, *op. cit.,* I, 33-35.
12. Dillin, *op. cit.,* 11-15.
14. Goddard, *op. cit., loc. cit.*
15. Alfred Mordecai, *Military Commission to Europe, in 1855 and 1856,* 172.
16. Goddard, *op. cit., loc. cit.*
17. Sawyer, *op. cit.,* I, 93.
18. *Ordnance Reports,* I, 16; Hicks, *op. cit.,* II, 15.
19. Clifford A. Miller, "Springfield Arms, 1794-1939," reprint from *Army Ordnance,* July-Aug., 1939, table facing page 14.
20. Miller, *op. cit.,* 16 and table cited.
21. Miller, *op. cit.,* table cited; Hicks, *op. cit.,* I, list of models following page 117.
22. Constance McL. Green, *History of the Springfield Armory,* in process.
23. Claud E. Fuller, *Springfield Muzzle-Loading Shoulder Arms,* 59.
24. *Ordnance Reports,* II, 495.
25. S. N. D. and Ralph H. North, *Simeon North, First Official Pistol Maker of the United States,* 174; Arcadi Gluckman, *United States Martial Pistols and Revolvers,* 63.
26. Sawyer, *op. cit.,* II, 2-3.
27. Hicks, *Nathan Starr,* 157-161.
28. Miller, *op. cit.,* 16; Fitch, *op. cit.,* 30.
29. Gluckman, *op. cit.,* 75.
30. Norton, *op. cit.,* 10.
31. Miller, *op. cit.,* 16.
32. Guy Hubbard, *Windsor Industrial History,* mimeograph, 55.
33. Hicks, *op. cit.,* I, 61, II, 112-113.
34. Fuller, *op. cit.,* 78.
35. Fuller, *op. cit.,* 77; Goddard, *op. cit., loc. cit.*
36. *Ordnance Reports,* II, 10, 122.
37. Hicks, *op. cit.,* I, 9.
38. Hicks, *op. cit.,* II, 136.
39. Gluckman, *op. cit.,* 76.
40. *Ordnance Reports,* II, 218, George Talcott to W. L. Marcy, March 18, 1848.

41. *Ordnance Reports,* II, 94; Goddard, *op. cit., loc. cit.*
42. *Ordnance Reports,* II, 94; Goddard, *op. cit., loc. cit.*
43. Fuller, *op. cit.,* 82.
44. Fuller, *op. cit.,* 82; Green, *op. cit.,* Appendix III; *Ordnance Reports,* II, 14-15; Carl W. Mitman, "Edward Maynard," *Dictionary of American Biography.*
45. *Ordnance Reports,* II, 495.
46. Miller, *op. cit.,* table cited.
47. Green, *op. cit.;* Miller, *op. cit.,* table cited.
48. Fuller, *op. cit.,* 113-115; *New International Encyclopaedia,* "Claude Minié"; Goddard, *op. cit., loc. cit.*
49. Hicks, II, 161-163.
50 John W. Lang, "Simeon North," *Dictionary of American Biography.*
51. Charles T. Haven and Frank A. Belden, *A History of the Colt Revolver,* 18-20.
52. Haven and Belden, *ibid.,* 47.
53. Philip B. Sharpe, *The Rifle in America,* 175, 177-178.
54. *Springfield Republican,* "The Smith and Wesson Revolver," June 18, 1893.
55. *Springfield Republican, ibid.*
56. Jack Rohan, *Yankee Arms Maker,* 176-177.
57. Remington Arms Company, *A New Chapter in an Old Story* (no pagination).
58. Norton, *op. cit.,* 173.
59. Sharpe, *op. cit.,* 209; *Springfield Republican,* June 18, 1893: Norton, *op. cit.,* 173-174; SAR, Colt Company to Commanding Officer, June 5, 1871.
60. *Hampshire Gazette,* Feb. 7, 1838.
61. *Ibid.*
62. Fitch, *op. cit.,* 32; Carl W. Mitman, "Richard Lawrence," *Dictionary of American Biography.*
63. Mordecai, op. cit., 172.
64. Winchester Repeating Arms Co., *Interesting Facts on Winchester Repeating Arms Co.,* Jan. 19, 1944, typescript.
65. Fitch, *op. cit.,* 30; *New International Encyclopaedia,* "Cartridge."
66. Springfield Armory Records, hereafter cited as SAR, T. T. S. Laidley to A. B. Dyer, June 3, 1865.
67. Hicks, *op. cit.,* I, 11.
68. *New International Encyclopaedia,* "Cartridge."
69. *Ibid.*
70. SAR, Reports to Commanding Officer by S. W. Porter, Dec. 19, 1870, and by E. S. Allin, Dec. 13, 1870.
71. Miller, *op. cit.,* table cited; SAR, Laidley to Dyer, Nov. 17, 1865.
72. SAR, Contract between Ordnance Department and J. T. Ames and J. C. Palmer, Nov. 9, 1867; D. F. Clark to Commanding Officer, Aug. 24, 1868; J. R. McGuiness to Major-General Seymour, Sep. 22, 1869.
73. Mitman, "Edward Maynard," *Dictionary of American Biography.*
74. Roe, *English and American Tool Builders,* 170.
75. *Ordnance Reports,* II, 604.
76. *Ordnance Reports,* II, 590, Henry K. Craig to Jefferson Davis, Nov. 11, 1856.
77. SAR, John B. Floyd to Craig, Feb. 28, 1860, enclosed in Craig to James S. Whitney, Mar. 1, 1860.
78. Green, *op. cit.*
79. Sharpe, *op. cit.,* 268.
80. Norton, *op. cit.,* 14.
81. SAR, Commanding Officer to S. Crispin, Mar. 1, 1865; Commanding Officer to Dyer, Sep. 5, 1865.
82. SAR, Commanding Officer to F. Guido Katzendojer, July 26, 1865; Commanding Officer to E. K. Root, Apr. 14, 1865; Laidley to Dyer, Sept. 4, 1865.
83. Miller, *op. cit.,* 17; SAR, C. C. Chaffee to Alfred Mordecai, Aug. 4, 1866; James G. Benton to Dyer, Feb. 2, Apr. 5, and Nov. 20, 1867.
84. Hicks, *op. cit.,* I, 90-91.
85. James G. Benton, *The Fabrication of Small Arms for the United States Service,* 2 *et seq.*
86. Hicks, *op. cit.,* I, 90-91.
87. Miller, *op. cit.,* table cited.
88. SAR, Capt. Penrose to Ordnance Department, July 23, 1868; Dyer to Benton, July 13, 1868.

89. Norton, *op. cit.*, 15.
90. SAR, Benton to Remington & Sons, Oct. 18, 1867.
91. SAR, Dyer to Benton, Mar. 13, 1870, Dyer to Benton, Oct. 17, 1870.
92. SAR, Dyer to Benton, Oct. 10, 1868; S. Van Fliet to W. R. Schoemaker, July 30, 1869.
93. Hicks, *op. cit.*, I, 94.
94. SAR, Report of a Board of Officers Convened Oct. 23, 1869, Dyer to Benton, July 26, 1870.
95. SAR, Stephen V. Benét to Ordnance Department, May 9, 1872.
96. SAR, Crispin to Benton, Sept. 12, 1872.
97. *Ordnance Reports,* III, 507; SAR, J. R. Edie to G. N. Billings, Sept. 22, 1873.
98. Miller, *op. cit.*, table cited.

CHAPTER III

1. Albert A. Pomeroy, *History and Genealogy of the Pomeroy Family,* 132-207, 327.
2. Sawyer, *United States Single Shot Martial Pistols,* 32.
3. *Hampshire Gazette,* May 23, 1848.
4. Sawyer, *op. cit.*, I, 31; Norton, *American Inventions and Improvements in Breech-Loading Small Arms.* 320.
5. Sawyer, *op. cit.*, I, 30.
6. Sawyer, *ibid.*, 30.
7. Sawyer, *ibid.*, 30.
8. Sawyer, *ibid.*, 71.
9. Sawyer, *ibid.*, 98.
10. Mordecai, *op. cit.*, 100.
11. Sawyer, *op. cit.*, 145.
12. Derwent S. Whittlesey, *A History of the Springfield Armory,* 64.
13. Whittlesey, *ibid.*, 82.
14. *American State Papers, Class V, Military Affairs,* I, 66, Document 14, "Arsenals and Armories."
15. J. Leander Bishop, *A History of American Manufacturers from 1608 to 1860,* I, 485-486.
16. Bishop, *ibid.*, 494.
17. Dillin, *op. cit.*, 19.
18. Roe, *English and American Tool Builders,* 119-120.
19. SAR, Cash Book, 1798-1811, 61, 55, 57.
20. *American State Papers, Class V,* I, 131, Document 37, "Armory at Springfield," James McHenry to Vice President of the United States, Jan. 6, 1800.
21. *American State Papers, ibid.*, 131.
22. SAR, Cash Book, 1798-1811, payment to S. Rockwell & Brothers, Nov. 27, 1798, *et seq.*
23. Herbert C. Keith and Charles H. Harte, *The Early Iron Industry of Connecticut,* table at end of pamphlet.
24. Whittlesey, *op. cit.*, 61.
25. SAR, Roswell Lee to Thomas Eams, Feb. 4, 1824.
26. Sawyer, *op. cit.*, I, 31.
27. SAR, James Byers to Callender Irvine, Sep. 30, 1803.
28. SAR, Cash Book, 1798-1811, 14-77.
29. SAR, James Williams to Samuel Torrey, May 20, 1802; Nathaniel Goodrich to Lee, May 21, 1816; Decius Wadsworth to J. C. Neilson, Nov. 16, 1816; Thomas Hart & Co. to Lee, Mar. 1, 1820.
30. Sawyer, *op. cit.*, I, 118-119.
31. North and North, *op. cit.*, 14.
32. North and North, *ibid.*, 15.
33. Hicks, *Notes on United States Odnance,* I, 9.
34. Hicks, *ibid.*, 9.
35. Hicks, *op. cit.*, II, 11-13.
36. Hicks, *op. cit.*, I, 14.
37. North and North, *op. cit.*, 19.
38. Hicks, *op. cit.*, II, 13-14.
39. Hicks, *op. cit.*, I, 19.

40. *American State Papers, Class V*, I, 65-66, Document 14, "Arsenals and Armories."
41. Fuller, *op. cit.*, 12, 16.
42. Miller, *op. cit.*, 12; Fuller, *op. cit.*, 11-15; Sawyer, *op. cit.*, I, 202.
43. James G. Benton, *Total Expenditure of Money and Fabrication of Arms, Equipments, &c. at the National Armory, Springfield, Mass.*, Abstract F.
44. Hicks, *op. cit.*, II, 15.
45. Bishop, *op. cit.*, II, 77.
46. Hicks, *op. cit.*, I, 19-20; Whittlesey, *op. cit.*, 240.
47. Hicks, *op. cit.*, I, 20.
48. Hicks, *op. cit.*, I, 20.

CHAPTER IV

1. Hicks, *Notes on United States Ordnance*, II, 29.
2. *American State Papers, Class III, Financial*, II, 22, Document 193, "Encouragement to Manufactures."
3. Hicks, *op. cit.*, II, 20, 157-158.
4. Hicks, *op. cit.*, II, 18, 25; *Ordnance Reports*, I, 193.
5. Fuller, *op. cit.*, 41.
6. Hicks, *op. cit.*, I, 32; North and North, *op. cit.*, 74.
7. *Ordnance Reports*, I, 133.
8. Hicks, *op. cit.*, II, 88-103.
9. Bishop, *op. cit.*, II, 77; *Ordnance Reports*, I, 109; *Sawyer, United States Single Shot Martial Pistols*, ix-x.
10. Hicks, *op. cit.*, II, 41, 44.
11. Hicks, *op. cit.*, II, 19.
12. Whittlesey, *op. cit.*, 123; SAR, Wadsworth to Secretary of War, Jan. 27, 1817; Wadsworth to Lee, Mar. 7, 1817.
13. SAR, Wadsworth to Lee, Mar. 15, 1817.
14. *Ordnance Reports*, I, 1.
15. SAR, Wadsworth to Lee, Mar. 15, 1817.
16. SAR, Smith Cogswell to Lee, Mar. 27, 1817; Lee to Robert Johnson, Dec. 5, 1817; Lee to Nathan Starr, May 1, 1817 and Oct. 12, 1818; Lemuel Pomeroy to Lee, May 5, 1817; Starr to Lee, Mar. 14, 1817; Asa Waters to Lee, Apr. 18, 1817.
17. SAR, Adam Kinsley to Lee, Apr. 7, 1817; Lee to Alva Keep, Jan. 6, 1820.
18. *Ordnance Reports*, I, 112-113.
19. Sawyer, *Firearms in American History*, I, 204; C. W. Mitman, "Eli Whitney," *Dictionary of American Biography*.
20. Starr Papers, hereafter cited as SP, notice of appointment of Nathan Starr as armoror of the regiment commanded by Captain Comfort Sage, June 20, 1776.
21. Hicks, *Nathan Starr*, 19.
22. SP, N. Starr Day Book, 1799-1832, notation of May 16, 1799.
23. SP, *ibid., passim.*
24. North and North, *op. cit.*, 25, 27, 56.
25. SAR, Lee to Robert Johnson, Dec. 28 ,1818; R. Johnson to Lee, Feb. 27, 1819; Lee to Wadsworth, Mar. 1, 1819.
26. L. D. Satterlee and Arcadi Gluckman, *American Gun Makers*, 20.
27. Satterlee and Gluckman, *op. cit.*, 17, 26, 47, 122, 155, 172; Hicks, *United States Ordnance*, I, 20, and II, 119-120.
28. Satterlee and Gluckman, *op. cit.*, 10, 19, 94.
29. SAR, Lee to E. H. Mills, Dec. 26, 1818.
30. SAR, "Table establishing the number, dimensions and power of the Water Wheels, with the head and fall of Water for each wheel, at the U. S. Armory, Springfield, Mass., Nov. 27, 1823."
31. William P. Blake, *History of the Town of Hamden, Connecticut*, 291.
32. Grace Fuller, *An Introduction to the History of Connecticut as a Manufacturing State*, 16.
33. SAR, Eli Whitney to Lee, Feb. 14, 1822.
34. SAR, Lee to Holly & Coffing, Dec. 20, 1821; Holly & Coffing to Lee, May 20, 1822; Pomeroy to Lee, June 11, 1822; A. Peet and Samuel Church to Lee, Jan. 14, 1826; SP, N. Starr Day Book, 1823-1852, entry of Nov. 29, 1823.
35. SAR, Benjamin Jenks to Lee, Aug. 28, 1822; Lee to George Bomford, Sep. 24, 1822.
36. SAR, James Carrington to Lee, Sep. 24, 1829; SP, Starr Day Book, 1823-1852, entry of Mar. 16, 1824.

37. SP, Starr Day Book, 1823-1852, entries of Apr. 2, 1818 and Sep. 23, 1824.
38. North and North, *op. cit.*, 65.
39. SAR, J. M. Morton to Lee, Mar. 4, 1818.
40. *Ordnance Reports*, I, 177.
41. Blake, *op. cit.*, 133.
42. *Ordnance Reports*, I, 177.
43. *Ordnance Reports*, I, 177.
44. See Appendix A, Table 4.
45. Hicks, *Notes on United States Ordnance*, II, 24.
46. Blake, *op. cit.*, 112-116.
47. Hicks, *op. cit.*, I, 20, 32; North and North, *op. cit.*, 35; Satterlee and Gluckman, *op. cit., passim.*
48. Margaret E. Martin, *Merchants and Trade of the Connecticut River Valley*, 176.
49. Hicks, *op. cit.*, I, 23-24.
50. Hicks, *op. cit.*, I, 45.
51. North and North, *op. cit.*, 95-99.
52. North and North, *ibid.*, 136-137.
53. Denison Olmsted, *Memoir of Eli Whitney*, Esq., 48.
54. *Ordnance Reports*, I, 26.
55. Carl W. Mitman, "Eli Whitney," *Dictionary of American Biography*.
56. Hicks, *Nathan Starr*, 123.
57. *Ordnance Reports*, I, 177.
58. Hicks, *Nathan Starr*, 82-84.
59. Hicks, *Notes on United States Ordnance*, II, 104-112; Blake, *op. cit.*, 298.
60. Blake, *op. cit.*, 298.
61. North and North, *op. cit.*, 137-138.
62. North and North, *ibid.*, 79, 95.
63. SAR, see note in contract between the Springfield Armory and the Springfield Manufacturing Company, Aug. 8, 1826; Benjamin Jenks to Lee, Feb. 13, 1827.
64. SP, E. W. N. Starr's Day Book, 1819-1860, entry of Nathan Starr, Feb. 25, 1819.
65. Blake, *op. cit.*, 133.
66. *Ordnance Reports*, I, 113.
67. *Ordnance Reports*, I, 113.
68. Hicks, *op. cit.*, II, 29, Tench Coxe to William Eustace, Oct. 20, 1810. Reprinted by permission of the author.
69. Hicks, *ibid.*, II, 35-36.
70. *American State Papers, Class V*, I, 328, Document 116, "Arms Provided for, and Issued to, the Militia."
71. *Ordnance Reports*, I, 65, 112-113, 178.
72. Hicks, *op. cit.*, II, 29.
73. Olmstead, *op. cit.*, 48-49; *Ordnance Reports*, I, 15.
74. Hicks, *op. cit.*, II, 42, 45.
75. SAR, Wadsworth to Secretary of War, Jan. 27, 1817.
76. *Ordnance Reports*, I, 176-177, Bomford to Peter B. Porter, Jan. 7, 1829.
77. SAR, Wadsworth to Lee, July 13, 1820.
78. SAR, Eli Whitney to Lee, Aug. 28, 1821.
79. SAR, "Estimated Cost of Labor and Materials for a Musket," undated, but apparently about 1829; Lee to Wadsworth, Jan. 16, 1817; Lee to R. L. Baker, Mar. 14, 1827; Lee to Lieut. Bell, Mar. 22, 1830; Lee to George Talcott, Aug. 24, 1830.
80. SAR, "Annual return of Muskets, Pistols, Screw Drivers, Gun Boxes, etc., Manufactured at the United States Armory, Springfield, Mass., in the Year 1818."
81. *Ordnance Reports*, I, 50.
82. SAR, Lee to Wadsworth, Feb. 6, 1817.
83. SAR, Lee to Bomford, Aug. 14, 1817.
84. SAR, "Cost of Arms at Springfield, 1822."
85. SAR, Lee to Nathan Starr, Aug. 15, 1822.
86. Eli Whitney, codicil to will, Jan. 7, 1825.
87. *Ordnance Reports*, I, 181.
88. James G. Benton, *Total Expenditure of Money and Fabrication of Arms, Equipments, &c. at the National Armory, Springfield, Mass.*
89. SAR, Bomford to John Robb, Jan. 10, 1837.
90. See Appendix B, Table 2.

91. SAR, J. M. Morton to Lee, Mar. 4, 1818.
92. Martin, *op. cit.*, 112-114, 171-173.
93. SP, Memo Book of N. Starr, 1810, entries of Nov. 20, 1808 and Oct. 18, 1809.
94. SP, Memo Book of N. Starr, 1810, entry of Oct. 16, 1810 *et passim*.
95. Martin, *op. cit.*, 179-183.
96. SP, Letter Book, 1829-1849, Nathan Starr to Levin D. Johnson, July 23, 1843, and to E. T. Starr and H. Brewer, Dec. 2, 1843.
97. SAR, Lee to Wadsworth, Feb. 26, 1817.
98. North and North, *op. cit.*, 92.
99. SAR, John Rogers to Lee, Mar .19, 1828.
100. Satterlee and Gluckman, *op. cit., passim.*

CHAPTER V

1. Hicks, *Notes on United States Ordnance,* II, 11, 15.
2. Hicks, *ibid.*, II, 17.
3. Hicks, *ibid.*, II, 39.
4. SAR, Lee to Eli Whitney, June 18, 1816.
5. Hicks, *Nathan Starr,* 88.
6. Hicks, *ibid.*, 131.
7. Hicks, *ibid., passim.*
8. SAR, Lee to Justin Murphy, Oct. 25, 1827.
9. SAR, J. M. Morton to Lee, June 1, 1816; Waters to Lee, Feb. 5, 1819.
10. SAR, Lee to Senior Officer of Ordnance Department, Nov. 20, 1817.
11. SAR, Lee to Moses Morse, Aug. 2, 1819.
12. SAR, Bomford to Lee, Aug. 27, 1829.
13. *American State Papers, Class V,* II, 609-611, Document 248, "Contracts Made Since Jan. 1, 1824, for Cannon, Cannon shot, Muskets and Other Small Arms," *Regulations for the proof and inspection of small arms made under contract with the United States;* SAR, Lee to Elisha Tobey, Oct. 26, 1818; Lee to Moses Morse, Aug. 2, 1819; Lee to Pomeroy, Dec. 3, 1829.
14. SAR, Lee to Luther Sage, Feb. 24, 1817.
15. SAR, Contract Book, 1818-1830.
16. SAR, Lee to Henry Burden, Sep. 12, 1829.
17. SAR, *ibid.*
18. SAR, Lee to Justin Murphy, Dec. 30, 1816.
19. SAR, Lee to Bomford, Feb. 20, 1818.
20. SAR, Diah Allin to Lee, Jan. 25, 1830.
21. Hicks, *Notes on United States Ordnance,* II, 49-71.
22. SAR, Lee to Pomeroy, Dec. 10, 1816.
23. Hicks, *op. cit.*, I, 13.
24. SAR, Eli Whitney to Lee, Mar. 19, 1818.
25. SAR, *ibid.*
26. Hicks, *op. cit.*, II, *passim.*
27. SAR, Eli Whitney to Lee, Apr. 23, 1818.
28. SAR, Whitney to Lee, Mar. 19, 1818.
29. Hicks, *op. cit.*, II, 43, Callender Irvine to John Armstrong, Nov. 30, 1813. Reprinted by permission of the author.
30. Hicks, *ibid.*, II, 67, Irvine to H. H. Perkins, Aug. 4, 1814. Reprinted by permission of the author.
31. Hicks, *ibid.*, II, 64.
32. SAR, Eli Whitney to Lee, Mar. 19, 1818.
33. SAR, Lee to Whitney, May 9, 1818.
34. SAR, Lee to Wadsworth, Oct. 3, 1820.
35. SAR, Lee to Whitney, May 9, 1818.
36. *New International Encyclopaedia,* "John Armstrong."
37. SAR, Lee to Whitney, Mar. 15, 1818.
38. SAR, Lee to Simeon North, July 11, 1818.
39. SAR, Lee to Wadsworth, Mar. 30, 1819.
40. SAR, Craig to Bomford, May 4, 1830. (copy).
41. SAR, Pomeroy to Lee, Dec. 10, 1818.
42. SAR, Lee to Pomeroy, Dec. 19, 1818.

43. SAR, *ibid.*
44. SAR, Pomeroy to Lee, Dec. 28, 1818.
45. SAR, J. Baird to Bomford, May 18, 1824.
46. SAR, *ibid.*
47. SAR, Pomeroy to Lee, June 18, 1822.
48. SAR, copy of Elisha Tobey's Report, July 23, 1824.
49. SAR, Pomeroy to Lee, July 23, 1824.
50. SAR, Lee to Bomford, July 24, 1824.
51. SAR, James Carrington to Lee, Aug. 12, 1824.
52. SAR, Carrington to Lee, Oct. 7, 1824; Lee to Bomford, Oct. 8, 1824.
53. SAR, Lee to Pomeroy, Sep. 27, 1827.
54. SAR, Carrington to Lee, Oct. 20, 1827.
55. SAR, Bomford to Lee, July 12, 1830; W. Wade to Lee, July 13, 1830.
56. SAR, Carrington to Lee, Sep. 6, 1830.
57. SAR, Bomford to Lee, Sep. 18, 1830; Lee to P. and E. W. Blake, Oct. 25, 1830.
58. *Ordnance Reports,* I, 31.
59. SAR, Nathan Starr to Lee, Jan. 30, 1826.
60. SAR, James Carrington to Lee, July 29, 1830.
61. SAR, Wadsworth to Lee, Jan. 6, 1820; Bomford to Lee, July 12, 1827.
62. SAR, Lee to Eli Whitney, June 18, 1816; Robert Johnson to Lee, Feb. 27, 1819; Pomeroy to Lee, Apr. 19, 1823; Starr to Lee, Jan. 30, 1826.
63. SAR, Lee to Whitney, Feb. 20, 1818 and Apr. 30, 1819; Waters to Lee, Nov. 11, 1822 and Jan. 30, 1828. Regulations Book, 1829-1830, Lee to J. Weatherhead, Oct. 20, 1830.
64. SAR, Lee to Lyman and Clark, June 19, 1817; Lee to Adonijah Foot, May 15, 1822; Waters to Lee, Sep. 24, 1822; Lee to Halbach & Bros., Dec. 22, 1825.
65. SAR, Lee to Waters, Oct. 14, 1819; Pomeroy to Lee, May 20, 1820; Waters to Lee, Dec. 16, 1820; Lee to William Shields, Oct. 16, 1827; Lee to Bomford, May 21, 1828; R. and J. D. Johnson to Weatherhead, June 14, 1828.
66. SAR, Lee to Pomeroy, June 29, 1816; Lee to Starr, June 28, 1817; Lee to Starr, Nov. 2, 1817.
67. SAR, Jenks and Wilkenson to Lee, Feb. 13, 1818.
68. SAR, Springfield Manufacturing Company to Lee, Nov. 23, 1819; Whitney to Lee, Oct. 1, 1821.
69. SAR, F. N. Holly to Lee, Nov. 4, 1829; Pomeroy to Lee, Feb. 3, 1830; P. and E. W. Blake to Lee, Aug. 23, 1830; Starr to Lee, Sep. 8, 1830.
70. SAR, Lee to North, Nov. 17, 1818; Whitney to Lee, Aug. 23, 1821; Pomeroy to Lee, Oct. 15, 1821; Pomeroy to Lee, Feb. 26, 1823; Lee to Pomeroy, Oct. 3, 1823; Lee to R. and J. Johnson, June 18, 1828.
71. SAR, Lee to Waters, North, Starr, Johnson and Whitney, Apr. 18, 1818.
72. SAR, Lee to Wadsworth, Apr. 13, 1816. Quoted in part by Whittlesey, *op. cit.*
73. SAR, Bomford to Lee, Oct. 5, 1825.

CHAPTER VI

1. SAR, John Fellowes to Lee, Nov. 1, 1817.
2. SAR, J. Williams to Samuel Torrey, Mar. 6, 1801.
3. SAR, Holly & Coffing to Lee, Apr. 17, 1826.
4. SAR, Peter Schoenberger to Lee, Apr. 18, 1816.
5. SAR, Edward B. Dorsey to Lee, Apr. 19, 1816.
6. SAR, Lee to Peter Schoenberger, May 14, 1816.
7. SAR, E. Ward to Lee, May 4, 1821.
8. SAR, "Estimated Quantity and Weight of Materials Used Annually at Springfield Armory and the Expense of Transportation," undated, but among miscellaneous incoming letters, 1829.
9. Martin, *op. cit.,* 9-10.
10. SAR, Outgoing Letter Book, Notation of July 10, 1828; Lee to C. A. Bradford, Apr. 7, 1830.
11. SAR, Lee to Alfred Smith, Feb. 15, 1825.
12. SAR, Lee to Lewis Enters, Nov. 9, 1817.
13. SAR, Eli Whitney to Lee, Jan. 27, 1818.
14. SAR, Lee to P. and E. W. Blake, Sep. 7, 1829.
15. SAR, Lee to Thomas Richards, July 29, 1815.

16. SAR, Wickman & Co. to Lee, June 30, 1818; Lee to O. D. Cook & Co., Nov. 8, 1828.
17. SAR, *passim.*
18. *Ordnance Reports,* I, 99, Report of Superintendent of Springfield to Ordnance Office, 1822.
19. SAR, Lee to Senior Officer of Ordnance, Oct. 22, 1816.
20. *Ordnance Reports,* I, 49.
21. SAR, Lee to Wadsworth, Nov. 18, 1816.
22. SAR, Bomford to Lee, Oct. 2, 1822.
23. SAR, Bomford to Lee, Mar. 22, 1823.
24. SAR, Lee to John Barber, May 16, 1823.
25. SAR, Lee to Holly & Coffing, June 30, 1815; Lee to Jacob M. Halderman, June 13, 1816; notice of contracts for supplies, superintendent's office, Jan. 20, 1823.
26. SAR, Joseph Williams to Samuel Hodgdon, Jan. 20, 1800.
27. SAR, James Byers to William Simmons, Oct. 11, 1806.
28. SAR, William Lee to Roswell Lee, May 22, 1817; J. Chaffee to Senior Officer of Ordnance Department, Oct. 18, 1817.
29. SAR, Byers to William Simmons, Jan. 24, 1810.
30. SAR, J. Chaffee to Secretary of War, Jan. 30, 1815.
31. SAR, Roswell Lee to Bomford, July 15, 1815; Lee to Senior Officer of Ordnance, Sep. 15, 1816.
32. SAR, Byers to William Simmons, Jan. 16, 1805.
33. SAR, Jonathan Leonard to Henry Lechler, Dec. 24, 1814.
34. SAR, Lewis Enters to Adonijah Foot, Jan. 12, 1825; E. Warner to Lewis Enters, Feb. 1, 1826; Lee to I. and J. Townsend, May 31, 1827.
35. SAR, I. and J. Townsend to Lee, May 18, 1827.
36. SAR, Lee to Bomford, July 15, 1815; Jacob M. Halderman to Lee, May 28, 1816; Ripley & Deming to Lee, Oct. 18, 1816; Lewis Enters to Lee, July 21, 1824.
37. SAR, Lee to James Baker, Apr. 21, 1826; Lee to Halbach & Bros., Aug. 8, 1826; Lee to Townsends, Jan. 9, 1828; Lee to Lewis Enters, Jan. 31, 1828.
38. Arthur H. Cole, *Wholesale Commodity Prices in the United States, 1700-1861,* 135-136, Appendix B., Table 45.
39. SAR, Outgoing Letter Book, 1815-1818, 228-230, "List Prices of the Component Parts of the Musket Manufactured at the United States Armory, Springfield, Mass." No date, but about Jan. 1, 1817.
40. *Webster's Dictionary.*
41. SAR, Holly & Coffing to Lee, Jan. 30, 1826; Lee to J. Richardson, Oct. 31, 1829.
42. SAR, Lee to James Stubblefield, Mar. 12, 1829.
43. SAR, Lee to Bomford, Aug. 1, 1825.
44. SAR, Jonathan Leonard to Lee, July 25, 1825.
45. John C. Pease and John M. Niles, *A Gazetteer of the States of Connecticut and Rhode Island,* I, 15.
46. Keith and Harte, *op. cit.,* 14.
47. SAR, Lee to Commissioners of Navy Board, Mar. 8, 1826.
48. SAR, Solomon Rockwell Bros. to Lechler, June 15, 1814.
49. SAR, Byers to Moses Swett, Apr. 23, 1804.
50. SAR, Jacob M. Halderman to Lee, Apr. 4, 1816.
51. SAR, Lee to Bomford, Oct. 20, 1815.
52. SAR, Lee to Bomford, Nov. 20, 1815.
53. SAR, Jonathan Leonard to Lee, May 9, 1816.
54. SAR, Lee to Eli Whitney, June 18, 1816.
55. SAR, Jonathan Leonard to Lee, Jan. 10, 1818.
56. SAR, Eli Whitney to Lee, Jan. 12, 1821.
57. *American State Papers, Class III,* II, 429, Document 325, "Manufactures."
58. SAR, circular sent by Lee to S. Rockwell, J. Boyd, Reuben Cook, Merritt Bull, Holly & Coffing, Dec. 20, 1816.
59. SAR, Eli Whitney to Lee, Feb. 14, 1822.
60. SAR, Lee to Clement & Buckley, Nov. 12, 1821.
61. SAR, Lee to James Boyd, July 16, 1819.
62. SAR, Lee to Holly & Coffing, James Boyd, Bull & Cook, Hall & Pithin, Dec. 12, 1820.
63. SAR, Eli Whitney to Lee, Jan. 12, 1821.

64. SAR, Holly & Coffing to Lee, Dec. 20, 1820.
65. SAR, Lee to J. Boyd, July 18, 1816; Lee to S. Rockwell, July 18, 1816, and Jan. 18, 1817.
66. SAR, Lemuel Pomeroy to Lee, June 11, 1822.
67. SAR, Lee to Springfield Armory, May 6, 1824.
68. SAR, Lee to M. B. Belknap, Feb. 8, 1825.
69. SAR, Lee to R. C. Napier, Aug. 18, 1825.
70. SAR, Jonathan Leonard to Lee, July 25, 1825; Pennfield & Taft to Lee, June 3, 1828.
71. SAR, Thomas Copeland to Lee, July 30, 1825.
72. SAR, Lee to Bomford, Aug. 1, 1825.
73. SAR, John Hall to Lee, Dec. (no day) 1827.
74. SAR, Lee to John Hall, Dec. (no day) 1827.
75. SAR, Lee to J. Boyd, Dec. 8, 1829.
76. SAR, circular sent by Lee to Holly & Coffing, Canfield & Stirling, S. Rockwell and J. Boyd, Dec. 3, 1829.
77. SAR, Lee to Richard Walkley, Dec. 28, 1829.
78. SAR, Report of Richard Walkley to Lee, Dec. 28, 1829.
79. SAR, Outgoing Letter Book, 1815-1818, "List Prices of the Component Parts of the Musket Manufactured at the United States Armory, Springfield, Mass." 228-230. No date, but about Jan. 1, 1817.
80. SAR, "Estimate of the Quantity and Cost of each of the several kinds of material that compose a Musket." Undated, but among miscellaneous incoming letters, 1829.
81. *Webster's Dictionary.*
82. Charles H. Fitch, *Report on the Manufacture of Hardware, Cutlery and Edge-Tools*, 14.
83. SAR, Halbach Bros. to Lee, Nov. 9, 1826.
84. SAR, Cash Book, 1798-1811, 51, account in favor of Rockwells, Sep. 1799.
85. SAR, David Watkinson and Co. to Lee, Nov. 11, 1826.
86. SAR, John Odin to Lechler, Mar. 8, 1814.
87. SAR, Abraham Gibson to Lechler, Oct. 25, 1813.
88. SAR, Lechler to Jonathan Leonard, Sep. 18, 1813.
89. SAR, Abraham Gibson to Lechler, Oct. 25, 1813.
90. SAR, J. Leonard to Lechler, July 25, 1814; J. Leonard to Lee, July 13, 1815.
91. SAR, J. Leonard to Benjamin Prescott, May 15, 1815.
92. SAR, Lee to J. Leonard, Jan. 18, 1819.
93. SAR, Lee to Stubblefield, Nov. 30, 1824.
94. SAR, Lee to Bomford, Apr. 30, 1825.
95. SAR, Lee to Bomford, Nov. 30, 1824.
96. SAR, Lee to Godfrey Boker, Apr. 16, 1825.
97. SAR, Lee to Godfrey Boker, Apr. 16, 1825; Lee to P. and E. W. Blake, Dec. 13, 1825.
98. SAR, Boker to Lee, Feb. 5, 1826.
99. SAR, D. Watkinson and Co. to Lee, Nov. 27, 1826.
100. SAR, Joseph Weatherhead to Lee, Mar. 30, 1826.
101. SAR, Lee to Joseph Dutcher, July 10, 1828; Thomas Richards to Lee, Dec. 24, 1828; Lee to Thomas Richards, Mar. 5, 1829; Devens & Thompson to Lee, Aug. 14, 1829.
102. SAR, Lee to Thomas Richards, Mar. 5, 1829.
103. SAR, John A. Sullivan to Lee, Apr. 23, 1823.
104. SAR, John A. Sullivan, *ibid.*
105. SAR, Index of outgoing letters, 1821-1825: Lee to John Sullivan, Apr. 30, 1823.
106. SAR, Lee to Thomas Eams, Feb. 4, 1824.
107. SAR, Lee to B. L. Clark, Jan. 20, 1825.
108, SAR, Jacob Richards to Lee, Dec. 1, 1817.
109. SAR, Lee to John Richards, Nov. 2, 1817.
110. SAR, Lee to Bomford, Apr. 23, 1823.
111. SAR, James Byers to Callender Irvine, May 29, 1805; Lee to Bomford, Dec. 12, 1815.
112. SAR, Jacob Richards to Lee, Nov. 24, 1815; Lee to John Richards, Nov. 2, 1817; Jacob Richards to Lee, Nov. 18, 1822.
113. SAR, Jacob Richards to Lee, Nov. 19, 1822.

114. SAR, Lee to John Bassett, Feb. 18, 1825; Lee to W. Mayweg, Sep. 10, 1828; Lee to George Richards, Jan. 13, 1829.
115. SAR, Lee to Thomas Eams, Feb. 4, 1824; Lee to Lewis Enters, Feb. 12, 1825.
116. SAR, Jacob Richards to Lee, Dec. 1, 1817 and Aug. 21, 1819; Samuel Rowland & Co. to Lee, July 29, 1822.
117. SAR, Lee to Decius Wadsworth, Sep. 10, 1819.
118. SAR, Lee to Edwin Hains, Dec. 19, 1827.
119. SAR, Lee to Elizabeth Richards, Apr. 19, 1826.
120. SAR, Daniel Kellogg to Lee, Sep. 24, 1824.
121. SAR, Lee to Elizabeth Richards, Apr. 19, 1826; Lee to George Talcott, June 7, 1826.
122. SAR, Jacob Richards to Lee, June 9, 1823.
123. SAR, Lee to Chester King, Oct. 21, 1825.
124. SAR, Ezra Ward to Lee, Sep. 4, 1820; Colton Vinton to Lee, July 15, 1821.
125. SAR, Incoming Official Letter Book, 1827-1833, charcoal contracts list.
126. SAR, Joseph Weatherhead to Lee, Jan. 13, 1827.
127. SAR, Lee to James Stubblefield, Oct. 26, 1820.
128. SAR, Lee to Bomford, Aug. 1, 1825.
129. SAR, James Williams to Samuel Hodgdon, May 4, 1820.
130. SAR, William Van Deusen to Lee, Sep. 20, 1816.
131. SAR, Lee to Chapin & Northam, Mar. 13, 1828.
132. SAR, Weatherhead to Lee, Feb. 21, 1827.
133. SAR, Lee to Lemuel Pomeroy, Apr. 25, 1828.
134. SAR, Diah Allin to Lee, "Expense of Coal for Welding Barrels," among Miscellaneous Incoming Letters, 1829.
135. SAR, D. Wilkinson to Lee, May 3, 1828.
136. SAR, Capt. A. Jenks to Lee, May 17, 1831.
137. SAR, Pomeroy to Lee, Apr. 22, 1828; Asa Waters to Lee, Oct. 3, 1828.
138. SAR, Joseph, Warren & Wright to Lee, Dec. 15, 1828.
139. SAR, Bills for files: from Thomas Richards, July 24 and Dec. 9, 1815; from Blake & Cunningham, Aug. 7, 1816; from James Baker, Aug. 29, 1826 and Apr. 13, 1827.
140. SAR, Lee to W. H. Dwight, June 18, 1815.
141. SAR, Springfield Armory Announcement, Apr. 19, 1821.
142. SAR, L. H. Bates and William Lacen to Lee, Feb. 5, 1829; Lee to Benjamin Morse, July 30, 1829.
143. Green, *op. cit.;* SAR, Charles Signourney to Lee, Nov. 6, 1816; Lee to James Stubblefield, Dec. 2, 1816; Lee to T. Wickham, Apr. 10, 1817; Lee to Senior Officer, Ordnance Department, Jan. 24, 1818; Lee to John Colley & Co., Aug. 13, 1827.
144. Claud Fuller, *op. cit.*, 68; SAR, Charles Signourney to Lee, Nov. 16, 1816; Wickham & Co. to Lee, Aug. 4, 1819; Signourney to Lee, May 24, 1824; Lee to Blossom & Williams, Aug. 11, 1827; John Dillingham to Lee, Sep. 24, 1829.
145. SAR, Hotchkiss & Burdett to Lee, July 20, 1816; Samuel & H. Fowler to Lee, July 10, 1821; W. H. Imlay & Co. to Lee, Apr. 19, 1824; Lee to Samuel Fowler, Jan. 18, 1828.
146. SAR, A. A. Bernard to A. B. Dyer, Dec. 18, 1862; I. G. Palmer to Dyer, Jan. 27, 1864.
147. SAR, Hotchkiss & Burdett to Lee, July 20, 1816; W. H. Imlay & Co. to Lee, Apr. 19, 1824.
148. SAR, Outgoing Letter Book, 1821-1825, p. 189, "Estimated Amount & Weight of Stock & Materials Necessary to Make 12,000 Muskets," undated, but about Apr. 6, 1823.

CHAPTER VII

1. Roe, *English and American Tool Builders,* 129-130.
2. Blake, *op. cit.*, 138.
3. Blake, *ibid.*, 296.
4. Blake, *ibid.*, 138.
5. North and North, *op. cit.*, 80.
6. SAR, Lee to Adonijah Foot, Mar. 24, 1818.
7. SAR, Lee to Asa Waters, June 8, 1819. Quoted in part by Whittlesey, *op. cit.*
8. SAR, Eli Whitney Jr. to P. C. Watson, Sep. 9, 1863.

9. *American State Papers, Class V, Military Affairs*, II, 543-54, Document 246, "Armory at Springfield."
10. *Ordnance Reports*, I, 150, Bomford to James Barbour, Jan. 31, 1827.
11. Fitch, *Report on the Manufactures of Interchangeable Mechanism*, 4.
12. SAR, Bomford to Lee, Sep. 21, 1821.
13. SAR, Bomford to Lee, Aug. 3, 1827.
14. SAR, Callender Irvine to Henry Lechler, June 22, 1814; Lee to Bomford, Sep. 11, 1821.
15. SAR, Bomford to Lee, Aug. 7, 1821; Lee to Stubblefield, Oct. 31, 1827.
16. SAR, Lee to James Carrington, Oct. 25, 1827.
17. SAR, William Wade to Lee, Sep. 28, 1824.
18. *American State Papers, Class V, Military Affairs*, II, 544, Document 246, "Armory at Springfield. Communicated to the House of Representatives by Committee on Military Affairs, March 3, 1823; A description of the United States' Armory at Springfield, Massachusetts, with a statement exhibiting the number of arms manufactured and repaired, and the amount of expenditures annually, from the commencement of the establishment in 1795, to the close of the year 1817." Report of Major James Dalliba, (or Dalaby) in Oct. 1819, to Col. Decius Wadsworth, U.S. Ordnance.
19. SAR, Bomford to Lee, July 26, 1822; Lee to Bomford, Feb. 1, 1823.
20. Hicks, *Nathan Starr*, 165.
21. SAR, Lee to Starr, Jan. 31, 1828; Lee to Jacob Russell, Mar. 26, 1828.
22. SAR, Pomeroy to Lee, Feb. 24, 1829.
23. SAR, Lee to Jacob Russell, Mar. 26, 1828.
24. SAR, Lee to Starr, Jan. 31, 1828.
25. *Ordnance Reports*, I, 15.
26. Olmsted, *op. cit.*, 53-54.
27. John W. Lang, "Simeon North," *Dictionary of American Biography;* North and North, *op. cit.*, 10; Roe, *English and American Tool Builders*, 136.
28. North and North, *op. cit.*, 64.
29. *American State Papers, Class V, Military Affairs*, II, 543, Document 246, "Armory at Springfield," report of James Dalliba cited *supra.*
30. SAR, Lee to Captain Pattridge, Apr. 22, 1817.
31. *Webster's Dictionary.*
32. Roe, *English and American Tool Builders*, 142.
33. Fitch, *op. cit.*, 21.
34. SAR, Pomeroy to Lee, Mar. 17, 1820.
35. SAR, Bomford to Lee, Jan. 23, 1828; Bomford to Lee, Nov. 6, 1830.
36. Roe, *op. cit.*, 142.
37. Roe, *Connecticut Inventors*, 4-5.
38. North and North, *op. cit.*, 84.
39. Roe, *English and American Tool Builders*, 142.
40. Fitch, *op. cit.*, 4.
41. SAR, Lee and Stubblefield to Senior Officer, Ordnance Department, Mar. 20, 1816.
42. Roe, *English and American Tool Builders*, 132.
43. SAR, Lee to George Blake, Aug. 29, 1821; Lee to Bomford, Sep. 15, 1821.
44. Fitch, *op. cit.*, 11; SAR, Jenks & Wilkinson to Lee, Feb. 13, 1818.
45. Fitch, *op. cit.*, 11.
46. SAR, Lee to William Holmes, Sep. 23, 1822.
47. SAR, Lee to William Holmes, May 17, 1820.
48. SAR, Stubblefield to Lee, Aug. 23, 1821 and Oct. 21, 1822.
49. SAR, William Holmes to Lee, June 22, 1818; Lee to George Blake, Aug. 29, 1821.
50. SAR, Stubblefield to Lee, Aug. 23, 1821; Lee to Bomford, Sep. 15, 1821.
51. SAR, Lee to Bomford, July 13, 1815; Wickham & Co. to Lee, Aug. 24, 1821.
52. Tench Coxe, *A Statement of the Arms and Manufactures of the United States of America, for the year 1810*, Part I.
53. *Digest of Accounts of Manufacturing Establishments in the United States and of their Manufactures*, 1822.
54. SAR, Lee to Senior Officer, Ordnance Department, Apr. 20, 1816; Lee to Eli Whitney, July 19, 1824.
55. SAR, Eli Whitney to Lee, Aug. 2, 1824.

56. SAR, Lee to Whitney, Dec. 30, 1816; Jonathan Leonard to Lee, June 26, 1818.
57. SAR, Jonathan Leonard to Lee, June 26, 1818.
58. SAR, Jonathan Leonard, *ibid.*
59. SAR, Lee to Bomford, Aug. 1, 1821.
60. SAR, Lee to Bomford, Aug. 1, 1821.
61. Asa Holmes Waters, *Biographical Sketch of Thomas Blanchard,* 6; SAR, Lee to Bomford, June 27, 1818.
62. SAR, Lee to Bomford, June 27, 1818.
63. SAR, Jonathan Leonard to Lee, June 26, 1818.
64. SAR, Jonathan Leonard, *ibid.*
65. SAR, Lee to Eli Whitney, June 30, 1815; Lee to Senior Officer of Ordnance, Apr. 20, 1816.
66. *American State Papers, Class V, Military Affairs,* I, 848-855, Document 175, "Contracts Made in the Year 1818"; SAR, Wadsworth to Lee, Nov. 16, 1818.
67. SAR, Lee to Senior Officer, Ordnance Department, Apr. 20, 1816.
68. Fitch, *op. cit.,* 10.
69. Fitch, *ibid.,* 10.
70. *American State Papers, Class V, Military Affairs,* II, 552, Document 246, "Armory at Springfield," report of James Dalliba cited *supra.*
71. Fitch, *op. cit.,* 11.
72. SAR, Lee to Bomford, Feb. 26, 1818.
73. SAR, Adonijah Foot to Lee, Mar. 10, 1818.
74. SAR, Eli Whitney to Lee, Jan. 3, 1818.
75. SAR, Lee to Stubblefield, Feb. 8, 1817; Sylvester Nash to Lee, Apr. 28, 1818.
76. Fitch, *op. cit.,* 11.
77. SAR, Thomas Blanchard to Lee, Oct. 13, 1818.
78. SAR, Lee to Stubblefield, July 11, 1818.
79. Waters, *op. cit.,* 6; SAR, Blanchard to Lee, Oct. 13, 1818.
80. SAR, Lee to Brook Evans, Apr. 3, 1821; Lee to Blanchard, Mar. 29, 1823; M. T. Wickham to Lee, Dec. 12, 1825.
81. SAR, Lee to John Morton, Dec. 6, 1817; Lee to Pomeroy, Dec. 12, 1827.
82. SAR, Adonijah Foot to Lee, Mar. 10, 1818.
83. SAR, Lee to Bomford, May 27, 1818.
84. SAR, Lee to Bomford, June 19, 1822.
85. Fitch, *op. cit.,* 16.
86. Fitch, *ibid.,* 17.
87. Fitch, *ibid.,* 15.
88. Bishop, *op. cit.,* II, 264; SAR, Blanchard to Lee, Feb. 17, 1829.
89. Edward W. Byrn, *The Progress of Invention in the Nineteenth Century,* 368.
90. SAR, Wadsworth to Lee, June 4, 1819; Stubblefield to Lee, Aug. 14, 1819.
91. SAR, Lee to Blanchard, June 18, 1819.
92. SAR, Blanchard to Lee, Feb. 19, 1821.
93. SAR, Lee to Bomford, June 19, 1822.
94. SAR, Lee to Blanchard, July 16, 1822; Lee to Bomford, Aug. 1, 1822.
95. SAR, Lee to Bomford, July 16, 1825.
96. SAR, Pay-Roll Books, *passim.*
97. SAR, Lee to Blanchard, Jan. 19, 1827.
98. SAR, Pay-Roll Books, 1828-1829.
99. SAR, Foot to Lee, Deb. 21, 1820.
100. SAR, Lee to Bomford, Nov. 12, 1825.
101. Fitch, *op. cit.,* 15; *Ordnance Reports,* I, 161-162.
102. North and North, *op. cit.,* 84; Mitman, "Eli Whitney," *Dictionary of American Biography.*
103. Fitch, *op. cit.,* 27.
104. *American State Papers, Class V, Military Affairs,* II, 551, Document 246, "Armory at Springfield," report of James Dalliba cited *supra;* Fitch, *op. cit.,* 26-27; inventory of Eli Whitney's estate, May 14, 1827, attached to codicil of his will; SAR, Foot to Lee, Dec. 17, 1824; "Table establishing the dimensions & power of the Water for each Wheel, at the U. S. Armory, Springfield, Mass., Nov. 27, 1823."
105. Dillin, *op. cit.,* 31-99.
106. SAR, Ruple & Parkinson to Lee, Dec. 29, 1827.
107. SAR, James Williams to Samuel Hodgdon, Mar. 12, 1800.

108. SAR, Lee to Whitney, July 18, 1818.
109. *American State Papers, Class V, Military Affairs,* II, 552, Document 246, "Armory at Springfield," report of James Dalliba cited *supra:* SAR, Lee to Senior Officer, Ordnance Department, Jan. 10, 1818.
110. SAR, Lee to Bomford, Aug., 1825. (No day given).
111. SAR, Lee, *ibid.*
112. SAR, Lee to Thomas Dunn, Sep. 16, 1829.
113. SAR, Lee to Whitney, July 19, 1824.
114. SAR, Lee, *ibid.*
115. SAR, Lee to John Symington, Feb. 16, 1829.

CHAPTER VIII

1. SAR, Lee to Bomford, Aug. 6, 1817.
2. SAR, Lee to William Riddell, Feb. 13, 1825.
3. *Ordnance Reports,* I, 395.
4. Hicks, *Nathan Starr,* 76; SAR, Work Returns, *passim.*
5. SP, Nathan Starr's Day Book, 1799-1832, *passim.*
6. Hicks, *Nathan Starr,* 76.
7. SP, Nathan Starr, Sr., *Memorandum Book of Contracts;* Nathan Starr's Day Book, 1823-1852, entry of June 22, 1825.
8. SAR, Josiah Thorp to Lee, Nov. 30, 1826.
9. SAR, Work Returns, Dec., 1814, Jan., 1815.
10. *American State Papers, Class V, Military Affairs,* I, 132, Document 37, "Armory at Springfield."
11. *Ordnance Reports,* I, 396, "Notes on the Springfield Armory," Talcott to Secretary of War, July 30, 1841.
12. *Ordnance Reports,* I, 396, Talcott, *op. cit.:* SAR, Erastus Clark to Lee, 1820 (no day or month).
13. *Ordnance Reports,* I, 396, Talcott, *op. cit.*
14. *American State Papers, Class V, Military Affairs,* II, 543, Dalliba, *op. cit.*
15. *American State Papers, Class V, Military Affairs,* II, 543, Dalliba, *ibid.*
16. SAR, Notice, Dec. 5, 1825; Lee to David Ames, Joseph and Allen Bangs, Dec. 17, 1825.
17. SAR, Lee to Bomford, July 3, 1824; "Regulations relative to warming the shops," Jan. 21, 1826.
18. SAR, Lee to Joseph Weatherhead, Dec. 18, 1817.
19. SAR, Lee to Waters, North, Johnson, Whitney, Starr, Apr. 18, 1818.
20. SAR, Lee to O. Bangs, July 18, 1817.
21. *Ordnance Reports,* I, 395, Talcott, op. cit.
22. SAR, Lee to Senior Officer of Ordnance, Dec. 1, 1817.
23. SAR, Benjamin Prescott to James Monroe, Feb. 4, 1815.
24. SAR, Benjamin Prescott, *ibid.*
25. SAR, Lee to Wadsworth, July 9, 1815. Quoted in part by Whittlesey, *op. cit.*
26. SAR, Lee to Bomford, Jan. 25, 1816.
27. SAR, Joseph W. Wright to Lee, Oct. 12, 1824.
28. SAR, Lee to Silas Fuller, Jan. 26, 1820; Lee to David Welch, Oct. 27, 1821; Lee to Josiah Finch, Apr. 29, 1822.
29. SAR, Diah Allin to Lee, Mar. 15, 1823.
30. SAR, Lee to William Riddell, Feb. 12, 1825.
31. *Ordnance Reports,* I, 396, Talcott, *op. cit.*
32. *Ordnance Reports,* I, 395, Talcott, *op. cit.*
33. SAR, Armory Regulation, Mar. 18, 1823; Notice of Superintendent, Sep. 13, 1827.
34. *Ordnance Reports,* I, 396, Talcott, *op. cit.*
35. SAR, Benjamin Moore to Lee, June 6, 1815; Oliver Allen to Lee, Feb. 3, 1821; Pomeroy to Lee, Sep. 8, 1829; Charles Ball to Lee, Dec. 7, 1829.
36. SAR, Eli Whitney to Lee, Apr. 23, 1818.
37. SAR, Armory Regulations, Mar. 8, 1816.
38. SAR, Armory Notice of Nov. 1816.
39. SAR, Lee to O. Bangs, May 14, 1816.
40. SAR, Lee to Pomeroy, Oct. 18, 1820; Pomeroy to Lee, Aug. 23, 1821; Nathan Starr to Lee, Mar. 28, 1826; James Carrington to Lee, Mar. 30, 1826.
41. SAR, Pomeroy to Lee, Jan. 7, 1819.

42. SAR, Lee to Bomford, Feb. 18, 1822.
43. SAR, Pomeroy to Lee, Jan. 7, 1819; Superintendent's Office, Order to Springfield Armory, Apr. 8, 1820; Lee to Charles Wood, Mar. 18, 1826; Bomford to Lee, Feb. 27, 1829.
44. SAR, Lee to Eli Whitney, Sep. 25 and Dec. 22, 1815; Lee to O. Bangs, May 24, 1816; James Dalaby to Lee, Apr. 25 and June 20, 1821; P. and E. W. Blake to Lee, Jan. 2, 1826; Lee to P. and E. W. Blake, Jan. 6, 1826; Asa Waters to Lee, 1829 (no day or month).
45. *Ordnance Reports*, I, 396, Talcott, *op. cit.*, SAR, Superintendent's Office, Order to Springfield Armory, July 8, 1818; Lee to Wadsworth, July 24, 1820; Bomford to Lee, May 28, 1821.
46. SAR, Lee to James Dalaby, Apr. 30, 1821.
47. SAR, Bomford to Lee, Sep. 28, 1826.
48. SAR, Lee to Charles Wood, Mar. 18, 1826.
49. SAR, Pomeroy to Lee, Feb. 20, 1820.
50. SAR, Lee to Bomford, Apr. 18, 1821.
51. SAR, Superintendent's Office, Order to Springfield Armory, Apr. 8, 1820. Quoted in part by Whittlesey, *op. cit.*
52. SAR, Bomford to Lee, Feb. 17 and 27, 1829.
53. SAR, Lee to Bomford, Nov. 15, 1821.
54. SAR, Lee to Talcott, Dec. 31, 1828.
55. Whittlesey, *op. cit.*, 82; SAR, Cash Book, 1798-1811, 51-149.
56. *American State Papers, Class V, Military Affairs*, IV, 364, Document 446, "On the Claim of Daniel Johnson, Apprenticed to the Superintendent of the Armory at Harper's Ferry, for Injuries From the Non-Performance of the Contract," communicated to the House Mar. 26, 1830, by Mr. Drayton, from the Committee of Military Affairs.
57. SAR, Work Returns for 1806, *passim.*
58. SAR, Edward Nichols to Lee, Oct. 22, 1817.
59. SAR, Lee to William Riddell, Feb. 12, 1825.
60. SAR, Note of sustenance stores sold at auction, Nov. 10, 1819.
61. *Ordnance Reports*, I, 395, Talcott, *op. cit.*
62. *American State Papers, Class V, Military Affairs*, I, 173, Docupment 53, "Rations Commuted."
63. *Ordnance Reports*, I, 395, Talcott, *op. cit.*
64. *Springfield Republican*, May 15, 1898, 10; SAR, Weatherhead to Lee, June 26, 1829.
65. SAR, Work Returns, 1818, *passim.*
66. *Ordnance Reports*, I, 395-396, Talcott, *op. cit.*
67. *American State Papers, Class V, Military Affairs*, II, 542-543, Dalliba, *op. cit.*
68. Harold G. Moulton, *Income and Economic Progress*, 181.

CHAPTER IX

1. Claud Fuller, *op. cit.*, 41; Hicks, *Nathan Starr*, 15, 137.
2. SAR, Bomford to J. W. Ripley, Dec. 4, 1841; J. T. Ames to Ripley, Mar. 25 and May 16, 1853.
3. SAR, Talcott to Ripley, Apr. 10, 1845; W. A. Thornton to Ripley, July 25, 1846.
4. SAR, W. A. Thornton to James S. Whitney, Dec. 6, 1858; Thornton to Whitney, Jan. 25, 1859.
5. *Ordnance Reports*, II, 524.
6. SAR, Pomeroy to John Robb, July 14, 1834, quoting letter of G. N. Briggs, June 10, 1834.
7. SAR, circular, Bomford to Robb, July 10, 1834.
8. Hicks, *Nathan Starr*, 151-153; SAR, Circular, Bomford to Robb, Oct. 24, 1834.
9. Hicks, *ibid.*, 153; Bomford to Starr, Oct. 24, 1834. Reprinted by permission of author.
10. SAR, Pomeroy to Robb, May 10, 1839.
11. SAR, Talcott to Robb, May 2, 1839.
12. *Ordnance Reports*, II, 524-525.
13. SAR, Robb to Elizear Bates, Apr. 17, 1834.
14. SAR, Waters to Robb, Aug. 5, 1835; Robb to Henry W. Edwards, Aug. 14, 1840; J. W. Ripley to Henry Derringer, Apr. 30, 1841; E. W. N. Starr to Ripley, Jan. 18, 1842; Ripley to Robbins, Kendall & Lawrence, Sep. 20, 1847.

15. SAR, Robb to P. and E. W. Blake, Dec. 16, 1833; Bomford to Robb, Aug. 16, 1837; Henry D. Smith to Robb, Nov. 4, 1840; Bomford to Ripley, Jan. 21, 1841; E. W. N. Starr to Ripley, May 19, 1841; Pomeroy to Ripley, Jan. 27, 1842; N. P. Ames to Ripley, Feb. 14, 1843.
16. SAR, Bomford to Ripley, Nov. 23, 1841; circular sent by Ripley to H. D. Smith, E. W. N. Starr, and Edwards & Goodrich, Dec. 14, 1841.
17. SAR, Craig to Whitney, Feb. 10, 1859.
18. SAR, E. Lucas to Robb, Nov. 25, 1837; Craig to Whitney, July 30, 1855; A. M. Barbour to Whitney, May 9, 1859; Craig to I. H. Wright, Oct. 29, 1860.
19. SAR, Samuel Byington to Jerome Young, Oct. 23, 1854.
20. *Ordnance Reports,* III, 2, S. Adams to John Floyd, Nov. 24, 1860.
21. *Ordnance Reports,* III, 2.
22. Hicks, *Nathan Starr,* 153-155.
23. Hicks, *Notes on United States Ordnance,* I, 67; North and North, *op. cit.,* 152, 167; Hicks, *Nathan Starr,* 163-166; Charles T. Haven and Frank A. Belden, *A History of the Colt Revolver,* 281; SAR, Craig to Robb, Oct. 31, 1836; Craig to Robb, Sep. 24, 1837; R. Johnson to Robb, May 10, 1839; Ripley to W. A. Thornton, Aug. 8, 1854; Craig to E. Allin, Apr. 10, 1860.
24. Pomeroy, *op. cit.,* 328, 466.
25. Hicks, *Nathan Starr,* 148, Starr to Bomford, Mar. 11, 1837. Reprinted by permission of the author.
26. Pomeroy, *op. cit.,* 328, 466; SAR, Talcott to Robb, July 9, 1840; Lemuel Pomeroy to Robb, Feb. 25, 1841.
27. SP, Nathan Starr's Day Book, 1823-1852, accounts of E. W. N. Starr & Co., 1845.
28. David D. Field, *Centennial Address,* 130.
29. Gluckman, *op. cit.,* 65-66.
30. See list of New England small arms manufacturers and gunsmiths, Appendix A.
31. Hicks, *Nathan Starr,* 166.
32. SP, Nathan Starr's Day Book, 1823-1852, accounts of E. W. N. Starr & Co., 1945.
33. Aston Papers, hereafter cited as AsP, book of letters, *passim.*
34. AsP, agreement of partnership between Henry Aston, Sylvester C. Bailey, Peter Ashton, John North, and Ira N. Johnson, Mar. 21, 1851; notice of termination of partnership of Henry Aston & Co., Nov. 4, 1852.
35. Hubbard, *op. cit.,* 55.
36. Hubbard, *ibid.,* 60-61.
37. Hubbard, *ibid.,* 61.
38. Roe, *English and American Tool Builders,* 186-192; Satterlee and Gluckman, *op. cit.,* 136.
39. Carl W. Mitman, "Samuel Colt," *Dictionary of American Biography.*
40. Haven and Belden, *op. cit.,* 18-20.
41. Rohan, *op. cit.,* 165-167.
42. Harold G. Hart, "The Colt Revolver in the Arthur L. Ulrich Museum," *Hobbies,* Aug., 1844, 106-107, Colt to C. P. Lebriskee, Dec. 11, 1847. Reprinted by permission of the publisher.
43. Haven and Belden, *op. cit.,* 88, 352.
44. Hart, *op. cit., Hobbies,* Aug., 1944, 108; Bishop, *op. cit.,* II, 741.
45. Hart, *op. cit., Hobbies,* Aug., 1944, 108.
46. Opinion of Mr. Harold G. Hart; Mitman, "Samuel Colt," *Dictionary of American Biography.*
47. Rohan, *op. cit.,* 138.
48. Hart, *op. cit., Hobbies,* Aug., 1944, 107.
49. Colt Papers, hereafter cited as CP, Samuel Colt to Richard Hubbard, Oct. 23, 1856; Book of Domestic Newspaper Clippings, I, *New York Weekly Herald,* July 18, 1840. Mitman, "Samuel Colt," *loc. cit.*
50. Haven and Belden, *op. cit.,* 83.
51. CP, Colt to William B. Hartley, Jan. 13, 1860; Book of Domestic Newspaper Clippings, I, *New York Herald,* Jan. 22, 1850; *Boston Daily Times,* June 30, 1851; *Hartford Daily Courant,* Apr. 27, 1852.
52. CP, *London Weekly News Chronicle,* Jan. 17, 1850.
53. CP, Colt to C. Wendal, Apr. 14, 1854.
54. CP, Colt to Arnold Harris, Apr. 9, 1859; Colt to John B. Floyd, Apr. 10, 1859; T. W. Talioferro to Colt, Apr. 12, 1859.

55. CP, agreement between Amos B. Colt and William B. Hartley, Oct. 11, 1859.
56. CP, printed circular, Jan. 2, 1860.
57. CP, Colt to John P. Morse & Son, A. W. Spies Co., Smith Crane Co., William Reed & Son, Dec. 3, 1859.
58. CP, folder of contracts with the allies; agreement between Colt Company and Kittredge & Folsom, Jan. 1, 1860.
59. Charles W. Chapin, *Sketches of the Old Inhabitants and Other Citizens of Old Springfield of the Present Century,* 162; Harold U. Faulkner, "Edmund Dwight," *Dictionary of American Biography.*
60. Ames Papers, hereafter cited as AP, N. P. Ames to J. K. Mills & Co., Apr. 18, 1836; N. P. Ames to J. K. Mills & Co., June 14, 1836, and Feb. 4, 1837; N. P. Ames to George Talcott, Feb. 8, 1837; N. P. Ames to Thomas Davis, Mar. 8, 1837; N. P. Ames to E. A. Clary, Mar. 10, 1837; N. P. Ames to W. M. Crane, May 27, 1845.
61. *Springfield Republican,* Jan. 15, 1899.
62. Mordecai, *op. cit.,* 107. AP, N. P. Ames to Benjamin Moore, Jan. 24, 1845; J. T. Ames to James Burton, Nov. 20, 1856.
63. AP, N. P. to J. T. Ames, Jan. 30 and Feb. 21, 1834, and Feb. 14 and Feb. 18, 1835; N. P. Ames to J. K. Mills & Co., Jan. 28, 1836; N. P. to J. T. Ames, Apr. 14, 1846.
64. AP, N. P. to J. T. Ames, Feb. 14 and 21, 1835.
65. Louis Hacker, *The Triumph of American Capitalism,* 235-238, 327.
66. *Springfield Republican,* Jan. 15, 1899.
67. AP, N. P. to J. T. Ames, Sep. 8, 1841; N. P. Ames to W. M. Crane, Mar. 21, 1845.
68. Satterlee and Gluckman, *op. cit.,* 168-180; Mitman, "Oliver Winchester," *Dictionary of American Biography.*
69. Mitman, "Eliphalet Remington," *Dictionary of American Biography.*
70. Carpenter and Morehouse, *The History of the Town of Amherst, Massachusetts,* 297.
71. Rohan, *op. cit.,* 177; Sawyer, *Firearms in American History,* II, 77. SAR, A. C. Burnside to Craig, July 9, 1853, enclosed in letter of Craig to Ripley, July 11, 1853; J. S. Whitney to John Taylor, Oct. 3, 1859; Whitney to Waters, Apr. 16, 1860.
72. Hubbard, *op. cit.,* 55; Sawyer, *Firearms in American History,* II, 80, 82-83, 168, 170.
73. SAR, Christian Sharps to Ripley, Dec. 13, 1852.
74. SAR, John C. Symmes to Ordnance Department, Sep. 9, 1864; Craig to Ripley, Sep. 11, 1854; J. S. Whitney to Craig, Oct. 23, 1854.
75. SAR, Craig to J. S. Whitney, Apr. 1, 1858; E. S. Allin to Craig, July 27, 1858; Craig to Whitney, July 30, 1858; John Brown to Whitney, Aug. 10, 1858; Whitney to Craig, Oct. 22, 1858; Craig to Whitney, Oct. 30, 1858; Brown to Whitney, Nov. 8, 1858, and Jan. 9, 1859.
76. *Ordnance Reports,* II, 232.
77. Haven and Belden, *op. cit.,* 389.
78. Haven and Belden, *ibid.,* 889.
79. Norton, *American Breech-Loading Small Arms,* 13.
80. Bishop, *op. cit.,* II, 429-474.
81. Hubbard, *op. cit.,* 55; Rohan, *op. cit.,* 174-175, 233.
82. Haven and Belden, *op. cit.,* 380; SAR, Justice & Steinmetz to J. S. Whitney, Feb. 12, 1858.
83. Rohan, *op. cit.,* 174-175.
84. Haven and Belden, *op. cit.,* 86.
85. Haven and Belden, *ibid,* 54-82.
86. Mordecai, *op. cit.,* 165.
87. Barnard, *op. cit.,* 360; Rohan, *op. ctt.,* 179, 223.
88. Harold Faulkner, "Nathan Peabody Ames," *Dictionary of American Biography.*
89. Fitch, *op. cit.,* 5.
90. Fitch, *ibid,* 6.
91. SAR, Henry Aston to Ripley, Oct. 12, 1847.
92. SAR, Ordnance Department to Ripley, Apr. 12, 1854; Ordnance Department to J. S. Whitney, May 9 and June 15, 1857.
93. Mordecai, *op. cit.,* 107.
94. SAR, Ordnance Department to J. S. Whitney, Dec. 15, 1854; Ordnance Department to I. H. Wright, Mar. 18, 1861.

95. SAR, Philos B. Tyler to J. S. Whitney, June 4, 1857.
96. Louis McLane, *Documents Relative to the Manufactures in the United States,* I, 280-281.
97. SAR, "Average Cost of Muskets Manufactured at the Springfield Armory 1825-1835 inclusive," statement enclosed in letter of Bomford to Robb, Jan. 10, 1837.
98. SAR, J. S. Whitney to Ordnance Department, Feb. 3, 1858.
99. Green, *op. cit.*
100. SAR, Robb to Talcott, Nov. 30, 1840.
101. Green, *op. cit.*
102. Green, *ibid.*

CHAPTER X

1. Thelma M. Kistler, *The Rise of Railroads in the Connecticut River Valley,* 41.
2. Kistler, *ibid,* 41.
3. SAR, Frederick Tyler to Ripley, May 21, 1841.
4. SAR, J. H. Williams to Lee, Oct. 29, 1832.
5. SAR, Elizabeth Barry to J. S. Whitney, Apr. 16, 1857; A. Heckman to Whitney, June 10 and July 23, 1857.
6. Kistler, *op. cit.,* 40.
7. SAR, Henry Edwards to Robb, May 20, 1839.
8. SAR, Henry Edwards to Ripley, Jan. 15 and May 18, 1842; J. Ellison to Ripley, Jan. 19, 1845.
9. SAR, Naylor, Hutchinson, Vickers & Co. to Ripley, Feb. 23, 1842.
10. Kistler, *op. cit.,* 39.
11. SAR, Landon, Moore & Co. to Ripley, Mar. 14 and June 15, 1842, and Nov. 6, 1844; Canfield & Robbins to Ripley, Aug. 27, 1845.
12. SAR, William Yates to Ripley, Jan. 2, 1844.
13. Kistler, *op. cit.,* 40.
14. Kistler, *ibid,* 43.
15. SAR, Lewis Enters to Lee, Nov. 24, 1832; Robb to Hiram Steel, Oct. 21, 1834; David Freed to Robb, Aug. 23, 1839; A. T. Durell to Ripley, Nov. 18, 1850; T. H. Baird to J. S. Whitney, Nov. 24, 1855; A. Heckman to Whitney, July 23, 1857.
16. SAR, J. Baker to Lee, May 13, 1833.
17. SAR, Noble & Co. to Ripley, June 18, 1850.
18. SAR, M. W. Chapin to Robb, Jan. 13, 1837; Timothy Sawyer to Robb, Aug. 12, 1837.
19. SAR, M. W. Chapin to Robb, Dec. 8, 1835.
20. SAR, Robb to Bomford, Sep. 23, 1837.
21. SAR, outgoing letter book, 1828-1834, memorandum of grindstone purchase, Jan. 20, 1831; A. C. Lombard & Co. to Robb, Aug. 8, 1836.
22. SAR, James Boyd to Talcott, Sep. 27, 1833.
23. SAR, George Shields to Robb, Apr. 5, 1839; Burgh & Boughton to Robb, May 27, 1840; H. Brainard & Co. to Robb, Oct. 29, 1840.
24. SAR, Masters, Markoe & Co. to Robb, Apr. 1, 1835; A. C. Lombard & Co. to Robb, Aug. 8, 1836, and June 9, 1838; George W. Shields to Robb, Apr. 7, 1839; A. C Lombard & Co. to Robb, Aug. 4, 1840; Naylor & Co. to Ripley, Nov. 10, 1841.
25. SAR, Lee to Salisbury Iron Co., Oct. 7, 1832.
26. SAR, Archer & Ellison to Robb, Sep. 20, 1836; Leverett & Thomas to Robb, Jan. 9, 1837; Thomas Barry to Robb, June 3, 1837, and Sep. 22, 1837; Thomas Barry to Robb, May 24, 1839; A. C. Lombard & Co. to Robb, Aug. 4, and Dec. 7, 1840; Robb to Talcott, Aug. 4, 1840; W. A. Thornton to Ripley, July, 1849 (no day); Paymaster's letter book, E. Ingersoll to Stillman Moore, Jan. 8, 1852.
27. SAR, Levi Woodbury to J. R. Poinsett, Aug. 11, 1840.
28. SAR, Bomford to Robb, circular, July 14, 1838.
29. SAR, William Bell to Robb, Oct. 18, 1836.
30. SAR, E. Ingersoll to Richard C. Dale, Apr. 5, 1852.
31. Keith and Harte, *op. cit.,* table facing p. 67.
32. SAR, Canfield & Robbins to Ripley, Oct. 28, 1845; SP, E. W. N. Starr Day Book, 1819-1860, entry of Apr. 17, 1841; CP, William J. Canfield to S. R. Sargent, May 28, 1859.
33. SAR, Canfield & Robbins to Ripley, Oct. 28, 1845.
34. SAR, Lee to Holly & Coffing, Canfield & Sterling, S. Rockwell, and J. Boyd, Feb.

7, 1831; David Rice to Robb, Jan. 10, 1834; Robb to Canfield & Sterling, Nov. 25, 1834.

35. SAR, Holly & Coffing to Lee, Feb. 12, 1831.
36. SAR, Lee to Holly & Coffing, Feb. 23, 1831.
37. SAR, Robb to Bomford, Jan. 23, 1841.
38. SAR, Canfield & Robbins to Ripley, Sep. 19, 1853.
39. SAR, Canfield & Robbins to Ripley, Sep. 19, 1853; S. C. Scoville to Ripley, Sep. 19, 1853.
40. SAR, Canfield & Robbins to Ripley, Jan. 18, 1853.
41. SAR, J. S. Whitney to S. B. Moore & Co., Dec. 12, 1854 and Dec. 26, 1855.
42. SAR, Bomford to Lee, July 29, 1831; Lee to Dorsey & Co., Oct. 3, 1831; Lee to Irwin & Smith, Oct. 3, 1831; Lee to Peter Schoenberger, Oct. 3, 1831; Lee to Michael Edge, Oct. 17, 1831; Lee to A. Cordon, Nov. 8, 1831; Lee to John Lyon, Nov. 8, 1831; Peter Townshend to Lee, Dec. 14, 1832; Robb to Bomford, Jan. 23, 1841; letter of S. Miles Green & Co. enclosed in letter from Weatherhead to Ripley, Nov. 20, 1843.
43. SAR, Robb to Bomford, Jan. 23, 1841.
44. SAR, Timothy Dwight to Ripley, Sep. 18, 1841.
45. SAR, Timothy Dwight to Ripley, Sep. 18, 1841; J. Ellison to Ripley, Jan. 19, 1845; Ripley to Edwards & Goodrich, May 19, 1842; Naylor, Hutchinson, Vickers & Co. to Ripley, Aug. 5, 1843; Ripley to J. Ellison, June 30, 1844; Naylor & Co. to Ripley, Jan. 2, 1849; Edward E. Finch to Ripley, July 20, 1849.
46. SAR, Naylor & Co. to Ripley, Feb. 14, 1849.
47. SAR, E. S. Allin to A. W. Prestadius, Nov. 29, 1849.
48. SAR, Naylor & Co. to Ripley, Jan. 2, 1850.
49. SAR, S. V. Scoville, S. B. Moore & Co., Landen & Co., and Albert Moore to Jefferson Davis, Feb. 20, 1855, enclosed in letter from Craig to J. S. Whitney, Mar. 8, 1855.
50. SAR, J. S. Whitney to Craig, Mar. 15, 1855. Quoted in part by Whittlesey, *op. cit.*
51. SAR, Whitney to Edward Halicht, Apr. 8, 1859; Whitney to T. Heyerdahl, Sep. 27, 1859; Whitney to J. T. Ames, May 21, 1860.
52. SAR, P. B. Tyler to Whitney, Aug. 3, 1857.
53. SAR, Ripley to Talcott, Mar. 5, 1842; Whitney to Edward Halicht, Apr. 8, 1859; Whitney to T. Heyerdahl, Sep. 27, 1859; Whitney to J. T. Ames, May 21, 1860.
54. SAR, E. S. Allin, Cyrus Buckland, William Cadwell, William Dickinson to Ripley, Mar. 4, 1850.
55. SAR, Damascus Steel & Iron Co. to Whitney, Sep. 4, 1858; S. C. Bemis to Whitney, Dec. 13, 1858; Whitney to Ordnance Department, Sep. 19, 1859.
56. Barnard, *op. cit.*, 224-225.
57. SAR, Jonathan Leonard to Lee, Oct. 22, 1832.
58. SAR, Masters, Marcoe & Co. to Ripley, Feb. 9, 1842.
59. SAR, Asa Waters to Robb, Apr. 7, 1834; Ripley to Masters, Marcoe & Co., Feb. 12, 1842; Ripley to Atkinson & Rollins, Aug. 11, 1845; AP, N. P. Ames to Alfred Mordecai, Dec., 1839 (no day).
60. AP, N. P. Ames to Alfred Mordecai, Dec., 1839 (no day).
61. SAR, Fullerton & Raymond to Robb, Apr. 26, 1849.
62. Mordecai, *op. cit.*, 108.
63. AP, N. P. Ames to William Crane, Mar. 21, 1845.
64. AP, N. P. Ames to Capt. Fraser, Mar. 22, 1845.
65. *Ordnance Reports*, II, 240, "Abstract of the Recommendations of the Ordnance Board at the Meeting of 19th June, 1848," Talcott to Secretary of War, Aug. 31, 1848.
66. *Ordnance Reports*, II, 240, Talcott, *ibid.*
67. North and North, *op. cit.*, 184-189.
68. SAR, Ordnance Department to Ripley, June 26, 1852.
69. Barnard, *op. cit.*, 229.
70. SAR, Weatherhead to Lee, Mar. 30, 1832.
71. SAR, Talcott to Robb, Jan. 23, 1840; Bomford to Robb, Feb. 16, 1841.
72. AP, N. P. Ames to William Crane, Mar. 21, 1845.
73. SAR, Ripley to Elizabeth Barry, Sep. 20, 1847; J. S. Whitney to Walter Heywood, Apr. 16, 1856.
74. SAR, David Freed to Robb, Nov. 24, 1840.
75. SAR, A. C. Bradford to Lee, Sep. 19, 1832; Talcott to Robb, Dec. 15, 1840.

76. SAR, William Yates to Ripley, Jan. 2, 1844.
77. SAR, Official Letter Book, 1827-1833, list of charcoal purchases.
78. SAR, J. S. Whitney to William Hodge, July 9, 1857.
79. SAR, Ripley to Simeon P. Smith, Dec. 20, 1842; Ripley to Nathan Starr, Jan. 24, 1849.
80. SAR, W. B. Lang to Ripley, Oct. 22, 1841.
81. SAR, W. B. Lang to Ripley, Oct. 22, 1841.
82. SAR, Nathan Starr to Ripley, Jan. 1, 1849.
83. SAR, Starr to Ripley, Jan. 19, 1849; Ripley to Starr, Jan. 24, 1849.
84. SAR, Starr to Ripley, Nov. 29, 1850.

CHAPTER XI

1. *American State Papers, Class V, Military Affairs*, VI, 108, Document 4, "Extracts from the report of a board of commissioners, in Jan. 1827, consisting of practical armorers and intelligent gentlemen, appointed by the United States Ordnance department to examine the machinery invented for fabricating the Hall's Rifles."
2. SAR, Weatherhead to Lee, June 20, 1831.
3. *American State Papers, Class V, Military Affairs*, V, 519, Document 608, "On the Expediency of Establishing a National Foundry."
4. SAR, Bomford to Robb, Jan. 7, 1835.
5. *American State Papers, Class V, Military Affairs*, V, 519, Document 608, "On the Expediency of Establishing a National Foundry," communicated to the House of Representatives Mar. 3, 1835, by W. Cost Johnson.
6. SAR, Ripley to Talcott, June 28, 1843.
7. Fitch, *op. cit.*, 4-5.
8. Fitch, *ibid.*, 4-5.
9. Fitch, *ibid.*, 4-5.
10. Fitch, *ibid.*, 5.
11. Roe, *English and American Tool Builders*, 203.
12. Haven and Belden, *op. cit.*, 356-357.
13. Claud Fuller, *op. cit.*, 61.
14. SAR, Talcott to Ripley, Oct. 19, 1843.
15. Haven and Belden, *op. cit.*, 356.
16. SAR, Bomford to Lee, Sep. 15, 1831; Bomford to Lee, Dec. 19, 1831; R. L. Whitely to J. S. Whitney, May 30, 1857.
17. SAR, Bomford to Robb, June 2, 1836.
18. SAR, Ripley to Talcott, Nov. 18, 1842; Whitney to Craig, Feb. 9, 1859.
19. AP, N. P. Ames letter book: Ames to Benjamin Moore, Jan. 24, 1845.
20. SAR, William Wade to Lee, Nov. 19, 1831.
21. SAR, Joshua Crospby to Lee, Jan. 31, 1830.
22. SAR, Robb to William Wade, July 16, 1835.
23. SAR, Samuel Wadsworth to Robb, Dec. 20, 1834.
24. SAR, Robb to Many & Ward, Feb. 27, 1835.
25. SAR, J. S. Whitney to P. V. Hagner, Mar. 30, 1855.
26. SAR, Talcott to Ripley, Apr. 20, 1843; Report of General Operations for Year Ending June 30, 1845, sent by Ripley to Talcott, Nov. 7, 1845; J. S. Whitney to Phineas Stevens, Aug. 31, 1855; Whitney to unnamed addressee, Mar. 24, 1856.
27. SAR, Ripley to Ordnance Office, Oct. 8, 1852.
28. SAR, Report of General Operations for Year Ending June 30, 1845, Ripley to Talcott, Nov. 7, 1845. Quoted in part by Whittlesey, *op. cit.*
29. Haven and Belden, *op. cit.*, 353.
30. Miller, *op. cit.*, 14.
31. Norton, *American Breech Loading Small Arms*, 186; Roe, *English and American Tool Builders*, 140.
32. *Ordnance Reports*, II, 243; SAR, P. V. Hagner to Whitney, May 12, 1856; Whitney to Hagner, Dec. 16, 1856; Craig to Whitney, Mar. 20, 1857.
33. Haven and Belden, *op. cit.*, 86.
34. Haven and Belden, *ibid.*, 358-359; SAR, D. W. Pardee to Whitney, Dec. 1, 1858.
35. Fitch, *op. cit.*, 13, 14; SAR, Whitney to Craig, Dec. 13, 1854; Craig to Whitney, Dec. 15, 1854; D. W. Pardee to Whitney, Dec. 1, 1858.
36. Waters, *op. cit.*, 14.

37. Hubbard, *op. cit.*, 113.
38. Mordecai, *op. cit.*, 107.
39. Hubbard, *op. cit.*, 69-70; Roe, *English and American Tool Builders,* 140.
40. Hubbard, *op. cit.*, 57.
41. Fitch, *op. cit.*, 34.
42. Hubbard, *op. cit.*, 116.
43. Fitch, *op. cit.*, 22.
44. *Ordnance Reports,* I, 336.
45. Fitch, *op. cit.*, 22.
46. Roe, *English and American Tool Builders,* 137.
47. Fitch, *op. cit.*, 22-23.
48. Haven and Belden, *op. cit.*, 354.
49. Fitch, *op. cit.*, 21.
50. Mordecai, *op. cit.*, 107.
51. SAR, Lee to George Rust, Nov. 14, 1831.
52. SAR, Henry Burden to Lee, Jan. 1, 1831.
53. SAR, Henry Burden, *ibid.*
54. SAR, Lee to Burden, Oct. 22, 1832.
55. SAR, Burden to Lee, Nov. 3, 1832.
56. SAR, Robb to Talcott, Aug. 23, 1839.
57. SAR, Joseph C. Vaughn to Robb, Feb. 23, 1841.
58. SAR, *Machines Fabricated and in Progress,* report for year ending June 30, 1850, sent by Ripley to Ordnance Department, Aug. 30, 1850; *Yearly Fabrication Report,* for year ending June 30, 1851, sent by Ripley to Ordnance Department, Sep. 1, 1851.
59. SAR, J. T. Ames to Whitney, Nov. 3, 1857.
60. SAR, J. T. Ames to Whitney, Nov. 3, 1857; Whitney to Ames, Jan. 1, 1858.
61. SAR, Whitney to Ames, Jan. 1, 1858.
62. SAR, contract between William Onions and J. T. Ames, May 27, 1858.
63. SAR, Whitney to Ames, Nov. 1, 1858.
64. SAR, Whitney to Craig, Jan. 17, 1859.
65. SAR, Whitney, *ibid.*
66. SAR, Whitney to John Gardner, Apr. 23, 1859.
67. SAR, Whitney to A. M. Barbour, Mar. 12, 1859.
68. Herbert D. Hall Foundation, *The Machine Tool Primer,* 199.
69. Fitch, *op. cit.*, 27.
70. SAR, Robb to Elizear Bates, Apr. 17, 1834.
71. Fitch, *op. cit.*, 27.
72. Fitch, *ibid.*
73. SAR, Springfield Armory Statement, May 13, 1842.
74. *Ordnance Reports,* I, 396, "Notes on the Springfield Armory," Talcott to Secretary of War, July 30, 1841.
75. Hubbard, *op. cit.*, 94; SAR, William Wade to Lee, Nov. 19, 1831.
76. SAR, Robbins & Lawrence to Whitney, Sep. 1, 1855.
77. Herbert D. Hall Foundation, *op. cit.*, 217.
78. SAR, Whitney to Massachusetts Arms Co., Mar. 14, 1857.
79. Herbert D. Hall Foundation, *op. cit.*, 214-215.
80. Fitch, *op .cit.*, 28.
81. Fitch, *ibid.*, 28.
82. Fitch, *ibid.*, 29.
83. SAR, Whitney to Colt's Patent Fire Arms Manufacturing Co., May 16, 1857.
84. Roe, *English and American Tool Builders,* 143.
85. Herbert D. Hall Foundation, *op. cit.*, 134.
86. Roe, *op. cit.*, 143.
87. Fitch, *op. cit.*, 29.
88. Fitch, *ibid.*, 13.
89. SAR, H. W. Clowe to Robb, Mar. 25, 1836.
90. Fitch, *op. cit.*, 13.
91. SAR, H. W. Clowe, Mar. 25, 1836.
92. Fitch, *op. cit.*, 13, 14.
93. Haven and Belden, *op. cit.*, 355.
94. SAR, Whitney to P. V. Hagner, Mar. 23, 1855; Whitney to Craig, Mar. 31, 1855.

95. Fitch, *op. cit.*, 13.
96. SAR, Whitney to P. V. Hagner, May 23, 1856.
97. SAR, Whitney to P. V. Hagner, Dec. 16, 1856.
98. SAR, Whitney to Craig, Jan. 3, 1857.
99. Fitch, *op. cit.*, 11.
100. SAR, Lee to Charles Leonard, Nov. 15, 1832.
101. Fitch, *op. cit.*, 11-12.
102. SAR, Lee to Nathaniel French, Dec. 24, 1831; Whitney to J. T. Ames, Oct. 3, 1855.
103. SAR, Craig to J. T. Ames, Dec. 16, 1852.
104. Fitch, *op. cit.*, 10.
105. Fitch, *ibid.*, 11.
106. Fitch, *ibid.*, 8-9.
107. SAR, Craig to Whitney, Nov. 11, 1857.
108. SAR, Samuel D. Sizer to Ripley, June 7, 1843.
109. SAR, Robb to Talcott, Apr. 16, 1839; Samuel D. Sizer to Ripley, June 7, 1843; Ripley to Talcott, Oct. 14, 1843.
110. Fitch, *op. cit.*, 16.
111. Hubbard, *op. cit.*, 88.
112. SAR, Alexander Jones to Robb, Dec. 30, 1840.
113. SAR, Talcott to Ripley, Nov. 2, 1850; Ripley to Talcott, Nov. 20, 1850; Talcott to Ripley, Nov. 27, 1850.
114. SAR, Ames Manufacturing Co. to Whitney, Sep. 4, 1855.
115. Hubbard, *op. cit.*, 69-70.
116. Barnard, *op. cit.*, 224; SAR, R. L. Baker to Ripley, Aug. 14, 1846; Ripley to Craig, June 23, 1854; Stevens Brothers & Co to Whitney, July 19, 1859; Whitney to Stewart Chase, Aug. 12, 1859.
117. Fitch, *op. cit.*, 29; SAR, Craig to Whitney, Nov. 11, 1857.
118. SAR, Robb to Bomford, May 18, 1836; Robb to Bomford, Jan. 2, 1837; Bomford to Robb, May 23, 1837; Bomford to Robb, Dec. 20, 1837.
119. SAR, Samuel Sizer to Robb, June 28, 1834.
120. SAR, Robb to Talcott, Nov. 5, 1839; Talcott to Robb, Nov. 21, 1831.
121. AP, J. T. Ames to James Burton, Nov. 20, 1856.
122. SAR, Craig to Whitney, Nov. 11, 1857.
123. Fitch, *op. cit.*, 30.
124. SAR, Lemuel Pomeroy to Lee, May 7, 1832; James Baker to Weatherhead, June 24, 1833.
125. SAR, Whitney to P. V. Hagner, Dec. 16, 1856.
126. Fitch, *op. cit.*, 12.
127. SAR, "Statement showing the expense for machinery, at Springfield Armory, from Jan. 1, 1820 to June 30, 1841."
128. Benton, *Total Expenditure of Money and Fabrication of Arms, Equipments, &c. at the National Armory, Springfield, Mass.*, Abstract A.
129. Green, *op. cit.*
130. SAR, Bomford to Lee, May 21, 1832.
131. Samuel Colt, *On the Application of Machinery to the Manufacture of Rotating Chambered-Breech Fire-Arms*, 19, 20.
132. Colt, *ibid.*, 17; Haven and Belden, *op. cit.*, 358.

CHAPTER XII

1. Haven and Belden, *op. cit.*, 361.
2. *Ordnance Reports*, I ,396, "Notes on the Springfield Armory," Talcott to Secretary of War, July 30, 1841.
3. *Springfield Republican*, May 15, 1898.
4. SAR, Robb to Bomford, Feb. 3, 1838.
5. Barnard, *op. cit.*, 214; Haven to Belden, *op. cit.*, 353; Sawyer, *Firearms in American History*, II, 188.
6. Barnard, *op. cit.*, 214.
7. Rohan, *op. cit.*, 188-189.
8. *Ordnance Reports*, I, 400.
9. SAR, E. S. Allin to A. M. Barbour, June 29, 1859.
10. SAR, E. A. Allin, *ibid.*

11. SAR, circular, Bomford to Robb, Oct. 22, 1838.
12. McLane, *op. cit.*, I, 280-281.
13. Barnard, *op. cit.*, 211; SAR, Talcott to Robb, Mar. 31, 1840.
14. SAR, "Mode of Averaging the Hours of Labor—Established 1st March 1842."
15. *Ordnance Reports,* I, 396.
16. Green, *op. cit.*
17. Miller, *op. cit.,* 14.
18. *Ordnance Reports,* I, 401, "Report of the Board Convened at Springfield, Mass., August 30, 1841, to Examine into the Condition and Management of Springfield Armory." Submitted by Charles Davies, John Chase and Daniel Tyler.
19. *Springfield Republican,* May 15, 1898.
20. *Springfield Republican, ibid.*
21. SAR, "A Table showing the Average Number of Hours devoted to Labor in 1841 by the Armorers at Springfield Armory," July 30, 1842.
22. *Ordnance Reports,* I, 397.
23. Carter Goodrich, *The Miner's Freedom, passim.*
24. Haven and Belden, *op. cit.,* 92.
25. SAR, book of instructions and regulations: John Wool to Master Armorer, July 17 and 24, 1833.
26. *Ordnance Reports,* II, 10. SAR, Talcott to Robb, Jan. 5, 1835; Ripley to Craig, Oct. 24, 1853.
27. SAR, Whitney to Craig, May 2, 1855.
28. Hicks, *Nathan Starr,* 147.
29. AP, N. P. Ames to Talcott, Dec. 19, 1839.
30. SAR, Marine T. Wickham to Lee, Mar. 15, 1832.
31. *Ordnance Reports,* I, 482, Talcott to J. M. Porter, Apr. 15, 1842.
32. *Ordnance Reports,* I, 482, Talcott, *ibid.*
33. SAR, Regulations Book, 1829-1840: Regulation Number 4 of 1834.
34. SAR, Ripley to Craig, Oct. 4, 1853.
35. *Ordnance Reports,* I, 396, "Notes on the Springfield Armory," Talcott to Secretary of War, July 30, 1841.
36. *Ordnance Reports,* I, 396, Talcott, *ibid.*
37. SAR, Asa Wood, John E. Stebbins, Charles Packard, Joseph Hopkins, Lewis Foster, Jr., and Micah Thayer to Lee, Jan. 23, 1832.
38. *Ordnance Reports,* I, 396, Talcott, *op. cit.*
39. *Ordnance Reports,* I, 396, Talcott, *ibid.*
40. *Ordnance Reports,* I, 397, Talcott, *ibid.*
41. *Ordnance Reports,* I, 400.
42. *Ordnance Reports,* I ,405.
43. *Ordnance Reports,* I, 403, 405, Charles Davies, *et. al., op. cit.*
44. Charles Stearns, *The National Armories,* 8.
45. Stearns, *ibid.,* 9.
46. SAR, Pomeroy to Robb, Aug. 22, 1835.
47. SAR, Robb to P. and E. W. Blake, Aug. 9, 1836.
48. SAR, Asa Waters to Bomford, Feb. 15, 1836.
49. *Ordnance Reports,* II, 536.
50. SAR, Pomeroy to Robb, Mar. 3, 1836.
51. SAR, Pomeroy to Ripley, Apr. 6, 1843.
52. SAR, Albert S. Nipper to Ripley, July 30, 1849.
53. SAR, Whitney to Cyrus Buckland, Jan. 21, 1860.
54. SAR, Instructions and Regulations Book, order of John Wool, July 29, 1833.
55. SAR, Binea Spurry to Robb, Jan. 21, 1834.
56. SAR, Instructions and Regulations Book, "Inspections and Report of Springfield to the Ordnance Department," Dec. 10, 1832.
57. SAR, Instructions and Regulations Book, William H. Ball to Lee, Jan. 7, 1833. Quoted also by Whittlesey, *op. cit.*
58. SAR, Instructions and Regulations Book, Bomford to Lee ,Mar. 9, 1833.
59. SAR, Robb to Edward Lucas, Oct. 8, 1839.
60. SAR, Robb to Bomford, Aug., 1836 (no day); Robb to Bomford, Aug. 10, 1837.
61. J. Deane Alden, *Proceedings at the Dedication of Charter Oak Hall,* 11, speech by W. J. Hammersley.
62. Haven and Belden, *op. cit.,* 361-362; Rohan, *op. cit.,* 187, 189.

63. Whittlesey, *op. cit.*, 139; SAR, Craig to Whitney, Apr., 1855 (no day).
64. *Ordnance Reports*, II, 537. SAR, Bomford to Robb ,Mar. 17, 1841.
65. SAR, Daniel Tyler to Lee, Aug. 31, 1832.
66. SAR, Talcott to Lee, Dec. 31, 1832.
67. SAR, Book of Instructions and Regulations, Bomford to Lewis Cass, Apr. 7, 1833.
68. SAR, Robb to Bomford, Aug., 1836 (no day).
69. SAR, Robb, *ibid.*
70. SAR, Bomford to Robb, Sep. 28, 1836.
71. *Ordnance Reports*, I, 405, Charles Davies *et al.*, *op. cit.*
72. SAR, Master Armorer to John Wool, July 24, 1833.
73. SAR, Master Armorer to John Wool, July 27, 1833.
74. Haven and Belden, *op. cit.*, 88.
75. SAR, Work Returns, *passim.*
76. SAR, Asa Waters to Lee, Mar. 17, 1832.
77. SAR, Book of Instructions and Regulations, Bomford to Lee, May 11, 1832; Talcott to Lee, Dec. 31, 1832.
78. SAR, Bomford to Lewis Cass, Apr. 17, 1833.
79. SAR, Bomford to Talcott, June 11, 1833; John Wool to Lee, June 28, 1833.
80. SAR, John Wool to Lee, June 14 and July 12, 1833.
81. *Ordnance Reports*, I, 396; SAR, Robb to Bomford, Aug., 1836 (no day).
82. SAR, Bomford to Robb, July 20, 1837.
83. *Ordnance Reports*, I, 402, Charle Davies *et al.*, *op. cit.*
84. *Ordnance Reports*, I, 396, "Notes on the Springfield Armory," Talcott to Secretary of War, July 30, 1841.
85. Green, *op. cit.*

CHAPTER XIII

1. SAR, Craig to Whitney, Dec. 31, 1859.
2. Frank Moore, *The Rebellion Record*, II, Part II, 234.
3. Moore, *op. cit.*, II, Part II, 234.
4. Moore, *op. cit.*, I, Part II, 72.
5. Victor S. Clark, *History of Manufactures in the United States*, II, 42.
6. Gluckman, *op. cit.*, 66, 82.
7. Clark, *op. cit.*, II, 45.
8. Opinion of Major James E. Hicks.
9. Moore, *op. cit.*, VI, Part II, 517.
10. Moore, *op. cit.*, VIII, Part II, 276.
11. Clark, *op. cit.*, II, 45.
12. *Ordnance Reports*, III, 442-445.
13. *Ordnance Reports*, III, 445-446, Ripley to Stanton, Nov. 21, 1862.
14. *Ordnance Reports*, III, 446.
15. CP, Colt to Gideon Welles, Apr. 20, 1861; Colt to Simon Cameron, June 10, 1861.
16. CP, Colt to Ashman, July 15, 1861.
17. SAR, S. Crispen to Dyer, Jan. 4, Feb. 8, Feb. 14, and Aug. 9, 1862; George Ramsay to Dyer, Oct. 15, 1862.
18. SAR, T. T. S. Laidley to Dyer, Mar. 29, 1866.
19. SAR, Howland & Aspinwell to Dyer, July 22, 1862; John Pendiz to Dyer, Oct. 16, 1862.
20. SAR, Ripley to Dyer, Jan. 27, 1862.
21. SAR, Ramsay to Dyer, Jan. 1, 1864.
22. SAR, letter to C. A. Davies, Jan. 14, 1865, enclosed in letter from Dyer to Laidley, Jan. 23, 1865; W. Raadoff to Laidley, Mar. 23, 1865.
23. Satterlee and Gluckman, *op. cit.*, 110.
24. Green, *op. cit.*
25. SAR, W. and L. E. Gurley to Dyer, Sep. 24, 1861; Stanley Rule and Level Co. to Dyer, Jan. 30, 1862; A. Merredy's Sons to Dyer, Mar. 12, 1862; Trenton Locomotive and Machine Manufacturing Co. to Dyer, Apr. 5, 1862; Wetherby Tool Co. to Dyer, Sep. 16, 1862; Dwight, Chapin & Co. to Dyer, Dec. 17, 1862; William M. Hawes & Co. to Dyer, Aug. 9, 1864.
26. Barnard, *op. cit.*, 199; Benton, *Total Expenditures of Money and Fabrication of Arms, Equipment &c. at the National Armory, Springfield, Mass., Abstract F.*
27. Sawyer, *Firearms in American History*, II, 187.
28. Claud Fuller, *op. cit.*, 116, 121.

29. *Ordnance Reports,* III, 555.
30. SAR, Craig to George Dwight, Feb. 9, 1861.
31. SAR, Ripley to Dwight, May 15, 1861.
32. SAR, Ripley to Dwight, June 7, 1861.
33. SAR, Ripley to Dwight, June 7, 1861.
34. *Ordnance Reports,* III, 442-443; SAR, Telegraph Book, 1861-1868, Ingersoll to Ripley, Sep. 8, 1861.
35. *Ordnance Reports,* III, 442-443.
36. Benton, *op. cit.,* Abstract F.
37. Claud Fuller, *op. cit.,* 116, 121.
38. *Ordnance Reports,* III, 443.
39. Bishop, *op. cit.,* 691, 745, 755, 773; Elstmer Publishing Co., *Inland Massachusetts Illustrated,* 148; Norton, *American Inventions and Improvements in Breech-Loading Small Arms,* 320; Sharpe, *op. cit.,* 268; *Hampshire Gazette,* Sep. 7, 1858 and July 2, 1861, and Oct. 30, 1866.
40. Claud Fuller, *op. cit.,* 116, 121.
41. Norton, *American Inventions and Improvements in Breech-Loading Small Arms,* 175.
42. Mitman, "Oliver Winchester," *Dictionary of American Biography.*
43. *Ordnance Reports,* III, 4.
44. *Ordnance Reports,* III, 86.
45. *Springfield Republican,* Jan. 15, 1898.
46. Claud Fuller, *op. cit.,* 116, 121.
47. *Ordnance Reports,* III, 4.
48. *Ordnance Reports,* III, 86.
49. Norton, *American Breech-Loading Small Arms,* 14.
50. SAR, C. A. Dana to Ramsay, July 28, 1864, enclosed in letter from Ramsay to Dyer, July 29, 1864.
51. SAR, William M. Hawes to Laidley, Jan. 19, 1865; Collins Co. to Laidley, Mar. 15, 1865.
52. SAR, E. K. Root to Laidley, Nov. 16, 1864.
53. *Ordnance Reports,* III, 445.
54. SAR, Armsby & Harrington to Dyer, Jan. 27, 1863.
55. Norton, *American Breech-Loading Small Arms,* 14.
56. SAR, Ripley to Dwight, June 15, 1861.
57. SAR, John Jones to Dyer, Nov. 1, 1861.
58. SAR, J. T. Ames to Dyer, Dec. 27, 1861.
59. SAR, P. V. Hagner to Dyer, June 10, 1862.
60. SAR, Ramsay to Dyer, Nov. 24, 1863; Dyer to R. P. Bruff, Nov. 28, 1863; Dyer to Bull & Williams, Nov. 28, 1863; Dyer to Ramsay, Dec. 25, 1863; Ramsay to Dyer, Dec. 30, 1863; Dyer to Merwin & Bray, July 8, 1864.
61. SAR, Ramsay to Dyer, Nov. 24, 1863; Dyer to R. P. Bruff, Nov. 28, 1863; Dyer to Bull and Williams, Nov. 28, 1863; Dyer to Merwin & Bray, July 8, 1864.
62. SAR, E. D. Townsend to Laidley, Dec. 20, 1864.
63. SAR, W. A. Nichols to Laidley, Jan. 11, 1865.
64. SAR, Laidley to A. Harrown, Jan. 3, 1865.
65. SAR, Laidley to O. F. Winchester, Jan. 24, 1865.
66. SAR, Dyer to J. T. Ames, Aug. 2, 1862; Dyer to J. T. Ames, Feb. 17 and July 23, 1863; Ramsay to Dyer, Jan. 26, 1864; Joseph Davy & Co. to Dyer, June 13, 1864; inspection certificate signed by Dyer, Aug. 23, 1864.
67. SAR, Dyer to Ridgeway & Rufe, June 27, 1864.
68. SAR, Commanding Officer's Book, entry of Nov. 11, 1861.
69. SAR, Laidley to P. O. Bush, Dec. 10, 1864.
70. SAR, Ripley to Dyer, June 30, 1863.
71. SAR, Dyer to Laidley, Apr. 13, 1865.
72. SAR, William Mason to Dyer, Aug. 29, 1864.
73. SAR, Colt Co. to Dyer, May 24, 1862; Dyer to P. V. Hagner, Aug. 7, 1863; Dyer to Laidley, Sep. 17, Sep. 24, Oct. 10, Oct. 31 and Nov. 4, 1864; Laidley to E. K. Root, Nov. 10 and Dec. 21, 1864; E. K. Root to Laidley, Nov. 16, 1864; Laidley to Armsby & Harrington, to Samuel Norris, and to A. H. Waters & Co., Dec. 21, 1864; Telegraph Book, 1861-1868, Ramsay to Dyer, Sep. 7, 1863.
74. SAR, Ripley to Dyer, Jan. 7, 1862.

75. Wesley C. Mitchell, *Gold, Prices, and Wages Under the Greenback Standard,* 23, Table 4.
76. Mitchell, *ibid.,* 5-13, Table 2.
77. SAR, Charles Evans, agent of W. Jessop & Sons, to Dwight, June 1, 1861;
   T. Heyerdahl to Dyer, July 12, 1862; Gray & Danforth to Dyer, Jan. 13, 1863.
78. SAR, Naylor & Co. to Dyer, Nov. 21, 1861.
79. SAR, John A. Kernochan to Dyer, July 22, 1862.
80. SAR, C. Habicht to Dyer, Feb. 12, 1863; R. S. Stenton to Dyer, Aug. 17, 1863;
   Collins Co. to Dyer, Jan. 14, 1864; Perkins & Livingston to Dyer, Mar. 17, 1864.
81. SAR, Cornett & Nightengale to Dyer, Jan. 2, 1864.
82. SAR, Salmon P. Chase to Simon Cameron, copy sent by Ordnance Department
   to Dyer, Oct. 22, 1861.
83. SAR, Secretary of Treasury to Secretary of War, copy sent by Ordnance Department to Dyer, Jan. 9, 1862.
84. SAR, T. M. Sackett to Dyer, Dec. 12, 1862; A. Hawkins to Dyer, Jan. 19, 1863;
   Bigelow Manufacturing Co. to Dyer, July 20, 1864.
85. SAR, Harmon & Crowl to Dyer, Mar. 11, 1864.
86. SAR, Dyer to G. and L. H. Scherberger & Co., May 15, 1862.
87. SAR, Dyer to Ramsay, Oct. 27, 1863.
88. SAR, Samuel D. Nye to Dwight, Aug. 29, 1861; A. Penfield to Dyer, Dec. 30,
   1862; Hailman, Rahn & Co. to Dyer, Apr. 28, 1863; Dyer to Brown & Co.,
   Wayne Iron and Steel Works, Mar. 14 and May 30, 1864.
89. SAR, Dyer to Colt Co., Nov. 22, 1862; Colt Co. to Dyer, Jan. 6, 1863; Dyer to
   Cooper Hewitt & Co., Aug. 19, 1864.
90. SAR, James M. Hopkins to Dyer, Sep. 20, 1862.
91. SAR, Joel Farist & Co. to Dyer, Jan. 26, 1863.
92. SAR, P. H. Watson to Dyer, Sep. 10, 1862.
93. SAR, Edwin M. Stanton to Cooper Hewitt & Co., Sep. 16, 1862.
94. SAR, Dyer to Marshall & Mills, Nov. 16, 1863.
95. SAR, Dyer to Ramsay, Oct. 27, 1863.
96. SAR, Perkins & Livingston to Dyer, May 4, 1864.
97. SAR, C. B. Hoard to Dyer, Feb. 29, 1864.
98. SAR, Dyer to Ramsay, Oct. 27, 1863.
99. SAR, E. Remington & Sons, Mar. 11, 1864, enclosed in letter from Ramsay to
   Dyer, Mar. 12, 1864.
100. SAR, William Onions to Laidley, Dec. 31, 1864.
101. SAR, Laidley to Cornett & Nightengale, Dec. 15, 1864; Copper Hewitt & Co., to
   Laidley, July 26, 1865.
102. SAR, Wilson, Hawksworth, Ellison & Co. to Dyer, Aug. 13, 1862.
103. SAR, Collins Co. to Dyer, May 9, 1864.
104. SAR, Thomas Prosser & Son to Dyer, Apr. 2, 1864.
105. SAR, S. E. Seymour to Dwight, June 14, 1861.
106. SAR, Park Bros. & Co. to Dyer, May 10, 1864; Walter Gregory & Co. to Dyer,
   June 24, 1864.
107. SAR, Laidley to John A. Kernochan, Feb. 2, 1865.
108. SAR, C. C. Haven to Dyer, June 17, 1862.
109. SAR, Kimball & Robinson to Dyer, 1862 (no date of day or month); A. Barnard to
   Dyer, Dec. 18, 1862; Isaac Newton to Dyer, Dec. 23, 1862; Laidley to W. Fuller,
   Dec. 3, 1864.
110. SAR, Silliman & Co. to Dyer, Jan. 15, 1864; Asa Smith to Dyer, Feb. 23, 1864.
111. SAR, I. G. Palmer to Dyer, Jan. 27, 1864.
112. SAR, Edwin H. Parks to Dwight, Apr. 29, 1861; N. G. Thom to Dyer, Aug. 4,
   1862; P. M. Preble to Dyer, Feb. 20, 1863; S. M. Dunning to Dyer, Sep. 9, 1863;
   Dyer to Hester Miles & Co., Dec. 4, 1863.
113. SAR, N. G. Thom to Dyer, Aug. 4, 1862.
114. SAR, David Freed to Dwight, June 20, 1861.
115. SAR, Requisition for Files, July (no day) 1862.
116. SAR, Dyer to Ordnance Department, Oct. 13, 1865.
117. SAR, Whipple File Manufacturing Co. to Dyer, Dec. 26, 1861; Dyer to Frederick
   Butler, Jan. 17, 1862; American File Co. to Dyer, Apr. 7, 1864; Kearney & Geiger
   to Laidley, Nov. 19, 1864.
118. SAR, R. Hoe & Co. to Dyer, Feb. 11, 1862.

119. SAR, Whipple Manufacturing Co. to Dyer, Apr. 9, 1864.
120. SAR, Ripley to Dwight, July 15, 1861.
121. SAR, Ripley to Dyer, Jan. 7, 1862.
122. SAR, T. W. Carter to Dwight, Aug. 17, 1861.
123. SAR, Ramsay to Dyer, Oct. 28, 1863.
124. SAR, Ripley to Dwight, July 13, 1861; Ripley to Dyer, Feb. 5, 1862; Savage Revolving Fire Arms Co. to Dyer, June 1, 1864; Dyer to Laidley, Nov. 4 and 12, 1864.
125. SAR, Norwich Arms Co. to Dyer, July 10, 1863.
126. SAR, Ripley to Colt, Oct. 25, 1861; Henry A. Chapin & Co. to Dyer, Jan. 8, 1862; Dyer to Lamson, Goodnow & Yale, June 21, 1862.
127. SAR, N. C. Niles to Dyer, Aug. 19, 1862; Wood, Light & Co. to Dyer, July 17, 1863.
128. SAR, T. W. Carter to Dyer, Feb. 22, 1862; George Crompton to Dyer, Oct. 10, 1862; J. C. Whiten to Dyer, Feb. 3, 1863; Barstow Stove Co. to Dyer, Oct. 17, 1863; American Watch Co. to Dyer, Dec. 7, 1863; George Lincoln & Co. to Dyer, Dec. 10, 1863; T. Lincoln & Co. to Dyer, Feb. 1, 1864.
129. SAR, C. L. Perkins to Dyer, Apr. 9, 1863.
130. SAR, Miscellaneous Outgoing Letter Book, 1863-1864, entry of about June 25, 1863.
131. SAR, R. Hoe & Co. to Dyer, Mar. 8, 1862; Dyer to J. T. Ames, Mar. 11, 1862; J. T. Ames to Dyer, Mar. 12, 1862; Dyer to J. T. Ames, Mar. 13, 1862; Dyer to R. Hoe & Co., Mar. 13, 1862; Dyer to William Sellers, July 3, 1862; R. Hoe & Co. to Dyer, July 15, 1862; A. M. Freeland and William Sellers to Dyer, July 23, 1862.
132. Fitch, *op. cit.*, 22.
133. SAR, Work Returns, 1862.
134. SAR, Dyer to Harvey Waters, June 23, 1862; Birmingham Iron Foundry to Dyer, Mar. 14, 1864.
135. SAR, Harvey Waters to Dyer, Jan. 13, 1864; Birmingham Iron Foundry to Dyer, Mar. 14, 1864.
136. Herbert D. Hall Foundation, *op. cit.*, 184, 222-224; SAR, J. C. Palmer to Dyer, May 22, 1862; R. L. Lawrence to Dyer, Sep. 29, 1862; Dyer to T. F. Taft, Dec. 12, 1862; Dyer to T. W. Carter, Dec. 8, 1863; Bull & Williams to Laidley, Dec. 13, 1864; Andrew Moody to Laidley, June 12, 1865.
137. Fitch, *op. cit.*, 31.
138. SAR, R. Hoe & Co. to Dyer, Nov. 14, 1861.
139. SAR, Samuel Colt to Dyer, Oct. 7, 1861; Ramsay to Dyer, Oct. 28, 1863.
140. Fitch, *op. cit.*, 11.
141. Barnard, *op. cit.*, 213, 229.
142. SAR, Note of July 17, 1863.
143. SAR, Colt Co. to Dyer, Aug. 7, 1862.
144. SAR, Work Returns, 1861-1862.
145. SAR, Ripley to Dwight, June 3, 1861; Springfield Gas Light Co. to Dyer, May 24, 1862.
146. SAR, Orders from Commanding Officer, 1861-1893, order of Aug. 31, 1861.
147. SAR, Dyer to Laidley, Apr. 12, 1865.
148. *Springfield Republican,* Mar. 27, 1898; SAR, Laidley to Dyer, Dec. 2, 1864.
149. Barnard, *op. cit.*, 211.
150. SAR, Dyer to Ripley, Feb. 6, 1862; Colt Co. to Dyer, Aug. 7, 1862.
151. SAR, P. B. Tyler to Dyer, Jan. 21, 1864.
152. SAR, American Machine Works to Dyer, Nov. 30, 1861; Laidley to Mason Manufacturing Co., Feb. 18, 1865.
153. SAR, Dyer to Ripley, Feb. 6, 1862.
154. SAR, Smith & Wesson to Dyer, Apr. 1, 1863.
155. SAR, Orders from Commanding Officer, 1861-1893, 1861 (no date of day or month).
156. SAR, Dyer to Lamson, Goodnow & Yale, Jan. 6, 1862.
157. SAR, J. T. Ames to Dyer, Apr. 16, 1864.
158. SAR, Laidley to D. D. Taylor, Dec. 14, 1864.
159. SAR, Laidley to Jeremiah J. Sullivan, Dec. 31, 1864.
160. SAR, Laidley to S. V. Beach, Dec. 30, 1864; Laidley to S. Crispin, Dec. 31, 1864, and Jan. 4, 1865; Laidley to George Burdick, Feb. 1, 1865.

161. SAR, Laidley to S. V. Beach, Dec. 30, 1864; Laidley to S. Crispin, Dec. 31, 1864, and Jan 4, 1865; Laidley to George Burdick, Feb. 1, 1865.
162. SAR, Naylor & Co. to Laidley, Dec. 8, 1865.
163. SAR, Dyer to Cooper Hewitt & Co., Mar. 28, 1862.
164. SAR, Dyer, *ibid.;* Dyer to Cooper Hewitt & Co., Apr. 18, 1862; Dyer to Phoenix Iron Co., Apr. 18, 1862.
165. SAR, Providence Tool Co. to Dyer, July 28, 1863.
166. SAR, Eli Whitney to Dyer, Mar. 16, 1864; Dyer to Colt Co., Mar. 17, 1864; Dyer to Providence Tool Co., Mar. 17, 1864; E. K. Root to Dyer, Mar. 19, 1864; Dyer to J. C. Palmer, Apr. 29, 1864; Dyer to E. K. Root, Apr. 29, 1864; James Burden to Dyer, June 11, 1864; Dyer to E. K. Root, June 30, 1864.
167. SAR, Orders from Commanding Officer, 1861-1893, order of Aug. 31, 1861.
168. SAR, T. Treadwell to Dyer, Dec. 4, 1861; Dyer to S. Crispin, Jan. 31, 1863.
169. SAR, P. B. Tyler to Dyer, Jan. 21, 1864; Dyer to Densmore Hartshorn, Mar. 17, 1864; Orders from Commanding Officer, 1861-1893, pay rates, July 23, 1864.
170. SAR, Dyer to George Boutwell, Dec. 29, 1862.
171. Mitchell, *op. cit.,* 89, Table 28.
172. SAR, Orders from Commanding Officer, 1861-1893, order of July 8, 1862.
173. SAR, *ibid.,* order of Oct. 19, 1861.
174. SAR, *ibid.,* order of Mar. 26, 1862.
175. SAR, *ibid.,* order of Nov. 21, 1861.

CHAPTER XIV

1. Appendix A, Table 2.
2. Appendix A, Table 4.
3. Norton, *American Breech-Loading Small Arms,* 15.
4. SAR, J. G. Benton to Dyer, Oct. 8 and 22, 1867; Benton to T. C. Palmer, Dec. 20, 1867; Reports to Commanding Officer, by Master Armorer, Mar. 25, 1868, and by S. W. Porter, Dec. 20, 1872.
5. SAR, Benton to Dyer, Nov. 30, 1867; Reports to Commanding Officer, by S. W. Porter, May, 1868.
6. SAR, Benton to Chief of Ordnance, June 5, 1873.
7. SAR, Reports to Commanding Officer, by H. Stockton, Nov., 1870.
8. Roe, *English and American Tool Builders,* 211. SAR, Outgoing Press Letter Book, 1875, 269, letter by H. Metcalfe (undated, no addressee).
9. SAR, "Extent and Value of the Plant necessary to manufacture 100 Rifles Cal. .45 per day of 8 hours, as determined from the actual practice of the National Armory, Springfield, Mass." unsigned report to Commanding Officer, June 16, 1873.
10. SAR, Remington Co. to Benton, Feb. 8, 1870.
11. Fitch, *op. cit.,* 7.
12. *New International Encyclopaedia,* "Calipers."
13. Fitch, *op. cit.,* 12.
14. Fitch, *ibid.,* 10.
15. SAR, Cooper Hewitt & Co. to Benton, Feb. 6, 1871.
16. Fitch, *op. cit.,* 22.
17. SAR, C. D. DeLaney & Co. to Benton, Feb. 28, 1873.
18. Appendix B, note on Table 1.
19. Appendix B, Table 1.
20. SAR, Reports to Commanding Officer, by S. W. Porter, Sep. 3, 1868.
21. Barnard, *op. cit.,* 231; Fitch, *op. cit.,* 10; SAR, Laidley to Dyer, Mar. 6, 1866; Adee & Son to Benton, Aug. 3, 1866; Ordnance Department to Benton, Jan. 9, 1869; Leng and Ogden to Benton, June 11, 1872; Remington Co. to Benton, Jan. 1, 1873; R. Woeff to Benton, June 5, 1873; Reports to Commanding Officer, by W. G. Chamberlain, May 8, 1871, "Report of Observations at Remington's Armory, Ilion, N. Y."
22. Barnard, *op. cit.,* 224-225; SAR, Benton to Leng & Ogden, May 28, 1873; R. Woeff to Benton, June 5, 1873; Benton to A. R. Egbert, Jan. 6, 1875. CP, Berger & Co. to Colt Co., May 22, 1869, June 17, 1869, June 28, 1869, Sep. 28, 1870, and Feb. 28, 1871.
23. SAR, Reports to Commanding Officer, by E. S. Allin, Oct. 18, 1866.
24. SAR, Benton to Cooper Hewitt & Co., Jan. 15, 1870; Cooper Hewitt & Co. to Benton, Feb. 15, 1870; Benton to George E. Gourand, Apr. 12, 1870; Benton to Chief of Ordnance, Feb. 13, 1873.

282

25. SAR, Gregory & Co. to Benton, price list, Jan. 7, 1871.
26. Appendix B, note on Table 1.
27. Appendix D, Table 2.
28. SAR, Justin Merrill to Benton, Oct. 15, 1869.
29. Fitch, *op. cit.*, 7.
30. SAR, Benton to Dyer, Apr. 29, 1870.
31. SAR, Benton to Dyer, Aug. 20, 1868.
32. SAR, Benton, *ibid.*
33. SAR, Felix Chillingworth, W. G. Carning, J. Richards, J. S. Brown, A. F. Adams, J. F. Cranston, G. K. Jacobs, B. Lyon, E. D. Stack, and E. B. Wilson to Henry Wilson, Dec. 14, 1868.
34. SAR, Benton to T. J. Treadwell, Dec. 9, 1868, and Jan. 11, 1869.
35. SAR, statement signed by J. Chattaway, R. Hathaway, C. W. Bales, A. Stone, and E. W. Clarke, Dec. 30, 1868; Benton to T. J. Treadwell, Jan. 11, 1869.
36. SAR, Benton to T. J. Treadwell, Feb. 15, 1869.
37. SAR, Benton to T. W. Russell, June 4, 1869.
38. SAR, S. V. Benét to Benton, Dec. 13, 1872.
39. SAR, Orders from Commanding Officer, 1861-1893, order of Feb. 29, 1884.
40. SAR, Benton to J. S. Merrill, Oct. 15, 1869.
41. SAR, Reports to Commanding Officer, by W. G. Chamberlain, May 8, 1871, "Report of Observations at Remington's Armory, Ilion, N. Y."
42. Satterlee and Gluckman, *op. cit.*, 12; Sharpe, *op. cit.*, 214.
43. Norton, *American Breech-Loading Small Arms*, 15.
44. Whittlesey, *op. cit.*, 267.
45. SAR, Benton to Remington Co., Oct. 18, 1867; Dyer to Benton, Nov. 16, 1867.
46. SAR, W. B. Franklin to Dyer, Jan. 26, 1871; Dyer to Franklin, Jan. 31, 1871; Colt Co. to Benton, Aug. 18, 1871.
47. SAR, Benton to D. F. Clark, Nov. 7, 1867; Benton to J. C. Palmer, Mar. 24, 1868; contract between J. T. Ames and J. C. Palmer, and the Ordnance Department, Nov. 9, 1867.
48. SAR, J. T. Ames to Dyer, Feb. 20, 1869.
49. SAR, Reports to Commanding Officer, by S. W. Porter, Dec. 19, 1870.
50. SAR, Dyer to Benton, Oct. 10, 1868.
51. SAR, F. Van Vliet to W. R. Shoenaker, July 30, 1869; J. R. McGuiness to Mj.-Gen. Seymour, Sep. 22, 1869.
52. SAR, Benton to W. B. Franklin, Dec. 1, 1866; Benton to Dyer, May 23, and Aug. 20, 1867; Dyer to Benton, Feb. 21, 1870; W. B. Franklin to Benton, May 20, 1871; J. R. Edie to W. B. Franklin, July 30, 1873; Benton to O. W. Ainsworth, Oct. 27, 1873.
53. SAR, Dyer to Smith & Wesson, Dec. 28, 1870; Smith & Wesson to Dyer, Dec. 30, 1870, Aug. 10, 1872, and Mar. 10, 1873; Benton to J. R. McGuiness, May 14, 1873.
54. SAR, Ludlow Case to Dyer, Mar. 30, 1870; Benton to George Sanders, July 5, 1870; J. R. Edie to C. Morris, Aug. 8, 1873.
55. Satterlee and Gluckman, *op. cit., passim;* Sawyer, *Firearms in American History,* Vols. I, II and III, *passim.*
56. Sharpe, *op. cit.*, 270.
57. Hart, *op. cit., Hobbies,* Aug. 1944, 108; Winchester Repeating Arms Co., *Interesting Facts on Winchester Repeating Arms Co.* (typescript).
58. Opinion of Mr. Edwin Pugsley.
59. *Springfield Republican,* Jan. 15, 1899.
60. Norton, *American Breech-Loading Small Arms,* 175.
61. Norton, *ibid.,* 182.
62. SAR, extract of contract between Winchester Co. and Ottoman Government, undated, enclosed in letter from Dyer to Benton, Dec. 23, 1870; copy of letter from G. Aristarchi, Ottoman Delegation, to Secretary of State, sent by Benét to Benton, Nov. 25, 1873.
63. Norton, *American Inventions and Improvements in Breech-Loading Small Arms,* 77.
64. CP, diary of an unnamed director of the Colt Co., 1865-1867, entries from Oct. 24, 1866 to Dec. 24, 1867.
65. Roe, *English and American Tool Builders,* 177-179.
66. Roe, *op. cit.*, 179.

67. SAR, William Maynadier to Benton, Sep. 6, 1867.
68. SAR, J. R. Edie to George K. Jacobs, July 18, 1873.
69. Norton, *American Breech-Loading Small Arms*, 89.
70. SAR, Austin Baldwin & Co., to Benton, Dec. 27, 1870.
71. Norton, *op. cit.*, 50.
72. Sharpe, *op. cit.*, 269.
73. Sharpe, *ibid.*, 269.
74. Norton, *op. cit.*, 73; Remington Arms Company, Inc., *A New Chapter in an Old Story*. (no pagination).
75. Norton, *op. cit.*, 45.
76. SAR, Remington Co. to Benton, Aug. 17, 1870.
77. Sharpe, *op. cit.*, 275.
78. Fitch, *op. cit.*, 5.
79. SAR, Dyer to Laidley, May 5, 1866; Dyer to Commanding Officer of Armory, May 21, 1866.
80. SAR, S. Crispin to Benton, June 16 and 28, and July 7, 1869; I. Jasize to Benton, July 19, 1869.
81. SAR, Ordnance Department to Benton, July 22, 1869.
82. SAR, Charles Lea to Benton, Jan. 19, 1867.
83. SAR, Dyer to Benton, Dec. 15, 1869.
84. SAR, William Tharwood to Benton, Sep. 10, 1866; L. W. Broadwell to Benton, Nov. 1, 1866; Dyer to L. W. Broadwell, Nov. 7, 1866.
85. SAR, Dyer to Laidley, Mar. 3, and Apr. 18, 1866; Dyer to Benton, Oct. 3, 1866.
86. SAR, Ferdinand de Luca to Benton, June 8, 1867; Valentin Estrada & Co. to Benton, Nov. 19, 1867; Benton to S. Crispin, Jan. 25, 1870.
87. SAR, John Hitz to Benton, May 6, 1867.
88. SAR, Charles Ost to Benton, Sep. 13, 1869; Benton to O. F. Winchester, Dec. 7, 1870; Benton to A. O. Sinclair, Oct. 31, 1873; Benton to Benjamin Lyon, Nov. 3, 1873.
89. SAR, Benton to George K. Jacobs, Dec. 19, 1870.
90. Federal Census Enumerator's Report, New Haven County, Connecticut, 1870.
91. Opinion of Mr. Pugsley.
92. SAR, Benton to George S. Sanders, July 5, 1870.
93. Federal Census Enumerator's Report, Hampton County, Massachusetts, 1870.
94. Roe, *English and American Tool Builders*, 192-194.
95. Roe, *ibid.*, 207-210.
96. Federal Census Enumerator's Report, Hampton County, Massachusetts, 1870.
97. Satterlee and Gluckman, *op. cit.*, 145.
98. Sharpe, *op. cit.*, 269-278.
99. Hubbard, *op. cit.*, 109.
100. Hubbard, *ibid.*, 117-118; Fitch, *op. cit.*, 21.
101. Hubbard, *op. cit.*, 117, 242.
102. Roe, *op. cit.*, 177-179.
103. Hubbard, *op. cit.*, 114-115.

INDEX

Adironack Arms Co., 209
Allen & Wheelock, 128
Allin, Erskine, 30, 209
Allin system, 30, 31, 209
  See also Small arms: breech-loading
Alsop, C. R., 128
American Machine Co., 157
"American system," 11, 148
  See also Interchangeability
Ames, J. T., 152, 195, 199
Ames, N. P., 126, 129, 140, 146
Ames Manufacturing Co., vii, 117, 121
  passim
Ammunition, 20 Fig. 7
  ball and powder, 17
  bullet
    grooved, 28
    Minié, 25
  cartridge
    metallic, 27-29
      adoption by government, 29
      breech-loading dependent on, 28
      center-fire, 29, 209
      rim-fire, 27, 29
    paper, 27-29
    pin-fire, 28n
    "detonating" caps, 22
    "detonating" powder, 23n
    invention in, 17
  See also Small arms, percussion
Apprentices *see* Labor
Armories
  national, 42, *passim*
    cooperation between, 67, *passim*
    shortage of funds for, 164
    See also Harper's Ferry Armory,
      Springfield Armory
  Palmetto, 121, 177, 178
Arms makers *see* Small arms industry
Arsenals, government, 162, 164
  Frankford, 56, 156, 200
  New York, 200
  Rock Island, 218
  shortage of funds for, 164
  Watertown, 156
  Watervliet, 187
Aston, Henry, vii, 121, 122

Ball, William, 156
Benton, Major James G., 51, 203, 206, 207
Bibliography, 250-254
  government documents, 251-252
  newspaper files, 252
  primary sources, 250-252
  secondary sources, 252-254
Bidwell, Oliver, 43
Blanchard, Thomas, 96-98, 101, 157
Breech-loading arms *see* Small arms
Bristol Fire Arms Manufacturing Co., 128

Brown, John, 128
Brown & Sharpe, 204
Buckland, Cyrus, 149, 156, 157
Bullet *see* Ammunition
Burden, Henry, 151, 152
Burton, James H., 149

Caliber *see* Small arms
Capital *see* Financing
Carbine *see* Small arms
Carruth, Adam, 48
Cartridge *see* Ammunition
Case-hardening *see* Small arms
Charcoal *see* Raw materials
Civil War, Ch. XIII, 177-201
  arms, down-grading, 185
  armories, expansion, 183
  costs, 184
  effects
    increased interchangeability, 202, 204
    increased capitalization, 202
    increased costs, 203-207
  inspection problems, 187
  labor *see* Labor
  Machine tools *see* Machine tools
  new firms, 184
  parts manufacture, 180, 181
  production, 182-185
  raw materials *see* Raw materials
Clement Hawkes Manufacturing Co., 183
Coal *see* Raw materials
Cole, Arthur H., index of wholesale prices, 71, 109, 135, 188, 200, 238, 239
Collier, Elisha, 22
Colt, Samuel, vii, 121-126, 140, 148, 159, 168
Colt Patent Fire Arms Manufacturing Co., vii, 27, 117, *passim*
Connecticut River Valley, limits of, 14
Contract *see* Contract system
Contract arms *see* Contract system, Small arms
Contract system, 33, 37, 38, 41-43, Ch. V, 55-67
  contract, form of, 55, 56, App. A 227, 228
  contract arms
    compared with arms of federal armories, 118, 119
    early use of, 42n
    pattern arms *see* Interchangeability
    prices, 48, 56, 185, 187, 188, App. B 229-232
  contractors, 37, 38, 43
    capital *see* Financing
    failures *see* Financing
    qualifications, 45
    standards of cost and production, **3,** 38, 41, 46
  decline of, 117-118
  disadvantages, 66

effects, 55
government patronage, 3, 4, 41-43, 46, 47
government policy, 41-43
importance to small arms industry, 38, 55
inspection, 56-65, 146, 187
  gages *see* Interchangeability
  problems, 59
  proving, 57, 59
  parts contracting *see* sub-contract
  sub-contract, 44, 45, 161, 181
Cooper Hewitt & Co., 190-192
Cooperation *see* Small arms industry
Corporation *see* Financing
Cost accounting *see* Costs
Cost of living *see* Wages
Cost, overhead *see* Costs
Cost, unit *see* Costs
Costs, 47, 49, 54, 130-132, App. B 229-232
  change of model, 3, 56, 57, 131, 132
  consolidation, liquidaton of plants, 208, 209
  cost series, 51, 52, 132, App. B 229-231
  depreciation, 35, 49-51, 53, 54, 131, 132
  determination, 49-52, 130-132, 204
  freight rates, 44, 69, 134
  insurance, 49, 50, 54, 131, 132
  interest, 50, 51, 54, 131
  labor, 44, 50
  See also Wages
  mechanization, 132
  overhead costs, 4, 202-204, 206, 207
  raw materials *see* Raw materials
  transportation *see* freight rates
  unit costs, 44, 50, 51, 119, 131, 132, 203, 207, 208, App. B 229-232
Coxe, Tench, 41, 42, 45, 47, 48, 55
Credit *see* Raw materials, terms of purchase

Dalliba, Major James, 88, 90-92, 108
Depreciation *see* Costs
Derringer, Henry, 48
"Detonating" caps *see* Ammunition
"Detonating" gun *see* Small arms
Dyer, Captain A. B., 186, 190, 190n, 212

Eames, Albert, 149, 150, 157
Edge weapons, 17n, 58
Employment *see* Labor
Expansion and adjustment, Pt. 4, 175-216
Export of arms and ammunition, 3, 129, 130, 148, 149, 202, 212
  decline of, 210-212, 214
  gun machinery and machine tools, 130, 148, 149, 156, 157
  prohibited, 37

Failures *see* Financing
Federal contract system *see* Contract system
Financing, 126-128

Ames Manufacturing Co., 125
arms shops, early, 34
capital, 6-12, Figs. 1, 3, 4; 45, 46, 48, 126, 127, 203, 215, App. A 220-221
Colt Patent Fire Arms Manufacturing Co., 124
corporation, 127
credit, 47, 134, 189
depreciation *see* Costs
failures, 47-49, 52, 54
partnership, 47-49, 52
Flintlock arms *see* Small arms
Forging *see* Interchangeability
Freight rates *see* Costs

Gages *see* Contract system: inspection; Interchangeability
Gilbert, Daniel, 43
Government contracts *see* Contract system, Springfield Armory
Guns stocks *see* Raw materials
Guns *see* Small arms: carbine, musket, pistol, revolver, rifle
Gunsmith *see* Small arms industry: arms makers, gunsmiths

Hall, John H., 22, 99, 129, 150, 153, 155, 157
Harper's Ferry Armory
  apprentices, 107, 160
  capture of, 177, 178
  cooperation
    lack of, 67
    with Springfield Armory, 67, *passim*
  cost at, 44
  inside contracting, 101
  inspection, 60
  interchangeability, 90, 144
  isolation of, 44, 67
  labor, 160, 164
  production, 181
  Superintendent, 67, 93, *passim*
Henry, B. Tyler, 27, 29, 126
Hoe, R. & Co., 193, 195
Hollister, Isaac, & Sons, 44, 74
Howe, F. W., 13, 149, 154-156, 214

Import of arms, 36, 37, 41, 44, 178-180
  gun machinery, 196
Income tax, wartime, 200
Industrial independence *see* Small arms industry
Information, sources of, vii, 33, 33n
  Springfield Armory records, 5, 33, *passim*
  Ordnance Reports, 50, *passim*
  U. S. Census, *passim*
"Inside" contracting *see* Labor
Inspection *see* Contract system, Springfield Armory
Insurance *see* Costs
Interchangeability, 3, 11, 87-93, 144-146
  advances in, 144-146, 193, 194
  "American system," 11, 148

early attempts, 11
forging, 145, 146, 150, 151
gages, 13, 89-91
increase of, in Civil War, 193, 194
introduction of, 87-89
  to Europe, 148
Jefferson, Thomas, interest in, 87
jigs, 93
machine tools, relation to, 93-99
methods of achieving, 89-99
occupational specialization, relation to,
  91, 92
  See also Labor
opinion as to value of, 88, 89
overhead costs, relation to, 204
pattern arms, 56, 57, 89, 90, 194
precision measurement, 3, 13, 144-146,
  204
standards, 144-146
swages, 92, 93
Whitney, Eli, interest in, 87n 88n
Interest *see* Costs
International markets *see* Exports
Introduction, Pt. I, 1-38
Inventions, Inventors, 3, Ch. III, 17-32,
  168, 204, 205
  See also Ammunition, Machine tools,
  Small arms
Investment *see* Financing, capital
Iron *see* Raw materials
Irvine, Callender, 48, 55, 60-62

Johnson, Ira N., 122
Johnson, J. D., 43, 45, 140
Johnson, Robert, 43, 45, 120
Johnson, Sir William, 19
Joslyn Fire Arms Co., 128

Kendall, N. & Co., 122, 123
Kendall & Lawrence, 123

Labor, Ch. VIII, 100-114, Ch. XII, 160-
  174
apprentices, 34, 107, 160, 167
Civil War, 197-201
conditions, 102-104, 162-164, 168
cost of living, 105, 106
discharge, 105, 167, 168, 198, 199
employment, 6 Fig. 1, 7, 8 Fig. 2, 12
  Fig. 4, App. A 220, 221, App. D 245
hours, 206, 207
inside contracting, 101, 102, 149, 150,
  161, 162
mechanization, effect of, *see* technological unemployment
occupational specialization, 34, 91, 92,
  100, 197, 198, App. D 240
productivity of barrel welders, 113,
  114, 174, 201, App. D 246 Fig. 2,
  247
relations, 104, 105, 164-168
shortage, 197-200
strikes, 164, 200

technological unemployment, 132, 160,
  161, 164
wages *see* Wages
Laidley, Major T. T. S., 29
Lamson, E. G. & Co., 183
Lamson, Goodnow & Yale, 213
Lawrence, Richard S., 27, 28, 123, 149
Lee, Roswell, 56, 59, 62-65, *passim*
Location of small arms manufacture *see*
  Small arms industry

Machine tools, 3, 13, 93-99, 144-159
before 1800, 35
builders *see* inventors
development, 93-99, 146-159
exports, 148, 149, 156, 157
improvements in Civil War, 196, 197
inventors, 13, 146, 149, 150, 214
investment in, 158, 204, 205
  See also Costs
jigs, 93, 145
manufacture of, 215
manufacturers, 147n
in Civil War, 193, 194
occupational specialization, effect on *see*
  Labor
over-specialization, 158
shortages, 194, 195
types
  barrel boring, 94
    drilling, 156, 157
    rolling, 151-153
    turning, 96, 155, 156, 158
    welding, 94, 95
  bayonet rolling, 196
  lathe
    cam control, 13
    turret, 13, 146, 158
  milling, 145, 146, 154
  miscellaneous, 98, 99, 158
  profiling, 154-156
  rifling, 155, 156
  stocking, 97, 157
machinery and machines, 335
  manufacturers of, 147n
steam-power *see* Small arms industry
steam-engine manufacturers, 147n
Machinery, machines *see* Machine tools
Manufacture, small arms *see* Small arms
  industry
Market, marketing, 4, 124-126, 129, 130,
  202
Mass production *see* Interchangeability,
  Machine tools, Small arms industry
Massachusetts Arms Co., 27, 117, 183
Master Armorer, 30, 60, 83, *passim*
Maynard, Edward, 25, 26, 29
Maynard primer *see* Small arms
McRae, Alexander, 48
Mechanization *see* Interchangeability, La-
  bor, Machine tools
Mills, J. K., & Co., 125, 126
Mitchell, Wesley C., indices, 188, 200,
  201, 238, 239, 243

Model, change of, *see* Costs
Moulton, Harold G., index of real wages, 109, 200, 243
Musket *see* Small arms
Muzzle-loading *see* Small arms

Navy Agent, 55
Navy Department, 31, 55, 129, 140, 209
Navy Ordnance, Chief of, 55
New Haven Arms Co., 203
North, John, 122
North, Selah, 93
North, Simeon, 11, 24, 26, *passim*
North & Savage, 128, 214
Norwich Arms Co., 183

Occupational specialization *see* Interchangeability, Labor
Onions, William, 152, 197
Ordnance, Chief of, 24, 30, 48, *passim*
Ordnance, Chief of, Confederate, 177, 178
Ordnance Department, 24, 28, 42, *passim*
Ordnance Office, 42n *see* Ordnance Department
Orr, Hugh, 35
Overhead costs *see* Costs

Palmer, Courtland C., 123
Parker, Snow & Co., 183
Partnership *see* Financing
Parts contracting *see* Contract system: sub-contract
Parts manufacture *see* Small arms industry
Patent arms *see* Small arms
Pattern arms *see* Contract system, Interchangeability
Peabody Rifle Co., 211
Percussion, percussioning *see* Small arms
Piece-rates *see* Wages
Pistol *see* Small arms
Pomeroy, Eltweed, 33
Pomeroy family, 33
Pomeroy, Lemuel, 44, 45, 48, *passim*
Pratt & Whitney, 211, 214
Precision measurement *see* Interchangeability
Presentation arms, 124, 125, 130
Product, value of, *see* Small arms industry: value of product
Production *see* Small arms industry
Production, diversified, *see* Small arms industry
Productivity of labor *see* Labor
Profits, 47, 49, 52-54
Providence Tool Co., 196, 211, 213

Raw materials, 35, 36, Ch. VI, 68-86, Ch. X, 133-143, 187-193
    charcoal, 83, 84, 193
    coal, 83-85, 192, 193
    cost of, 50, 205, App. B 232
    files, 85, 142, 143, 193
    gun stocks, 81-83, 193

import of, 79-81, 139, 189, 190
iron, 72-79, 119, 136-139, 189-192
miscellaneous, 36, 85, 141, 142
prices of, 71, 72, 135-138, App. C 234, 237, 238 Fig. 1, 239
terms of purchase, 47, 69-71, 134, 135, 189
Real wages *see* Wages
References, 255-283
Remington, Eliphalet, 121, 122, 127
Remington, Samuel, 211
Remington Co., 27, 30, 157, *passim*
Remington system *see* Small arms: breech-loading
Revolver *see* Small arms
Rifle *see* Small arms
Rifling *see* Small arms
Ripley, Major J. W., 165, 166
Robb, John, 136, 160, 162, 167
Robbins, Kendall & Lawrence *see* Robbins & Lawrence
Robbins & Lawrence, 27, 117, 121-123, *passim*
Root, E. K., 149-151, 154, 155, 157

Savage Revolving Fire Arms Co., 183
Scoville, Hezekiah, 44
Secretary of War, 35, 37, 48, *passim*
Sharps, Christian, 30, 128
Sharps Rifle Co., 123, 128, 203, *passim*
Shaw, Joshua, 22, 23, 22n, 23n
Small arms
    breech-loading, 17, 18 Fig. 6, 27-32, 209
        systems
            Allin, 31, 209
            Morse, 30, 128
            Remington, 31, 209
        See also carbine, musket, revolver, rifle
    caliber, 21, 30-32
    carbine, 117, 128
        Burnside, 128
        Hall, 21, 22, 24
        Jenks, 127, 129, 157
        Joslyn, 209
        Maynard, 117
        Sharps, 31, 123, 128, 209
        Spencer, 31, 209
        Winchester, 210
        See also breech-loading, flintlock, percussion and percussioning
    case-hardening, 93
    die forging, 92, 93
    flintlock, 18 Fig. 6, 19-24, 26
        See also carbine, musket, pistol, revolver, rifle
    general purpose arms, 34
    guns, 18 Fig. 6
        See also carbine, musket, pistol, revolver, rifle
    Maynard primer *see* percussion, percussioning
    musket, 18 Fig. 6, 19, 21, 24, 25, 25n, 30, 31

288

See also flintlock, breech-loading, muzzle-loading, percussion, percussioning
muzzle-loading, 17, 30, 31, 209
See also carbine, musket, pistol, revolver, rifle
patent arms, miscellaneous, 128, 129, 209, 210
percussion, percussioning, 23-26
Maynard primer, 25, 26, 128
See also carbine, musket, pistol, revolver, rifle
pistol, 24, 26
Colt, 30
Remington, 31
Volcanic, 28
See also breech-loading, flintlock, percussion, percussioning
product
change of design, 3
standardization, 13
repeating and magazine arms, 19, 19n, 27, 31
See also revolver
revolver, 17, 18 Fig. 6, 22, 26, 27, 128
Allen, 128
Collier, 22, 26
Colt, 18 Fig. 6, 24, 26, 30, 123, 124, 129, 145, 209-211
Joslyn, 128
Leavitt, 27, 128
Remington, 27, 128
Savage, 128
Smith & Wesson, 31, 32, 128
See also breech-loading, flintlock, muzzle-loading, percussion, percussioning
rifle, 18 Fig. 6, 19-25, 27, 29-31
Hall, 22, 22n, 24, 129, 144, 153
Henry, 184
Jenks, 129, 157
Jennings, 26, 27, 123
Kendall, 122, 123, 129
Kentucky, 20, 21, 24, 25
Maynard, 183
Minié, 123
Missouri, 130
Peabody, 211
Remington, 30, 31
Robbins & Lawrence, 129
Sharps, 31, 183
Spencer, 13
Springfield, 31
See also breech-loading, flintlock, muzzle-loading, percussion, percussioning, repeating and magazine arms
rifling, 21, 25, 26
second-grade arms, 185
technical development of small arms, 1770-1870, Ch. II, 17-32
truing of barrels, 204
Small arms industry
adjustment to peace, Pt. 4, 117-216,

App. A 221-226
arms makers, 121-126, 127n, 221-226
distribution in New England, 15 Fig. 5, 16, 43, 44
early nineteenth century, Ch. IV, 41-54
origin of, 43
capital see Financing
characteristics, 3, 4, 9, 215
concentration in New England, 12 Fig. 4, 13, 14, App. A 218
consolidation of plants, 208, 209, App. A 221-226
contract arms see Contract system
cooperation of
early arms makers, 3, 67, passim
decline of, 119
lack of, with Harper's Ferry Armory, 67
with Springfield Armory, 66, 67
national armories, 119, passim
See also Harper's Ferry Armory, Springfield Armory
credit see Financing
demand, 33, 34
foreign, 3, 129, 130, 148, 149, 202, 210-215
See also Export
government, 38
private, 123, 128, 129
depreciation see Costs
development of, Pt. 2, 41-114, 202
dilemma of, 214, 215
employment see Labor
expansion, 4, 7, 9, 36, 180-184
failures see Costs
government patronage, development under, Pt. 2, 41-114
guns see Small arms
gunsmiths and gunsmithing, 4, 7n, 15 Fig. 5, 16, 33, 36, 221-226
industrial independence, Pt. 3, 115-174
inelasticity of demand, 215-216
inside contracting see Labor
inspection see Contract system
interchangeability see Interchangeability
investment see Financing: capital
liquidation of plants, 208, 209, App. A 221-226
location
Connecticut River Valley, 3-5, 14, 43, 44, 184
New England, 5, 12 Fig. 4, 15 Fig. 5, 16
machine tools see Machine tools
manufacturers, new, Ch. IX, 117-132
manufacturers, old, disappearance of, 120, 121
mass production, 4, 13, 202
See also Interchangeability, Machine tools
mechanization see Costs, Interchangeability, Labor, Machine tools

model, change of, 3, 56, 57, 131, 132
occupational specialization *see* Interchangeability, Labor
organization of, 44
overhead costs *see* Costs
over-specialization, 122
partnership *see* Financing
parts contracting *see* Contract system:
sub-contract
parts manufacture, 42, 44, 45, 180-182
post-war adjustment and development,
Ch. XIV, 202-216
precision measurement *see* Interchangeability
price of arms *see* Contract system: contract arms
product, value of, *see* value of product
production, App. A 220, 221
diversified, 4, 125, 202, 213-216
New England system, 34
productivity *see* Labor
quantitative aspect, 4, 5, 6-12 Figs. 1-4,
App. A 217
roots of the industry, Ch. III 33-38
small arms contract *see* Contract system
small arms manufacture, place of, in
American industry, Ch. I, 3-16
southern branch of, 41n
specialization, 128, 129
statistics, App. A 217-221, App. *passim*
steam-power, 3, 99, 146-148
sub-contracting *see* parts manufacture,
Contract system
unit costs *see* Costs
value added by manufacture, 6 Fig. 1,
9, 10 Fig. 3, App. A 217
value of product, 6 Fig. 1, 9, 10 Fig 3,
App. A 217, 220, 221
water-power, 44, 93
Small arms manufacture *see* Small arms
industry
Smith & Wesson Co., vii, 27, 28, 121,
128, 184, 199, 210
Spencer, Christopher, 13, 214
Spencer Repeating Rifle Co., **209**
Springfield Armory
Commanding Officer, 29, 186, 191, *passim*
costs *see* Costs
efficiency, 201
experimentation, 32, 128
financial problems, 189
importance, 37
machine tools *see* Machine tools
parts, manufacture and repair, 187
production, 128, App B 233
raw materials *see* Raw materials
records, 5, 120
Superintendent, 49, 50, 60, *passim*
wages *see* Wages
"yardstick" function, 5, 118
Springfield Arms Co., 128
Springfield Manufacturing Co., 44

"Stand" of arms, 37n
Standardization *see* Interchangeability
Starr, Elihu, vii, 121
Starr, Nathan, Jr., vii, 43, 53, *passim*
Starr, Nathan, Sr., vii, 43-45, *passim*
State Armorer of Virginia, 119
Steam-power *see* Small arms industry
Steel *see* Raw materials
Stevens, J., Arms Co., vii
Stevens, J., & Co., 203, 213
Stone, Henry D., 13, 149, 158
Sub-contract *see* Contract system

Talcott, Lieutenant-Colonel George, 108,
165, 173
Technological unemployment *see* Labor
Transportation, 43, 44
canal, 69, 83
freight rates *see* Costs
railway, 133, 134
river, 68, 69, 83
sailing packet, 134
steam-boat, 133, 134
Trenton Iron Co. *see* Cooper Hewitt &
Co.

Uniformity of parts *see* Interchange-
ability
Union Metallic Cartridge Co., 213
Unit costs *see* Costs

Value added by Manufacture *see* Small
arms industry
Value of product *see* Small arms industry
Volcanic Repeating Arms Co., 126, 127

Wadsworth, Captain Decius, 87
Wages, 8 Fig. 2, 9, 48, 100, 165, 167,
169, 170, 172, 200, App. A 220, 221,
App. D 240-243, 244 Fig. 1, 249
apprentices, 34, 35
bimodality, 111, 174
cost of living, relation to, 105-107,
119, 168, 173, App. D 244 Fig. 1
course and structure, 106, 109-111, 172-
174
delays and discounts on, 103
different occupations, 180
differentials, 171, 172, App. D 249
incentive, 106, 107
journeymen, 34, 35
mean and modal, 172, App. D 241-243,
244 Fig. 1
non-money, 107
other income, 107
piece rates, 108, 169, 170, App. D 240,
246 Fig. 2, 248, 249
policies, 105, 107
real, 4, 9, 109, 110, 172, 173, 200, 201,
App. D 241-243, 244 Fig. 1
time rates, 108, 109, App. D 240
War Department, 30, 38, 42, *passim*
Warner, James, 128
Warner, Thomas, 102, 145, 149, 153, 154

Wars,
  Civil, 25, 30, Ch. XIII, 177-201, *see
    also* Civil War
  Crimean, 129
  First World, 7
  Franco-Prussian, 210
  Mexican, 24, 26, 123, 129
  of 1812, 88, 93
  Revolution, 21, 33, 36
  Spanish-American, 7
Water-power *see* Small arms industry

Waters, Asa, 48, 94, 96, 120
Waters, Harvey, 196
Waters Armory, 121, 167, 177
Waters family, 33
Whitney, Eli, Jr., 117, 124, 136, *passim*
Whitney, Eli, Sr., vii, 11, 43-48, *passim*
Whitney Armory, vii, 120, 145, 156
Wickham, Marine T., 48, 49, 55
Winchester Repeating Arms Co., vii, 121,
  126, *passim*
Windsor Manufacturing Co., 213